THE END OF
BASEBALL
AS WE KNEW IT

SPORT AND SOCIETY

Series Editors
Benjamin G. Rader
Randy Roberts

*A list of books in the series
appears at the end of this book.*

THE END OF
BASEBALL
AS WE KNEW IT

THE PLAYERS UNION, 1960-81

Charles P. Korr

Foreword by Bob Costas

University of Illinois Press
Urbana and Chicago

Unless otherwise noted, the photographs in the
book are reproduced courtesy of *The Sporting News*.

Library of Congress Cataloging-in-Publication Data
Korr, Charles P.
The end of baseball as we knew it : the players union,
1960–81 / Charles P. Korr ; foreword by Bob Costas.
p.   cm. — (Sport and society)
Includes bibliographical references (p.) and index.
ISBN 0-252-02752-3 (cloth : alk. paper)
1. Baseball players—Labor unions—United States—
History—20th century. 2. Major League Baseball Players
Association—History. 3. Industrial relations—
United States—History—20th century. I. Title. II. Series.
GV880.2.K67   2002
331.89′041796357′0973—dc21   2001007535

To Anne,
for so many reasons

Contents

Foreword by Bob Costas   ix

Acknowledgments   xv

Introduction   1

1. A "House Union"   15

2. The Association Chooses Change   35

3. A New Focus for the Association   54

4. The Union Asserts Itself   68

5. Curt Flood and the American Dream   84

6. Only One Chance at a First Strike   102

7. A Loss in Court and a Gain at the Bargaining Table   121

8. Different Roads to Free Agency   130

9. Messersmith and McNally:
Two Pitchers and One Big Win   147

10. Protecting Free Agency   168

11. 1980—The Strike That Didn't Happen   186

12. The Union's Sternest Test 210

Conclusion 231

Epilogue:
1990s—Parallels Abroad and Problems at Home 249

Notes 267

Sources and Further Reading 309

Index 317

Foreword

THESE DAYS, IT'S DIFFICULT TO even imagine baseball without a union and with players who were tied to a team for life and made whatever money the general manager was willing to give them. Free agency, million-dollar contracts, and work stoppages have been facts of major league baseball life for twenty-five years. But that's only a fraction of baseball's long history. *The End of Baseball As We Knew It* explains the events that changed baseball forever. It's not an overstatement to say that between 1966 and 1981 there was a revolution in baseball that in turn changed all of professional team sports in America.

In the decade after 1966, the accepted procedures and legal structure of the sport were questioned by the players, challenged by their union, and left in rubble by the decisions of arbitrators and courts. When the players decided to use their union to take on the owners, it was an uneven playing field, with both power and tradition on the side of the owners. Most of the players took it for granted that the system that existed was what always would be in place. Even those who most felt the need for change held little hope that something as ingrained as the reserve system would ever be ended. For their part, the owners were so wrapped up in their own version of what was best for baseball that they never thought that change, let alone compromise with the players, was either desirable or necessary.

Until the 1970s, the extent of most baseball fans' interest in the front office was to wonder why their general manager didn't make better trades or how the farm clubs were doing. Lou Brock for Ernie Broglio was baseball news; how much a player was paid, the issue of free agency, or what was happening with the players' pension fund belonged in the business section of the newspaper. That all changed in 1972 when the players union staged a short, successful strike. Baseball might not be as much uncomplicated fun for people once they'd been exposed to the business side of it, but the reality had always been there. However, before we complain about how the changes might have harmed the game, let's not forget how stacked the deck was against the players in "the good old days" or that in the era of free agency the measurable popularity of the game and its overall revenues have increased enormously.

A quote from Paul Richards, long-time baseball man and a strident foe of everything the union tried to do, provides the title of Chuck Korr's book, a volume that shows us how the players union changed baseball. Richards was right, of course. Once the union gained a foothold, it did start the end of baseball as he had known it. Baseball became both a better game and a fairer one to everyone involved in it. For the first time, the business of baseball took on the values of what the game had always claimed to be, namely, America's "national pastime."

There is a temptation to look at the after-the-fact successes of the players union and make a couple of assumptions: that its victories were inevitable (one baseball historian called the union's activities from 1966 to 1981 "the longest winning streak in baseball history") and that they were solely the product of Marvin Miller, the union's executive director. *The End of Baseball As We Knew It* shows us that the first point is wrong and the second is much too simple. Korr presents the story of how the union brought about such huge changes with the skills of a historian and the sensibilities of a long-time baseball fan. How many people are there who have written about the political and economics aspects of sports on four continents, who saw one of Jackie Robinson's first games as a Dodger, and, as an almost obsessive Phillies fan, feels that Dick Sisler's 1950 pennant-clinching home run was almost as important as Bobby Thomson's "Shot Heard 'Round the World" a year later?

Korr's book begins with the decision by the players to transform a loosely knit group into a focused, aggressive force to improve their situation. It ends with the 1981 strike, which guaranteed that the union would not allow the owners to roll back free agency. This period could also be called the "Miller Years" since it coincides with almost all of his tenure as the first executive director of the Major League Baseball Players Association. It's difficult to overestimate Miller's skills as a strategist as well as his uncanny ability to understand what the opposition was doing and to capitalize on its mistakes. This slight, soft-spoken man had a profound impact on the players. He became the public face of the union, the man that owners, executives, and most writers and fans loved to hate. But Korr shows us that Miller's greatest skill might have been that of a teacher, someone who helped the players understand their situation, recognize the need for change, and see that they had the power to make a difference in their lives if they chose to work together. Most of all, he never underestimated the players' ability to see and do things for themselves. It was not Miller's union, it was the players union. For decades, it's been easy for some to dismiss the players as either pawns of Miller or unwitting beneficiaries of his skills. But Korr shows us just how much the players mattered and how their ability to maintain a solid union made all the difference.

This book demonstrates that the union and the players had choices to make. There was no clearly defined way for the union to get from one place to another, and sometimes the toughest part was trying to figure out where it wanted to go. There were risks to be considered: players were traded or released because of their union activities; powerful reporters consistently criticized and ridiculed the union; and fans made it clear how much they disliked the union and disapproved of the players who were active in it. The idea of Baltimore fans booing Brooks Robinson might seem outlandish, but they did exactly that because he took an active role in the 1972 strike.

Korr gained the kind of access that every historian dreams about: free rein to go through the papers and correspondence of the union with no restrictions on how he used what he found. Besides the letters and proposals and records of the negotiations, there are personal moments. The high drama of the San Juan meeting of player reps in 1969, when they decided to support Curt Flood in his challenge of the reserve system, and a while later when they responded to a presentation by Bowie Kuhn by telling him he was the owners' commissioner, not theirs. There is the no-holds-barred 1972 meeting when the reps decided to vote for a strike despite the warnings from Miller and Dick Moss, the union's counsel, about the dangers involved. There are quirky moments when the future of baseball was changed by something as simple as the owners forcing Peter Seitz to render a judgment about the meaning of the word "one."

This is also a story of players like Robin Roberts, whom executives described for years as the man who brought Marvin Miller into baseball—and they didn't mean it as a compliment. Jim Bunning, currently a conservative Republican U.S. senator and one of the driving forces in the crucial early years of the players union. Ted Simmons, a catcher with Hall of Fame credentials and the first player in the twentieth century to start a season without a signed contract. Al Downing, best known as the man who delivered the pitch that Henry Aaron hit for number 715 but also the man who could have broken the reserve system years before Andy Messersmith and Dave McNally did. Bob Boone, one of the most respected men in the union but whose involvement (with the Phillies) in the 1980 pennant race meant that negotiations over proposed modifications in free agency had to be postponed. And, of course, the more familiar names: Messersmith and McNally, whose case marked the end of the reserve system; Catfish Hunter, who became a free agent thanks to Charlie Finley's bungled efforts to get out of contractual obligations; and most of all, Curt Flood. Flood's quiet courage was remarkable, especially since his stance was scorned by the vast majority of commentators and fans. As a historian, Korr is after the realities of a situation rather than the romantic version that has taken hold years after the fact.

The End of Baseball As We Knew It is a book about baseball, about change, about the role baseball plays in American culture, and about men working together off the field to win. Here we have a chance to get behind the newspaper accounts of what happened. We can be present at the discussions that took place within the union and between the negotiators for both sides. This book is distinguished by the willingness of so many of the participants to talk with Korr about these events. For the first time, Judge Cannon, Miller's predecessor, explained what he was trying to do. Men like Joe Torre, Brooks Robinson, and Sal Bando talked about the problems they faced and the decisions they made. Marvin Miller and John Gaherin, opponents for a decade, gave Korr their versions of what happened and why. Executives like Buzzie Bavasi, owners like Ewing Kaufman, and Commissioner Bud Selig all provided their own unique perspectives. This may be a book about the union, but Korr also shows us the importance of understanding how its opponents dealt with it.

As a young observer of baseball, I'd always felt that the players were exploited and that baseball's rules concerning labor were unfair and outmoded. A strong and effective union was necessary for the players to achieve any real equity. As it happened, they succeeded beyond even their own dreams. The union did represent the interests of its members, it did win in the battles against ownership, it did change the structure of sports—and it accomplished all of that against the backdrop of public hostility and the unique legal status of baseball. How all that happened is a fascinating piece of the history of baseball and of American society during a period of massive social change. This is a book that understands baseball and the culture surrounding it. It's a book that captures the drama of the events and the long-term significance of what happened during those years in which the union held both the intellectual and moral high ground.

In the past decade the baseball landscape has changed considerably. As I've said and written elsewhere, it's no longer possible for fair-minded baseball observers to back the union 100 percent. Many of the present positions of the players are, I believe, vestiges of the past and products of a mindset that served the game well during the Miller years and beyond but should be modified now, provided that the owners present honest and reasonable proposals of their own. As I write this, that chapter of baseball is yet to be played out. When it is, let's hope that someone as capable as Chuck Korr is there to help shape history's judgment.

Bob Costas
NBC and HBO Sports
March 31, 2002

Acknowledgments

My research for this book was dependent on the generosity and assistance of a great many people. None of them were under any obligation to speak with me, and all who did so placed no restrictions on either the questions I asked or how I used their comments. Each of these interviews added new perspectives. From these conversations I also gained a new appreciation of the complexities and special qualities of their chosen professions.

Marvin Miller and Don Fehr gave me the kind of access that is usually the unrealized dream of a historian. They allowed me to go through the correspondence and other files of the Major League Baseball Players Association. The only limitations on how I used this material were the conventions of client-attorney confidentiality, provisions surrounding some contracts and *in camera* hearings. Throughout my research and writing, they made it a point not to discuss the interpretations I was forming, whom I interviewed, or what kinds of documents I was choosing. The Players Association let me use the facilities in their offices and kept out of my way while I did the work.

Maryanne Ellison Simmons first suggested to me the possibility of doing a history of the union and pointed the way for me to take the next steps. Leonard Koppett has been a special friend—a source of encouragement and information and a unique combination of knowledge, insight, experience, humor, and generosity. Ted Simmons never does things by half measures, and the support he gave me was just as complete. He introduced me to the people at the Players Association and made sure I got to meet the participants who were involved on both sides of the issues.

The Washington, D.C., office of a conservative Republican congressman might seem a strange place to start the research on a labor union. Jim Bunning played a pivotal role in the development of the union, and he was the first former member of the Players Association whom I interviewed. He is a man of strong opinions, forcefully and articulately stated. Talking with him showed me that the research on this book would never be dull.

Judge Robert Cannon spent hours with me. He presented his detailed memory of events and gave me a perspective that was unavailable anywhere else. A day with Buzzie Bavasi was a history of the sport adorned with anecdotes, reflections, and a special view of the world of baseball. It is easy to see why he has retained so many friendships within baseball.

Many of the former players I interviewed had gone on to successful careers in management and/or sports broadcasting. They might have been expected to phrase their views about the union, or at least their criticisms of ownership, in euphemisms. This was definitely not the case. Tim McCarver, Ralph Kiner, Al Downing, Steve Boros, Sal Bando, Reggie Smith, and Brooks Robinson minced no words in their opinions about how the union had changed baseball, their support for what it had done, and how much ownership did to influence the course of events. Bob Barton and Milt Pappas provided very interesting perspectives.

No one was more forthcoming than Joe Torre, whom I interviewed while he was managing the Cardinals. Although he might have had reason to downplay his involvement in the union and the disputes involving him, he showed no inclination to do so. This had an unexpected result for me years later. I have rooted against the Yankees since I saw my first baseball game in 1945, but in 1996 I wanted Joe's team to win a World Series.

Dick Moss went out of his way to provide background and to put "flesh and blood" on many of the documents that I had read. Dick's unique sense of humor and irony and his ability to cut to the heart of an issue were as clear during our conversations as they were in the records of his performances in court and at arbitration hearings.

Bud Selig and Harry Dalton also made a special effort to fill in gaps in the written record. They gave me a personal view of circumstances in which they were involved and talked about implications of events that took place after 1981.

Four men who were special to this book died before I completed it.

Mark Belanger had the same grace off the field that he showed as a brilliant shortstop. His comments were helpful, and he made me comfortable working at the Players Association. Steve Hamilton showed why everyone who knew him in baseball remembers him as someone who combined honesty, intelligence, professionalism, and humor. The time I spent with John Gaherin was the most surprising part of the research. A meeting that started with him saying, "Nobody ever wants to get our side of the story," ended more than four hours later with him saying, "Remember, I haven't talked like that before . . . make sure you ask me if you need any more help." It was easy to see why so many of the men who sat across the table from him praised his skill and integrity. The history of baseball might have been very different if the owners had recognized the need to give him the kind of support that Miller received from his members. In person, Judge John Oliver showed the same kind of dry wit and legal realism that he demonstrated as a trial judge hearing an appeal of the 1975 Messersmith-McNally arbitration ruling that created free agency. He made it clear how much he was enjoying his first opportunity to discuss the case and to put it into a broader perspective. I often wonder about what Oliver and Gaherin would have made of my interpretation of their roles in the changing structure of baseball.

I received support for this project from the National Endowment for the Humanities, the American Council for Learned Societies, the American Philosophical Society, and the Office of Research and the Center for International Studies of the University of Missouri–St. Louis. The directors of the latter two institutions, Doug Wartzok and Joel Glassman, respectively, were helpful far beyond the financial assistance they provided.

Many friends and colleagues played significant roles at various stages of this work. I received suggestions, comments, and encouragement from Jerry Cooper, Steve Hause, Wray Vamplew, Bruce Kidd, Brian Stoddart, Steve Gietschier, Asa Briggs, Art Shaffer, John Rawlings, Joe Fresta, Rob Ramage, Bill Gould, Mike Harris, Bert Moorhouse, Dick Holt, and Pierre Lanfranchi. Dick Waters and Joe Losos kept asking questions, often pointed and always instructive and supportive.

A conversation about baseball with Bob Costas is always special. Besides asking probing questions and making observations, Bob also went out of his way to encourage some of his many friends to share their recollections and ideas with me.

Andy Rothschild, Mel Adelman, and Paul Staudohar read the manuscript and made useful suggestions. It's difficult to find a suitable way to thank the "Baker Boys," Bill and Norrie. They not only read the whole manuscript at various stages, they went through it with the care that marks their own scholarship.

Don Fehr did much more than let me into the files of the Players Association. We talked about his role within the union and broader issues of labor law. Some of the most interesting afternoons and evenings I can remember in New York were when Don and I talked about things having little to do with baseball—politics, science, travel, and universities.

Over the past thirty-five years, Marvin Miller's accomplishments have given him almost mythic status and helped to create an impression that he is austere and unapproachable. I quickly learned that neither could be further from the case. Humor and perspective are as much a part of his character as are the qualities associated with his public persona. There was never a dull moment spent with him or Terry, whether the setting was E. 70th Street or the Frick Gallery, the topic labor law or international cultural differences. It took more than fifteen years for me to meet Marvin after I invited him in 1972 to be part of a conference in St. Louis. I wish it had not taken that long, but it was worth the wait.

Gene Orza is a person whose range of interests and knowledge is matched only by the passion with which he approaches them. But that runs a distant second to his generosity and hospitality. He welcomed me to his home, made me comfortable among his friends, and allowed me to feel a part of the city that is so much of his life. My friend Cli was with me throughout all the drafts of the book. His suggestions were made quietly but forcefully. A look from him always got the serious attention it deserved.

This is the first book that I've dedicated solely to Anne; it should have been the third. She understood immediately why this subject was so important to me. She recognized, before I did, why I should set aside the work I was doing and concentrate on it. She supported my decisions to take on some responsibilities that meant postponing research and writing, but she never allowed me to forget that the book had to be done and had to be done right. She never has developed a proper appreciation for the game of baseball, but she certainly understands how much it means to so many other people. She could stand back and provide a different perspective. In Anne's case, always being there means being active and involved, exactly what someone would expect from their best friend.

THE END OF BASEBALL AS WE KNEW IT

INTRODUCTION

"'THIS WILL BE THE END OF BASEBALL, AS WE KNEW IT,'"
announced Paul Richards, the general manager of the Atlanta Braves, at
a press conference held during the 1967 winter meeting of Major League
Baseball club owners.[1] A veteran of more than thirty years in organized
baseball, Richards had been a major league player, manager, and general
manager. He was warning his fellow executives, owners, and the assembled baseball writers against the dangers of negotiating an industry-wide
collective bargaining agreement between the clubs and the Major League
Baseball Players Association (MLBPA).

The MLBPA was the legally constituted bargaining agent for the major league players, a union in all but name. It certainly did not fit popular definitions of a labor union, since most people did not regard major
league players as workers. It is not clear how many players, even those
involved in the association, thought of it as a union. Even the word
"union" did not come easily to the vocabulary of the players; "association" and "players' group" were the preferred terms. The association had
been in existence for more than a decade, but it attracted little attention
until April, when it appointed Marvin J. Miller, an executive with the
Steelworkers Union, as its first full-time executive director.[2]

The union was composed of hundreds of men who were competitive
by nature. Their job was to beat other members of the union on the field.
The players had short careers, and they scrambled to maintain their position on the roster. The threat of being released or sent down to the minor
leagues hung over many of their heads, and being traded was an occupa-

tional hazard that faced all but a few of them. Even stars were not immune. From the time players were in the minor leagues, they knew they were part of a system where it made little sense to challenge the power of their clubs and even less to think about organizing to challenge the system itself.

The historian of early baseball Warren Goldstein has pointed out the dual nature of the sport's development. Fans got an emotional lift from the performance of the players, and owners were recognized as civic-minded sportsmen and reaped profits from what the players did on the field. But the players were involved in much more than a game or contest. They were "playing for keeps," trying to earn a living, maintain a lifestyle, and ensure a special status for themselves.[3] They needed the sport for their success, but the sport, the fans, and the owners needed players for profit and pleasure. When the players recognized the possibility of capitalizing on this equation, they transferred their "playing for keeps" attitude beyond the field. After 1966 they created their own team to win a contest against the owners, teams, and structure of Major League Baseball.

From 1954 the MLBPA represented the players in dealings with the owners on issues including the pension fund and some working conditions. Frank Scott, who was the part-time director of the association for almost a decade, commented in 1992 that before 1966 the association had been "a 'House Union' guided by a member of the Commissioner's office and the most influential owner of that time."[4]

In 1960 the MLBPA hired a part-time legal consultant, Judge Robert Cannon of Milwaukee, to work with Scott. For the next six years Cannon represented the public face of the organized players. He has become an important footnote in the history of baseball. A serious fan of the sport might see some similarities between Cannon and Wally Pipp, the Yankee first baseman who sat down for Lou Gehrig and never got back his position. The historian Robert Burk is dismissive of Cannon, stating that the "new counsel craved the magnates' respect and approval," and Marvin Miller describes him as a man "who never met an owner he didn't like."[5] Some of Miller's most thoughtful and articulate allies among the players have a less harsh assessment of Cannon. One of the leaders in the association, Joe Torre, stated that Cannon was "the necessary prelude to Miller" and that the judge's cozy relationship with the owners gave them "a false sense of security" that enabled Miller and the new-style association to "sneak up on them." That might be reading some of the post-1966 world into Cannon's actions. Torre's view that Cannon "was likeable and probably trying to do what he thought was best" recognizes that Cannon had genuine, however misguided, feelings about the need to protect the traditions of baseball.[6]

After 1966 the MLBPA transformed itself from a loose group with no full-time staff and no positive agenda into an assertive force that set a whole new pattern for labor relations in baseball and achieved all of its important objectives. It set the standard and the goals for unions in other professional sports. Over the next fifteen years there was a power struggle between the association and ownership during which the union maintained what a prominent labor economist characterizes as the longest winning streak in the history of baseball.[7]

The changes that resulted from the union's activities were enormous. In 1966 a player had no right to have an attorney or agent represent him in contract negotiations. When a player received his contract for the following season he had limited options: he could sign the contract, he could hold out and try to force the club to change the terms or trade him, or he could retire from the profession. He could not market his services to any other club within the realm of organized baseball; he could be traded or sold to any other major league club. He had no control over the process, nor did he gain any financial benefits from it. The club could fine or suspend him for disciplinary purposes, and his only right of appeal in such cases was to the league presidents or the commissioner of baseball, all of whom were selected and employed by the owners of the clubs.

In 1981 every player had the contractual right to be represented in negotiations by anyone of his choice, and the clubs had to meet with that person. Any player who had been in the major leagues for ten years and with his current club for a minimum of five had the right to turn down a trade involving him. Any player who had been in the major leagues for at least two years had the right to demand that the salary offered to him for the following season should be referred for binding arbitration by an impartial party agreed upon by both sides. Any player who was fined or suspended by his club had the right to appeal that action to a grievance panel, whose deciding vote would be cast by an impartial arbitrator chosen from a panel of names agreed upon by the two bodies.

The most noticeable change for the players between 1966 and 1981 involved their salaries. In 1966 the minimum salary for major league players was six thousand dollars, seven thousand if they were on the roster by the end of June. It had increased by only one thousand dollars in more than a decade; the average salary was nineteen thousand dollars. In 1981 the minimum salary was $32,500, and the average salary was $185,651.

Even when adjusted for inflation, it is clear that the players had made enormous economic gains.[8]

Once the players decided that the association was in a contest against the owners, "playing for keeps" became the essence of the union. Its leadership was playing for high stakes, and winning was essential. It was the job of the union's Executive Board (made up of the player representatives elected by each club) and the executive director and counsel, whom they employed, to seek out every legitimate weapon in the arsenal of labor law.

When this contest started, there was a huge power differential between the players and their employers and a history of failed efforts on the part of the players to get concessions from the owners. The bedrock of baseball ownership's control over the players was the reserve system. It had originated in 1879, when the club owners in the recently formed National League agreed that each team could "reserve" five of its players for its roster. The other teams agreed not to employ these reserved players or compete against teams that did. Within a few years, the concept was extended to include all the players on every club. The reserve system stabilized the business side of baseball. It allowed the owners to control salaries and other aspects of the players' lives and gave the players no alternative but to accept the terms offered to them or find another occupation. Between 1900 and 1903, the newly formed American League presented a challenge to the monopoly status of the National League, but when the leagues merged, a new version of the reserve system was instituted.[9]

Various aspects of the system had been tested in court. In 1922 the Supreme Court ruled that organized baseball was exempt from the provisions of federal antitrust legislation. Justice Holmes's decision was more a panegyric to the virtues of baseball and its important role in American culture than an informed commentary on antitrust law.

By the late 1960s there were different opinions about the desirability or necessity of the reserve system but little disagreement about its effect. John Gaherin, the owners' representative, accurately pointed out that the reserve system "permits each club to retain exclusive employment rights to a player within organized baseball until and unless the player is released, retires, or until his contract is assigned to another club."[10]

Miller brought to the union the belief that it had to change "an employment relationship held together by compulsion and the power of the employer [that] inevitably results in certain abuses."[11] This went against the prevailing sentiment, typified in a 1970 New York radio station editorial: "Professional sports is facing a challenge that threatens its existence. . . . Under the existing system, a baseball player must perform for the club that owns him if he plays at all . . . professional sports can not work without it [the reserve system] or something like it. More to the point, any player not in favor of the ground rules has no business entering the game."[12]

The combination of the reserve system, the limited number of major league jobs, and the extremely short careers gave the owners enormous leverage—the financial and psychological advantages all lay with the ownership. Players were proud to be major leaguers and thought of themselves as professionals who did not see union activities as part of their lifestyle. Many players gave little consideration to the business realities of being a ballplayer. They were in the big leagues, where they were making good money and living out boyhood dreams. One veteran player and manager, Harry Walker, summed it up in 1971: "When we enter the profession, we know the conditions, including the reserve clause."[13] Walker's comment echoes one made twenty years earlier by one of baseball's most popular players, his brother Dixie: players "should not run it [baseball] into the ground through neglect or arrogance."[14]

Baseball officials who had grown up with the sport regarded the reserve system as much more than contractual provisions to retain economic advantage and ensure stability. It was what made baseball special. Baseball without a reserve system was almost a contradiction in terms. In 1967 the New York journalist Leonard Shecter correctly predicted that if the union raised issues about the current situation, the owners would do everything possible to ensure that no one "tampers with their holy grail, the reserve clause."[15]

The depth of management's attachment to the reserve system was enunciated articulately and forcefully over the years by Bob Howsam, the highly successful and respected general manager of the Cardinals and the Reds. He was part of the inner councils of baseball, and his opinions carried enormous weight with other executives and baseball writers. In 1973 he warned about men who threatened baseball, "the institution that reflects all that is America . . . the freedoms we cherish and the liberties we defend."[16] His solution was "to ensure that the reserve clause and territorial rights be protected." Howsam expressed dismay that Commissioner Bowie Kuhn was willing to consider any changes in the reserve system, especially those that would allow "free agency after a certain number of years' service in the major leagues if a club was unwilling to meet a minimum salary."[17] Howsam was reassured when negotiations with the players resulted in "no concession towards free agency, not even a study of the reserve system." He made it clear that he was "against any form of free agency" that limited "the freedom [of a club] to use veteran players so you can build the kind of club you want."[18]

While the battle between the association and the owners was about power, legal restrictions, and money, their differences were fundamental. They had two incompatible visions of the history of baseball and what was necessary to ensure its future success. Whatever other divisions existed among the owners, they shared a common concept that they alone had the responsibility to protect "the good of the game." Bowie Kuhn, a long-time attorney for the National League and the commissioner of baseball from 1969 to 1984, made this point clear in 1980: "'I will say that the greatest long-term interest in the game is held by the club people. Their financial interest is longest and deepest. They'll still be around as the generations of players pass.'"[19] Compare this with Miller's belief that "players will always be the core of the sport, even if it's different players,"[20] and one can see the difficulty of reconciling the positions of the union and the hierarchy of baseball. In 1967 Jack Fisher, a player who was active in the union, told a meeting of players and owners, "It's a matter of taking pride in your profession. . . . We don't think we'd be fighting for ourselves. We'd be fighting for baseball."[21]

Commissioner Kuhn believed he would render decisions that were impartial, fair, and "in the best interests of baseball." Miller made his differences with the commissioner clear: "My problem with Bowie . . . is his constant refusal to admit what he is—spokesman for management. He insists on projecting the myth that he is a judge who listens to all parties objectively, when in fact, he speaks for the people who pay him— the owners."[22]

A year after Miller's selection by the players, the owners created the Player Relations Committee (PRC) to handle their relationship with the union. The PRC hired a veteran labor negotiator, John Gaherin. One of the first newspaper articles to analyze the new situation in baseball greeted the arrival of Gaherin with the comment, "having such capable and intelligent men [Miller and Gaherin] doing the negotiations should, in the long run, be a good thing for baseball. It certainly would be something new." Even this reporter underestimated the seriousness of the issues that faced Miller and Gaherin when he concluded that "a pair of overqualified labor relations experts are nose to nose over the conference table . . . each receives $50,000 a year. Seldom has so much gone into solving so little."[23]

For a decade, Miller and Gaherin worked together on the problems facing baseball. They were on opposite sides, but they shared a common background in labor-management relations. Neither seemed prepared for some of the peculiarities of baseball. Almost thirty years later, they both retained a strong memory of one particular phrase that was used by owners and executives when Miller or Gaherin questioned an existing policy or proposed some changes: "That's baseball."[24] Outsiders supposedly could not grasp the essence of baseball. If baseball did not fit in with the norms of the outside world, then the latter would have to accommodate itself to the former.

Bud Selig, the owner of the Milwaukee Brewers and later the commissioner of baseball, has spoken often about his background as a history major and how much the history of baseball has shaped his actions. In 1991 even Selig found it puzzling when he tried to explain the difficulties so many baseball men had in dealing with the players' union. He described the situation with a question and a conclusion, "Why would owners who had unions in their other businesses like they did have problems dealing with them [the MLBPA]? . . . I can't understand it. . . . But granted, it's different in baseball."[25]

Bob Howsam personified the view of baseball traditionalists who wanted to stop the union dead in its tracks. They were convinced that any changes were certain to harm baseball. In 1975 he warned, "We may just have passed the golden age of athletics."[26] The concept of a golden age is always imprecise, and historians treat it with great caution. The term usually is a combination of a wish to return to some ill-defined previous circumstances and a self-interest in denying, or changing, the current realities. After 1966 it became increasingly clear that if the players were asked to describe a "golden age" they would have responded that baseball was just entering into one.

Howsam's version of the golden age ended two days before Christmas in 1975, when the almost century-old relationship between the players and the owners was turned on its head. An impartial arbitrator ruled that the way the owners had utilized the renewal provision in the standard player's contract was invalid. In effect, the reserve system was dead, and every player could become a free agent in a year or two. The owners were unsuccessful in their efforts to get this decision overturned in the federal courts, and over the next few months they tried to achieve at the bargaining table what they had failed to do in court. The players and their union accepted some changes, but they were not willing to go back to the old system.

After 1966 the players would not accept the two fundamental premises of the owners—that baseball could not exist if the reserve system were modified and that baseball had been run well and equitably under the pre-

1966 rules. Free agency was the most dramatic sign of how much the union changed the nature of baseball and altered the status of its members. The arbitration ruling that created free agency was the product of a decade of incremental changes that the union had extracted from the owners.

It is important to recognize the role of the press during the fifteen years under consideration. Baseball was one of the few industries that received almost daily coverage, and this is how the public learned about the changes that were taking place. The press not only covered events, it also influenced actions taken by both sides. Most of the men who covered baseball had little background and even less inclination to examine issues like pensions, arbitration rules, or grievance hearings. For many sportswriters, the introduction of these issues was an unwelcome and unnecessary intrusion. Baseball was a sport with a romantic history of its own, and there was no need to burden it with everyday problems. It was not surprising that once the Players Association and its executive director pressed hard for changes, they faced a media that were antagonistic to the issues and to the union's tactics.

Many players would have agreed with Jackie Robinson's statement in 1972: "the owners have the writers in their pockets . . . after all, a player might get a hamburger for a writer . . . but the owners feed them steak." The real reasons were more complex and less venal. Many writers were fans and maintained a romantic notion about the game. They assumed that owners and executives were the constant aspect of baseball and that individual players were transitory. Writers depended on their access to the clubs for their stories, and many of them had cultivated a good working relationship with management. Bob Hertzel, a reporter with the *Cincinnati Enquirer*, made this point in a letter to Miller. After reminding Miller that he was one of the "more sympathetic journalists towards your organization," Hertzel made some suggestions about how the union could develop a better relationship with the press. Miller should recognize that "facts, sometimes, are hard to get. You deal with the club owner in your own town, of your own team. He is a news source and you can't check every fact and figure he gives you." It was clearly easier for writers to relate to owners and executives than to players, especially those who had little respect for the traditions of baseball.[27]

One of the most perceptive observers of baseball, Roger Angell, discussed the resentment "not a few senior baseball writers" felt when some control of baseball turned "over to the lucky, well-paid, and unforgivably young men who can actually play it." Miller shared this view. In a letter to a journalist, Miller talked about sportswriters who were "neutral on the owners' side" and who had succeeded in getting "a large section of sports fans to empathize with multi-millionaire owners . . . [who were] flouting their legal obligations to bargain."[28]

The idea of players, let alone a union of them, challenging the structure of the sport was an unforgivable blow at common sense and tradition. Writers took it upon themselves to help ownership protect baseball from intruders who were trying to ruin it or players who had no real stake in its continued success. The 1976 comments of Tom Callahan in the *Cincinnati Enquirer* summarized the situation: "Baseball writers as a breed anyway seem more patriotic to the game than writers on other beats. . . . Perhaps it speaks well for baseball that it elicits such concern in the press box, but it speaks poorly for objectivity."[29]

In 1999 Paul Staudohar, a leading labor economist of sports, commented, "there has been no more successful union in modern American history and no more influential labor leader than Marvin Miller . . . and [the years from 1966 to 1981] were the crucial years in the existence of the MLBPA."[30] I agree with his assessment, and that is why the union during that period is the focus of this book. It was the time in which the Players Association transformed itself from an informal "players group" with no organizational structure, no philosophy, and no detailed program of action into a union that bargained aggressively with management for a whole series of beneficial changes in the lives of its members.

Ironically, some of the owners who were most antagonistic to the union became assets for the union's leadership. They helped to create an atmosphere that encouraged the players to get involved with the union and to push it to become more aggressive. At least one owner, Bill Veeck, understood and spoke publicly about that aspect of baseball: "A lot of players figured that anyone the owners disliked that much couldn't be all that bad . . . it has helped Miller rally support when he's needed it. He's been like a funeral director sitting back and waiting for the bodies to come to him."[31]

Bowie Kuhn, the commissioner during most of that time, pointed out that the arbitrator's decision ending the reserve system "not only changed baseball, but it changed all sports." On the twenty-fifth anniversary of the decision, Bud Selig, the current commissioner, commented, "'That was one of the most momentous days in baseball history. . . . I think one can make the case that we've spent the last two-plus decades trying to re-establish some reasonable equilibrium.'"[32] The changes described by Kuhn and Selig were the result of policies initiated by the union and actions taken by the players to protect them. In 1994–95, baseball faced the longest work stoppage in the history of American professional sports, which caused the cancellation of the World Series and parts of two seasons. Many commentators referred to it as the most important event in the history of the union. I do not share that opinion. The strike was a replay of earlier disputes. The issues involved and the bitterness with which they were addressed in 1994–95 indicated the scope of the changes that took place in Major League Baseball between 1966 and 1981.

This book concentrates on the union because it was the union that forced the changes on baseball against the efforts of the owners to retain the status quo. This is clear in the sworn court testimony given by baseball officials and their comments during negotiating sessions with the union. The owners and their employees had every reason to keep the structure of baseball unchanged and to try to prevent the players from having an effective union.

The book explains how the union restructured itself, how it decided which issues to address, how it approached those issues, and how it used the tools that were available to win its battles. The most important sources for this discussion are the files of the union, which include the internal correspondence, minutes of meetings, and other papers of its officials and members. I used the material at the union as a foundation for my research and built upon it through the use of newspapers and periodicals and interviews with men involved on both sides of the negotiations as well as journalists. I have been able to address subjects that have received little or no attention heretofore—the discussions and divisions within the ranks of the union as well as the role played by Frank Scott and Judge Cannon. A lengthy interview with Judge Cannon allowed me to present his view of the early years of the association as well as his perspectives on what happened after 1966.

Because the union achieved such great success, it has been too easy to look at its achievements as part of an unbroken string of advances that were part of some detailed scheme created by Miller and some of the players. My analysis makes it clear that the union's policy was pragmatic and dealt with circumstances as they arose. The leadership of the union certainly had a set of principles and long-range goals, but it took a measured approach toward what seemed possible at the time. The union pushed matters but never to the point of endangering the unity of the players. This book analyzes how the bargaining process worked as well as its results. In addition to those sources mentioned above, I have examined public releases, briefing papers and synopses prepared for the Executive Committee of the union, the notes of participants, and the manuscript minutes of bargaining sessions. The last were usually taken by a representative of ownership. I also had access to the minutes of various joint study committees. I have used contemporary journalistic accounts to gain a broader understanding of what took place and how press accounts might have affected the negotiations and what the public understood about the situation. I also took the opportunity to get the retrospective reflections and insights of journalists who covered the events between 1966 and 1981.

This book emphasizes how the union established goals and how the players' ideas of what was possible and what tactics were acceptable changed dramatically. It calls three commonly held assumptions into question: that the success of the union was inevitable, that it had some well-defined master plan, and that it was Miller's union.

The most serious popular misinterpretation of the union concerns Miller's role. The struggles between the union and ownership have often been portrayed as a kind of morality play: St. Marvin versus the dragon of entrenched, paternalistic ownership or the Machiavellian "Merchant of Menace"[33] leading selfish, gullible players headlong into destroying the foundations of America's national pastime. There is no question that Miller played a pivotal role in transforming the union from a venue for players' gripes into an agent for change. But it was the players union, not something that Miller created and ran for them. He, Dick Moss, the counsel for the union, and Don Fehr, Moss's successor (and later the executive director of the association) were the spokesmen and tacticians for the players. The players determined what they wanted to accomplish and what they were willing to risk.

The idea of Miller as Edgar Bergen to the players' Charlie McCarthy achieved common currency in the sports pages and among many fans. The comments of a Boston writer in 1973 were typical of this opinion: "players have no real grasp of what is going on. . . . It is to Miller's advantage, of course, to keep the players dependent on him and his office. The less the players know, the more dependent they will be."[34] It might have been comfortable to portray men who make a living playing a game as overgrown adolescents, but this misreads the players and the association. It underestimates significantly the ability of the players to recognize what was best for them.

The popular perception of Miller's power ignores the role of individual players, especially those who were active within the association. It consigns them to the background, like extras in a film who were there to be manipulated and used by their executive director. In fact it was the *players'* association, a point made forcefully by Joe Torre: "It was our union . . . his strength was only as strong as we were."[35]

Most of the important work of the union took place behind closed doors in the meetings between the players and the staff of the union, in team meetings where player representatives briefed other players, and in negotiating sessions between the union and the representatives of the owners. The union was a complex organization composed of people with different opinions about goals and tactics. The way in which the players resolved these differences and how Miller, Moss, and Fehr mobilized the human assets of the union is the story of how the union transformed itself and baseball.

The first chapter discusses how the association operated under the leadership of Judge Robert Cannon and Frank Scott. This is essential in order to understand the scope of the changes that took place after 1966. Chapter two examines the decision of the players to take a new direction and to hire a labor executive as the first executive director of the association and looks at the relationship that developed between Miller and the players. Chapter three discusses how the union changed its approach and how the owners and the press reacted to that.

Succeeding chapters concentrate on specific issues and events that became the basis for the new relationship between the players and the owners. Some of these were obvious turning points for the union—the Basic Agreements (baseball's terminology for a collective bargaining agreement), Curt Flood's court challenge of the reserve system, the decision of the union to strike in 1972, the 1976 arbitration decision that ended free agency, and the lengthy 1981 strike. Some of the other issues were nowhere near as apparent to the public. These include the range of opinions that existed among the players, the need for the union to find a way to finance itself, the changing attitude of the players toward the commissioner and ownership, and the relationship between the union and the media.

The union did not change itself or challenge the owners in a social or political vacuum. The players made the decision to change their situation in the context of dramatic challenges to hitherto accepted norms in many areas of American society. As Jim Bunning, one of the pivotal figures in changing the union, pointed out at the time, "today's player . . . isn't about to take anything the owners offer and be grateful for it. The new attitude on the part of the players brought the association to where it is, not vice versa."[36]

Throughout American society in the 1960s, there was a growing reluctance to accept the status quo and an increasing willingness to question authority. The Players Association was part of the cultural and social milieu of the era, but the union changed within a set of circumstances that were shaped by baseball and its history.

As the French social historian Pierre Bourdieu reminds us, "'The history of sports is a relatively autonomous history which, even when marked by major events of economic and social history, has its own tempo, its own evolutionary laws, its crises, in short, its specific chronology.'"[37] Bourdieu's observation certainly applies to the sport that laid claim to America's national pastime.

Miller and Paul Richards rarely agreed on anything, but Richards's 1967 prediction might have been an exception. The big difference between the two men and the groups they represented is that ownership regarded Richard's prediction as something to fear, while the union regarded it as exactly what they were striving to accomplish.

In any case, Richards was absolutely correct. When the first Basic Agreement was signed in 1968, it was the start of a process that culminated in the end of baseball as it had been known to owners, players, writers, and fans for almost a century. The effects of these changes were felt on the field of play and in the perceptions of the fans as well as in the front offices and the lives of every player. How and why that took place is the story that follows.

A "HOUSE UNION"

THERE IS A LONG HISTORY, starting in the late nineteenth century, of efforts on the part of professional baseball players to form labor organizations to improve their situation. One of the most significant took place right after baseball resumed at the end of World War II.

On April 17, 1946, Robert F. Murphy, a Massachusetts-based lawyer and labor organizer, registered the American Baseball Guild in his home state. At the press conferences that followed, Murphy made clear that he planned to establish a union of major league players that would bargain with the owners for higher wages, a pension fund, and improved working conditions. The turning point of this proposed union took place in early June when the players, trainers, and coaches for the Pittsburgh Pirates took a strike vote. Pittsburgh was a heavily unionized city, and Murphy and his supporters thought that the Guild stood the best chance of succeeding with the Pirates. The vote disappointed them.

The vote was 20-16 in favor of a strike, but it failed because the participants had agreed that it would take a two-thirds vote to call a strike. In retrospect, the Guild seems quixotic. It appeared serious enough at the time that the owner of the Pirates made a rare visit to the clubhouse and ensured that Murphy was barred from visiting the players. The Pirates had a semi-pro team ready to perform as replacement players. Some of the players, led by Rip Sewell, a veteran pitcher, made it clear that they would go on the field no matter how their teammates voted.

Major league players in 1946 were not thinking about changing labor relations in baseball. Many of them were returning to a career after military service. They were aware of the insecurity of the job and how quickly a career could be ended. They were competing against mature minor leaguers, many of whom were also returning from the service and were hungrier than usual for even a brief chance at the fame and salaries of the major leagues. The owners had a pool of players from whom to choose, and they left no doubt that malcontents, so-called clubhouse lawyers, had no future. It was also difficult for players to shake free of the decades-old culture of baseball that claimed that clubs "would take care of former players." Writers and executives went out of their way to remind players that in the old days, they really had it rough. They should thank their lucky stars that they got to be major leaguers, and if they complained, things would get a lot worse.

In 1946 the nation was at a new level of prosperity, and baseball was reaping its share of it. Outside baseball, membership in unions had reached an all-time high. Murphy's platform talked about a rise in the minimum salary and improvements in conditions of employment. He mentioned the reserve system, but he was more concerned with issues that affected the everyday lives of the players. The weekly baseball paper *The Sporting News* was almost a house organ of Major League Baseball, but it probably was close to accurate in stating, "not one per cent of the player personnel brought up the matter of the reserve clause in meetings."[1] Their concerns were much more basic. One member of the 1946 Pirates cited tip money for spring training and covers for the bull pens as the most pressing issues. The same player remembered that Murphy "was careful not to call it [the Guild] a 'union,' he always had a euphemism."[2]

At the same time, there were developments in Mexico that affected the players. When Jorge and Alfonso Pasqual tried to start a new league, they introduced novel features into the relationship between major league players and their clubs. They offered big raises coupled with the idea that players should be free to accept a better deal if someone offered it. Ralph Kiner, a rookie with the Pirates in 1946, remembers that it was the Pasquals who "got the players to thinking about big money," but at the same time, "none of us ever thought we would get out of baseball law, whatever it was then."[3] The Mexican League might have started players thinking, but few of them acted.

Murphy's effort to organize the players failed completely, but it convinced some of the owners that it would be prudent to head off potential difficulties in the future by making some changes. This group, led by Larry MacPhail of the Yankees and Lou Perini of the Braves, started talking with some of the players. A series of meetings took place during the summer between a committee of owners led by MacPhail and a group of player representatives including Johnny Murphy of the Yankees, Dixie Walker of the Dodgers, and Marty Marion of the Cardinals.

The gains made by the players in 1946 might seem insignificant by later standards, but they were important at the time. A minimum salary of fifty-five hundred dollars was established. It was less than the players expected, but it established the principle that a minimum should exist.[4] There was a limit placed on how much the team could reduce a player's salary from one year to the next. Spring training expense money was an important part of the new deal for players. This became known as "Murphy Money" by generations of ballplayers, most of whom knew nothing about Murphy or his 1946 guild.[5]

For most players, the big change in 1946 was the creation of their pension plan. It was originally funded by a contribution from the players that was matched by money from World Series radio and television. It emerged into something financed from revenue from the All-Star Game, which the players participated in without payment. The players took the pension plan very seriously, but it was not well funded. By 1949 the plan did not have the money to meet some of its obligations.

In 1953 some players started to ask questions about the pension fund. A group of respected veteran players met at the All-Star Game to form a new organization. It was primarily an ad hoc arrangement set up by the players to monitor the pension fund and to bring some questions to the attention of the owners. Each club selected a player representative, but there was no formal mechanism for the process. In theory, the player reps were elected, but in practice it varied widely from club to club. On some teams the general manager or manager suggested who would be the best choice. On others the position was held by a veteran player who had the respect of his teammates or a player who could not figure out a way to decline the position. There was one tangible benefit to the player rep, the free loan of a Chrysler automobile from the manufacturer for the duration of his service in the job.

The player reps met a couple of times each year among themselves and designated a player from each league to meet annually with a group of the owners. The player reps nominated the players who served on the pension committee, where they met with representatives of the owners. Some star players were involved with the organization, most prominently, Bob Feller, its first president, Allie Reynolds, and Ralph Kiner. Reynolds and Kiner were elected by player reps to represent the American and National Leagues, respectively. The players assessed themselves minimal dues that enabled them to pay some of the expenses of the player reps to attend meetings and to distribute some written material to all the players. The association entrusted the operation of the group to a part-time retainer, Frank Scott. He had been the traveling secretary for the Yankees. After leaving that job, he set up guest appearances and a few endorsements for some players. He handled the few chores that were necessary to run the Players Association. That kept him involved with the players, and he received expenses for his troubles. Most discussions of the MLBPA make little mention of Scott's role over the years. He described himself as a "player representative and coordinator of all baseball matters involving the Players Association in relation to the club owners and the baseball Commissioner's Office."[6]

Ralph Kiner is in a unique position to comment on how the association evolved and how baseball has changed since 1946. He was a veteran of World War II, and in 1946 he became the first rookie in forty years to lead the National League in home runs, playing on the Pirate team that had taken the strike vote. Kiner became the Pirates' player representative "almost by default, since I was the only guy who had the stature to stand up to the owners. . . . There was a general feeling that they would ship you out if you were disruptive . . . and even though I didn't have much education, at least I had enough not to be intimidated by owners."[7]

For most of his career with the Pirates, Kiner was virtually a one-man team. He was paid well by baseball standards. He also knew first-hand how powerless the players were to determine anything other than what happened on the field. After tying for the league lead in home runs in 1952, he was told that his contract for 1953 would include a 25 percent pay cut, the maximum allowable. There were no negotiations. When Kiner pointed out to Pittsburgh General Manager Branch Rickey that the Pirates drew good crowds to watch a bad club only because fans wanted to see him hit home runs, Rickey responded, "We can finish last without you." That reply was a big hit with baseball reporters. After all, Rickey was a baseball genius and good copy; Kiner was a ballplayer who thought too much of himself. None of the writers pointed out that it was Rickey who had acquired the players that made the Pirates a last-place team. No one in baseball knew more about the importance of gate money than Branch Rickey, but he ignored that part of Kiner's value when it came to contract time.

Kiner was instrumental in creating the predecessor of the current Players Association, but he had no idea of forming a union. In 1953 his counterpart in the American League, Allie Reynolds, had addressed that possibility: "I would be as opposed to a labor boss in baseball as would the owners. We can only hope for the best and rely on the fairness of the men who run baseball."[8] The next year he made his position even clearer: "I have nothing against union in industry. But if I had any suspicions that we in baseball were moving towards a union, I would not have anything to do with the enterprise. . . . The union pattern does not promise anything good for our profession."[9]

Reynolds and Kiner created a stir in 1953 when they brought a lawyer, J. Norman Lewis, with them to attend a regularly scheduled pension committee meeting with the owners. They wanted Lewis to explain some of the issues that they were going to discuss in the meeting. The owners responded that Lewis was welcome to be part of the discussions as long as he would sit in the hall outside the room. Shirley Povich, the widely read Washington sports columnist, praised the owners for recognizing that "the players are grown up people, with the right to hire a lawyer," and pointed out that "it required more than a bit of courage for such as Reynolds and Kiner to lead their fight. Theirs was a completely unselfish project . . . [and] they were risking the wrath of the owners . . . [and] they had less to gain . . . than any of the athletes they represented."[10]

Dixie Walker, a long-time star outfielder, wrote an article to remind his fellow players that they should be satisfied to protect what they have "and find out how to hold it, instead of running it into the ground through neglect or arrogance . . . [and] through unreasonable demands." A retired player and manager, Bill Terry, went even further in a 1954 *Sporting News* article. He warned the players that they had no right to complain. They didn't know how tough things used to be, he claimed, and complaints about conditions were leading to "a soft race of major leaguers." They were unwise to interfere, since "baseball has made great advances because of control by the owners. . . . [Kiner and Reynolds] will find themselves in a bad spot if they do not halt right now."[11]

A few months after the Lewis episode, a sketch at the annual dinner of the New York Baseball Writers gave this version:

A lawyer is everyone's right
Whenever he gets in a fight
But make sure your lawyer stays in the foyer
While Frick guards, he SAYS, players' rights.[12]

Years later, Kiner still is angry about what happened and is convinced that it was symptomatic of the situation in baseball: "In the '50s, we were powerless, [the player reps] out there on a springboard with no help . . . and players tend to be self-satisfied . . . I got mine, now you get yours. . . .

There was a general feeling that they would ship you out if you were disruptive." Kiner was not sure exactly what Lewis could have done for the players, but he was bothered by something that "was un-American, not to be allowed to have your lawyer there. [We] were competitive by nature and were angry, . . . but we were in over our heads. After all, we were ballplayers, not businessmen. . . . We needed some continuity at the 'head' of our guild."[13]

After 1954 the player reps continued to meet two or three times a year, and their designees met annually with a group of owners to talk about the pension fund. The owners did not alter their policy about the players having a lawyer present. Lewis became an advisor to the players and did some research concerning salaries and pensions. In 1955 he published a report that discussed some changes that might take place without disrupting baseball.

Newspaper reports coming out of the 1958 winter meeting of the owners prominently mentioned the Players Association for the first time in years. Some owners and executives went out of their way to talk to the press about the arrogance and ingratitude of the players. One owner commented how "the players have reached the limit [in their demands] and the fever will run its course and leave. They never have had it so good and they know it." Another owner concluded, "I don't want to get mixed up in this mess. But the players are moving closer and closer to a union. That twenty per cent is union stuff." What enraged the owners was a "demand" (the phrase used by *The Sporting News*) made by the players, which paralleled a suggestion made by Lewis, that they might consider a system where player salaries should equal 20 percent of the clubs' revenues.[14] In reality, the association was in no position to "demand" anything.

Tom Yawkey, the owner of the Red Sox, had the last word in an article in *The Sporting News.* The paper described him as a man who "always treated his players fairly," who never used his right to cut salaries by 25 percent, and who was "the highly principled senior owner and vice president of the American League." Yawkey wondered out loud whether it was worth the time and money to stay in baseball because of the "undemocratic principle of the players' proposal." In case anyone did not understand Yawkey's definition of democracy, he added, "To me the greatest example of American democracy is the right a player has to sit down with a general manager and negotiate his contract."[15]

In late 1958 the players decided that they no longer needed Lewis's services. There appears to have been no connection between the decision and the 20 percent suggestion. The leadership of the Players Association had become convinced that it had not received enough from Lewis to warrant paying him a retainer.

The organization had a casual quality about it. Scott sent letters to more than four hundred players asking for comments. He reminded them, "This is *your* Association." He received responses from a total of thirty-nine players. One player commented, "Write some bylaws to govern the Association to build as strong an association as possible."[16]

In the spring of 1959 Robin Roberts, a college-educated star pitcher with the Phillies, was a member of the Pension Fund Committee and a National League player representative. He tried to convince his fellow player representatives that there was enough possible work for the association to warrant a permanent office with a full-time staff.

Some of the player reps encouraged Roberts to become a spokesman for the association. He corresponded with owners and general managers about playing conditions and urged Scott to take up issues of scheduling, field conditions, meal money, and other concerns directly with the owners. Little came out of Roberts's efforts. He maintained a low-key approach but did enough to prompt one veteran player to tell Scott that the association was a "tremendous step in the right direction." This player also said there was a need for better public relations "when a fellow like Robin Roberts must shoulder the brunt of newspaper attacks—such as Dick Young has written in his N.Y. paper—I think he should receive the proper support from us and at least make the public read our side of any controversy which has been brought up in the papers."[17] The members did nothing to implement the suggestion. Coincidentally, when the association became an active union, Young was its most consistent and acerbic critic in the press.

In 1960 Scott presented a document, "A Central Office for Major League Baseball Players," to a meeting of the player representatives. Scott stated that although the player reps were "well selected and competent men," they did not have the time or expertise to communicate with all the other players or to deal with important issues that might arise. "What was lacking . . . was a central clearing house for all baseball player matters and an active liaison man whose function was to represent baseball matters and baseball matters only . . . [and who would] be ready to travel between clubs to discuss whatever matter has arisen within a particular club." There were problems "often ignored unintentionally by club owners because they are not presented properly and are not regarded as indicative of the majority of the baseball players . . . problems which if presented in the right manner and with the proper approach to club owners or the Commissioner of Baseball, they can be solved with little or no fuss."[18]

Scott concluded that no adversarial or confrontational relationship should exist between the players and the owners. In an appended report concerning public relations, he took time to reject the idea that anything in it was part of an "anti-owner" campaign. His plan combined a response to Roberts's ideas with a way to increase Scott's job. When Scott recommended himself for the position, he stressed, "Above all, I can attain respectability for such an office."[19] Scott's solution to whatever unspecified problems might exist was to have someone who could work within the present framework of baseball and be a link with ownership and league executives.

Roberts wanted to go further than Scott. Whoever ran the office should confer with the commissioner, deal with player endorsement contracts, hold press conferences, and handle other matters. He should retain a law firm, and "after careful examination by the players group . . . we can let the players decide after a year if it should continue." Roberts stressed that it was the responsibility of the players to determine what the "office" should do and that it was up to them to monitor the performance of whoever ran their association for them.[20]

The step that transformed the association into a potentially viable organization was the decision, announced by Roberts and Harvey Kuenn, to establish a central office in New York. The office was housed in hotel rooms rented by Scott out of which he also conducted his own business as an agent. The stated purpose of the central office was to "make it feasible for ball players to register their views and opinions on any matters pertaining to Association policy or player welfare." This was the first time that the Players Association had identified itself in that role. At the same time, Scott's role as an employee of the association specifically "did not pertain to the player's relationship with the club which employs him."[21]

The most important aspect of Scott's new activity was the announcement that he was taking applications for the position as part-time legal counsel for the association. The duties of this person were not stated, but clearly they would be something more than Lewis had done. Among the candidates who either applied or were nominated were former Commissioner A. B. Chandler ("needs no introduction"), Richard Moss ("young Pittsburgh attorney . . . is interested in baseball . . . can give the position the time and energy it needs"), Edward Bennett Williams ("he has represented clients such as Costello, Hoffa, and others not because he leans in any way towards this kind of client"), and Judge Robert C. Cannon of the Circuit Court of Wisconsin.[22]

Cannon had an impressive resume and an even more interesting pedigree. His father, Raymond, had been a lawyer for players, including Shoeless Joe Jackson, and had made some efforts to organize a players' union. As a congressman from Wisconsin, the elder Cannon had tried, and failed, to get the attorney general to investigate the monopoly aspects of baseball and had considered introducing legislation to end baseball's 1922 antitrust exemption.

Bob Friend, the Pirates' pitcher, was the National League player representative and one of the most influential leaders of the association. He wired Scott, "Please give considerable attention to a recent applicant for player attorney Judge Robert Cannon from Milwaukee. Of all applicants I would favor this one."[23] Friend made clear that he wanted the legal consultant of the association to ensure that the pension fund was kept safe and to see that the players would have some way to address complaints about conditions that could affect their performance on the field.

Cannon's 1959 letter of application pointed out that although he was not an authority on pensions, he was "cognizant of the problems which the major league players have experienced in the past number of years, and which may face them in the near future." He presented no specifics about those "problems." His expressed philosophy was that "baseball is and must forever be an integral part of developing the youth of America. . . . [Players must] also set a good example off the field." Cannon was selected by the Executive Committee for the position after a brief discussion among the player reps. He was pleased that his appointment was "well received by baseball authorities and the club owners in general. . . . I know that by working together, we will continue to make baseball the greatest sport in America."[24]

During Cannon's first year in office, the Players Association was approached about hiring a Washington lobbyist to attempt to change the legal status of the sport. Cannon replied that the ballplayers should not endanger the tremendous gains they had made and "that if the Association, in the future, proceeds cautiously and carefully many more deserving benefits will accrue to the individual player." He wanted to do nothing that would "jeopardize the fine relationship existing between the players and the club owners. . . . I am satisfied that the Commissioner and the Presidents of the respective leagues sit as quasi judicial officers and *it is presumed that they will accord fair treatment to both the player and the club owner.* Until such time as it is proven to the contrary, it is best that we not associate ourselves with any organization" (emphasis added).[25]

Cannon mirrored the attitudes of the players in his distrust of allying the association with other organizations. But he went far beyond them in his effusive respect for the fairness and integrity of the owners. He had never been subjected to one-sided contract negotiations or being traded, actions that the players had grown to accept as commonplace, however disturbing they might be. Cannon believed that the owners would act benevolently and that the commissioner and presidents they hired and paid would act impartially. In his version of major league baseball, there were no issues that were serious enough to divide the players from the owners.

Cannon knew that it would require money to run the new permanent office and the association's part-time staff. He rejected the suggestion that the owners fund the Players Association, since this would not "be a wholesome situation [making] the players to a certain degree beholden to the club owners and this would not be good for anyone."[26] He recommended that the office be financed in the same way as those of the commissioner and the league presidents, through revenue generated by the World Series.

By 1960 the association had an office, a part-time director, and a legal advisor who spoke publicly as the representative of the players. In one of his first appearances for the association, Cannon testified before a congressional committee reviewing legislation about the proposed Continental League. Cannon saw absolutely no need for congressional interference in the current legal structure of baseball. He assured everyone that the club owners and the commissioner would work out any problems, and "whatever determination or decisions they came to would be for the best interest of baseball and the ball players in general."[27] *The Sporting News* had a positive impression of Cannon. The paper told its readers that within Cannon's first few months as advisor to the players, there was a new harmony between players and owners that was especially important since the low point that had occurred the previous year. *The Sporting News* was convinced that Cannon would be more realistic than the player reps, because he would "make no demands, no public statements."[28]

After Cannon's appointment, Roberts and a few other interested player representatives continued to talk about the need for a permanent office run by someone whose qualifications went beyond those of Scott. A study committee was created, composed of Bob Allison, an outfielder with the Twins, Friend, and Roberts. At its first meeting it decided "to discuss the

Judge Robert C. Cannon, legal advisor to the MLBPA for six years, visiting the Cardinals clubhouse to talk with the players. Seated next to him is the association's director, Frank Scott. In 1966 Cannon turned down the opportunity to be the MLBPA's first full-time executive director. (AP/Wide World Photos)

proposal and to secure Commissioner Frick's approval." The committee reported to the player representatives and then joined Cannon and Scott at a meeting with Frick, National League President Warren Giles, and American League President Joe Cronin "to further discuss this new plan for a permanent office and methods for financing same." Roberts still wanted the association to hire a full-time director and a full-time legal representative to deal with the pension fund and "all business matters pertaining to baseball players." After a lengthy discussion the player representatives tabled his motion by a unanimous vote. At the same meeting, the Executive Committee reported an interesting development—the owners would permit Judge Cannon to sit in with the players on the pension committee.[29]

Cannon felt it was inappropriate for him to voice opinions about the structure of baseball, but there were some times when he thought he could play a constructive role. When a player sarcastically criticized the president of the National League for fining Milwaukee infielder Eddie Mathews, Cannon responded that the remarks were in bad taste and that the player should be glad that former Commissioner Landis was not in office because the player would have been in serious trouble. Cannon wrote that "everyone has the right" to criticize a league president or a commissioner, but "For *anyone to question* the honesty or integrity of an administrative official of baseball . . . is neither good for the game nor an aid to good player-club relationships" (emphasis added).[30]

Cannon found one public issue where he thought he could, and should, intervene. Baseball received bad publicity when the Reds second baseman Billy Martin, a player famed for his temper and using his fists, charged the mound and delivered a punch that broke the jaw of the Cubs pitcher Jim Brewer. Martin and his general manager asked Cannon to appear at the disciplinary hearing held by Warren Giles. The judge answered that since he represented all the players, he could not take sides. He came up with a way to put the matter behind everyone by asking Martin and Brewer to walk across the field and shake hands. He assured Brewer that it would show that the pitcher was a "big league gentleman" while telling Martin that shaking hands was not admitting that he was wrong.

Cannon wanted to avoid any lingering problems between the players and to protect the image of the sport.[31] Brewer had threatened a suit for damages, and Cannon was especially anxious to keep lawyers out of the situation. Cannon's proposed solution had the sentiments of a fan, one who grew up in the tradition that "boys will be boys." The players had to be protected from the consequences of their actions, and baseball had to be kept apart from the consequences that operated in the real world.

The three meetings each year gave the player representatives the opportunity to discuss matters that affected their own teams and other players. There was a report about the pension fund and a list of things that the players wanted Cannon and Scott to present to the owners. Better mounds in the bull pens in Yankee Stadium, "the odor in Philadelphia dugouts," more lights in Houston for night games, covered runways in Minneapolis from the visitors' clubhouse to their dugout, and "more toilet facilities in Cincinnati park for players" might not seem like the issues that would change baseball.[32] But they mattered a great deal to the players, who thought they might be able to get the attention of the owners by bringing up such issues at their meetings.

Reporters and the public might not be interested in the "suggestions" made to the owners that all parks have telephones from both dugouts to the bull pens and that "the second base umpire in the National League be positioned behind the second base bag," but if the association could not get results about things that affected the everyday professional lives of its members, it was not good for anything else. Years later, players who were involved in the association remembered the agenda of the joint meetings. They pointed to it as symptomatic of the minimal expectations they had for the association.

It appears that few players gave much thought to changing their relationship with the clubs. It was baseball as it had always been. Steve Boros, who was involved in the pre-1966 Players Association and remained in baseball until the 1990s, summed it up:

> Players had no leverage. . . . They were taken advantage of, but nothing to do. There were lots of horror stories, distrust, and anger, but we had no weapons. . . . After all, lots of players never thought about anything other than they were getting paid good money to play a kids' game. . . . It's basically a selfish business, not really a team sport. You can be selfish and succeed, and that's why so few players wanted to get involved. . . . [We] hurt ourselves by not wanting to share information about salaries. . . . There was something unfair about being locked into a system. It was so ingrained, that they never thought about it. Later, I thought how stupid it was not to have realized this was the U.S. . . . in the sixties we didn't think we had a hope to change things, even if we thought about what should be changed. You could only petition the owners and hope that there were more people like Yawkey and Wrigley who might graciously agree to what the players wanted.

Boros chose his words carefully, and the sarcasm of "graciously" portrayed a situation that Scott and Cannon perceived as natural, as well as in the best interests of the game.[33]

Cannon toured the spring training camps after taking the position as advisor to the association in 1960. At his first stop, Scott asked Cannon if he would mind if an employee of the Yankees stayed in the clubhouse, and Cannon replied, "Who the hell am I to tell Joe D what to do?" Cannon went out of his way to tell players how lucky they were to have a job "that 10,000 men making a lot more money would give anything to do." He told the players that he "was not there to fight ownership. After all, you had to recognize that the other side had problems. . . . [You] can't do anything to damage the good of baseball, like calling a strike and getting fans sore at you. . . . [You] have to make sure that [they] didn't endanger the cash flow of the clubs." Owners and players were in it together.[34]

Cannon saw his role as an intermediary during the rare times when there might be problems. His first appearance as a spokesman for the Players Association had been at a joint owners-players meeting. When he went into the room he was faced with Joe Cronin, Warren Giles, and "all those great players, . . . [a situation] that left me a little bit starry eyed." Cannon did not talk with the player reps before making a presentation in which he enunciated his philosophy: "My primary concern will be what's in the best interest of baseball. Second thought will be what's best for the players." As he left the room, Cannon promised himself that in future meetings things would be different. He would sit at the head table with the commissioner, and the players would sit at the same table with the owners, "not across from them with swords in their eyes."[35]

Roberts's 1960 memorandum contained a phrase that was to prove prescient: "I am sure that if we make arrangements for such a set-up [a full-time director and a legal advisor], we will find other benefits and duties which are not so obvious at the present time." In 1962 the members of the association were satisfied enough with the performance of their part-time employees that Cannon was reappointed as legal advisor by a vote of 580 to 15, and Scott was reappointed as director of the general office by a vote of 430 to 137.[36]

In 1965 the association decided to create a position for a full-time executive director. It authorized Scott to solicit applications and nominations. The applicants for the new position included Judge Cannon, Marvin Miller, an economist with the Steelworkers Union, and Bob Feller. In their brief letters to Scott, Miller and Feller mentioned pension plan experience. Cannon emphasized his civic involvement and the many talks he gave "on behalf of baseball" and advocated maintaining the fine relationship between the players and the owners.[37]

The association established a screening committee for the position. Not all of the members of the committee interviewed all of the candidates. Most noteworthy, Bob Friend chose not to meet with Miller. This was not so much a commentary on Miller as a statement by Friend that he was convinced that Cannon was the right man for the job. The Executive Committee selected Cannon for the position in January 1966. He had a track record, and they knew what to expect from him.

Cannon accepted the position but immediately began to have second thoughts about the job. He realized how much pension he would lose if he left the Wisconsin bench, and he began to talk about that and other financial hardships. He discussed setting up the office of the association in Milwaukee but then compromised to the point where Chicago was an acceptable location for him. Some members of the Executive Committee wondered about his conduct, and they responded by insisting that the association's office should be in New York.

In 1991, Cannon claimed that the expectations of the players either had changed or that he had misjudged them: "the leadership of the Association, not the rank and file, wanted [me] to go punch the owners in the nose, but don't tell them we told you to do it." Cannon believes that a militant attitude had entered into the leadership of the Players Association and that "Roberts and [Jim] Bunning [a pitcher with the Phillies] somehow had become radicals." Cannon believed they thought that he had developed too close a relationship with the owners. Cannon described Roberts as "a fine person, good morally, and a great player, but he had ideas [that] were little bit anti-owner."[38] Cannon's viewpoint probably is colored by the recognition that it was Roberts who brought Miller's name to the association's attention.

Robin Roberts (testifying at a Senate committee, July 9, 1958) led efforts to transform the association into an organization with an active agenda and a full-time staff. In 1966, he brought the name of Marvin Miller to the attention of the MLPBA.

Jim Bunning (with Commissioner Kuhn and President Nixon in 1969) was one of the veterans who provided strong leadership for the union after 1966.

In 1987, Bunning had a darker view of Cannon's conduct: "the judge was playing hard to get because the job he really wanted was commissioner of baseball, not executive director of the Players Association."[39] However, in 1966 it was Bob Friend, Cannon's strong supporter, whose views seemed to give the judge the most reason for caution. Three years earlier Friend had denounced publicly anything resembling union activities by the association, saying, "'the reserve clause is an absolute necessity for the survival of baseball [and] . . . during the thirteen years I have been in the National League, I know of no player who has been exploited.'"[40] Cannon thinks that Friend's willingness to go along with the two more radical pitchers was a product of his disillusionment over his trade in December 1965 from the Pirates to the Yankees, which had "made Friend become a little bit militant."[41] If Cannon is correct, it was certainly not the first time that being traded had shown an established player the harsh realities behind the romantic ideals of baseball. Nor, as Curt Flood was to show a few years later, would it be the last.

One reporter attempted to explain that pension issues and moving to New York were not all that influenced Cannon to decline the job. Jack Clary reported that Cannon was disturbed by the fact that although he received a clear majority of the votes, it had been "far from the 'unanimous choice' announced at the time." Clary had nothing but praise for Cannon's intelligence and ethics and thought he was wise in thinking he could not accept a position of representation "with that faction of disapproval within the union."[42]

Bunning is convinced that he was not the only player who had second thoughts about Cannon. In 1990, when Bunning was a U.S. congressman, he claimed that the move away from Cannon was a sign of how frustrated some players had become. "We would take our requests to the owners at a joint meeting and then they would just laugh at us and say 'sure, we'll look at it,' and that was the end of it. We didn't know labor law, we didn't know collective bargaining."[43]

Cannon certainly did not think in those terms. Years later, he described his situation as being able "to pick up the phone and talk to the owners. I could tell the Baltimore owner, 'You're a fair and decent man . . . this is an unfair situation and has to be changed.' . . . Things were tough for the owners in 1966, no matter what Miller says."[44] Bunning's memories agree with Cannon's in one respect: in 1966 the vast majority of players did not talk with one another about problems and did not want confrontation with the owners.

If Bunning is correct that the players needed someone to challenge the "friendly, father image" of the owners, Judge Cannon was the wrong man for the job. Cannon was proud of his close relationship with the owners and saw no problems with it. He thought briefly about reconsidering his decision not to accept the position when he received an offer to guarantee him a pension that was equivalent to what he would be giving up by leaving the bench. The fact that the offer was made by the owner of the Pirates, John Galbreath, did not trouble Cannon. After all, Galbreath had the interests of baseball at heart. Rather than being wary of a possible conflict of interest, Cannon says that he did not accept the offer because he had "got it up to here with players who kept talking about money."[45]

Even if Cannon had changed his mind again, there is serious doubt that influential players like Friend and Bunning would have been willing to give him a second chance to restructure the job for himself. It was not so much his conditions as his attitude that led them to question whether they had made the right decision. Once Friend stopped supporting Cannon, there was no chance that the judge would become the first executive director of the Players Association.

There is a remarkable consistency between the private and public views Cannon expressed while he worked for the association and his version of them almost thirty years later. Those opinions make it difficult to see how he could have treated seriously the complaints of the player representatives who, in the words of one of them, "sat around at meetings and talked about which of us would be traded because of our actions with the association."[46] There is no question that if Cannon had become executive director, he would not have done it "with a chip on his shoulder and [been] anti-management and anti-ownership," which is his description of Marvin Miller.[47]

Cannon would have had trouble mounting a serious challenge to the reserve system, which he had described to Congress as a "necessary evil." He claims that his approach would have been to go with a small group of players to the commissioner and ask him to set up a commission that would include owners, players, and baseball's attorney, Lou Carroll, "a wonderful, fair man." They would come up with possible modifications. Cannon did not want to get people angry and turn the discussions into an adversarial situation. He believes that he would have "gotten changes because they [the owners] owed me something and I would have been able to collect." He thinks he could have convinced the owners that the current system "was repugnant to all Americans," and the "kind of relationship I had with the owners" meant they would listen. He could tell men like Ewing Kauffman "that it's not fair, and [changes] are going to come sooner or later," and Kauffman would have listened to him.[48]

Cannon was sincere in his faith in the willingness of the owners to establish a harmonious relationship. But the events of the next few years show that the relationship he envisioned would have allowed the owners to avoid any meaningful changes in the power they held over the players. Cannon's attitude was a combination of wishful thinking and an unrealistic, romantic idea of the owners. The fact remains that the owners were determined not to consider any changes in the reserve system, and he was not willing or able to understand either that or the need for changes.

Cannon contends, "Had the players authorized me, I would have gone all the way . . . would have issued an ultimatum . . . but would not use the word 'strike' because the players would not have accepted the idea and it was the wrong thing to do." He was right that the idea of a strike had no place in the tradition of baseball. He was equally correct that in 1966 there was no evidence that the players would have considered the idea of a strike. He felt that he had a better way to deal with a potential conflict. "Why should I make a damned fool of myself by making demands? After all, I was winning more than I was losing, especially with the pension fund. . . . I knew how far to push because I knew how far they [the owners] could go."[49]

Cannon's view of how far the owners *could* go coincided with how far they were willing to go. He consistently put himself in their position, never seeing himself as the independent voice of players who had justified grievances. In 1966 Cannon did not see the important changes that had already taken place in baseball. Corporate involvement in the sport had begun to alter the attitudes of owners, and that affected the players. Cannon still believed in a baseball where the owners ran things with a firm, just hand limited only by a fair-minded commissioner like Judge Landis. Ford Frick was, in Cannon's terms, "a good man . . . baseball all the way, but did not have the training to be commissioner." Cannon thought that what baseball needed in the next commissioner was someone with judicial training who loved baseball and could be as "fair as a state judge hearing a suit against the state." Cannon thus considered himself superbly qualified for the job he described as "the biggest job in America besides the Presidency."[50] Two years earlier Dick Young had predicted, "Robert Cannon . . . who is apprenticing as legal counsel for the ball players, will wind up commissioner of baseball in two or three years, if he plays his cards right."[51]

It's tempting to look at Cannon's somewhat tepid advocacy of the Players Association as part of a campaign to become commissioner. He was almost elected when the owners chose General William Eckert to succeed Frick. But the reality is probably less Machiavellian. Cannon wanted to be commissioner because he had a romantic view of baseball. This was precisely the same reason that he could not be a strong advocate for the players. His world of baseball had no place in it for a category called "players' interests." There was no room for hostilities that would endanger the traditions of baseball, even if these hostilities arose from situations that were unfair to the players. He could be an effective head of the association only if it remained a combination of debating groups for miscellaneous complaints and a company union. Cannon could not countenance confrontation because he saw no need for something that was antithetical to his concept of baseball.

Years after Cannon left the association, some of his admirers in the press looked back fondly at his efforts to retain harmony between the players and the owners. One example was Furman Bisher, a veteran writer and sports editor of the *Atlanta Constitution*, who wrote, "Judge Robert Cannon of Milwaukee was the players' advocate for several years, and their most worthy one. When the players' demands were just, he prosecuted them vigorously. When he felt the demands were not just, he told them so." On the tenth anniversary of Miller's hiring, Bisher informed his readers that "Baseball Misses Judge Cannon" and agreed with Cannon's evaluation of the previous decade, "it's a pathetic world . . . not one-tenth of the players know what the issues are. . . . Once you've gone as far as Miller has, there's no way back. I have fears."[52]

Supporters of Judge Cannon have defended his actions by saying that it is unfair to condemn him for not taking actions like his successor because the players were not prepared to support any strong measures and Miller was willing to damage baseball for his own purposes. This version ignores the fact that the same players who supposedly would not back severe steps by Cannon supported Miller a few months later when he openly challenged both the integrity and competence of the owners.

THE ASSOCIATION
CHOOSES CHANGE

ONCE JUDGE CANNON did not accept the job, the search committee took another look at the other men on the list. The name that attracted the most attention was Marvin Miller. Robin Roberts originally had suggested Miller to the screening committee on the recommendation of George Taylor, a distinguished professor at the Wharton School of the University of Pennsylvania. At the same time that the screening committee was compiling its original list, Roberts had sent a list of candidates to Commissioner Eckert and had asked him to determine the suitability of each of them. Roberts told Eckert, "If there is anyone on the list you think we should not choose because he might be bad for the game, then he won't be chosen."[1] Eckert had not responded negatively to any of the names.

When the second search started, Roberts and Jim Bunning approached Miller, who was uncertain whether he wanted his name put forward again. He was particularly concerned about the attitude of Bob Friend and felt that if Friend was opposed to him it would not be worth proceeding any further. By this time, Friend had made it clear to other players that Cannon was no longer acceptable to him. Friend expressed no clear preference among the other candidates but did ask to meet with Miller. It took a while to organize a meeting, but the two got along well. Friend joined Bunning and Roberts in his support for Miller.

There is a compelling case that the new era of the Major League Baseball Players Association became apparent at a special meeting in Miami on March 5, 1966. Its purpose was to discuss the candidates for the position of executive director. The elected player reps were joined by Frank Scott, Robert Cannon, Robin Roberts, Bob Friend, and Harvey Kuenn. The meeting also included General William Eckert, the commissioner of baseball, and Lee MacPhail, his assistant. No one at this meeting of the player representatives seemed at all surprised when these two employees of the owners took part in the discussion.[2]

Eckert cautioned the players to exercise discretion in the selection of their executive director while giving assurances that he would cooperate fully with the new man. His definition of cooperation must be understood in light of his earlier remark that the office of commissioner "was intended to represent the players, *as well as* the owners" (emphasis added).[3] It is easy to joke about Eckert's brief tenure as commissioner, but his predecessors and his successor, Bowie Kuhn, shared the belief that the commissioner was the sole spokesman for everyone involved in Major League Baseball. Cannon had the same philosophy, which clearly was not acceptable to Marvin Miller, who was the topic of this meeting.

Two months after selecting Cannon, the screening committee recommended Miller. The recommendation was approved by the Executive Committee on the first ballot. The offer of the position was contingent on a majority vote of the total membership of the association. The vote would take place after Miller had toured all of the spring training camps to give players a chance to question him. Plans were made to distribute his name and biography to the press and the players. The basic facts about him were clear but open to widely differing interpretations. At the age of forty-eight, he was a labor economist whose career had been spent working for the federal government and the Steelworkers Union. Some players and writers raised questions about how this qualified him to deal with baseball and its unique history and status in American life. He was a life-long fan who could amaze baseball veterans with his knowledge of the history and trivia of the game. In many ways he was the antithesis of anyone who had been involved with the players. His politics were liberal Democratic, his attitude toward the hierarchy of baseball was distinctly nonreverential, and even his mustache seemed too close to the counterculture radicalism that was symbolic of the nation's social and political divisions.[4]

Bunning quickly became a strong supporter of Miller. The Phillies pitcher had spoken a year before about the need to create a permanent office and to hire a full-time executive director because the players "needed continuity" to get any concessions from the owners. Bunning knew that Miller's background with the steelworkers might frighten people in baseball, but that was not important because it "wouldn't take him long to learn the answers . . . [and soon] he would know more about baseball than ownership did." This runs counter to the view of baseball insiders and their allies in the press who claimed that Miller took the job under false premises and then used his position to manipulate unsuspecting players into taking militant antimanagement positions that harmed baseball to satisfy his ego and biases. If it was important to Bunning and other player reps that "Miller knew labor-management law better than anyone the other side ever hired," then they were thinking about taking a different course than Judge Cannon had pursued.[5]

In 1966 it appeared that many players were influenced by two phrases that had always been an important part of management's vocabulary: "we'll take care of you" and "the good of the game." Even players who were disillusioned after retirement have a special emotional feeling for "the game." Players loved playing the game, and almost all of them felt extremely lucky to be making a good living. They were well aware that they were a small elite doing something that millions of other young men would give almost anything to do.

Steve Hamilton was a pitcher for the Yankees and the team's player representative. For years he shared the belief with other players "that we were lucky to be playing baseball . . . [owners and general managers] were concerned with what was good for the game." In many other respects Hamilton was atypical. He was a college graduate who was prepared to teach after he retired from baseball. He had a parallel if short-lived career in the NBA with the Minneapolis Lakers as "the *other* forward they drafted the same time as Elgin Baylor." He wanted to play baseball "because it was fun and it was a good living. . . . All of us had a dream, and mine was to play in Yankee Stadium . . . it was more of an innocent era . . . we didn't make waves, we just played."[6] But even Hamilton realized that baseball was a demanding, uncertain way to make a living that gave him little control over his future.

Players might be thankful to be major leaguers, but they had little starry-eyed sentiment about the job. Don't tell major leaguers about the romance of the bush leagues and the character-building qualities of riding buses between small towns. The minor league experience was merely a necessary rite of passage. Writers could rhapsodize about the minor leagues, but they did not have to live through it. Leonard Koppett noted wryly that "it never seemed true that players were happy just to play."[7]

Players knew that baseball is a game of numbers. To fans, that phrase conjures up batting averages, home run totals, and earned run averages. To players, it means limited spots on rosters, short careers, and very few coaching and front office jobs. Players understood a simple principle about their job as major leaguers—many of them were disposable, and they couldn't stay in baseball forever. Management often assured a player that there would be a place in the organization for him later, but all but the most unsophisticated players knew that there weren't that many jobs.

Bob Barton, a marginal catcher with a few teams who became a player representative and an active member of the Players Association, put it in simple terms: "I might not have been an Einstein, but I was no dummy." This analysis has an interesting echo in the words of Buzzie Bavasi, the Padres' executive with whom Barton had constant problems concerning the union: "Players might be stupid, but they're not dumb." Barton admits that he did not "really know very much about the system [because players] never thought about it until they got stymied by it." His first sense that something might be wrong was when he was a third-string catcher with the Giants. The Giants wanted to keep him as a reserve even though he could start for other teams. He began to think about that and "realized that they knew they had control of you and they could do whatever they wanted with you." When he tried to make a change in his career, "I was treated like a peon. Number one, I was a human being; number two, I was a major league baseball player. I had fought my ass off to get there. . . . At least they could show me some respect. . . . I thought I lived in this country. It just wasn't right."[8]

Shortly before Barton started to think about the "system," another much more successful catcher got involved in the association. Tim Mc-Carver was one of the bright young stars of the St. Louis team that won three pennants in the 1960s. It was an organization that had prided itself since the Branch Rickey days on teaching both fundamentals and standards to its players. This included what it meant to be a professional. McCarver remembers one of the veterans standing up at a meeting in 1966 and making "an impassioned plea" for the players to avoid turning the association into anything resembling a union. That would mean "strikes and strife" and would destroy the great relationship with management.[9] How much did the players know about that relationship? The player that McCarver mentioned did not convince any of his veteran teammates. The Cardinals produced some of the most tough-minded and involved members of the union.

Years later McCarver said, "We were naive. We had no idea about unions. . . . More than that, we had no idea of how powerful we were. . . . I was stupid enough to swallow the idea once that 'I'd be taken care of.' There is no taking care of you." He thinks that the players did not know exactly what was happening and were unsure of the future, but they knew they had to do something to "buck the system. . . . When we negotiated for the first basic agreement, we had to be led, and we had the right guy to lead us. We may have been inexperienced, but we were not dumb. We just needed to have things explained." Years after the negotiations, his strongest memory was "how mad I got listening to writers make ridiculous and untrue assumptions about Svengali [Marvin Miller] leading us. . . . [It was] far from objective journalism. . . . The owners made it easier for us to convince the players [about the need for a Basic Agreement]. You didn't have to be very bright to see that."[10]

The historian Warren Goldstein describes the history of baseball in terms that parallel McCarver's remarks: "For most fans, baseball history is a combination of remembered feelings and facts. . . . [For the players] the baseball world has never been very far removed from the world of work."[11]

The owners could count as well as the players, and they used the situation to exercise control over the players' actions and attitudes. Miller's first task was to see if the players wanted to think about their situation in a different manner and gauge how much they wanted to challenge the existing norms of the game. During his visits to the training camps, Miller fielded questions about his background in organized labor. He could not disown his past, nor would he have tried to do so. There were management-inspired rumors that he was a "labor goon," but the idea of Miller as "goon" seemed so laughable that the charge became an asset to him. His demeanor and quiet patience were the antithesis of the stereotype of a union boss. He inspired confidence in the players who took the time to meet him. Miller kept reminding the players that he was going to be the executive director of their association, not the leader of some union that happened to include baseball players. He spent most of his time listening to players. At virtually every training camp they expressed the same concerns—the season was too long, the travel schedule was brutal, and playing conditions in certain ballparks were terrible. Previous complaints by the association had accomplished little. Players talked a lot about the pension fund, but Miller discovered that most of them had no idea how the fund operated or how it compared to retirement programs in other industries. What impressed Miller the most was how many players talked about the "relationship with the owners" but seemed to know little about its details.

Miller got the strong feeling that the players thought that "certain benefits enjoyed by the players were gracefully presented [by the owners] with no effort on the part of the players." The message he repeated in every camp was his assumption that if the players were going to approve his selection, that meant they had chosen "to have an effective association to represent their interests, [which meant that] the most important factor was player support of decisions arrived at democratically."[12] Miller made it clear that he saw himself as the head of a union whose members had a long string of unanswered, sometimes unstated grievances. Those were the terms under which he wanted the job, and those were considerations that should determine how each player voted. From the perspective of management, the specific points that Miller raised in his discussions with the players were not as important as what was already evident about him—he was a union official, he had no background in baseball, and he was not Robert Cannon. During the first part of Miller's spring training tour he visited the teams that trained in Arizona. He ran into significant opposition there, much of it encouraged by the clubs. He saw how little the association resembled a traditional union. His meeting with the Indians players was organized by Birdie Tebbetts, their manager, rather than Max Alvis, the long-time player rep. Tebbetts stayed throughout the meeting, and his main activity was to heckle and to ask Miller about his appropriateness in baseball. This included inquiring whether Miller had ever been investigated by the FBI. Years later, when the two men met at a spring training game, Tebbetts told Miller that the team had instructed him to make things difficult for Miller. A few years later a mutual friend wrote Miller a lengthy note conveying Tebbetts's respect for the gains the association had made for the players and thanking him for the increased benefits he received from the pension fund.[13]

Few players talked openly with Miller during the 1966 meetings. More often, players who had been silent would seek him out after the meeting to talk about things that affected them deeply and personally. Reggie Smith, a young player with the Red Sox in 1966, later described why players began to have confidence in Miller: "Marvin was there to help players learn how to think for themselves."[14] Much of Miller's problem in 1966 was that he was an outsider. Steve Hamilton, who became one of his strongest supporters in the union, and Bob Hunter, one of his opponents in the press, both remember that their first impression of Miller was that he "looked like he was slick [and] he wasn't part of the fraternity."[15]

By the time Miller got to the Florida camps, some of the more influential players heard about how he had been treated in Arizona and resented it. After all, their judgment and prestige were being called into question. The meetings in Florida were organized by the player reps. Coaches

and managers played little if any role in them. The final vote on his ratification reflects the difference. The total was 489 in favor and 136 opposed.
The vote among the four Arizona-based clubs was 17 in favor and 102
opposed. In a vote held at the same time, the players approved the creation of a permanent office by a vote of 576 to 24, with 30 abstentions.
All of the abstentions on the issue of the permanent office were from the
San Francisco Giants, who trained in Arizona. The Giants also voted
against Miller's selection 27 to 0, with 3 abstentions. The player rep sent
a cover letter with the tabulation that described the "other ballot" (about
Miller) as "self-explanatory."[16] Within a few weeks this player rep was
vocally supporting Miller at the stormy meetings with the owners, which
set the tone for the independence of the association.

Although it is possible to put too much emphasis on the personality
of a leader like Miller, it is important to understand the relationship he
established quickly with the players that comprised the union. First
impressions were crucial since the players knew little about him. He had
to infuse a sense of confidence in the players for them to take the association seriously. The fact that the association was a loose organization
with no track record and no agenda meant that Miller had a formidable
task from the outset. He had to find a way to change attitudes before
anything could be accomplished. Would players be willing to take risks
to support an organization that had not yet accomplished anything? Until
enough of them, especially some stars, stepped forward, there was little
chance that the association could do anything more for the players than
they had been able to do for themselves.

Some of the player reps recognized the potential of the union to make
changes in the lives of the players. Their confidence in Miller got a boost
before the union and its new executive director could point to any specific
gains. It is important to look at how some players remember their impressions of Miller with the caveat that such reflections are colored to
some degree by the knowledge of what took place throughout his tenure
at the union.

Steve Hamilton is representative of how players have talked over the
years about Miller's most notable characteristics. What struck Hamilton
was how quickly "Marvin gave you a sense of trust . . . he got us talking
about things we'd never considered, like how things should be . . . and
his level of confidence was so great, you had to believe in him. . . . The
players finally found someone to be our guy."[17] Former players often
mention that Miller was "little," "low-keyed," and "soft-spoken." These
are precisely the qualities that don't show up in the locker-room atmo-

sphere. He was the opposite of the managers and coaches who had pushed and prodded the players since the minor leagues. He was certainly not what they expected from the newspaper portrayals of the new executive director of their association. Miller was not there to holler at them, to humiliate them, or even to tell them what to do. He was there to identify issues that the players had not considered and to recommend tactics. Bunning described this trait: "We lacked direction, and that's what Marvin gave us. He focused on things that were important."[18]

Miller wanted the players to think about their situation, not to have an emotional reaction to it. Sal Bando talks about how Miller's demeanor inspired confidence, a "fantastic calmness [that was] important when dealing with immature egotistical athletes. . . . [Miller was] so low-keyed that I never saw him rattled."[19] Bunning got so annoyed that Miller never lost his cool that he "asked him to say 'shit' just once to see him get mad." Bunning didn't get his wish, at least in this respect.[20] When Joe Torre saw Miller for the first time in 1966, the Braves' player rep was uncertain about how to vote. Torre thought that Cannon had "been likeable, and Miller had to do some talking to change minds." Torre kept looking for "the devious labor vulture" that the owners had portrayed. In his place, there was this "small, soft-spoken man who mesmerized you because he kept making sense."[21] Steve Boros, who was a coach in 1966, was amazed that Miller "could say the most revolutionary things in the quietest possible voice. . . . He could even make an actuarial discussion seem interesting. . . . It was not Mr. Miller, but Marvin, someone who was interested . . . in us as individuals, even the coaches. . . . This wasn't someone who swooped in to give a talk, [Miller] did not demand the respect of the players, rather he held it . . . for what he said and what he wanted to do."[22]

Players sometimes give him credit for more than he could have done. In 1961, for example, the player reps discussed "the Negro housing problem during spring training" and asked clubs to summarize what efforts have been made, or would be made in the future, to solve the problems faced by black players who trained in Florida. The most detailed response came from the Cardinals, who described the integration of the club's facilities and outlined the efforts it was making to change the situation off the field.

Bing Devine, the general manager, summarized the history of blacks in Major League Baseball and concluded that when "they [black players] come to spring training, they are not just segregated—they feel downgraded and embarrassed." Devine outlined an ambitious program of reforms that he thought would be necessary "if Major League baseball is to continue its training program in the south." This program included providing housing at the same headquarters hotel, travel conditions on an equal basis, and including all players in invitations extended to the club, and "games played in ball parks during spring training must be on a non-segregated basis for spectators. This has been the situation in St. Petersburg for a number of years, without incident of any kind." In this private letter addressed to Frank Scott, Devine concluded, "We cannot continue to claim for baseball that it is the 'great American game' when, in fact, some players are treated differently than others because of the color of their skin and for no other reason."[23]

The Cardinals took matters into their own hands. A group of players asked Devine and Gussie Busch to do something, and they responded by purchasing motels in which the players would live as part of a team. The success of their policies was assured when the most respected veteran, Stan Musial, moved his family out of the residence they normally used so he could move in with his teammates. Years later, a prominent player from that team spoke about how the players had approached Miller to discuss what was happening. The only problem is that the events took place in 1963, and Miller arrived at the union in 1966.

The association's choice of Miller met with immediate open antagonism from baseball executives and the baseball press. The media played a significant role in shaping the attitudes of ownership and fans toward the players. Many players obtained some of their impressions about what their union was doing through the press. One of the most important functions of the player reps was to counteract what they felt was the increasingly hostile and inaccurate portrayal of the union by baseball writers.

Dick Young was probably the best-known and most widely quoted baseball reporter in the country. His views about the union and Miller were common among writers, but his skill as a writer and his popularity made him a potent force. His most quoted portrayal of Miller was entitled "Ballplayers Mesmerized by an Old Smoothie": "He [Miller] runs the players through a high-pressure spray and . . . they come out, brainwashed." In other columns Miller was "Comrade Miller" and "Marvelous Marv."[24] To a Maryland writer, Miller was "Marvin Millerinski," a quasi Bolshevist who was trying to convince players to stop being old-fashioned and to support a strike. To the majority of the baseball press, he was a dangerous annoyance who was willing to challenge upholders of baseball morality and tradition, someone who "must think the game of baseball was invented the same time he came onto the scene."[25]

The sports editor of the *Atlanta Journal*, Furman Bisher, was troubled that the players had tried to "con" the writers into convincing the public that they were victims of "inequities" and "maltreatment." Why, asked Bisher, should anyone have sympathy for men who are paid an average of twenty-two to twenty-three thousand dollars a year, get to live in fine hotels, and spend each spring in Florida? The players get trainers, doctors, legal assistance in divorce suits, and "even religious concessions known to few other American workers." The last probably referred to Sandy Koufax's refusal to pitch on the Jewish High Holy Days.

Bisher wanted the players to stop complaining about the hardships of the sport and stop asking for outlandish concessions like moving expenses and an increase in the minimum salary of seven thousand dollars. He reminded them and his other readers that every job has its drawbacks. Journalists have to take late-night flights and arrive unshaven, disheveled, and tired. What would players do if they had a tough job like driving a mail truck, working in a scientific lab, or fighting fires? The real issue to Bisher was "that professional baseball players are going to have to decide if they are common laborers or professional men. If they are going to be dealt with as laborers then they should accept all the conditions of the laborer. If they are going to be professional men who practice a special craft, then they should travel on their individual merits." In case readers could not understand Bisher's disgust with a group of ballplayers led by a trade unionist, he made it clear. "I cannot see the major league baseball player *demeaning* himself to the status of a unionized laborer" (emphasis added).[26]

If players like Drysdale and Bunning wanted to be part of a union, then Bisher wanted them to return part of their handsome wages to "that righteously underpaid minority he and his group defend, the $7000 player." Even minimum-wage players got little sympathy from Bisher: "If I must say what I truly think, most of the $7000 major league players I have known have been overpaid," and most of the Atlanta Braves players "were accepting money under false pretenses." The players should be happy for the privilege to be major leaguers, they were paid too much, and they should have enough pride in their job to realize they should not associate with unions.[27]

A few years later, Bisher evaluated the union and concluded, "What I can't condone is the necessity of a Marvin Miller. He appears to be a nice enough fellow, oil-smooth, almost too oily to be accepted without reservations. I wish he'd shave that moustache and let's see what the rest of his face looks like. . . . It appears that Miller is there to coddle the players' every whim. If they demand five inning games, three day weeks, and three month seasons; bubble baths after night games; or locker room chamber maids, pat them on the head and tell them anything their little heart desires."[28]

In 2000 Bisher wrote an article entitled "Most Powerful Sports Figures of the Century," which concluded: "you can't overlook Marvin Miller, the union shepherd, whether you like the turn baseball has made or not."[29]

The favorable comments in the press about Miller were often muted or backhanded. One writer pointed out that "Miller is a thoughtful and pensive sort—*for a labor leader, especially*" (emphasis added). When Miller was given a chance to present his own views, he stated, "'Of course, [the MLBPA is] a union.'"[30] This was a daring thing to say to a reporter from the *Cincinnati Enquirer*, the house newspaper of the Reds.

One article about Miller's appointment was unique, both in its philosophy and literary allusions. The *New York Times* reporter Robert Lipsyte discussed the arrival of "Marvin Miller, the unionist," into baseball and paraphrased a popular 1848 pamphlet, *"A specter is haunting the capitals of sport—the specter of unionism."*[31]

Bob Hunter, an influential West Coast writer, described himself as "part of a generation of writers" who "opposed the actions of the union . . . [and believed] there was no reason [for players] to hire someone like Miller . . . [and thought] Miller was an imposter at first, but we finally found out different . . . he always would give you a straight answer, if he gave you an answer. . . . [You] more or less got to like him, because you could trust him."[32] Reporters discovered an important quality about Miller: "he never said 'no comment.' He was skillful enough that he could say 'no comment' in a thousand well-chosen words. . . . There were times when he couldn't talk, and then you got things on background. He wanted to explain his position to you even if you disagreed with him. . . . Most of all, he had the facts, and he never lied to you."[33] The New York writer Leonard Koppett was one of the few writers who was favorable to the union's position. He had a simple description of how Miller went about the complicated task of winning the confidence of the players and even some writers: "he could be persuasive because he was right and had the facts right. It all comes back to that."[34]

Miller laid out his philosophy to the players in one of his first meetings as executive director, emphasizing that a good relationship was easy to maintain "when one party to it either did not ask for anything or accepted repeated rebuffs. The test of a good relationship lies, in part, in the results obtained."[35] He wanted players and management to know exactly where he stood. Miller wanted each player to question for him-self what results he had obtained from the existing relationship between the association and the owners. He was convinced that once the players did this, they would reject past practices and press for changes.

Miller took some opportunities to make the same point in public. When *The Sporting News* claimed that "the once-happy relations between management and athletes have been more than significantly strained since Miller entered the picture," he replied, "Very few men, faced with the choice of making unilateral decisions concerning their employees' conditions or working with them on a cooperative basis, will choose the latter." He made it clear that he saw nothing unusual or suspicious about employees, in this case major league players, wanting to use an attorney to clarify the terms of a contract they had been offered. He did not char-acterize the owners as wicked, merely as employers, many of them priv-ileged, who had operated in a unique legal climate that conferred upon them special powers that they would not relinquish until forced to do so. He wanted everyone to know that the situation had changed because "major league players have made known their decision. They have elected a full time executive director . . . [and] their executive director will carry out their mandate to work closely with them in working for their best interests and for baseball as a whole."[36]

Any successful efforts to transform this new philosophy into policies that could modify the existing relationship was going to need much more than rhetoric. No one understood this better than Miller. Once the play-ers decided to press for changes, their greatest weapon was going to be an aggressive approach through labor law and the collective bargaining process, something that had been untapped by the Players Association during its relatively brief existence. This meant that the union had to have an organizational structure, staff, and money. In 1966 all of those were in short supply.

The need for money to support the association was a pressing concern for Miller. In 1960, when the union established a permanent office and employed Cannon as a legal consultant, it had a bank balance of less than nine thousand dollars. The union had a balance of approximately fifty-seven hundred dollars when Miller arrived in 1966. The association had been operating on the basis of an annual grant of $150,000 from the pro-ceeds of the All-Star Game. This money was essential to the existence of the association, and in April 1966 it became an important issue divid-ing the association and the owners. This was one of those rare times when not getting money was better than getting it.

In 1966 owners and their executives underestimated Miller and the players and were unprepared to deal with an opponent who questioned their motives and competence. Bob Addie, a long-time columnist for the *Washington Post*, was one of the first observers to see how things were changing and how ownership might be accelerating that. He pointed out that the selection of Miller, "whose credentials appear to be impressive," could well be a sign "that talk of unionism is getting stronger. . . . [The] owners immediately begin to sniff a union . . . [they] act as if Miller didn't exist and they would like nothing better than to sweep him under the rug." Addie's predictions that "the odd sequel is that the owners could drive the players into a union" proved to be accurate. He pointed out that the players had reasons to be worried about the future of the pension fund, since they "had contributed over $194,000 of *their own money* . . . to the pension fund" (emphasis added).[37]

Even before Miller had an office of his own the owners presented him with a dramatic way to show the players why they needed a strong, independent association. The issue was the "financing of the permanent office" to be run by the executive director. At a meeting attended by the player reps, management, and the commissioner, Miller accused the owners of acting in bad faith. He made it a point to remind everyone that his selection had been ratified by an overwhelming vote of the players in April 1966, "but on May 3rd the owners attempted to assert a veto by reversing the actions of the Pension Committee and the recommendation of the Executive Committee." Miller was referring to a private meeting on May 3, where the commissioner had informed him that the proposed funding scheme for the association's operation was prohibited by the Taft-Hartley Law. The way the commissioner and his lawyers handled the matter gave Miller the opportunity to question the sincerity of the owners and their ability as businessmen. When he described the situation to the player reps, he stressed that the issue was not the money but what the owners were trying to do to the association and why. Miller also pointed out that by using the Taft-Hartley argument, the owners were saying that "baseball was an industry affecting commerce" and that the association was a labor organization.[38]

The new executive director of the association leveled another charge against the owners that was bound to get the attention of the players because it dealt with the pension fund. Miller said that the way the commissioner had described the funding of the association made it clear that the owners believed that the money in the pension fund belonged to them rather than the players; they could use it as they pleased, and they had no obligation to give the players any say in that. Miller was attacking the good faith of the owners and setting the union up as the defender of the pension fund. The players who were present did not appear surprised. According to Miller, at one of his early meetings with the screening committee "the players advised me that they suspected that Game of the Week valuation [money that went to the owners] was artificially inflated and that the value put on the World Series and the All-Star Game [money in which the players shared] was seriously deflated."[39]

Miller's skill in formulating a position for the association and his willingness to embarrass the owners showed that a new man and new attitudes were in place at the association. That had been obvious a few weeks earlier at the first meeting between Miller and the owners. Judge Cannon remembered that "I asked Walter O'Malley [the owner of the Dodgers], 'What the hell is going on?' and his reply was that he [Miller] was the cause of it all. . . . What he [Miller] did was in poor taste. Instead of being conciliatory, he blasted them right away."[40]

How the owners must have wished for the good old days of J. Norman Lewis waiting in the hall or the conciliation of Judge Cannon! The owners might not have liked dealing with the new realities, as personified by Miller, but they would have little choice. He was there as the chosen representative of the players' organization that had legal standing. He had the clear support of the players. It did not take long for the player reps to understand the significance of what was happening and to impress upon other players the need to support the association.

The spectacle of Commissioner Eckert lecturing Miller on the subtleties of Taft-Hartley would be hilarious were the issues not so serious. The owners contended that they were doing nothing more than backing away from a previously illegal position. Many of the player representatives must have been surprised by the owners' admission, since the owners had consistently asserted that the players did not need a strong organization because they could trust the owners' judgment and instinct to do what was best for everyone. The timing of the owners' mea culpa regarding the Taft-Hartley Act gave Miller the opportunity to question their sincerity, their ability as businessmen, and the scope of their paternalistic control of the sport. He did all of that with an issue that the owners had raised.

The lump sum contribution of $150,000 would have solved the immediate needs of the association, but there was more wrong with its source than the violation of federal labor law. Accepting the money would continue the dependence of the union upon the owners. This was not Miller's idea of establishing a relationship of equals. His remarks to the players stressed that there were ways to solve the financial problem without depending on the owners. The real issue was the motives of the owners in stopping the allocation when they did. He could not have choreographed a better situation for himself than the one the owners had created. The timing of the owners' action infuriated many of the player representatives. Miller's explanation was unambiguous and devastating: "I am not alone in my opinion that these difficulties about financing the Players Office had come about because I am not the choice of the owners for the job as Executive Director of the Players Association."[41] The players saw that they had hired someone who had a competitive streak at the table that matched what they had on the field. The owners were unprepared for that kind of behavior.

During the meeting with the owners, the player representatives raised the possibility of financing the association with a two-dollar-per-day contribution from each player in place of taking $150,000 per year from the proceeds of the All-Star Game. The commissioner replied that the owners would need more time to consider the matter. Walter O'Malley, the real power in baseball, said that there was no reason to discuss the proposal. Tom Haller of the Giants, the team that had cast no positive votes for Miller, followed O'Malley's remarks by asking if any of the owners would like to respond to the proposal made by Miller "on behalf of the player representatives" (emphasis added).[42] There was complete silence. Finally, Donald Grant of the Mets said that the owners, commissioner, and counsel would caucus and meet later with the players.

During the recess, the players returned to their own room to discuss what one described later as "a meeting [that] was a farce. . . . It was clear that the Commissioner and the League President and the owners felt they had no authority to work out a solution with the Players Association. They had been given the authority to present their own proposal, but not to consider any other."[43]

The reconvened meeting gave the players even more reason to distrust management's response to recent developments. Paul Porter, counsel for the owners, reasserted that the former funding of the association was illegal and that the owners "considered All-Star Game funds to be legally the property of the clubs." The players had been shown the business equivalent of "the Lord giveth, and the Lord taketh away." Porter assumed that the association would need his help to figure out a "proper, lawful, and legitimate" way to finance the office and suggested a "payroll checkoff system on the basis of a voluntary revocable plan."[44]

In a few sentences, Porter had destroyed whatever faith the players might have had in the owners, condescended to the executive director of the union, and brought up precisely the source of funding that Miller already thought was best for the association. A checkoff was, after all, the way a real union operated.

When Miller spoke again, he reviewed the history of the discussions about the $150,000. He pointed out that during two years of meetings and correspondence, no attorney for the owners had ever suggested that the arrangement was a violation of the law. How could they account for the sudden concern over legal problems? The question was rhetorical. Miller followed with the answer that was suggestive of the future relationship between the association and the owners: "It had not escaped the attention of the players that the 'legal' problems allegedly present first came to light when it appeared that the new Executive Director of the Players Association was to be someone whom the owners were unable to hand pick. These 'legal' problems which counsel, Mr. Porter, admitted had been ignored for years by the owners, suddenly became a matter of concern when the players decided to name their own choice for the new job."[45]

The counsel for the National League responded that the "lack of diligence" was not a sign of bad faith, and the commissioner said that "no one questions the actions of the players in selecting a man of their choice." This only intensified the resentment of the players and convinced them to press for answers. Ed Fisher, the White Sox pitcher, went unchallenged when he said that "not a single thing had been accomplished and that the Player Representatives would like to know when our proposal would be considered."[46]

In one important respect Fisher was wrong. Something important had taken place during the five-hour-and-forty-five-minute joint meeting. The players had shown that what had been standard conduct by the owners for years was no longer acceptable. They had asserted their independence. Their executive director had shown no respect for the owners, the commissioner, or the traditional relationship that had existed between them and the Players Association. From that time forward, Miller would use the words and actions of the owners and their representatives as a potent tool to create unity in the MLBPA.

The next important step for the union was to complete its professional staff by finding a labor lawyer who would be compatible with the executive director and the new thrust of the organization. At an Executive Board meeting in November 1966, Miller introduced the new counsel for the association, Richard Moss.[47] He was the same man who had applied to be the part-time legal advisor in 1959, when the association had cho-sen Cannon to fill that position. It is hard to think of two men more dif-ferent from one another than Moss and Cannon, other than the fact that they were both attorneys and baseball fans. A few months after accept-ing the job, Moss thanked Warren Giles, the president of the National League, for having "fulfilled one of the boyhood ambitions of this life-long National League fan." This was after Giles had sent Moss a 1967 National League season pass.[48]

Moss was thirty-five years old, had served as assistant attorney gener-al for the State of Pennsylvania, and was currently an associate general counsel of the United Steelworkers. It seemed as though the doomsday predictions made when Miller was hired were coming true. Now the union was staffed by two CIO-trained men whose backgrounds and atti-tudes were different from anything the owners had seen before. Moss was hired to work full time for the union and "to provide legal advice . . . to individual members, as may be appropriate."[49] The baseball men who had feared what might happen once the association had the look of a union must have thought their worst fears were coming true.

Moss became an aggressive and ingenious advocate for the union and the players. The appraisal of one of Moss's colleagues in Washington proved to be true: "he will certainly give you a great lift and have an opportunity to play an important role in the pioneering effort to democ-ratize relations between players and their masters."[50] Within a few months, the changes were apparent to anyone who bothered to look at the letterhead of the association. It listed Marvin J. Miller as executive director and Richard M. Moss as general counsel; 375 Park Avenue had replaced The Biltmore (the site of Frank Scott's office) as the headquar-ters of the association. There was a new team and a new setting, and there were new goals.

Moss was more than a good attorney; he enjoyed the work and went at it with zeal. He also had a rare knack for focused sarcasm and the in-stinct to seize on the vulnerability in an opponent's case or personality. He struck many people as less patient than Miller and more willing to go on the attack. Part of his role as a successful number two was to take positions that allowed the executive director to appear to be above the nastier parts of the arguments and to remain deliberate, thoughtful, and considered in his demeanor.[51] Tactically, they were a balanced team. They appeared to share completely the feeling that the players had been de-ceived by the owners for decades and that labor relations in baseball (if that was not an oxymoron) had not yet reached the situation that had existed in most other industries in the early 1930s. They also shared a delight in puncturing pretensions and in reminding baseball officials, executives, and writers how much the situation had changed.

Moss seemed to enjoy making a serious point in a flippant, cutting manner, whether it was reminding Dick Young that "I [Moss] am legal counsel. . . . Marvin is not a lawyer and he has not been practicing law without a license";[52] telling Sandy Hadden, the counsel for the commissioner, "constructive problem solving is not a concept which interests your office . . . so we will not waste any time trying to avoid an embarrassment to baseball";[53] or writing the mayor of Pittsburgh to complain that the Pirates did not provide parking spaces for their players while Moss was able to park in the places they needed "by displaying to the policemen on duty no credentials other than two one-dollar bills."[54] He could be more direct when he thought someone was trying to take advantage of him or the union. One example was a letter to a prominent sportswriter in which Moss stated, "you chose to distort everything I said and to call me a few names to boot. While I could never quarrel with your right to have opinions, I do find your inability to report facts accurately a cause of distress." The letter got more pointed when Moss, a Pirates fan, discussed the events of 1946: "you quoted me as saying '[Rip] Sewell was the fink who prevented the strike.' I do not give Sewell that much credit. Sewell was a fink . . . a classic 'labor spy.'"[55]

Most of the players appreciated Moss's style and attitude long before they had the chance to understand his skills as an advocate. Writers had very different feelings about him, which were reflected in Bob Hertzel's comment to Miller: "if you ever want or need the sympathy of the public and the press, you'd better put a muzzle on Dick Moss . . . his constant belittling of the press, his arrogant, aggressive attitude aren't needed. I'm sure in his job he is capable, but as a spokesman for the Players Association he causes nothing but ill will."[56]

Moss's job was not to act as a public relations spokesman for the union. In any case, he and Miller both believed that the majority of the press had not given the players a fair hearing. Moss used public forums to get across his views about the press. At one university conference, he said that "with some exceptions, it [the baseball press] was a hostile and uninformed press." He then explained that he thought the great majority of baseball writers "were not *deliberately* hostile. Rather, sports writers reflected the fact that they had no particular expertise in the subject matter . . . a labor dispute story, and they understandably relied on their traditional sources of information, the club management."[57] Moss's explanation was little comfort to writers who thought that outsiders like him and Miller had even less understanding and appreciation of baseball than the writers supposedly had of labor issues.

With Miller and Moss at 375 Park Avenue, not only would changes take place, there would be many uncomfortable moments when baseball executives and sportswriters who were used to going unchallenged opened their morning mail.

A NEW FOCUS FOR THE ASSOCIATION

THE UNION HAD GAINED an important psychological boost when the owners withdrew the $150,000 in operating funds. The union was also now free to operate independently of the owners. The short-term problem was still there, however; the association needed money to operate. Miller had a series of meetings with Eckert and MacPhail to discuss it, and he told them "that all the players want to do is to spend their money in a way that they desire." Miller was referring to the percentage of the World Series radio and television revenue that had gone to the pension fund. That raised the issue of to whom the money belonged. Did the players own it, or did they receive it as a gift that could be revoked any time the owners thought that it was in their best interests to do so? Questions like these drove Miller and the Executive Committee to make sure that a collective bargaining agreement would be concluded that would spell out the precise terms of the contractual relationship between the parties. The days of informal cooperation and players acting as supplicants were about to end.

How was the union to operate until the dues checkoff went into operation in the 1967 season? "The player reps considered [joint All-Star Game sponsorship] the most appropriate method," but there was little chance that the owners would give up control of the proceeds of the All-Star Game. Miller, with the assistance of Frank Scott, negotiated a contract that allowed Coca-Cola to use players' pictures inside bottle caps in return for a cash payment of sixty thousand dollars to the association. That might not seem like much money in the current era of multi-million-dollar endorsements, but it was in 1966. Within a few years, the association had signed other agreements and created a significant source of income for the players. The purpose of the 1966 arrangement with Coca-Cola was simple. As one member described it, the union was able "to survive."[1]

Companies were interested in the likenesses of stars, and these players could have refused to participate or insisted that they get a percentage of the income. Instead the money went directly to the Players Association to support whatever efforts its membership thought were important. There was also 100 percent authorization for the dues checkoff. The whole process was an important step toward building a sense of solidarity among the players.

Miller also brought a new regimen of fiscal standards to the union. He insisted that his expense allowance be "limited to reimbursement of . . . actual expenses" with a ceiling placed on the total. Over the next few years, those expenses always were less than were allowed. This attention to financial detail and a desire to do things inexpensively reflected Miller's personal standards. They also served to blunt possible attacks against his stewardship of the association. He went out of his way to make the financial arrangements public, as he did in a letter to Bob Addie of the *Washington Post*. Addie had written a complimentary article about Miller, but Miller wanted to correct Addie's portrayal of a supposed fifty-thousand-dollar expense account and to clarify the details about his own salary: "I am happy to say that I am not working without a salary."[2]

The financial turnaround of the Players Association was remarkable. At the end of the first year of operating with a full-time executive director and legal counsel, the association showed a budget surplus of $28,970. This was in addition to $265,000 obtained in commercial contracts.[3] By the end of 1967, players were receiving back from the association almost fifty thousand dollars more than they were paying into it in dues. Endorsements, which had provided the life's blood for the union, might have had another possible use that no one thought about in 1967: a fund in case players should stop receiving their paychecks for any reason. By 1969 the first six-month statement showed that the union had received $78,950 in dues and $84,817 in licensing revenue with an additional $45,555 remaining to be collected. The union, which had a current account of less than ten thousand dollars in 1967, showed a fund balance of $168,294 and current assets of more than $157,000 by June 30, 1969.[4] The authorization for licensing that each player approved had a specific clause ensuring that money would be returned to the individual players unless the Executive Board decided it needed the money to meet problems facing the union.

The association was operating under the constitution and bylaws that Judge Cannon had written in 1960. Each club elected a player representative and an alternate for two-year terms. These elections were supposed to take place by secret ballot. The player reps, in turn, elected a representative for each league. The league player representatives were charged with organizing the three regular meetings of all the reps held each year. They also were responsible for transmitting the concerns of the players "to the appropriate authorities." The club player reps acting collectively as an executive committee had the authority to employ people and to select two players to serve on the Pension Committee. The player reps were to consult with the legal advisor and to keep the players on their clubs aware of actions taken by the association, as well as "any new developments." The new constitution, written in 1967, showed that the association had developed a new sense of purpose. It emphasized the need to bring together all players, managers, coaches, and trainers, "regardless of race, creed, color, or nationality."[5] The most substantive changes recognized the existence of the executive director and the permanent office. The constitution provided that the league player representatives did not have to be club player representatives. The league representatives were co-treasurers who would arrange for an annual independent audit of the association's finances. It used a new title, Executive Board, to describe the organization made up of the club reps, the league reps, and the Pension Committee reps.

The Executive Board had the authority and responsibility to establish policy and direct the affairs of the Players Association. It became the responsibility of the board to identify problems and vigorously push for solutions. The players had hired Miller to take the association from talk to action, however much that might upset the traditions of baseball or infuriate owners, writers, or fans. The Executive Board took a symbolic action by unanimously approving further changes in the constitution and bylaws of the association. One of these empowered the Executive Board to suspend a member "from the Association for proper cause." Prior to 1967 it was difficult to imagine the association doing anything to upset a member and harder to describe how it would be damaging for a player to be suspended.[6]

During the first year of Miller's tenure, the association had focused most of its attention on internal matters. Miller took opportunities to state his philosophy of the union publicly. He discussed broader goals and attacked the way in which ownership had treated the players and the association. He picked his targets carefully. Nothing could be more harmful to the uncertain future of the association than lashing out wildly. He concentrated on specific issues identified by the players. These included minimum salary, grievances, fines, scheduling, hotels, per diems, and the pension fund. He made a concentrated effort to ensure that individual players realized that the association was their representative and that an important part of his job was to listen to them. That meant more than only making a perfunctory circuit of the spring training camps. He made sure to see players throughout the season, to stay in touch with the player reps, and to have a listed phone number (despite the obvious inconvenience that might present) to make it easier for any player to contact him.

Joe McGuff was a reporter covering the Kansas City A's in 1966 when he met Miller briefly. When Wes Stock, the A's player rep, spoke with McGuff about Miller's candidacy, McGuff replied that if Stock wanted more rights and more confrontation with the owners he should support Miller. McGuff was right on both counts. He described himself later as being "one of the more sympathetic writers [to Miller], and I wasn't very sympathetic."[7]

Two months after his arrival at the union, Miller saw first-hand just how different baseball was from any other industry with which he was familiar. It was his first meeting of the Executive Council of the Pension Fund. The commissioner (an employee of the owners) presided over it, acting as an impartial chairman. Miller must have squirmed when Eckert opened the meeting by declaring, "you men who represent the players . . . [want] nothing [to] happen which could possibly alter *the fine relationship which exists in baseball among the Player Representatives, the owners, and the Commissioner*" (emphasis added). The level of paternalism was high even by the standards of baseball when the commissioner reassured the players that no one was "questioning the propriety of the Players Association employing a full time Executive Director and staff in conjunction with or in lieu of the original concept of 'Legal Advisor' if the players feel this is *seriously* needed" (emphasis added).[8]

Given the backround of Miller and Moss, it's probable that when they heard the rhetoric of baseball's management they were reminded of one of the most famous quotes in the history of the American labor movement. In 1902, George Baer, the president of the Reading Railroad, declared, "the rights of the laboring man will be protected, and cared for, not by the labor agitator, but by the Christian men to whom God has given control of the property interests of the country."[9]

In 1966 the commissioner made it clear that he could work with any "qualified representative" of the players, but he offered no definition of "qualified." Eckert added his "understanding" that none of the changes in the association "will change or alter the authority and responsibility of the Commissioner of Baseball." Nothing could have been further from the truth. He did not realize that that concept was as unacceptable to Miller as it was natural to Scott and Cannon. One of baseball's lawyers, Bowie Kuhn, later summarized the situation: "Our repeated attempts to create a good relationship with the Association never really worked and never would so long as Miller was there." Kuhn said that dealings between Miller and General Eckert were like trying to get the lion to lie down with the lamb and that Miller, the lion, would devour the lamb before morning.[10]

In February 1967 Miller outlined to a journalist what he thought were the most important concerns of the association. They included the length of the season, the minimum salary, split doubleheaders, the unsatisfactory travel schedule, and the need to modernize the standard players' contract. The idea of free agency or the possibility of a work stoppage did not enter into the discussion. But the association had come a long way from 1963, when its requests had included that more getaway games be played during the day, that up to eight warm-up pitches be allowed, and that each major league park have "standard foul poles."[11]

The independence of the union was a constant refrain of Miller's, something he repeated in a number of places. He reminded the players of it and used it as part of his conversations with the press. But he and Moss proclaimed it with greater force to an audience that seemed unprepared to accept the implications of the message, namely, the owners and their employees. Miller and Moss capitalized on a seemingly trivial episode to assert the rights of the union to monitor the actions of ownership, an action calculated to show just how much had changed.

On May 3, 1967, the Players Association returned a check for $1,032 to Arthur Allyn, the owner of the Chicago White Sox. The check had been sent by the White Sox as dues for three members of the association—the manager and two coaches. Miller sent a curt note to Allyn that the method of payment did not "conform to your obligations under the agreement of December 1, 1966, which was to deduct dues from members' salaries, and furthermore that the delivery of the money violated Section 302 of the Labor Management Relations Act . . . money is incidental. . . . [T]he issue at hand is the obligation of the owners. . . . [Your assertion] that the club cannot permit coaches and managers to pay dues or to be active members of the Association represents a position which constitutes unfair labor practices under the law."[12]

In case Allyn did not get the message, Miller concluded with the comment that the MLBPA was willing to initiate the appropriate legal action to rectify the situation. He then sent a lengthy letter to the player reps reminding them of the struggle over the establishment of the permanent office and warned that the owners were trying to sabotage it. Miller stressed that the White Sox were ignoring their contractual obligations. This was one of those cases where the issue was the principle, not the money. Players who were constantly reminded by club executives that rules had to be followed must have enjoyed the conclusion to Miller's letter: "If a formal written contract can be rendered meaningless by one party to the contract, then all contracts are in jeopardy—including the Major League Baseball Players Benefit Plan which, after all, is merely a piece of paper that is given meaning only through the signatures of the parties and their carrying out the agreement expressed in that piece of paper. . . . The matter of whether or not a few persons do or do not pay membership dues is not of overriding importance. The matter of whether or not a contract agreed upon in good faith is to be complied with or violated is of very great importance."[13]

The actions of the White Sox gave Miller and Moss a useful target. They probably took a special pleasure in using that franchise as an object lesson. There were repeated instances where the association got complaints from its players about the racial attitudes that existed on the club, how management treated black players differently, and how the manager made no secret of his support for the candidacy of George Wallace at a time when the Alabama governor had become symbolic of a white backlash against civil rights gains. The association was not in a position to take any action on these charges, but Miller and Moss thought they were important enough to monitor.

Owners might regard what the White Sox did as a trivial administrative problem or a good-faith effort to enable three old-time baseball men to handle their objections to the checkoff system. It was their money; couldn't they handle it as they saw fit? In any case, who was harmed by their actions? Judge Cannon might have been willing to give the owners every benefit of every possible doubt, but Miller was not. Time and again, throughout his career, Miller emphasized the importance of the reciprocal nature of contractual obligations. It became a standard part of his correspondence with numerous sportswriters, many of whom chided him for looking for technicalities and not trusting in the good faith of the owners. They were right on both counts.

Miller felt the need to dramatize the differences between the two sides and show the players that they could beat the owners at their own game.

This meant applying the rules equally to both sides and tapping into the competitive instincts of the players. Threatening legal action against the White Sox, intervening in disciplinary cases, and making demands based on the strict interpretation of labor laws was how Miller and Moss asserted the legitimacy and the untapped power of the association.

In the spring of 1967 the owners made a major change in how they ran their businesses. They recognized that they had to deal with the union and that the commissioner was not the person to run that part of baseball. The owners established a committee of executives, the Player Relations Committee, to handle labor-related issues. There was a division among the members of the PRC about whom they should hire to supervise its efforts. One group thought that bringing in a baseball man would "be less likely to provoke confrontation with the union." When they could not find anyone who combined the knowledge of labor law with a background in baseball, they selected a veteran negotiator, John Gaherin, to do battle with Miller. Gaherin was a pragmatic, street-wise veteran of labor negotiations. Most of his recent experience had been with multi-ownership organizations, including New York newspapers and the railroad industry. Nevertheless, he was not prepared for the situation in Major League Baseball, where there was no tradition of labor relations, and individual employers interfered publicly with the efforts of their negotiator.

From the start of his tenure, Gaherin had difficulty convincing his employers of the elementary fact that he and Miller both knew—the MLBPA had the powers and responsibilities of a union. As such, it had a wide range of potential legal devices to force change on the owners. In Gaherin's view, it might have been comfortable for veteran executives like Buzzie Bavasi, the general manager of the Dodgers, to talk "about his boys, but [the belief] that it was an Association of professional men was bullshit. It's a *union!*"[14] A year before Gaherin came on the scene, Miller had said in a public statement, "The Players Association has always been a labor organization."[15] Gaherin agreed completely with that.

Gaherin assumed that Miller did not have in mind the company union of Frank Scott or a situation where an employee of the union would discuss important issues on an informal basis with the owners and without any players present. Miller's reminder that the owners had "the obligation to negotiate in good faith" was a statement of the obvious to Gaherin. The owners preferred the advice that Joe Cronin, a Hall of Fame player, the president of the American League, and a member of the PRC had given to Miller: "players come and players go, but the owners stay on forever." Miller granted that Cronin might have been well intentioned, but he thought that he was dead wrong because although "individual players have short careers, the players as a group go on forever."[16] This idea that the players were the foundation of baseball is crucial to understanding Miller's career.

Gaherin and Miller developed a relationship of mutual respect and understanding as fellow professionals, although Gaherin was convinced that "Miller intended to destroy the whole goddamned temple that I was paid to hold up [since he thought] the whole structure of baseball was evil."[17] Shortly after the two men met, Miller gave Gaherin a present to

Marvin Miller

John Gaherin

introduce him to the realities of baseball, which offered a preview of the problems he was going to face in response to the actions of some of the men who employed him: copies of *Sports Illustrated* that contained a series of articles by Buzzie Bavasi in which he discussed the way he negotiated contracts and paid special attention to the 1966 contract holdout of the two Dodger star pitchers, Sandy Koufax and Don Drysdale.

Koufax and Drysdale refused to accept the contracts offered to them or to report to spring training. They had made eighty-five thousand dollars and eighty thousand dollars, respectively, in 1965. They hired an agent supposedly to arrange film work for them and a lawyer to handle contract negotiations with the Dodgers. Their original request was for a million dollars over three years for the two of them. The whole situation was unacceptable to the Dodgers. The players were asking for too much money and a multiyear contract. They were negotiating jointly and were using a third party to act for them. Worst of all, from the club's view, the two pitchers were using their leverage to try to force the Dodgers to change how they did business. There even was some talk that the attorney for the players might file suit to test the validity of the reserve system. When a settlement was reached, Koufax received $125,000 and Drysdale got $115,000. But there were no multiyear arrangements, the players settled for different amounts, and the club gave the impression that dealing with a lawyer had been incidental.[18]

Bavasi has said many times over the years that it was the issues surrounding the negotiations, not the money, that most troubled him and Walter O'Malley, and there is good reason to believe him. Koufax and Drysdale's raises did not damage the club's budget, since the money came out of the raise pool that the club had decided it would allocate for the 1966 season. The reserve system gave the general manager the power to set the salary scale for the whole club, making raises a zero-sum game among the players. The Dodgers had decided that the budget would go up by one hundred thousand dollars, and that is exactly what happened in 1966. Koufax and Drysdale got seventy thousand dollars of it, and that meant that much less for the rest of the players. In Bavasi's words, "I'd liked to give the other players more, but a budget is a budget, and I stuck to it."[19]

Other owners saw nothing positive coming out of how the Dodgers handled the holdout. The idea of dealing with agents went against the ethos and the interests of the owners. It was much better to have players who believed they would get the fairest possible deal by working directly with the general manager. The joint nature of the holdout was even more worrisome to the owners. They feared a repetition of this more than they feared a legal challenge to the reserve system. The owners wanted to prevent another Koufax-Drysdale situation, and they took steps to ensure that the collective bargaining agreement precluded a repetition of the tactics employed by Koufax and Drysdale. This became a public issue years later when it was the basis for the massive judgment against the owners for their own collusive activities to artificially reduce salaries undertaken during Peter Uebberoth's tenure as commissioner.

The headline in Bavasi's *Sports Illustrated* articles described how "baseball's most successful executive" dealt with the "joys and troubles in the front office." It was clear from the articles that control of players and the maintenance of the system meant much to him. Bavasi expressed concern that he had "opened the door to more trouble than baseball ever dreamed in its worst nightmare" by allowing Drysdale and Koufax to have agents negotiate their contracts for them. Bavasi proclaimed that "all's fair in negotiating, [and] . . . money is a big thing in baseball," and then he went on to prove what he meant. His second article, "Money Makes the Players Go," showed that since "some ball players just don't understand money at all, or don't stop to figure things out . . . you could take advantage of them something frightful." In case anyone thought Bavasi was talking idly, he stated, "we don't negotiate by the Marquis of Queensbury Rules, . . . [and] as far as I'm concerned, anything goes at salary time." A club's budget was worked out in advance, and he knew "almost to the penny what each player is going to get."[20]

Rather than real negotiations, what took place was a series of charades allowing Bavasi to do whatever he wanted. Bavasi had the power, and he exercised it, although he cloaked it in a paternalism that supposedly protected the players from themselves. The players had no leverage within the reserve system. Bavasi took special delight in the fact that he had "pulled that phony contract stunt ['letting' a player see how little a teammate supposedly was paid by showing him a phony contract] a dozen times, and I'll do it every chance I get, because this war of negotiations has no rules."[21] But there was not really a war, since only one potential combatant was armed, and the rules bestowed almost unlimited power on him.

Bavasi's conclusion was that "the easiest players to deal with are the ones who leave it all up to you. They have enough faith in me to know that they are going to be paid what they're worth."[22] This last sentence summed up much of what Miller thought was wrong in baseball—it was a one-sided system that was structured to allow ownership to operate without interference.

Bavasi had no second thoughts about writing the articles; he had no reason to think that they would cause any discontent among the players. The possibility that they might be used against him by the union was not part of his calculation. Bavasi's articles did wonders for Miller's credibility by showing the players why they needed a forceful and unified association. Miller and Moss made sure that the articles went to each player rep with instructions that they be distributed to as many players as possible. One player remembers how the Bavasi articles "opened a lot of eyes," and some players were surprised that it was "so brazen." Another player assumed that "every owner could have killed Buzzie at that point . . . you thought things like that, but you didn't say them."[23] Neither of these players were with the Dodgers, and both of them thought that other general managers admired Bavasi.

Bavasi spent thirty-six years as an executive in baseball. He was "very comfortable" with a pre-1966 situation, when he "used to suggest who should be the player rep so I got along with them very well. They used to come to me to work out problems." He had no compunctions in writing Frank Scott to complain that the general manager wasn't getting copies of letters between the association and the Dodgers' player rep or to tell the association how to run its affairs. When the Dodgers responded to a 1961 questionnaire from Judge Cannon about housing and other facilities for black players, O'Malley sent a straightforward letter. Bavasi wrote his own letter to Scott, which ended, "You folks must be out of your mind. We eat, sleep and drink under the same roof. . . . You must know that. . . . Now get lost!"[24]

Long after Bavasi retired, he reflected on the changes that had taken place and why they took the form that they did. He had particular insight into the union's tactics, since Bavasi was a repeated target of grievances filed by the union on behalf of players. At first, he said, Miller "made me mad as hell by dwelling on small things, not pensions or salaries. Why should we fight on things like [who was] paying the spring training room tax in 1966?" The reason was straightforward to Miller and Moss. They were doing their job, and they were taking every chance to show the players that the union was fighting for them.

Bavasai looked back on his relationship with Miller: "Marvin may be a no-good son of a bitch to a lot of people . . . and there were lots of times I wanted to knock him on his ass, . . . but he never lied to me and I don't think to anyone else. . . . [From] the beginning, Miller understood their [the players'] problems, and they followed him. . . . He guided them where they wanted to go."[25]

A few years before the Bavasi articles, Yankees players discovered that George Weiss, the general manager, received a percentage of every dollar he cut from the payroll established by the owners for the coming season. The players were furious, but there was no way to focus that anger.[26] Similar situations probably existed in other clubs, but it was not until after 1966 that players realized there might be ways to change things. It was ironic that the Dodgers, the best-run club with a far-sighted owner and a veteran general manager, gave the union so much valuable ammunition.

Miller and Moss bombarded the player reps and the membership with information. The association started a newsletter, and Moss found an additional use for it. The first issue had a long article on the benefit plan, accused the owners of being unwilling to negotiate on the minimum salary, and went into detail about the Bavasi articles. The second issue was numbered three, prompting some executives to complain that the union had acted in bad faith by not sending them earlier issues. This was exactly the response Moss hoped would materialize. It gave him a chance to have some fun at the expense of ownership, but something more serious was involved. The fact that executives asked about the second issue showed that they were paying attention to what the players were saying among themselves.

During the 1967 All-Star Game break, the Executive Board of the Players Association met to discuss what actions it should take to start the process to create a collective bargaining agreement with the owners. A couple of years later, Miller reflected back on the situation in 1966, when he told the board about the difficulty that "fans and veteran observers of baseball" had in understanding why the players needed an organization. He realized that fans viewed baseball as a diversion. There was no reason for them to understand that baseball was a job for the players. He dismissed the idea that players had no reason to be concerned as harmful "myth." If doctors and attorneys organized to protect their interests, and entertainers had their union, why shouldn't major leaguers?[27]

In case anyone was unsure where the union was going, he made it clear in a public statement: "For many years the players have elected player representatives who are intelligent, capable, and sincerely concerned about carrying out their responsibilities, but the complexity of the duties facing them had gone beyond their ability. . . . I don't know why there is confusion about this, but the Major League Baseball Players Association is a union in structure, in purpose, in its functioning, it is a union under the law, and it has all the rights, duties, and obligations of any other bona fide union."[28]

While the pennant races were being fought out in the 1967 season, these two outsiders to baseball, Miller and Gaherin, started negotiations that showed how much baseball had changed and started the process to accelerate that change.

How are we to account for what had happened between April 1966 and the end of the 1967 season? First of all, it is necessary to recognize that baseball did not exist in a world sealed off from the broader currents of the society. The late 1960s saw dramatic changes in American life, including the questioning of traditional authority and institutions. It seems natural that this note of scepticism also would enter into the thoughts of baseball players. Players no longer had the Depression-era mindset of the previous generation. By 1967 there were many who thought they had the right to get a fair hearing on issues that mattered to them.

The players were aware that new types of owners had bought into baseball. These ranged from the CBS corporation, which owned the Yankees, to flamboyant self-publicizing entrepreneurs who had made their money in other fields and wanted to be part of baseball, for ego or profit or both. Charlie Finley of the A's and Gussie Busch of the Cardinals were two of the most noticeable. Owners had found a way to maximize their profits by either moving a team or threatening to move. They could obtain tax concessions and new facilities because they owned a scarce, valuable commodity. The Dodgers and Giants were the most dramatic moves, but other franchises had gone to more prosperous settings for the owners, the Braves from Boston to Milwaukee, the Browns from St. Louis to Baltimore, and the Senators from Washington to the Twin Cities. Some players saw the parallels between their own situation and those of the owners and wondered why the rules of baseball let only one side have the freedom to move.

Players who became union activists arrived there through different experiences. Mike Marshall is convinced that the union succeeded because the minor league experience, "where they treated you like dirt," had shown players the need to "bind together."[29] Joe Torre had some experience on Wall Street, which made him wonder about the reward system in baseball. He got involved in the union because he had to deal with a general manager who was vindictive and refused to deal with what Torre thought were legitimate questions.[30]

It might appear paradoxical that Jim Bunning, who went on to become a conservative Republican congressman and senator from Kentucky, was a driving force in pushing the union to challange the owners. He is only one example illustrating the fact that being active in the MLBPA had nothing to do with political philosophy. Players like Bunning, Torre, Brooks Robinson, Milt Pappas, Tim McCarver, and Steve Hamilton were not involved in ideological fights. They all had highly developed senses of self-interest on the field. What they were doing after 1966 was applying the same idea of self-interest to their activities off the field.

When players started asking questions in systematic ways and had someone like Miller or Moss to assist them, they were not pleased with the answers. They decided to break with decades of conditioning and tradition. That took the willingness to think for themselves and act on it, qualities that were more rare than taking an extra base or playing hurt. After 1966 star players took risks off the field with their careers that players formerly took only with their bodies on the field.

THE UNION ASSERTS ITSELF

BY THE START OF THE 1967 SEASON the union had established a new agenda. There was no question that it intended to press for changes. During the season and the winter that followed, the association was involved in a series of negotiations whose results would show whether the union could produce tangible benefits for its members.

On February 25, 1968, Joe Cronin, the president of the American League, wrote a letter to Marvin Miller that began, "Let us hope we can continue our association with mutual cooperation for the benefit and interest of our great national game."[1] He was writing about the recent signing of the first Basic Agreement between the owners and the Players Association. This was a collective bargaining agreement that spelled out in detail many of the contractual relationships between the two parties. Unlike Cronin's handwritten note, Miller's reply maintained a degree of formality and distance. He said that he agreed "wholeheartedly with your expressed hope that we continue our association with mutual cooperation for the best interests of baseball."[2] This was his way of reminding Cronin and the players who would see the letter that there were two equal sides at a bargaining table, each of which had a legitimate right to define what was meant by "best interests of baseball."

Passages in Miller's letter appear pedantic or even condescending. These were meant to impress upon the players and Cronin's employers that the Basic Agreement was not a gift from the owners. It had been fashioned in a bargaining process that had started at the insistence of the players.

The union wanted "this same approach [to] result in the successful administration of the Basic Agreement."[3] This was bound to give little comfort to any baseball executive who wanted to believe that the union regarded the Basic Agreement as an end unto itself. The crux of Miller's attitude and the strategy of the union was that "It [the Basic Agreement] demonstrated that problems can be resolved and progress made by reasonable men who are willing to consider fully each other's problems."[4] There was no question that the union's definitions of "problems," "progress," and "reasonable" differed widely from those held by the owners and their employees.

The first hurdle on the way to concluding an agreement had been to convince the owners that there was a reason, let alone a necessity, to have such a document. A collective bargaining agreement ran counter to the norms of professional sports. The fact that the Players Association had been able to get the owners to negotiate showed that the union would use its legal status to force changes.

John Gaherin's presence was essential to starting the process toward a Basic Agreement. In 1967 the idea of a collective bargaining agreement was perfectly natural to both Miller and Gaherin. Miller's employers believed that bargaining should take place and was in their best interests. Gaherin's employers had an opposite opinion, but he convinced them that the law left them no choice but to negotiate some form of agreement. His job was to fashion the best terms possible. Years later, Gaherin described his position in 1967: "If the Lords [of Baseball] wanted a man to kill the union in its crib, I was the worst possible selection."[5]

The path to the bargaining table was more difficult than the actual negotiations. In November 1967 a delegation from the association went to the winter meeting of the owners held in Mexico City. The players and Miller were under the impression that they had been invited to discuss possible changes in the minimum salary with a committee of owners. Upon their arrival, the players discovered that the owners had set aside no time to meet with them. The result of the trip to Mexico City was a set of rival press conferences, each trying to show that the other side was unreasonable. It was the worst possible scenario to inspire confidence for future negotiations. It did have one positive result for the union. The players who went to Mexico City were outraged at their treatment, and they told other players what had happened. This helped to create an even greater sense of unity among the players. It also had a direct impact on the career of Joe Torre, one of the players who had come to talk with the owners. Torre told his general manager what he thought about the owners' attitude concerning a player's role in the union, which "led to the best thing that ever happened to me. It got me traded [to St. Louis] on March 17, 1969."[6]

In Mexico City, Torre's general manager, Paul Richards, castigated Miller and the union in a series of public statements. At a press conference, Richards complained about men who want to drag baseball into court, "'and that'll be a sad day in the lives of 90 per cent of all the ballplayers.'"[7] He then went on to deliver a long series of comments about the need for the players to unite and get rid of the "outsiders" who had no interest in the players and were trying to destroy baseball for their own motives.

Miller thought that players might be worried if he sat back and took abuse without replying. After he returned from Mexico City, he drafted a letter to the Braves players. He characterized Richards's comments as "unreasoned attacks" probably caused by his need "to obtain some kind of internal release" by seeing himself quoted. He treated Richards with contempt and pity and described him as unable to cope with the changes in a fast-moving world, someone who couldn't "think young [and had to] berate the present and [was] living in the past . . . [an example of the] generation gap, [unwilling to understand] the values and life styles of younger people and others trying to cope with present day reality." Miller concluded his letter with a couple of gratuitous insults about Richards's record as an executive, paraphrasing remarks supposedly made by other executives. The letter gave Miller a chance to reflect on the situation and vent his anger. But as an experienced negotiator, Miller knew the potential cost of winning sympathy for his opponents. He decided not to send the letter.[8]

The immediate prelude to the negotiations for the Basic Agreement dealt with changes in the minimum salary. The current amount was seven thousand dollars for players who remained on the roster after June 1, a figure that had not changed significantly in nearly twenty years. The players wanted it raised to twelve thousand dollars, although they were sure that they would not get that. If inflation or the growing profits in baseball mattered, the players had a good case for a higher minimum salary. The owners established a committee to meet with the players, but when the players showed up, they were shocked to find that "instead of a committee of General Managers, the Clubs were represented by American League President Cronin, National League Secretary Flieg, and the two League attorneys." These were not the men who could make the decisions. The league attorneys turned a bad situation worse when "they took the position that they had only come to listen; they would not offer any facts, arguments, responses, proposals, or counter-proposals." The nonmeeting lasted three hours, and the answer to every proposal by the players was that it "served no useful purpose."[9]

The players at that meeting, Jim Pagliaroni and Steve Hamilton, were furious but not surprised. In Hamilton's words, "They had a way of putting us down . . . of ignoring us and assuming that, 'maybe they'll go away.'" This meeting gave Hamilton his first opportunity to see first-hand the way in which the owners dealt (or chose not to deal) with the new situation and reinforced his view that the owners "had no respect for the union."[10]

The Basic Agreement of February 19, 1968, established the credibility of the union. The Players Association had made specific gains rather than seeking some abstract goal. The agreement dealt with long-standing complaints like split doubleheaders, the length of season, and the structure and payment for the playoffs. This showed the players that their union could play a role in determining working conditions and what they would be paid. The agreement incorporated existing arrangements about the benefits program and the dues checkoff. Anyone who was familiar with contracts in other industries would consider the Basic Agreement to be remarkably ordinary. That is precisely what Miller and Moss wanted. The association was acting as a standard bargaining agent for its members.

The content of Article IV of the Basic Agreement was boilerplate to Gaherin and Miller, but it laid the foundation for every important gain the union made over the next decade. It stated, "The parties have adopted a Grievance Procedure, the purpose of which is to set forth an orderly and expeditious system for the handling and resolving of grievances."[11]

The complete text of the grievance procedure was appended to the document. From the first day of the negotiations, Miller had insisted that a specific procedure for raising, identifying, and adjudicating grievances was as necessary as it was normal. The reasons were clear to him. The existing procedures in baseball assumed that the players either had no grievances or that their complaints would be handled fairly by the clubs, the league presidents, or the commissioner.

The procedure in the 1968 Basic Agreement set up a process for handling grievances and retained some role for the commissioner. This might seem unusual, since Miller's first action as executive director had been to distance himself from the commissioner, and Miller continued to remind the players that the commissioner was an employee of the owners. But during the negotiations, Miller saw the tactical value of reassuring the owners that some traditions could be maintained. He emphasized that there was nothing to be feared by a grievance procedure that would not "interfere with the exclusive rights of the Clubs to manage their operations and direct their employees."[12] Of course, those terms needed definition, which would, in turn, be the product of further negotiation between the union and the owners. The important questions for the future were what issues would be decided in grievance hearings and how the process might be altered in the next Basic Agreement.

Why did the owners accept an innovation that went against the history of the game and gave new rights to the association? Certainly it was not an oversight. The grievance process ran almost five pages in the twenty-four-page Basic Agreement. The owners had discussed the question among themselves and had been assured by their veteran labor relations expert that the grievance procedure was a necessary part of the agreement. Gaherin saw no way around it. Nevertheless, Commissioner Kuhn objected to it. According to Gaherin, "it took a lot to get Kuhn to accept it," which he did only when he was assured that there were specific areas reserved for the commissioner.[13] Years later, Kuhn was still convinced that it was an unnecessary concession made by the owners and that it started baseball on a downward spiral of increasingly ill-tempered relations between the MLBPA and the owners.[14] Kuhn saw it as the first step in creating problems where none existed; Miller and Moss saw it as the first step toward solving problems that had existed for years.

The relative ease with which the association got the owners to accept the grievance procedure was one sign of how secure the owners were in the belief that nothing could challenge their control. The owners thought that players were satisfied. If the past was any indication, grievances would be limited to issues such as bull pen mounds and shower heads in the locker rooms. Clearly, the association had other ideas in 1968.

The new grievance procedure was incorporated into the uniform player's contract, the document that spelled out a player's terms of employment. It replaced the article in the contract that had stated, "In case of dispute between the Player and the Club, the same shall be referred to the Commissioner *as an arbitrator, and his decision shall be accepted by all parties as final*" (emphasis added).[15]

A few years later, Dick Moss discussed the importance of the grievance provision in a talk to the National Academy of Arbitrators. He demonstrated a combination of ongoing culture shock and whimsy. Moss informed them that the idea of "just cause for discipline [was] a thought contrary to baseball's prior history and sacred tradition . . . impartial arbitration was [assumed to be] one of those subversive devices Marvin Miller was bringing over from the Steelworkers Union as part of his plan to ruin baseball." In case his audience thought Moss was exaggerating, he reminded them that the grievance procedure had been run by "the Commissioner, an employee of the club owners—he is hired, paid by, and can, at will, be fired by the owners." In the forty-five-year history of dealing with complaints that a player might lodge against his club, "there is no record or hint of even one player-club dispute being appealed by a player to the Commissioner." Moss tried to describe what it was like to represent a player at an arbitration hearing when "you are massively outmanned by opposing counsel . . . [and] when the arbitrator has the same employer as all those [opposition] lawyers."

What Moss found in baseball was "a unique experience to engage in what I call 'partial' arbitration, as opposed to 'impartial' arbitration." Nothing better describes the unique qualities of baseball's attitudes toward the players than Moss's choice of "partial" to describe the process. He used it to a group of professionals who assumed that "partial" meant the opposite of "total" and that "impartial arbitration" was a redundant use of the adjective.[16]

The results of arbitration for the players were obvious and instantaneous. The players had a sense that they could get a fair hearing where they would be supported by the union. The number of grievances went from two in the past forty-five years to more than twenty in the next five years. The owners could take some comfort in the role left for the commissioner and in other language specifically maintaining elements of the past. The article entitled "Management Rights" stated, "Nothing in this agreement shall be construed to restrict the rights of the Clubs to manage and direct their operations in any manner whatsoever except as specifically limited by the terms of this Agreement."[17] The owners had some reason to believe that nothing would go to arbitration that could damage the sport.

While the union was working on the Basic Agreement, it was considering another important issue. The board discussed the contracts that players had signed with Topps Chewing Gum that allowed the company to use their photos on baseball cards. To the thousands of youngsters who collected the cards, they were a link with Major League Baseball. To the players, they were a source of incidental but very useful income. To the company, it was big business, and Miller and Moss turned their attention to that aspect.

The Coca-Cola arrangement had given the union and the players a whole new perspective on the importance of marketing. If Topps was making a good profit out of their cards, why shouldn't the players get as much as possible for their part of the product? What heretofore had been a private arrangement between a player and a company became an issue for the union. The player reps discussed what they described as the "inadequate payments made to players" as well as the control that Topps exercised over the use of the players' pictures. The staggered nature of the contracts with individual players made it impossible for the union to organize a competitive bidding process that would include companies other than Topps.

When Miller tried to speak with the president of Topps, the president sounded like the owners talking about the reserve system—this was the way we've always done things, the players are satisfied, and why is Miller sticking his nose into an arrangement between an individual player and the company? Miller could force the owners to deal with the union, since it was the legally certified representative of the players. Topps had no such obligation. The union found another way to get the company's attention. After Miller and Moss told the Executive Board that it was their opinion that "baseball players have a very bad deal with Topps," the board decided to do something.

Since Miller and Moss constantly reminded the owners and the press about the importance of reciprocal contractual obligations, it would have been hypocritical and tactically inept for the union to convince players to break their currently binding contracts. More than that, it would have been illegal. The board decided that Miller and Moss should immediately hold meetings with all of the players to "recommend that each player refuse to sign any additional renewals with Topps." That got the attention of Topps, especially when its long-time representative to the players found that he could not get any signatures on contracts. The resultant changes gave the players a percentage of the revenue for the first time, rather than a flat fee. This meant a significant increase in the payments made to the players. The Topps negotiations reinforced the lessons learned from the Coca-Cola contract.[18]

The bubble gum card settlement was a preamble to a much more important battle for the union, one fought over an issue that every player understood—the pension plan and its related benefits. The pension agreement was scheduled for renewal at the start of the 1969 season. The union tried to begin talks during the 1968 season, but management refused. Miller chose to present the worst interpretation to the players, pointing out that Gaherin and his colleagues were waiting until the players were dispersed and scattered to start the talks. He also wondered aloud why negotiations in the past had been completed during the season prior to the expiration of the agreements. He contended that the owners' new proposal was an attempt to turn back the clock, even to the point of no longer granting benefits to recently retired players. He impressed upon the players that the owners were testing the union's resolve. The clear implication was that this was one more instance of the owners changing the rules because the players had hired Miller and were taking a more aggressive stance. He wanted to remind the players once more about the 1966 battle over the $150,000.[19]

Negotiations on the pension and benefits finally began on October 23, 1968. Miller and Moss were joined by nine players and Gaherin by the two league presidents and two baseball lawyers, one of whom was Bowie Kuhn. The owners presented their proposal at the end of a third meeting, and it was "opposed with considerable vigor" by the players. The players were convinced that the money offered by the owners was grossly inadequate, especially in light of the increased television revenue generated by the All-Star Game and World Series. The new proposal would have increased the contribution of each club from $205,000 to $212,500, approximately $125 per player.[20]

The union appeared to be more troubled about the reason for the dispute than the money involved. The most disturbing feature was the owners' insistence that the players drop any claims that they had a right to share in the television revenues. Miller made the association's position clear. He wrote to the players that the owners claimed the right "to unilaterally terminate the plan in the future" and to decide what kinds of benefits would be available. He claimed that the owners were not interested in the history of the pension arrangements and that they intended to control it. On December 17, the owners submitted to the players what they described as a final offer.

The union submitted the proposal to every player, and they rejected it by a vote of 461 to 6. As negotiations dragged on, the owners rejected all of the union's counterproposals. According to Miller, the owners added a provision stipulating that they have "a unilateral right to liquidate the Plan for any reason at all or for no reason." This gave Miller an unparalleled chance to depict the union as the protector of the pension fund and to claim, "The owners apparently believe they and they alone are baseball. . . . They seem quite willing to sacrifice fan interest, if in the process, they can 'teach the players a lesson.'" In case the players did not understand the seriousness of the issue, Miller reminded them that "it is the players' ability to bargain effectively through their Players Association which they [the owners] look to destroy."[21]

It was one thing to recognize the danger and alert the players to it; it was something else to devise a strategy to force the owners into making a pension proposal that was acceptable to the players. The lessons learned from the negotiations with Topps came into play. The Executive Board adopted a policy that players should not sign their individual contracts for the new season until both sides had agreed upon a new benefit plan. The union was orchestrating a massive holdout that dwarfed the Koufax-Drysdale episode. The players were using the most effective weapon they had. For the first time, actions by the players union pushed hot-stove league topics into the background of the sports pages. Individual holdouts had always been a feature of the off-season, but players seldom gained much by them. This time, more than four hundred players were involved. Players showed up at union-sponsored press conferences and public events. The clubs put pressure on individual players through personal contacts and the press. There were some defections, but the union held firm. Gaherin presented another set of final proposals, and the union rejected them.

As spring training approached, there was another unsettling feature. The owners had removed Commissioner Eckert and were trying to find a new commissioner, a process that dragged out longer than they intended. They finally chose Bowie Kuhn, an experienced baseball lawyer and a great fan of the game. Kuhn had been involved throughout the abortive negotiations over the Pension Fund, and he understood that the union was not bluffing. A spring training without most of the players was not the way he wanted to start his new job. A combination of player resolve and the new commissioner convinced the owners to make more changes in their proposal.

Once spring training opened in 1969, the public and management forgot about the player boycott. The players turned their attention to the season, but the union staff and a few players had additional concerns. The Basic Agreement included a provision entitled "Joint Studies," which described two areas that "the parties shall review jointly." One of these was a study that should "be completed prior to the termination date of this agreement . . . [about a] possible alternative to the reserve clause as now constituted. . . . [I]t is mutually agreed that the Clubs shall not be obligated to bargain or to seek agreement with the Players Association on either of the above matters [the reserve system] during the term of this Agreement."[22]

The owners had agreed to hold meetings, but they were free to ignore any proposals that the players might bring to the committee. The Joint

Study Committee was far more than window dressing as far as the union was concerned. The existence of the committee reminded the players that there was something that had to be studied and that the union was the mechanism for it. Some owners viewed the situation as further assurance of the status quo. However, coupling Miller's philosophy with the provision should have alerted people that the joint study was the union's first step in an effort to modify the reserve system. In this respect, Bowie Kuhn's suspicions of Miller's motives and tactics was realistic.[23]

The Joint Study Committee on the Reserve System held its first meeting on April 24, 1969, in the offices of the Players Association. The owners had five representatives, led by Gaherin, and the players had a three-man delegation: Miller, Moss, and Bunning. The opening remarks showed that the parties did not disagree about the effects of the system. What divided them were the questions raised by the union: Why was the system necessary? If restrictions on the movement of players were needed, why couldn't they be modified?[24]

The issue was joined at the start of the first session when Miller asked that the committee come up "with an agreement that both sides can support." He then asked, "Why do we need it [the current reserve system]?" The answer that came from the owners' delegation was just as straightforward. If the current system did not remain in place, the future of baseball would be full of more Koufaxes and Drysdales. This did not mean that baseball could look forward to great pitchers. What the speaker had in mind was the specter of future Hall of Famers who had found a way to force their teams to deal with them over salary. If it was dangerous for a few players to work together to raise salaries, it would be catastrophic if they gained some control over where they played or didn't play. The opening statement of the owners turned out to be their final position: "chaos would result, if there were any changes."[25]

The complexities facing the committee were clear. Ownership wanted to know why the players wanted to question something that everyone knew, or should know, was essential to baseball's success. The man who asked the question for the owners also supplied the answers. The association's leadership did not understand baseball and was trying to sabotage the system from ulterior motives. Lou Hoynes, one of baseball's attorneys, phrased the concerns of ownership succinctly when he asked Miller, "Are these suggestions [for changes] motivated by salary considerations only?"[26]

Hoynes's question was one of the first examples of what became the public strategy of the owners to portray the union as having no interests other than more money for the players. The conclusion he drew was bound to frustrate the players—the present system was a compromise that was equitable to both parties. He was never specific about the advantages the players got from it. But by raising the link between salaries and the reserve system, his question helped pave the way for the establishment of salary arbitration. After all, that was one way that the players could ameliorate the economic restrictions imposed by the reserve system.

Club executives, whose jobs were to make money for their employers, charged the union with acting in bad faith because it wanted more money for its members. Miller chose to ignore the money issue and took another approach. He asserted that the reserve system was about "opportunity to play and 'human dignity.'"[27] This might sound like a public relations ploy, but it was made during a closed negotiating session.

In the brief opening meeting, the participants showed why the existing power relationship in baseball meant that nothing positive would come out of the Joint Study Committee. Bunning talked about the need to protect players who did not have a chance to further their careers because of the reserve system. The lawyers for the owners responded that the players preferred to have a reserve system. Both sides discussed whether a player should have any say about where he played and mentioned some of the difficulties involved in trades. They were operating with different frames of reference. One Players Association proposal was that a player should be allowed to leave his team if his salary did not reach a certain level. Management rejected this because it "would create incentive to do poorly," which prompted Jim Bunning to respond that "no one tries to have a bad year."[28]

It's hard to imagine what was going through the mind of this pitcher, who was known throughout the game for his hard-nosed competitive fervor and a willingness to throw inside at his closest friends and ex-teammates. In one short sentence, the owners had challenged the integrity of the players, misunderstood the depth of their competitive instincts, and insulted their understanding of the economics of the game. Would a player be dishonest enough to play badly just for the possibility of leaving his current team? Didn't players take pride in their accomplishments and want to win? Didn't they feel responsibility to their teammates, and wasn't there peer pressure to perform? Didn't every player understand that if he didn't perform, he would be killing off any chance to profit economically by moving to another team? Who would want to sign a player who was having a bad season, especially if his performance was clouded by suspicion that he was not playing hard?

In virtually all succeeding negotiations the owners and their representatives failed to take into account the kind of reaction Bunning had shown. The competitive nature that players showed on the field was part of their basic character. It is hard to understand how managers and general managers who prized tough-minded competitors should be so surprised when those traits showed up at the bargaining table.

The future of the Joint Study Committee was clear from the start. Management stated that the control they presently exercised was necessary for the protection of baseball. It was the only way to equalize team strength, avoid tampering, and protect the investment involved in the development of players. If the union could come up with suggestions that would protect all of these, management might be willing to listen.

As the first meeting was concluding, Miller asked, "What will be the conclusion of the review?"[29] Management had a clear concept of what it wanted: no changes unless they made it even more difficult for a player to bargain or to move. The view of the players was more nebulous. They wanted some freedom to move or to pressure their current employers to bargain with them for salaries that reflected their potential market value. Given the huge gulf between the two parties and the clear intention of the owners to retain the current reserve system, was there any purpose for a second session? Two months later, the discussion got down to specifics and showed how difficult it would be to agree even on an innocuous document. From the association's point of view, the Joint Study Committee was useful because it made it easier for Miller to get information to the players about the current situation. He assumed that when more players thought about what was involved in the reserve system, they would support efforts to change it. He clearly believed that the system was wrong and that it harmed individual players. But his job was to deal with the pragmatic issues involved. If the owners cast doubts on the motives of anyone questioning the reserve system, it might rally player support around the union.

The insistence of the union to open the issue of the reserve system was the baseball equivalent of Galileo questioning the earth-centered universe. It challenged common sense and the power structure. Why overturn orthodoxy with no care for the consequences when the old system had worked so well? Wasn't the game thriving as a result of its unique set of rules? Why take the chance of ruining baseball to appease a few malcontents and their radical labor leader? Realistically, more was at stake than abstract principles. The reserve system was about power and money.

The work of the committee operated against the background of important changes that had taken place in the business of baseball during the 1960s, of which expansion and corporate involvement were the most noticeable. Players and owners interpreted these events through different experiences and self-interests. To the players, expansion meant more jobs and a new sense of job security for veterans, which had a huge effect on the attitudes of the players. Formerly marginal players were filling major league rosters. In 1961 the American League expanded from eight to ten teams, and the National League followed suit the following year. In 1969 both leagues added two more teams. In 1960 there were four hundred players on major league rosters. By 1969 there had been a 50 percent increase. The threat of being sent down to the minor leagues or released no longer had the same impact. The abortive efforts led by Branch Rickey to establish the Continental League had provided the impetus for expansion. It is ironic that Rickey, who used the restrictions of the reserve system more effectively than other executives, should play a role in fostering a new level of player militancy.

The new complexities involved in baseball convinced owners that they needed firm control of their primary asset. This was not the time to start experimenting. There was more reason than ever for an unchanged reserve system. Baseball appealed to new investors because its unique system enabled them to exercise more control than they had in any other enterprise. It would be foolish to invest in baseball and then bargain away one of its biggest assets.

Every meeting of the Joint Study Committee affirmed that the two sides were speaking a different language. Instead of narrowing the differences, new concerns appeared. The owners rejected every proposal, and the union leadership used those rejections to get more of the membership interested in the need for change. During the meetings, both sides talked about how they were representing the broader interests of baseball. The owners had always spoken in those terms; it was something new for the players.

At an early meeting, Gaherin had made an off-the-record comment that "all positions were retractable," but that did not appear to be the reality.[30] The committee decided to look at how versions of player control operated in other sports. The players talked about how positive lessons could be drawn from football and basketball, but the owners replied that they did not apply to the unique situation in baseball.

One of the first assertions made by the owners was that change would work against the players because any modified form of free agency would depress salaries. The owners on the committee claimed that they were protecting the job security of the marginal players and standing up for the rights of all players to prosper. Decades of paternalism died hard. Miller reminded them that it was the responsibility of the Players Association to deal with the needs of players.

The owners pointed out that even a third-string player had value to a club, even if only for trading purposes. It was good for a marginal player to be moved around from club to club because he could fit into the needs of several different teams. But that movement had to be controlled by the clubs, "Even if it was only one player [who moved on his terms] it would have the same long-term consequences," and that would be chaos.[31]

The owners said repeatedly that money played little role in their concerns about the reserve system. But the history of baseball showed that was not the case. Financial concerns had always been a major consideration for player movement. When there had been competition for players, salaries had risen. When that ceased, salaries had returned to previous levels. Teams had used their players as an asset to be sold on the market. Kansas City had become virtually a farm club for the Yankees as a way of making money for the club. Since the money had gone to the owners, and the players had nothing to say about either the movement or the cash, it's understandable that the owners saw no need to change the system.

The claim that the system was constructed to provide the maximum benefits for the players must have come as a surprise to the players. At one meeting the union responded that if the owners were right and that movement was in fact good for the career of a marginal player, wouldn't it be better if he had some freedom to control that movement? The tone of the discussion changed once and for all when Miller moved away from generalizations and used one player to illustrate what the association thought was wrong with the current system.

Bob Barton was scarcely the material of which baseball legends were made, not someone to revolutionize the game. Miller asked what conclusions could be drawn from a player whose career could be summarized as follows: "third-string catcher for the Giants. In four years, never became a regular . . . played only seven games." This was the textbook definition of a marginal player, precisely whom the owners claimed to be protecting.

When Miller asked, "What about Bob Barton?" to summarize the issues that had been introduced by the owners, the men across the table from him had no answer.[32] There was no way to fit Barton into the equation that the reserve system was protecting players like him and giving them a chance to succeed. This silence spotlighted the differences between the two sides and showed that the even the smallest changes that were necessary to cope with the reality of the problem would be considered a revolution.

Meetings continued for almost two years, but almost nothing changed. At the meeting held a few weeks after the Bob Barton question, one of the owners' lawyers made the point that "the clubs cannot allow players to decide where or for whom they will play." Miller put a marginal note in his copy of the minutes: "heart of the reserve clause not negotiable."[33] The succeeding meetings would show just how correct this was. Miller questioned the owners' assertion that the values of the reserve system were "reciprocal." He wondered what was reciprocal about the way owners and executives traded or released players who were active in the association. He used Paul Richards and Joe Torre as examples.

A baseball lawyer responded by pointing to cases where clubs had paid back taxes for players and had only traded them after years of using club attorneys to keep them out of jail. When the issue of salary emerged, the lawyers reminded Miller that every club had to maintain a salary budget. Miller pointed out that this meant that players in smaller cities were destined to get lower salaries throughout their careers. The response was that such differences were inevitable. There were variations in the ability of clubs to pay, which "is the essence of competition." Competition appeared to be a virtue in baseball in every area other than competing for the services of players.[34]

One of the lawyers challenged Miller's assertion that freedom of contract was an American ideal. The lawyer pointed out that soldiers, clergymen, and other professions had restrictions based upon their freedom to move. Miller rejected the comparison to nonprofit enterprises like the army and the church and stressed that "we're not fighting an ideological battle named 'clause'—we have problems."[35] That was almost a textbook definition of how the union operated. It was in the business of dealing with problems that affected its members. In the case of the reserve system there was no way to avoid the ideological context, since the owners had turned the maintenance of an unchanged reserve system into the touchstone for the survival of the sport.

For baseball fans 1969 will always be the season of the "Miracle Mets," the year when the team that was famous for its years of futility won the World Series. It was also the year when baseball revolutionized the pennant races by creating postseason playoffs. The most significant change in the league structure of baseball since 1903 had allowed a mediocre Mets team to go to the World Series. Their "miracle" would have been comparitively insignificant had the Joint Study Committee come up with any recommendations that were acceptable to both sides.

Succeeding meetings of the committee showed no changes on either side. When it concluded its deliberations, Miller sent out a memorandum to all of the players informing them of recent developments and summing up what he described as "two years [of] long, fruitless discussions with the owners' representatives on the subject of the reserve system." Miller reminded the players that the union had never asked for the abolition of the reserve system, and he included a set of detailed proposals the players had made to change the system. All of them had been rejected completely because, in his words, the purpose of the present system "is to inhibit competition by restricting a player to one market for his services during his entire career." Another point Miller raised in the memorandum was the fact that the players had no control over their lives, the "fact that some players are 'treated well' does not mask the lack of dignity in the relationship."[36] That phrase had a special significance since the preceding pages of the memorandum stated that the board had decided to support a suit by Curt Flood to overturn the reserve system.

5

CURT FLOOD AND THE
AMERICAN DREAM

"I AM A MAN, I live in a democratic society, and I believe I am entitled to participate in our free enterprise system."[1] Such sentiments were worthy of Walter O'Malley moving the Dodgers from Brooklyn to Los Angeles, Dick Young changing newspapers, or Gussie Busch presiding over the rise of Anheuser-Busch to become the largest brewery in the world. They would have been applauded widely had they been delivered by an owner, a businessman, or a politician. But the reaction to them in 1969 was outrage because the author was a black center fielder who was embarking on the most unequal contest of his career. They were spoken in 1969 by a man who quickly was branded as an ingrate and a radical threat to baseball.

This was Curt Flood speaking shortly after he sent a letter to Commissioner Kuhn rejecting his trade from the Cardinals to the Phillies and requesting that the commissioner grant him the ability to play for the team of his choice. Flood used another phrase that showed both the emotion and the thought that went into a decision that he knew almost certainly would bring his successful and financially rewarding career to a premature end: "I do not, however, consider myself to be a piece of property to be sold regardless of my desire."[2]

The name Curt Flood has come to represent an era and a cause. This almost has obscured the fact that he was a talented player on one of the most interesting teams of its generation. He batted over .300 six times and was the perfect second-place hitter batting behind the great base stealer Lou Brock. In 1968 the cover of *Sports Illustrated* proclaimed him to

Curt Flood, one of the best center fielders in the history of baseball, brought the reserve system to everyone's attention, prematurely ending his career.

be the best center fielder in baseball, a tribute to his talent as well as a comment on the effect of age on Willie Mays. He was supposedly a favorite of the Cardinals' president, Gussie Busch, in a city where the Busch family were local aristocracy. A Sunday supplement of the *St. Louis Post-Dispatch* had featured him on its cover sitting on the balcony of his high-rise apartment with St. Louis spread out below him, a comment on the fact that Flood was also somewhat of a civic celebrity. He was an example of a ball player who chose to live where he performed and who had interests outside of baseball. Flood was an accomplished artist and had other qualities that were supposed to show that he was anything but a potentially rebellious troublemaker.[3]

The same man who was described in 1965 as "a Baptist, reared and taught that persecution from the outside can be a measure of a man's inner strength" and in 1969 as "The Rembrandt of Baseball" had become by 1970 a "spoiled ingrate" and by 1971 "a cynic and unforgiving guy whose racial resentment runs deep" and a "wheeler dealer [moving] to the land of boozin and beddin."[4] There is little need to repeat details of the Flood case, but it is important to understand that he operated within the framework created by the revitalized Players Association. His decision to mount a legal challenge reflected the new atmosphere between players and owners. Flood was solely responsible for his decision to reject the trade and to sue for free agency if that was the only way to gain his freedom. But he informed Miller of his plans almost immediately.

Eleven days before Flood sent his letter to Kuhn, the regularly scheduled winter meeting of the association's Executive Board took place at the Sheraton Hotel in San Juan, Puerto Rico. Other things were special about the San Juan meeting besides Flood. It was the first time the players had met at a venue different from the owners' winter meeting. In Steve Hamilton's words, the previous year's experience at the Mexico City winter meeting made the players wonder, "Why did we have to go where they go?"[5] The union's decision to meet on its own was a statement that some members of baseball's hierarchy, including Commissioner Kuhn, thought was unfortunate and unnecessarily provocative.

The agenda for San Juan included a report about the negotiations for a new Basic Agreement, which stated that the owners had "rejected all Association proposals" concerning the reserve clause and related rules. The board later "reviewed in detail the history of discussions with the Owners' representatives regarding the reserve system" and said that although the owners had pledged in 1968 to give serious study to the issue, they had refused to discuss any proposal put forward by the players and "have not advanced one single idea of their own for reform. . . . It was the feeling of the board that the players' problems caused by the present reserve system represents the most serious issue in the present negotiations, and the issue can no longer be overlooked and must be resolved in these negotiations."[6]

The minutes of the meeting that were distributed later contained a superb piece of understatement: "In a related manner, the Board then heard from Curt Flood, who had requested an opportunity to appear at the board meeting to advise it of his impending action, and to enlist the support and cooperation of the Players Association."[7] The twenty-seven players in that room had all grown up in a system where what had happened to Flood was common. They were being asked to consider challenging the supposed foundation of the sport that brought them wealth and fame. The board members had been elected to represent their teammates. Every man who listened to Flood was an established major leaguer, and many of them were stars. They had a huge stake in the continued prosperity of baseball, and many of them went on to have careers as managers or in the front office.

Tim McCarver was a teammate of Flood's and part of the player package including Flood that had been consigned to the Phillies in return for Dick Allen and others. At the San Juan meeting McCarver was listed already as a member of the Phillies, while Joe Torre and Dal Maxvill represented the Cardinals. McCarver flew to San Juan with Flood, and during the trip he tried to understand why Flood was taking his actions. McCarver was concerned about what it meant "to Flood as a person" and wanted to know how sure Flood was about what he was doing. During the flight, Flood's determination and his realistic assessment of the consequences were obvious to McCarver, something that Flood made equally clear to the board members the following day.[8] When Maxvill saw Flood at the airport, he had asked him, "Do you know you're going to be out there like the Lone Ranger?" Flood nodded his head in agreement.[9]

Writers and fans might discount phrases like "great inequities to all the players" and "no longer willing to be bought and sold like a piece of property," but the players in Puerto Rico understood what Flood meant. Even if they did not share the depth of his outrage, many of them had gone through the same experience. They also had no doubts about what was at stake for him. As Steve Hamilton and Jim Bunning listened to Flood, they needed no reminder of the attitude of the owners during the abortive Joint Study Committee. Flood's proposed action was one answer, maybe the only answer to the owners' refusal to consider any changes. One of the board members, Joe Torre, recalled, "we weren't militant by any stretch of the imagination, but obviously we realized that the fabric of baseball was one-sided from the owners' standpoint."[10]

Hamilton was convinced that the owners would never pay attention to any proposals by the players about the reserve system, but until the San Juan meeting he saw no real interest among the players in trying to force changes. He did not initially want Flood to go forward with his action and thought that many of the board members shared this feeling. Nevertheless, when Flood made clear his intentions, Hamilton thought, "if he's going to do it, we have to back him." Hamilton thought that the meeting "was kind of exciting."[11] Other participants remember it differently. Gary Peters, the Red Sox pitcher, thought that it was "almost mundane" because nothing Flood said surprised or upset him; "it was a statement of the obvious."[12] Hamilton thought most players were ambivalent, but Milt Pappas contends that "99 percent of the players supported what Flood was trying to do, even though they knew it would be a tough fight."[13]

Everyone in the room knew that if Flood did not report to the Phillies his large income and his career were probably at an end. Flood's opening comments set the tone for what he would say later. He informed the board that he would soon make his position public. There was no doubt that he intended to go forward with his actions. He wanted to show the board members that his fight was that of all the players. He wanted the support of the Players Association, but he was not asking for its permission. His opening statement to the board was unambiguous: "regardless of what you decide, I plan to go ahead. . . . We are all here under the same yoke. I can't be bought off. Someone has to do it. . . . I feel I am qualified and capable of doing it."[14]

Miller thought that it was important to support Flood. The players at the meeting had lots of questions. Their discussion with Flood turned quickly to his motives. These concerns would be paralleled by later comments by reporters: how much was Flood interested in money rather than freedom and principles? Flood assured the board that "his motivation for taking action was not to use it as a bargaining technique for obtaining more money for himself."

The player reps understood that they had to be careful about what they endorsed. They could not get too far ahead of the membership. One long-time player rep pointed out, "we can be 100 percent [behind Flood], but that doesn't necessarily mean all the players will support [him]."[15] As another player rep described it, "we gave Flood the third degree . . . we had to . . . we had a concern that any player doing this should understand the consequences, personal and otherwise."[16] Jim Bunning repeatedly raised the question about what to tell the other players. He assumed that the owners and their supporters would put the worst possible interpretation on whatever the union did to support Flood. If they could portray him as a selfish malcontent, it might be possible for management to convince other players that they were being used by a radical minority on the board. That might break the unity of the organization.

Board members asked Flood if he realized that "he would be subjecting himself to personal attacks by the owners, and that he may well be endangering the remainder of his baseball career."[17] After more than an hour of questioning, Flood "was excused from the meeting" while the board discussed what to do. During the closed-door discussion, concerns were raised about what "dangers there might be if Curt Flood wins or what the cost would be if he lost." There were also questions about what financial cost would be involved for the union to support his case and help him to obtain high-quality legal representation. After its discussion concluded, the board issued a resolution that "Curt Flood's action will affect every player in baseball" and that the association's participation was necessary to see that an "appropriate result is achieved." It voted 25-0 to talk with him about the best way to proceed, to help him obtain high-quality counsel, to pay the costs, and "to publicly announce its support of him."

The board also said that it intended to "continue to negotiate appropriate revisions" to the reserve system but noted that the owners had refused to consider any meaningful changes. That left only two alternatives for the players. They could "take concerted action on the issue by withholding their services or test the matter in court." The latter was preferable, since it was "far less disruptive." Almost everyone who read the minutes of this crucial meeting concentrated on the statement about Flood and might have ignored the passing reference to "withholding their services." Many of the players who were there do not even remember the comment. This appears to have been the first time that the union spoke publicly about the possibility of a strike.[18]

The commissioner responded immediately to Flood's letter. Kuhn agreed that "you as a human being, are not a piece of property to be bought and sold. That is fundamental in our society and I think is obvious."[19] This might not have been as obvious to a man whose whole life had been changed when he received a twenty-eight-word letter trading him from the Cardinals to the Phillies, a letter written by Bing Devine, the general manager of the Cardinals, and a man for whom Flood retained fondness and respect.[20] The commissioner and the rest of the baseball establishment had no common ground with anything Flood said in his letter. They did take him seriously, even though they believed that "since baseball had never lost in court since 1922, there wasn't any danger now."[21] Kuhn's reply reflected the careful rhetoric of someone who wanted to deal only with the legal issues. Baseball executives and sportswriters made the broader case against Flood. Their responses to Flood were a combination of fears for the future of baseball, personal attacks, and accusations that the union leadership had seduced Flood while violating their contractual obligations.

The point men for the owners were the league presidents, Joe Cronin and Chub Feeney, both of whom had grown up in baseball and neither of whom saw any need to consider any changes in the reserve system. They talked about the "obvious" results of a world without the reserve clause— one in which "professional baseball *would simply cease to exist*" (emphasis added).[22] This was more than scare tactics or hyperbole. Baseball, as experienced by Cronin and Feeney, would end if Flood were to win. The arguments of the owners had three foundations—tradition, self-interest, and a belief that the reserve system was an all-or-nothing arrangement. A "modified reserve system" was an oxymoron to them. The response to Flood was based on the same beliefs that had made the Joint Study Committee irrelevant.

What were the "chaotic results" that ownership claimed would result from a successful challenge to the reserve system? Clubs would not pay to scout and develop players because "no club could build with assurance" for the future. "No intelligent person would continue to invest the large capital required" to run a major league club. In addition, the minor leagues would collapse because "Major League support would be destroyed" and "mutually advantageous trades would become impossible if the players' consents were required." This would deprive fans of one of the most exciting aspects of baseball as well as stopping management from managing. Everyone would lose. In case the players did not get the point, Cronin and Feeney told them that baseball would have to cut money from "an unmatched benefit plan" for the players.[23] This reference to the pension plan showed that the owners still regarded it as a gift from management. By merely hinting at cuts in the pension fund they assumed that the players would see that their support for Flood was misguided.

The two presidents also asserted, "The integrity of the game would be threatened as players could negotiate with one club while playing for another."[24] This made it seem that the players had no sense of integrity for the game or their profession and that they were willing to betray their teammates, themselves, and the sport. No player could accept this view. It was not calculated to give the public much confidence in either the players or the sport. Furthermore, if it was true, what did this say about the integrity of the owners and the executives? Tampering was not a solitary enterprise. The only way a player could compromise himself was if another club approached him. Did Cronin and Feeney have so low an opinion of their employers that they thought the owners would engage in wholesale tampering if the reserve system was changed?

The heart of the campaign against Flood was that the competitive nature of baseball would be destroyed if he and the union prevailed. Cronin and Feeney summarized their argument: "Without the reserve clause the wealthier clubs could sign an unbeatable team of all-stars, totally destroying league competition. . . . Clubs of more limited resources would be stripped of their stars and their ability to field teams which the public would accept."[25] This scenario went to the heart of baseball's traditions and its self-serving mythology.

At first glance, the claim that even a limited free market in players could result in the creation of a few all-star teams might seem plausible. But it flew in the face of the history of baseball. By 1970 the game's past was filled with the exploits of a few teams that won often and the wreckage of most teams that never won. Try explaining competitive balance to generations of fans of the Phillies, Reds, A's, Red Sox, Braves, and Pirates, or convincing an American League fan that any team could dominate more than the Yankees had for decades. While it was not as bad in the National League, after 1946 fans could count on the Dodgers and a couple of other teams to be in the hunt for the pennant every year. From 1919 to 1968, the Yankees, Dodgers, Giants, and Cardinals had won sixty-three of one hundred pennants. Owners like Connie Mack and Bill Veeck would have been surprised to learn that it would take the end of the reserve system to make it necessary for them to strip the playing assets of their clubs in order to survive financially, something they had done for decades.[26]

The statement by Cronin and Feeney showed no understanding that the players wanted to excel and be rewarded and praised for their talent and accomplishments. Was Tim McCarver going to sign a contract with Cincinnati, which had Johnny Bench, the best catcher in baseball, and then never get to play? Why would the two best relief pitchers split time on the mound or have one consigned to a supporting role? The issue of competitive imbalance was based on a set of seductive myths. This argument was based on economic factors only. It assumed that the only thing that interested players was the money in their contracts—that they had no sense of professional pride, no desire to compete, and no desire to be the best. More directly, it ignored another aspect of baseball's recent history. With the reserve system in place, some teams stockpiled players, either as reserves or minor leaguers, to deny them to other major league clubs. That also meant denying good players a chance to go as far as their talent and hard work might otherwise allow them to go.

There is no better way to demonstrate the personal dimension of the reserve system than a 1971 letter to Miller from Dave Leonhard, a pitcher with the Orioles. Leonhard asked if there was any way for him to get away from his current team, since "they have a wealth of pitching talent . . . Weaver [his manager] admits to me that he feels the way he has chosen to use me has hurt my career. . . . The Orioles don't deny that I could pitch in the big leagues nor that my career has been hampered by being with them. Nonetheless, they refuse to trade me, admitting they would rather have me at Rochester as insurance for them; in effect, mortgaging my career against the chance that one of their pitchers will be hurt or be ineffective this year." Leonhard was talented enough to be in the big leagues, unlucky enough to be with a pitching-rich team, and realistic enough to understand the problem: "Like Curt [Flood], I have the option of quitting the game, and like Curt, I can't afford to do so. Once you invest eight or nine years of your life you can't turn your back on them so easily."[27]

A few years later, the system changed. The men who changed it were Andy Messersmith and Dave McNally. The latter, a teammate of Leonhard's, commented: "'Another thing that kept me going was what happened to younger players. A lot of them were being held in reserve instead of being let go to a place where they could further their careers. We had a lot of young players in the Baltimore organization who couldn't break into our staff, but they couldn't do anything about it because they were locked up by the Orioles.'"[28]

Leonhard's letter did not deal with abstract principles, other than the fundamental belief that a player should be allowed to pursue his own career. It was hard to dismiss him as either an overpaid star or a black militant. Miller replied to Leonhard that the trial court had ruled against Flood despite documented proof of hardships "resulting from the restrictions of the reserve system. . . . The reserve rules work the greatest inequities on the less well known players as well as the overall institution of baseball."[29] Leonhard's letter "would be of educational value to many players," but Miller foresaw no possibility that public opinion could be mobilized to bring about any real changes. Nothing could be done to help the pitcher improve his career by giving him the right to change teams. The same alternatives available to Flood remained for Leonhard. He could stay in the Orioles organization, or he could retire. This was not much of a choice for a man who said that he "would rather play than retire since my enthusiasm for the game is almost boundless."[30]

In 1970 many owners believed that players who had been raised with the idea that the reserve clause was normal and necessary would reject Flood's position and his tactics. John Quinn was speaking for most owners when he said, "'I can only believe that Curt Flood's taking baseball to court is an idea prompted by Marvin Miller.'"[31] Like many self-serving myths, it damaged the men who believed it. Robin Roberts weighed in with a different view: "'The reserve clause has to be rewritten. But going to court is the wrong way. Anyway, I don't think it was Miller's idea.'"[32]

A few newspapers, like the *Wall Street Journal*, thought Flood had some justification for his actions, but even it was convinced that "most players and all owners oppose an end to the reserve clause." "Like any other big business, baseball is going to have to work out reasonable ways to get along with its employees."[33] This writer seemed to know little about the history of baseball and nothing about the Joint Study Committee. Some writers, including Red Smith and Leonard Koppett, supported Flood's position and his tactics. The majority opinion was represented by articles like that in the *Houston Chronicle,* which stated, "Baseball rules pretty well protect the players. . . . Knocking out the reserve clause could be a death blow to professional baseball or at least it could drastically cut the present high salary bracket and endanger the entire player pension fund source."[34]

Dick Young and Bob Broeg, the sports editor and columnist for the *St. Louis Post-Dispatch,* were among the prominent critics of Flood. In an early column on the subject, Broeg emphasized that Miller had said the previous spring that "the reserve clause was inequitable in its impact and not as essential in its present form as management says [but] I'm concerned that a chaotic situation could exist if a lawsuit overthrew the legality of the reserve clause. I believe a hard look might be taken at what substitute arrangement might be made that was fair to *both* the club and the player and would stand up in court" (emphasis added).[35] Broeg quoted Miller correctly but said nothing about how the Joint Study Committee had failed because the owners had rejected every proposed change. Broeg believed that the owners were willing to make changes to the current system that would benefit the players, but there was no evidence to support that opinion. Many writers of his generation placed their faith in the owners' desire to do right by their "boys." The discussion in San Juan made it clear that the leadership of the union had arrived at a different conclusion—if negotiation and conversation would not impress the owners, maybe legal action would get their attention.

One expert to whom Young turned was the Hall of Famer Ted Williams, who summarized the problem: "'The trouble is that the players have hired a union man now, and he's accustomed to pushing and pushing, and you wind up with a strike. Some players have told me there's going to be a strike. I'll tell you something, if there's a strike, it's the end of Marvin Miller.'"[36] Williams was better at analyzing hitting than he was at predicting the future of baseball. He and Young portrayed Flood's action as the efforts of a radical Players Association led by a self-serving labor boss who knew nothing about baseball and cared even less. In this version, Flood was almost incidental to the situation. He was a pawn whose decision to reject the trade to the Phillies was only a bargaining ploy for more salary. He was a negotiating chip for the union, not a person who wanted to control his own future. Young admitted that Miller and the union wanted to "modify" rather than abolish the reserve system but said that was a trivial distinction, since "What is modification to me may be outrageous to you. What is modified to Marvin Miller may be confiscatory to the Lords of Baseball."[37]

Serious discussions about the reserve system did not occur until Flood brought the issue to center stage. He based his actions on his own background and ethical standards and the circumstances that the Cardinals forced upon him. He was not a stalking horse for anyone. His personal situation was the product of complex social events that were changing American society. From the moment Flood went public, questions were raised about him that had nothing to do with the merits of the case. Questioning his motives and belittling him personally were convenient ways of trivializing what was involved. This type of criticism was typified by a headline in a St. Louis newspaper, "Does 'Principle' or 'Principal' Motivate Flood?"[38] It is paradoxical that a society that venerated winning and free enterprise pilloried Flood for wanting to prevail in court and possibly make more money. Two veteran New York–based writers, Milton Richmond and Red Smith, represented the extremes. Richmond stated that Flood's "'rights as a human being'" were not abridged in any way, while Smith said that "'Baseball demands incredulously, "You mean at those prices, they want human rights too?"'"[39]

The publicly distributed minutes of the Executive Board meeting were noteworthy for what they did not say. There was no mention of any racial issues. That omission ignored Flood's background, the broader setting in which his challenge was framed, and what actually had taken place at the meeting. Curt Flood was not only the highly paid, very successful center fielder of the St. Louis Cardinals. He was a black man who chose to describe his problems as being "a piece of property" at a time when people had to recognize, however begrudgingly, that sports was part of "the real world." Shortly after Tommie Smith and John Carlos shocked the American public by using the Olympics to spotlight racial injustice, and when Muhammad Ali's political stance had made him the most famous and controversial athlete in America, could anyone doubt that racial considerations would be part of the discussion about Flood? A younger black player reflected that he had known at the time that "any black player who stood up in any way was in danger of being labeled a troublemaker."[40]

The players at the meeting were in a difficult situation. Those who shared Flood's racial sensibilities tried to downplay the issue for fear of losing support for his cause. Those who were interested only in the issue of the reserve system hoped that racial attitudes would play no role in the public discussion. They feared that this would detract from the issues involved in the suit and would give the defenders of the status quo an opportunity to stigmatize the players as being the tools of racially motivated militants.

Almost thirty years later, some of the players who were at the meeting are convinced that the topic of race never did arise, but the question certainly was debated, although not at length. One of the longest-serving members of the board asked Flood how much of what he was doing was "a race thing."[41] Players wanted to assess Flood's motivation and convictions to figure out how he would handle circumstances. They wanted someone who did not appear to be too militant, but someone who would not be bought off.

The board contained two minority members, the young Reggie Jackson and the veteran Roberto Clemente. The latter was a recent addition, having become the Pirates' player rep in a complicated arrangement that reflected new racial sensibilities of some players. Shortly after Jim Bunning had been traded to the Pirates, there was a move among the players to elect him as their representative. He was an obvious choice, given his long record with the association and the important, uncharted areas into which the association was entering. Despite their different backgrounds and attitudes on many issues outside of baseball, Bunning and Miller were bothered by the lack of black participation on the board and were troubled by how blacks and Latinos viewed the organization. Bunning told Miller about his plan not to accept the nomination and to suggest that Roberto Clemente be elected. That would bring another respected veteran player to the board and would hopefully give new impetus to the involvement of blacks and Latinos. Bunning retained a position on the Executive Board, since he was the National League Pension Representative and was present in San Juan.[42]

The views of two former players present an interesting insight into what was involved. In 1969 they were both pitchers with the Yankees, both were convinced that some kind of challenge to the system was necessary, and both would be shipped out of New York shortly. They went on to successful careers outside baseball—Steve Hamilton as the athletic director at his alma mater, Moorhead State University, and Al Downing as a broadcaster in Los Angeles. They have often reflected about what happened in 1969, and they have very different memories about how much of a role race played in the discussion about Flood. Hamilton, who is white, said that "color was not an issue with me" and "hoped" that it was not part "of the calculations of other players."[43] At the same time, he was sure that racial concerns mattered to people outside the game and affected how the opposition talked about Flood. Downing, who is black, was less involved with the union and knew almost nothing about Flood as a person. He was positive that the press would be hostile toward Flood because "even to a certain degree, the press still [in 1986] treats black and Latin athletes as if they are not as intelligent as whites. . . . You have to remember, in 1970 it upset a lot of people if black athletes brought up social issues."[44]

As soon as Flood uttered the phrase, "I am not a piece of property to be bought and sold," he reminded everyone that he was a black man striving for rights at a time when racial injustice was the most important political and social issue facing the nation. It is disingenuous to try to divorce the Flood suit from the reality of his race and the importance of race in American culture. Flood's public statement, "A well-paid slave is no less a slave. . . . The death of the ancient practice of handling people as property is long overdue," brought race into the open. Years later, when Bob Hunter, a Los Angeles writer, reflected that "Flood's rhetoric didn't help," he was referring directly to the "slave" phrase.[45] After all, wasn't a well-paid slave a contradiction in terms?

In its crudest form, enemies of Flood and the union used racial stereotypes and code words to belittle what he was doing, as in Dick Young's reference to the trial as the "Dred Flood Case." Others merely ridiculed Flood's efforts to contend that he was not free. How could there be such a thing as a "ninety-thousand-dollar-a-year slave"? When one reporter said that it was hard to be sympathetic "to the little man" who spurned a hundred-thousand-dollar contract, he was echoing the views of many fans.[46] But the opinions of writers and fans mattered little to Flood. The audiences that concerned him were the other players and the federal judiciary.

When a black man challenged baseball tradition, he brought a new focus to problems and spotlighted divisions within baseball that had been ignored by almost everyone involved. It reinforced some of the cherished myths of owners, journalists, and fans—black athletes were troublemakers and/or ingrates, the Players Association could not be trusted, and players were being manipulated by Miller. One vocal critic of Flood was Harry Walker, a former player and manager and someone who should have had strong memories of the racial hatred that Jackie Robinson faced in Philadelphia in 1947. Walker told the *Birmingham News* that he was "burned up by some of his [Flood's] griping . . . [and] I can't stomach his crying that baseball mistreated him. . . . Mr. Busch pets his players." The article included a quote from Flood in which he had observed, "'if I had been a foot shuffling porter, they might at least have given me a pocket watch.'"[47]

Even though Miller and Moss had warned Flood that the press would find every possible way to discredit him, they became increasingly angered by what they thought was the biased treatment of Flood. Moss spoke about his frustration at what "thus far has been completely overlooked in all the writing on the subject, which is a commentary on our society." He was convinced that the reaction to Flood was "violent in nature and racist in quality. It is a reaction, I believe, of white America to a black man who has been permitted to 'make it' and then turned on his benefactors." He and Miller discussed "the fact that no writer has observed a racist element in the reaction to Flood's case." Moss approached a prominent columnist who dealt with political and social issues ("and admitted to a basic lack of interest in baseball") to see if she would like to address the matter. Gloria Steinem apparently did not follow up on Moss's comments, and nothing came of the letter other than to allow Moss to express his feelings about the reaction to Flood.[48]

The black press treated Flood quite differently. Bill Nunn Jr. wrote, "Flood should be commended for the battle he is waging. He isn't doing it for personal gain. He's fighting for something he believes in."[49] In another article, he compared Flood to "other black athletes who have placed principle above personal gain," including Muhammad Ali, Jim Brown, Arthur Ashe, and Bill Russell. The civil rights leader Bayard Rustin made the same comparison.[50] Jess Peters Jr. countered the ninety-thousand-dollar-slave argument, pointing out that "a man who makes $20,000 a year is entitled to no less constitutional protection than a man who makes $5,000."[51] *Ebony* magazine connected the reserve system to slavery, concluding, "It will be a pit of poetic justice should it turn out that a black man finally brings freedom and democracy to baseball. After all, organized baseball kept black players out of the game for 75 years just because they were black."[52]

The league presidents seemed especially upset that the association had chosen to support one of its members in a frontal attack on the judicial basis for the reserve system. Feeney and Cronin charged that "the position of the Players Association violates its pledge to the clubs in the basic agreement 'to ensure that all terms and conditions of all uniform Players' contracts signed by individual players will be carried out in full.'"[53]

Miller replied by publicly accusing the owners of manipulating Feeney and Cronin into "making libelous public accusations." He wondered how anyone could charge the players of acting "in bad faith," since it was the owners who had refused to bargain about the reserve system. He said publicly what the players had said to one another for years, that the owners "never did intend to change one comma in any of the restrictions which comprise the reserve system, despite any arguments or suggested approaches made by the Players Association or anyone else . . . [and it] had only one purpose—to save the clubs money and avoid competitive bidding."[54] Joe Torre said years later, "I might not have known very much about free agency because that seemed so far off, but I did know we had no negotiating tools for a contract. It was play or else, and that didn't seem fair."[55]

Even though the decision of the Executive Board in San Juan was unanimous, the veteran player rep Max Alvis was correct in predicting that some players would have serious questions about the issues raised by Flood and the board's action to support him.[56] Carl Yastrzemski wrote to Miller expressing concern about how the board decision had been taken and suggesting that it should have been deferred until the membership was canvassed. He also asked that a detailed questionnaire (like last year's "in connection with the strike") be sent to all the players asking for their views on the reserve system and what specific changes should be pressed by the union.[57] Miller replied to "Yaz" with an eight-page letter, copies of which were sent to all the major league players. Miller answered the points about the procedural issues, indicating that all the Red Sox players had been involved in a series of meetings dealing with the reserve system. Most of the letter was a reply to newspaper articles that quoted Yaz as saying that the player reps had acted improperly and he would resign from the union unless a vote about supporting Flood was taken during spring training. Miller reminded the player that the previous year the owners had tried to divide the players by asking for a vote on the "owners' 'last offer.'" Miller could only hope that the Red Sox star was not trying to do the same thing.

Miller assumed that Yastrzemski was acting in good faith, although he might be misinformed or letting his emotional attachment to his team get in the way of his judgment. Miller laid out the realities of the situation. Flood had the legal right to sue, thus, "The board had two choices— and only two. It could turn its back on a player seeking co-operation . . . or the Board could express its support." He hoped that Yastrzemski would run for player representative and, if not elected, would give his support to whomever was chosen. Miller asked him to continue to criticize the union when he thought fit, but he hoped that it would not be done through the newspaper.[58]

Shortly after this exchange, the Players Association received a proposal from a business marketing firm to send a questionnaire to all the players "investigating the attitudes on the reserve clause and other pertinent questions." This was prompted by public remarks made by Harmon Killibrew, a star with the Twins, suggesting that a poll was necessary because the Executive Board's support of Flood did not reflect the views of the membership.[59] After the player reps talked with other players the board chose to go no further, and Killibrew let the matter drop.

Even if some players were not ready for such a dramatic step, Flood left them no choice. The issue was out there to be discussed and decided. Attempts to dismiss Flood as an isolated militant or a puppet might appeal to the press and the public but carried little weight with other players. One player who "never felt strongly about being traded as a matter of principle [understood] why Flood felt so strongly about it since he had been traded before and was determined not to let it happen again."[60] Another player remembered that he "did not know Flood, but did know that a man had to do what was in his best interest."[61] Flood's demeanor and determination impressed Reggie Smith, who in 1969 had finished his third year with the Red Sox, the team that showed the least support for the association.[62] Gary Peters, a teammate of Smith, was one of the board members who enthusiastically supported Flood. He admitted years later that he thought the system would "never change. We'd lived with it a long time. It was so unfair, but it was a fact of life, a fact of life that we did not think about."[63] Once the association took a stand, the player reps were determined to involve as many players as possible.

In the wake of the reaction to Flood's suit and the union's support for it, some prominent members of the union brought up the idea of hiring a public relations firm. Jim Kaat, a veteran pitcher who was involved deeply in the union and worked for a sports film and marketing firm, suggested that it was time for the union to think of professional assistance because "it is imperative that we convey a more positive image of the professional baseball player to the public." He pointed out the need to show the public that a player is more than "someone who just plays baseball for six months a year and gripes about not getting more money the other six months." He wanted to do something that "will make for a more unified organization . . . [where] instead of quoting a half a dozen players on a particular subject, the Players Association would be responsible for making blanket statements." He identified two of the problems that became more serious over the next few months. Kaat pointed out that the union did not have the time "to truly tell our point of view" and that the players had a bad image because "your ordinary fan gets his news from the sports pages."[64]

In 1971 Miller "met with representatives of 5 or 6 public relations firms" and felt that only one was satisfactory. This proposal addressed the attitude of fans and the need to see if they believed "players are more interested in their own income than in the long term good of baseball. If I had to make a guess, I would say that a great many people resent the high salaries baseball players are getting today—not the superstars but the above-average players who are making today what the superstars were making just a few years ago. That, of course, attests to the effectiveness of the MLBPA, but it also indicates—if my assumption is correct—that a genuine need exists to explain to the public why such salaries are warranted and why owners can afford to pay them."[65] The proposal went into great detail about dealing with the press, setting up scholarship funds or an MLBPA charitable foundation, and a number of related issues. The author pointed out the problems facing the union in any effort to get its message to the public and how slim the odds were that it would have a positive response. This analysis was made in 1971, before the first strike, before any changes in the reserve system, and when the average major league salary was $31,543.[66]

The association decided not to employ any firm, a decision based on a combination of financial and tactical considerations. The union did not want to spend money that it might need for other purposes, possibly for a strike fund. It was almost an article of faith among the players that writers and fans had no interest in any complaints, however justified, the players might have and would support the owners in any dispute. In some ways this became a self-fulfilling prophesy. Players were reluctant to talk with most writers about the union. This conduct confirmed the writers' belief the players were dominated by Miller and that they had little interest in or knowledge about the affairs of the union or their own futures.

In recent years Flood has achieved almost martyr status in a way that parallels the respect accorded to Muhammad Ali. Part of the feeling about Flood was due to the passage of time, and part of it was a reaction to how much baseball had changed since 1970. Some of the men who questioned his sincerity, his intelligence, and his motives came to regard him as a heroic if somewhat foolish man. His refusal to whine about his defeat or to claim much credit for the association's later victories gave him even greater stature.

When Flood died in 1997, many articles spoke about his courage and foresight and how he was responsible for many of the changes that have occurred in baseball, despite the fact that he lost in the courts, his career ended, and he became the target of some of the choicest invective conjured up by sports journalists across the country. Some of the highest praise in 1997 came in the pages of the papers and magazines that had portrayed him as an ingrate, a dupe, a radical, and a hypocrite. Although Flood lost in court, he emboldened other players to pay attention to what was being done to them by the system. The more efforts there were to belittle Flood, the more sympathetic he became to players who had shown little concern about either the reserve system or the Players Association. The union tapped into resentments that were brought into the open by Flood's courage. His sincerity and determination went a long way to convince players that there was a battle worth fighting.[67]

If the hiring of Miller had not been a sufficient wake-up call for the owners, the unanimous decision of the board to support Flood should have been. Just the opposite happened. Flood's actions validated the owner's worst fears about Miller and hardened their reluctance to deal with the union. Since many owners did not believe that the players really wanted to change baseball, management chose not to deal with the merits of the issue. It responded by challenging the sincerity and intelligence of the men who supported Flood. A legal situation turned into an us-versus-them battle. No matter how the courts ruled, the sense of unity that existed among the players and their recognition that something had to be done were Curt Flood's legacies.

ONLY ONE CHANCE AT A
FIRST STRIKE

THE FIRST HOME GAMES of the 1972 season took place against
a background of events that would have been unthinkable only a few years
earlier. The significance of what was happening was illustrated by the reaction of the fans to their home teams' third basemen at the first home
games of the Baltimore Orioles and the St. Louis Cardinals. The players
involved were Brooks Robinson and Joe Torre. Robinson was a perennial
All Star and the most popular player in the history of the franchise, and
Torre was coming off of an MVP season and was a fan favorite in a town
that had deep feelings about its players. What was common to Robinson
and Torre on opening night was the torrent of boos that greeted the announcement of their names and their appearances on the field. In Torre's
case, what the *Montreal Star* described as "being booed by the mental
midgets in Busch Stadium" was instigated by Gussie Busch, the deeply
involved owner of the team that played in the stadium named after him.[1]
   Twenty years later, Robinson and Torre remember those April recep-
tions more vividly than they do many of the high points in their illustri-
ous careers.[2] The anger directed against them was a reaction to their active and public roles in ensuring that the first home games did not take
place on the date that the season was scheduled to start. Opening day in
1972 was delayed because the Players Association did what was supposed
to be both unthinkable and impossible. It staged a strike that brought
baseball to a halt.
   In December 1971 Miller regretfully declined an invitation to a sym-
posium sponsored by the University of Missouri–St. Louis, scheduled for

the following February, with the comment that "the Players Association likely will be involved in negotiations at that time with respect to the players' pension fund."[3] At the time he had no idea how dramatic the events of the spring would be and how much the future of baseball would be shaped by them. The players' strike of 1972 demonstrated publicly that the association could successfully challenge the control the owners had exercised for almost a hundred years.

Viewed in light of the next ten years, it might appear that the strike was inevitable, its success preordained, and that Miller and Moss encouraged it. The opposite is true on all counts. The strike was virtually forced on an association leadership that neither wanted a strike nor was confident of its ability to survive it. Like much of the relationship between owners and players, the strike was surrounded by a rhetoric unsuited to reasonable labor negotiations. The strike went well beyond the issue that precipitated it, the unwillingness of the owners to slightly modify the pension fund. The strike was not predominantly about money. The real issue was the power relationship between the two groups and whether the union would survive as a forceful negotiating tool for the players' interests.

Marvin Miller and Dick Moss announcing the start of the strike in 1972.

Dal Maxvill (left) and Joe Torre, the Cardinals' player reps, in an empty clubhouse during what was supposed to be the start of the 1972 season.

There were three important, interrelated aspects to the strike—the pension fund, the decision of the union to make a stand, and the reactions of the owners and the press. The strike brought public notice to the issues that had been involved in the negotiations for the Basic Agreement and the decision to support Curt Flood. Anyone who had paid attention to the union for the previous four years should not have been surprised at what happened in 1972. The owners and much of the press seemed amazed and almost insulted, however, when the players not only voted to strike but lived up to their word and refused to play.

The strike was the first industry-wide work stoppage in American professional sports. It became a topic for the media and public conversation. Unlike the negotiations that took place behind closed doors, no one could ignore the strike. There was no opening day, something that even non-fans noticed. Labor commentary took the place of game reports in the sports pages. Efforts to cast blame quickly replaced any serious attempts to understand why the Players Association felt compelled to strike. The simple and most repeated explanation was that Miller had caused it. One typical example was in an article in the *Cincinnati Enquirer*, which quoted Bob Howsam: "'Marvin Miller has said that I said there would be no strike if it were not for Marvin Miller. That statement stands. . . . Look at Mr. Miller's background. . . . I challenge his knowledge of baseball to represent to the players the need of a strike. . . . I believe strike has been in his mind ever since he became associated with the players' union.'"[4] This statement represented a fair cross section of both baseball executives and the working press.

The strike took place because the PRC would not allow Gaherin to settle a fairly trivial pension-related matter. The situation turned into a test of wills: the owners were convinced that Miller was the problem, and the players were convinced that the future of the union was at stake.

Negotiations had started shortly after the end of the 1971 season about a new formula for the pension fund revenues. The association requested a 17 percent increase in the owners' contribution, a figure in line with inflation of the preceding three years. That would bring the owners' share to approximately $6.5 million. The union proposed a way to handle it with little additional cost by using the surplus that had accrued in the fund. Outside actuarial experts agreed on the soundness of this approach. There also were issues of increased health care, the inclusion of more players who had retired before becoming eligible for benefits, and an increase in dependents' allowances for disabled members and widows. None of these involved much money.

Miller told confidants that he thought that the association's proposals were so modest that he did not foresee any problems in the negotiations. The pension fund was so important to all of the players that he could not imagine the owners challenging it. It seemed implausible to him that a major struggle would be fought over the one area where both sides seemed to have so many reasons not to fight, especially when a new Basic Agreement had to be negotiated soon, and the Flood case was pending.

Miller's evaluation of the situation was wrong. He was surprised by the response of the owners and Gaherin. The PRC rejected the proposals and decreased an earlier offer on medical benefits. It instructed Gaherin to take a hard line on all issues and charged Miller with endangering the fund just to make the players think he had won new gains for them.

Gussie Busch was the most quotable of the owners. His most noteworthy comment, "'We're not going to give them another goddamn cent. If they want to strike—let 'em,'" proved very useful to Miller and Moss.[5] At the time Busch spoke, no one in the association, least of all Miller and Moss, were even talking about a strike. However, they were preparing themselves to face the unpleasant reality that it might be necessary.

The hostile response to the union's pension proposals was the product of a belief shared by many owners that Miller had poisoned the atmosphere of a formerly harmonious relationship. As the impasse on the pension continued, many player reps saw it as part of a pattern that would extend to the reserve system and the Basic Agreement. Phrases like "respect" and "not being pushed around" began to enter into conversations between players. By March, many players thought that the owners were testing their courage and resolve to stand up for themselves. Once that sentiment took hold, the player reps became more upset than either Miller or Moss and began to think in terms of a strike.

In the early spring, Miller, Moss, and the Executive Board had discussed the idea of having a special meeting of all the player reps and alternate reps near the end of spring training. The purpose for the meeting was to let everyone know the status of the ongoing negotiations with the PRC. This would enable the player reps to go back to their teams and let the rest of the players get ready for whatever might happen at the end of spring training. The meeting was arranged at a hotel in Dallas. It was not planned as a strike meeting, but it became increasingly clear that it could very well become just that. As the meeting approached, Miller and Moss came up with multiple reasons why a strike wouldn't succeed and why the association should back off from an action that would be counterproductive at best.

The more Miller talked with the players about a possible strike, the more he showed the differences between him and his predecessor at the association. Even in the midst of a crisis situation, he did not presume to know what the players wanted. He listened to them rather than substituting his own views for theirs. If they did not know much about strikes, they had to be told the realities. What players did know was the importance of winning and supporting teammates. Ironically, the association benefitted from the virtues of teamwork and sacrifice that management had drilled into the players as they came up through the minor league system. The traits that management prized in players, like "taking one for the team," helped make them more willing to dig in their heels when they thought the owners were trying to take advantage of them.

Joe McGuff, a veteran sportswriter and columnist for the *Kansas City Star*, commented that one key to Miller's success was that "he did not get too far out in front of his constituency, and he understood very well the nature of the people he was leading . . . as well as the nature of the opposition."[6] At the Dallas meeting Miller was even more cautious than ever. Many factors convinced players to speak and vote in favor of a strike, but following Miller's lead was definitely not one of them. He and Moss had serious doubts about whether 1972 was the time to strike and whether the issues were important enough to risk using the union's ultimate weapon. They were unsure if the association could prevail in a strike, and Miller was sincere when he told the assembled players, "You only get one chance at your first strike, and if you don't win that one you have lost the union."[7]

Miller and Moss were experienced enough to know that a successful strike needed more than the resolve or enthusiasm of the participants. This would be a unique strike because the Players Association was a union like no other. There was no single facility, and the workforce was scattered throughout the country. The association had virtually no staff to coordinate activities, let alone to keep its dispersed membership involved.

The players who were in Dallas were at the peak of their earning capacity, were fast approaching it, or were trying to last one or two more seasons. They were in a profession where almost everyone had a short career and knew how many different circumstances could end it. Players might admire Curt Flood for his courage, but his fate was an object lesson about how a highly paid player could become an unemployed symbol and a distant memory.

The executives who thought they could appeal to a sense of loyalty to the club confused the business of baseball with what happened in the clubhouse and on the field. Players rarely equated their team with the organization. The former was something that involved them; the latter was something that tried to control them. As Al Downing put it, "What makes a player grow up more than anything else is being traded . . . otherwise, it's easy to remain in that infantile stage where the club continues to treat you like a kid."[8] It was the organization that traded and released players and whose chief operating officers had a vested interest in keeping down salaries. Any executive who thought that the players would rally around the club was even more isolated from the realities of baseball in 1972 than the players who supposedly were naive and impressionable.

Miller has concluded since 1972 that he had not understood how much the players had been thinking about a strike. One union activist put it more simply: "He underestimated them."[9] Miller did not realize how angry they were at the actions of the owners and how much it meant to the players to know that they could challenge and beat the owners. It was a natural mistake since even many player reps "didn't like the word 'union,'" and others had made clear that the word "strike" was not part of their vocabulary.[10]

As late as the evening before the Dallas meeting, Miller was sure that there would not be a strike vote. He, Moss, and Miller's wife, Terry, drafted a press release to be distributed after the meeting was over. Among the three of them, they called it the "Sacco-Vanzetti document," since it sounded to them like the letters in which the two convicted anarchists talked about the inability to defeat an opponent who had all the resources and the power. They did not show the press release to anyone else. They destroyed it after the meeting, when Miller and Moss had to write a vastly different one summarizing the events of the meeting.[11]

The Dallas meeting was a combination of a discussion of the issues, an educational experience, a bitch session, and a revival meeting. It was clear that during spring training, players had talked a lot among themselves about a possible strike. The participants came to the meeting prepared to present the views of their teammates in addition to making their own opinions known. Some players used the meeting to affirm their faith in the courage and the ability of the association to persevere. The player reps had to be careful since, as Tim McCarver phrased it, the idea of a strike "frightened people who didn't understand that they had the right to strike."[12]

In Dallas, it was the ability to strike rather than the right to strike that was at issue. Accounts of what happened vary, but all agree that Miller did everything possible to present the negative aspects of a strike. Miller and Moss saw it as their responsibility to make certain that the players were informed fully about the options that were open to them and knew the problems and consequences that could result. The player reps had to make an informed decision: it would be their decision, and no one could question that they had made it. The player reps needed to be committed to whatever decision they made. They had to be able to explain it to their teammates and to convince them to support it.

Among the problems Miller mentioned was the fact that players would be scattered across the country. This presented a logistical nightmare. The union did not even have an up-to-date list of addresses and phone numbers. There was no strike fund. Many players lived from check to check. There was bound to be an outpouring of negative publicity, and the union had no way to counteract that. The players had little idea what to expect. Their inexperience with strikes showed when one player asked Miller, "How long will the strike last?" The only answer was that no one could predict something like that.[13] Some of the players were equating a strike with a demonstration. Miller and Moss had to make sure that they knew that the two were very different.

There is an important unanswered question, especially in the minds of Miller's critics, about his role in the decision to call a strike. It has been suggested that his forceful presentation of the obstacles to a strike was motivated by something more than the need to inform the players of the realistic dangers they were facing. Was he playing devil's advocate for a cause he wanted to push? Was he challenging their "manhood" and playing on their competitive instincts in precisely the way he knew would push them toward a strike? Was he telling them they would fail because he knew it was the best way to convince them they were really a union and that a strike was how they should act?

After Miller turned the meeting over to the players, the tone and substance changed. Each rep gave a report of the attitude of his team. It appeared that three or four teams might be wavering. Miller left the room after making a statement, and then the main event began. Various players rose to give their version of why the strike was necessary, why they would win, and why the fainthearted had to be persuaded to support the union. A sense of personal involvement pervaded the remarks. If Gary Peters was right "that nobody knew what we were getting into," the player reps made up for a lack of labor experience with a surplus of passion and dedication.[14] One of the younger players, Reggie Jackson, became increasingly vocal and unleashed a string of profanities that gave the discussion the feel of a clubhouse. At least one rep shouted, "get 'em Reggie," while Jackson talked in detail about what kind of men would desert their teammates just because it looked like they might fail. Jackson and others seemed "to pinpoint guys who didn't want to strike," making clear that they were in it together. Milt Pappas, a self-described "vocal one in Dallas," shouted to all who would hear that "if we can't strike together, we might as well fire Miller and go back where we were."[15] That was a threat that meant something. By that time, no one in the room wanted to return to the world before Marvin Miller.

Miller was in this case uncharacteristically out of touch with his membership. Rather than getting too far ahead of them, he was lagging behind. Players took their turn explaining why it was necessary to strike and how their teams would support the action. Waverers disappeared, and only Wes Parker of the Dodgers went against the tide. By that time, no one was in the mood for dissension. Parker was shouted down, and a strike-authorization vote of forty-seven in favor and one abstention was recorded. The decisiveness of the vote and the fervor of the speeches should not blind us to the doubts of many of the players or the real problems they faced. They were going into completely uncharted territory. Some expressed the fear that "the owners will never talk to us again . . . they'll get minor leaguers to play . . . and they'll end the pension fund."[16]

Pappas's reaction was probably common: "I was scared, too. I didn't know if I'd ever play baseball again." Most of the players might not know what to expect, "but they did know they had arrived at a turning point . . . it was go forward or go backwards." The former might be frightening, but the latter was unacceptable. The meeting developed a dynamic of its own where players "got so mad, so tuned out the other side, that it's hard to remember who opposed the strike and why."[17] Years later, Miller reflected on "how badly the labor 'pros' on both sides had miscalculated" how much the issues mattered to the players and how much they were resolved not to be beaten or to lose what they thought they had gained since 1966.[18]

The membership of the union approved a strike authorization by a vote of 663 to 10. If the strike took place, they would have to face the problems that Miller and Moss had described. But for a few days, the reps and other players were still caught up in the emotion and euphoria of the meeting. They were doing what professional athletes do best, competing where there would be a winner and a loser. The intricacies of the pension fund and compromises that would be the basis for a settlement were pushed into the background. They focused on the strike and their ability to maintain unity rather than the specific issues for which the strike was called. They had hired professionals like Miller and Moss to handle such matters.

Al Downing's memory of the events reflects what other players have said: "It was up to you to decide. In 1972 [that meant] are you going to be an adult about it and say, 'we want better out of baseball than we've gotten'?"[19] One participant in Dallas was upset at the "bickering and insane crap that was being said." Everyone did get their say, and the vote reflected both their feelings and an understanding of what was taking place. Another player who spoke at the meeting became convinced that "the strike vote meant we had a *real* organization and wouldn't take any shit. The owners had to know we were for real."[20] Another player put it more simply: "the players had had more than enough."[21]

The comments made at the meeting were a good indication of how the strike would play out. There were logistical problems, but the players remained unified. Some of the most involved player reps had special problems to face. According to Torre, "the toughest thing [was] to tell Busch we were going on strike. . . . I loved him . . . but we had to show we could stick together, even if we didn't think things would have gone that far."[22] Gary Peters was in a touchy situation since the star of his team, Carl Yastrzemski, was a hero in New England, was close to Tom Yawkey, and had shown some hostility toward the association. Peters succeeded in getting him to say nothing about the strike. The Red Sox had the most players (four out of twenty-five) vote against the strike authorization. Peters felt that his teammate decided to support the union "once he was convinced we were opposing the hierarchy of baseball, not Yawkey."[23]

Peters remembers, "It wouldn't have taken much of an offer by the owners to get us to accept it." But there was no offer. Peters was able to convince his teammates to stand firm "thanks to someone like Busch, who just said, 'To hell with you, and that's putting it mildly.'" As Peters later reflected, "we probably shouldn't have been able to pull it off. We probably succeeded because we knew we were doing it for a reason and Marvin was there to give us the realities and the motivation."[24]

One of the teammates that Peters did not convince was Reggie Smith, who voted against the strike. He did not want "to vote against Yawkey [because] he cared about the players . . . [and there was] ignorance and naivete and some selfishness involved." Looking back, Smith says, "I didn't see the big picture [and] didn't think we could pull off a strike." Many who voted for the strike shared this view. Smith was "afraid of the consequences," since he was married, had started a family, and "baseball was all I had." But once the strike started, Smith felt that the players had to see it through and that the "owners always underestimated the competitive nature of the players."[25]

The stakes were high for most of the players. There was a real danger that owners would retaliate by trading or releasing players who were involved with the union. Even a staunch supporter like Steve Hamilton knew that many players, especially marginal ones, were scared. Many of the players did not have the money to sustain themselves through a long strike. The player reps kept telling everyone, including themselves, that the strike was not just about the pension. It was about challenging the system and about not losing. Many of them were not too sure about what the first meant, but they had lots of experience with the second.

The reality of the strike hit home when players had to pay for their flights home from spring training. But such expensive inconveniences were insignificant when compared to the fragile nature of a career that could end at any time. In Hamilton's case, "we lost eight days, I lost my fastball, my slider, the whole thing, [but] the strike was still the right thing to do."[26]

Most of the players who were involved with the strike would agree with Bob Barton's assessment that 1972 was "a challenge to the system" and Steve Hamilton's view that "we certainly were breaking new ground."[27] The Dallas meeting showed that the players were involved in every step of the process and were familiar with the issues and the consequences. It was hard to convince outsiders of this, however. The next year, a Boston writer claimed to be "appalled . . . that the players who voted for a strike last spring in Florida were admittedly so ignorant about a lot of the issues. They listened to Miller and his lawyer talk, and they voted." He reckoned that it was even worse in 1973, since the Red Sox player rep situation was "so muddled" because Gary Peters was gone, Ray Culp was released, and Phil Gagliano was new to the position.[28] The writer failed to note that the reason that Peters and Culp were no longer with the Red Sox might have been because they were player reps who had supported the strike.

Years later, Buzzie Bavasi's view that "the owners gave Miller the issues, and he picked them up" was echoed by others who felt that actions by the PRC and statements by owners in 1972 convinced the players that the strike was necessary and gave them the resolve to make sure it succeeded.[29] Leonard Koppett saw 1972 as "a totally self-inflicted wound by the owners . . . [who] should have known that the players were united." As a veteran of newspaper strikes, Koppett was amazed that the owners did not understand how strikers stay together and didn't realize how players would react to being pushed into a corner.[30] It was John Gaherin's job to educate his bosses about dealing with the union, but it was hard to convince enough owners of two new realities that existed by 1972. The Players Association was a legally recognized entity that would not go away, and the overwhelming majority of the players thought it represented their interests. The fiercely individualistic nature of the owners made Gaherin's job more difficult. They were not going to change because he told them it was necessary. He could not convince his most vocal employers that more was involved than getting rid of Miller and a few militant player reps. Reflecting on his situation, Gaherin thinks that "Miller probably knew our people better than we did."[31]

Ewing Kauffman, the owner of the Kansas City Royals, certainly was not a fan of the union. Years later, he summed up the background to the strike: "some of the owners were the best allies the union had. . . . The owners did not think they had to give in on anything. . . . In 1972, owners had the whip hand. The players were chattel. I didn't know of any industry as archaic as baseball was then. . . . Even the most paternalistic owners weren't sharing with the players. The owners were egotistical, used to getting their own way. . . . [Because of that] Gaherin had no real authority. The owners were always going different ways. . . . Nineteen seventy-two was the last chance that the owners had to break the union, and they failed . . . another union would have emerged because the owners were treating the players unfairly. Miller built a hold on the players by showing them what the owners did. . . . If the owners had treated the players fairly, maybe there would have been no need for the union."[32]

The press took a greater interest in the union than ever before. A *Cincinnati Enquirer* columnist represented the conventional view: "What the baseball strike was all about was really Marvin Miller. . . . It was Miller who fomented the strike, whose velvet tongue convinced the players, the majority of whom, by their own admission, did not know what they were getting into."[33] Some writers took a different view. Montreal's John Robertson pointed out, "Today's players are not bumpkins" led around by Miller, and "they had no reason to feel grateful to the owners for giving them a job."[34] Two New York writers took an approach similar to Robertson's. Phil Pepe described the players as "taking a bum rap," and Leonard Koppett headlined his column, "Baseball Bosses Blunder."[35]

In earlier years, Dick Young had been an outspoken foe of what he described as the arrogance and power of the owners. He coined the term "Lords of Baseball" to apply to them. After the New York newspaper strikes, he developed a deep distrust of unions and their leaders. Political and social turmoil disgusted him, and he turned his considerable talents against a whole range of what he saw as malcontents, traitors, and ingrates. By 1972 even the world of sports that he had covered for years was suffering from the same problems that disgusted him in the broader society. Most noticeably, Cassius Clay (the name Young continued to use for Muhammad Ali) personified what was wrong with sports and American society. Radicals like Miller and Moss and the players who supported them were another sign of decay.

Young could not stop radicals from protesting against his government and a war that he supported without reservation. He could protect the sport that he thought should reflect the best values of America from similar attacks. It was an intensely personal issue for him since he felt that he earlier had been on the side of the players and he had helped to make baseball better for them. Young became a self-appointed defender of the values of American sports, especially baseball. All the changes he saw were changes for the worse. He had no time for the new generation of athletes, especially baseball players, and the feeling seemed reciprocal. They seemed to have little or no respect for his opinions and even less appreciation of what he had done, or thought he had done, for them in the past.

Young and many of his colleagues had been troubled by the choice of Miller and even more disturbed by the Flood case. But a strike that was sanctioned by a players' vote of 663-10 was the last straw. Young believed that Miller was leading baseball into the abyss, urged on by arrogant selfish players. With the instincts of a first-rate reporter, Young ignored the minutiae of the pension issue that brought on the strike. He was perceptive in stating, "Clearly the enemy [of the owners] is not the players, whom the owners regard merely as ingrates. The enemy is Marvin Miller, general of the union. The showdown is with him. It is not over a few thousand dollars, not the few thousand demanded now for some obscure pension inflation, it is over the principle of who will run their baseball business, they, the Lords, or this man Miller."

Young tried to convince owners and fans that 1972 was the time to stand, fight, and destroy the union before it got too powerful. According to Young, "there is no reason for [the union to] strike. There is no issue remotely worth a strike." Young characterized Miller's advice that the players had to stand united against the owners as "tired cliches used by every union organizer. . . . To the young and impressionable, the words sound new and dramatic."[36]

It was relatively easy for Miller and Gaherin to settle the pension-related issues that had supposedly been the cause of the strike. They rearranged some numbers and came up with a solution that resembled what Miller had proposed earlier. The players had channeled their anger into teamwork; the owners had turned theirs into self-defeating displays of petulance.

The strike was an important lesson to Miller and the players about the divisions among the owners. These divisions were deeper than anything Gaherin had experienced with other multi-owner organizations like the railroads or the New York publishers. Now he was working for men, "each of whom not only thought he knew more than me about labor relations, but *knew* he was the smartest guy in baseball."[37] Years later, Harry Dalton, a long-serving and successful general manager, commented that 1972 was the victory that was essential for the future success of the union. Dalton said that ownership lost because "not enough of the owners saw the need to be moderate . . . and too many [of them] including me were too sure that the players would not remain solid and the owners could end the threat of Miller by letting the strike fall apart from its own weight." Dalton recognized, long after the fact, that the owners "put their man [Gaherin] in an untenable position. Miller was the acme of a union [that was united] and Gaherin was trying to deal with unstable forces. . . . The two of them could not meet on common ground."[38]

The season had been scheduled to open in the first week of April with the first nationally televised game on April 8. On April 11, Miller and Gaherin worked out the final details of the pension arrangement. They had to consider whether to reschedule the canceled games and whether to pay the players for games they missed before the strike ended on April 13. Eighty-six games had been canceled when the season finally opened on April 15. The union had prevailed on the issue that had caused the strike. That fact, and the speed with which the players had gotten what they wanted, was not lost on anyone involved.

The two sides drew very different conclusions from the events. The players were virtually unanimous in feeling that events showed the importance of supporting the cause. If they had shown Miller that he was wrong about their resolve, they should be able to prove it to anyone. The owners drew a wide variety of sometimes contradictory conclusions. Some thought that the mistake had been to make concessions and not let the strike run its course. Others felt that it had been Gaherin's fault. Few of them accepted Walter O'Malley's view that the owners were better off dealing with a unified group of players. The real problem for the future was whether the owners would understand that they had to bargain with the players' legally recognized representative, which was a union in action if not in name. Future negotiations would have to deal with issues rather than the question of whether the owners wanted to negotiate at all. Gaherin was sure there would be more problems in the future as long as "the players were influenced by someone [Miller] who believed that the whole baseball establishment and the system were evil . . . [and executives] who thought players were boys, nice kids . . . [and who] delighted in being able to screw these guys."[39]

After the strike, Miller summed up his thoughts in a letter to Dan Galbreath, the president of the Pirates: "the strike was largely unrelated

to the pension issue. . . . [It] was directly related to the fact that a significant number of owners allowed a small minority to try to insist on dic-
tating terms to the players rather than attempt to negotiate a fair settlement." Miller wanted to remind Galbreath's father, one of the most
influential owners, that "any owner who does not disavow the truculence
and profanity of Gussie Busch should not be surprised when collective
bargaining breaks down."[40] Miller was setting the stage for the upcoming negotiations for a Basic Agreement. He sent copies of the letter to the
player reps and the newspapers in which Dan Galbreath's comments
about the strike had appeared.

During the strike, the union concentrated on a few reporters whom they
thought would listen to their position. After the strike was over, Miller
responded to reporters and letter writers from the general public in an
effort to correct what he characterized as "foolish things," "misinformation of the owners," and "mistaken notions." Miller's letters were detailed and precise, leaving little for the recipient to assume or guess about
his meaning. He stressed that the strike had been forced on the players
by the owners. The players had made their own decisions. He also pointed
out repeatedly that the players no longer regarded the pension fund as "a
gift" from the owners. Instead, they viewed it as something that was part
of a collective bargaining agreement.[41]

There were some light moments, even when Miller was dealing with
a prominent journalist who was a determined and articulate opponent
of the union. In a letter to Jim Murray, Miller asked him to remember
that a "caricaturist misses the boat when he is forced to make up what
is not there." Miller said he was willing to consider some of Murray's
suggestions, but "when you get to the mustache, you've gone too far. . . .
my wife has the final word. . . . she does not think she would like living
with a man whose appearance would be unfamiliar to her."[42]

Why should Miller take time from a busy schedule to answer letters
from members of the public, especially when they could have no direct
effect on events? One reason was his frustration and anger at what he
thought was people's unwillingness to see that the union had a position
that deserved serious consideration. Another reason was his penchant for
trying to show people the righteousness of the cause. In any case, these
private letters give an interesting insight into his feelings and the attitudes of people who felt upset enough to write to him.

One intriguing example was an extended correspondence between
Miller and the Reverend William R. McGeary, a Presbyterian minister
from Pennsylvania. Baseball executives and sportswriters who thought

they were being singled out by Miller for scorn and sarcasm should have talked to McGeary, who received a second letter that began, "your knowledge of economic problems is on a par with my knowledge of the problems of the Presbyterian Ministry—absolute zero. The difference is that I am not proud of my ignorance and do not demonstrate it with foolish pronouncements, as you persist in doing."[43]

Miller could hardly restrain himself when someone condemned the players for making "too much money" and compared their salaries to "the endless list of *legitimate workers*" (emphasis added) without mentioning the profits made by the owners. The fact that McGeary was echoing the complaints of so many sportswriters struck a raw nerve in the supposedly unflappable Miller. If he couldn't get the writers to change their views, at least he could answer someone whose assertions were based on how Miller thought the press misrepresented the players. McGeary reflected public opinion when he condemned the players for getting paid good money for playing a child's game. They should be thankful for the fame and fortune they had, especially since they performed no useful social function.[44] Why should they be paid so well when nurses, teachers, prison wardens, doctors, and FBI agents made so much less? Players had been given a great pension fund that they did not deserve. Any mention that the players received something through the benevolence of the owners was a particularly sore point with Miller.

In a second letter, McGeary made clear that he was angry because "the little guy who buys a ticket will foot the bill by paying increased prices for tickets, which are already overpriced." The whole system was a perversion of American priorities, and the players were at fault for trying to get more. Strikes should be reserved for "real workers" who were doing something that mattered to the public. In Miller's reply, he pointed out that it never dawned on fans like McGeary that if baseball was so unimportant and no vital national priority was at stake, why should it matter if the players went on strike? Would people like him have preferred that nurses and FBI agents strike to obtain their fair reward?[45]

I have dealt elsewhere with the "too important/too trivial" standard that the public applies to high-profile, highly paid professional athletes.[46] This standard clearly applied in 1972: what players did on the field was supposedly too trivial to warrant high salaries or free agency, while baseball was too important to allow players to bring the games to a halt by striking. McGeary questioned how the players could expect the public to support a strike that was so wrong and a set of demands that were so ludicrous. There was no answer to that question, since the players would have been amazed if they had received any support. As one player put it, "we knew that the perception of the fans was that we were overpaid, greedy, and spoiled."[47]

Long after the strike, Joe McGuff made a simple point: "The press was peripheral to Miller. Like any good labor leader, he was interested in the rank and file. Let's face it, most of it [the strike] was unpopular with people writing about it. . . . I was one of the more sympathetic ones, and I wasn't very sympathetic."[48] Bob Hunter put it more directly: "Miller came across like a city slicker. . . . The role he was in, I had, rightly or wrongly, prejudged him as antibaseball. . . . He was going to have to prove the opposite to me. That might have been unfair, but that's the way it was." Hunter remembered his reactions to a Miller press conference: "I never entered into it . . . it may have been dumb, but I just didn't want to hear what he had to say. Maybe [because] I was so steeped in baseball tradition, or that I was pro-owner, or pro-baseball."[49]

The owners used their allies in the press to fight the wrong battle at the wrong time with the wrong tactics. It was shortsighted to try to inflame the opinion of the fans against the players. In the first instance, it was unnecessary. The public was predisposed to blame the players. Secondly, fan pressure was going to have no impact on the positions taken by the union. Its decisions were going to be based on what happened at the bargaining table, not what was discussed in the newspapers.

Management representatives correctly regarded Leonard Koppett of the *New York Times* and *The Sporting News* as an advocate for the players' views, but they should have taken note of his post-strike analysis. He pointed out that the owners kept talking about how the players were highly paid and were "forfeiting the 'sympathy' of the fans. . . . Players were 'selfish and ungrateful.'" The owners claimed that the players were going to alienate the fans and force higher ticket prices and that "players' demands were unjustifiable . . . since most clubs were already losing money." The union supposedly was forcing clubs to the brink of financial disaster and endangering the future of baseball. Koppett had been involved in enough labor disputes to understand that "much of the anger directed at the players [by the owners] was one way to bring pressure on them."[50]

Koppett pointed out something that should have been obvious: baseball was not like other industries. If owners continued to tell fans what bad people the players were, how could they expect them to identify with them when the season started? If baseball was in such bad shape, how could it expect the support of the local financial community and sponsors? Why would "any businessman in his right mind" trumpet the fact that he had to increase prices? Since baseball remained the cheapest ticket in sports, why didn't the owners emphasize that instead? Worst of all, why did the owners compare players to "the ordinary man"? If the "ordinary man" was equivalent to major leaguers, why should he pay to see them play? In Koppett's phrase, "Either a big league ballplayer is something very special like a movie star, or he's not worth the price of admission."[51]

In future strikes and negotiations, the owners continued to use the press as a battering ram against the players. This succeeded in poisoning negotiations and driving a bigger wedge between the players and the fans. After awhile, some executives like Harry Dalton came to the conclusion that "Criticism by the owners is silly. . . . Hollywood doesn't say, 'We've got some of the worst actors you've ever seen in this film, come see it.'"[52] However, the tactic of blaming the players was a difficult habit to break, and ownership continued to use it.

The short duration of the strike masked the importance of what was at stake. Once it ended, Dick Forbes, a vocal supporter of the owners in the press, drew some interesting conclusions. To him, the strike showed how easily the American people forgot the lessons of history. In the 1930s there was a need to stand up to Hitler, and in the 1970s there was the continued threat of communism: "There is somewhere a parallel between dictators and labor leaders. . . . And so we come to Marvin Miller." The comparison and the hyperbole were silly, but Forbes's conclusion was essentially correct: "What the baseball strike was all about was Marvin Miller."[53] This oversimplified matters a bit. More precisely, the strike was about the new situation in baseball that Miller personified. It was about the willingness of the players to recognize that the union was a necessary part of their future. It was about the ability of the union to call a strike and maintain it. It was about star players taking an active role and giving credibility to both the strike and the Players Association. It was about the inability of the owners to understand the necessity of dealing with the union, whether they wanted to or not. Forbes's conclusion that "the baseball strike was all about . . . Marvin Miller" was right if this meant that he was the symbol of the dramatic changes that the players had caused since 1966.

In the aftermath of the strike, Gaherin was worried about the climate that existed while negotiations were under way for a new Basic Agreement. The strike had caused bitter feelings on both sides. Just as those feelings seemed to be disappearing, another development threatened to derail the negotiations. The Supreme Court handed down its decision denying Curt Flood's appeal. The ruling reaffirmed the feelings of many owners that they were invulnerable. They were in no mood to make conciliatory gestures. They now thought that they had a chance to make up for what many of them believed had been an unnecessary capitulation to the players during the strike.

A LOSS IN COURT AND A GAIN AT THE BARGAINING TABLE

THE FIRST BASIC AGREEMENT set the pattern for future arrangements between the union and the owners. When negotiations began for the 1973 Basic Agreement, the union was determined to consolidate its position and to gain further concessions. The main area of concern for the players was to find some way to ameliorate the effects of the reserve system. If they could not end the system in a court challenge, they were determined to use the collective bargaining system to weaken it. After the union lost its appeal of the verdict in the Flood decision, it put its energies into the negotiations for the new Basic Agreement.

When Marvin Miller said, "We got a deal," the other nine men seated around the negotiating table on February 25, 1973, realized that months of negotiating and posturing had culminated in a new Basic Agreement.[1] The 1973 agreement might appear to be similar to the one it supplanted, but it significantly altered the relationship between the two parties. The negotiations had taken place against the background of two dramatic public events: the strike in April 1972 and the Supreme Court's decision on June 18, 1972, in *Flood v. Kuhn*. These appeared to be one triumph for each side. The players had held together in their strike and gotten some concessions in the pension plan. The owners had won in court, and the reserve system appeared safe.

The decision in *Flood v. Kuhn*, written by Justice Blackmun, was a commentary on baseball's place in American culture and its emotional hold on some men. Blackmun took the time to include a litany of great ballplayers from the past who had supposedly played an important role in shaping the values of generations of American youths.[2] Understandably, baseball's officials exulted in Blackmun's opinion, but they ignored its details, especially his invitation to Congress to make changes. While Blackmun had said that baseball had a unique status, he also had said that there was every reason to change that.

The decision itself hardened the resolve of those owners who had wanted to ignore the union. Gaherin saw *Flood v. Kuhn* in a different light. He tried to use it as a bargaining weapon. In his terms, that meant convincing his employers that "it was not a victory for us . . . [we] had barely gotten out with our skins. . . . The jurists said, 'This one's on us and we'll get you next time.' . . . Too many people used it as an applause meter for the sagacity of the legal establishment in baseball." He argued that this was the best time to approach the association and discuss changes that would bring results that "were less traumatic and better."[3] Some of Gaherin's later judgments about the owners must have been affected by the antipathy that developed between him and many of them after his contract was terminated in 1976. But it is true that Gaherin tried to convince them to use the ruling in the Flood case to make some concessions and to seize the initiative from Miller.

Gaherin wanted to create a new Joint Study Committee, this time to include owners who might find some change acceptable. He knew that the Players Association was going to seek other ways to force changes in the reserve system. He was aware that Miller and Moss already thought that they could mount a challenge to the renewal clause in the standard player's contract. If that worked, it could accomplish what Flood had attempted. Gaherin wanted management to take the initiative to combine modifications to the reserve clause and limited salary arbitration into a system that would enable the owners to retain control of the business and have some certainty over the distribution of players while encouraging the players not to make further efforts to weaken the reserve system.

A statement by the association that focused on the ambiguities in Blackmun's decision should have attracted the attention of the PRC. The association asserted that it would do whatever was necessary to encourage Congress to change the system or "to find an appropriate solution at the bargaining table. . . . This fall, for the first time the Players Association and the Clubs will be engaged in collective bargaining with regard to *all* terms and conditions of employment of major league players with the sole exception of salaries above the minimum."[4] Once negotiations started, it was clear that no changes in the reserve system would result from these talks.

On January 5, 1973, the association reformulated its position based on the premise that "we have bogged down on the whole Reserve system area . . . because you have proposed nothing touching real questions of free agency."[5] Miller proposed that negotiations focus on three specific issues: salary arbitration, assignment of contracts (the manner in which players were sold or traded), and a study committee on the reserve system.

Miller and Moss were looking to create a system where the players could bargain with their employers on equal terms, which had a mechanism to protect any rights the players might obtain. Both men distrusted management. They believed that since baseball had no tradition of reciprocal obligations between the players and the owners, any future committee should consider "not just the conditions of free agency, but enforcement of any such system." According to Miller, the players would not trust any system where the association "could not successfully resist concerted efforts to undermine [it]," something that sounded eerily like the collusion undertaken by the owners in the mid-1980s. Miller summed up the feelings of the union: "But given the absolute power [of the owners] over players, salary arbitration is a must."[6]

The union's insistence on the importance of salary arbitration introduced a crucial new element into the negotiations and the relationship between the two parties. The owners' opposition to salary arbitration took two basic forms. One was based on the idea that there was no role for outsiders in making baseball decisions. The clubs should take care of their own affairs. Bob Howsam articulated this view: "'Arbitrators don't have realistic ideas of what value players have to clubs.'" He added that it was necessary for owners to control salary structures and claimed that it would be a "'sad state'" for baseball when "'it's more important for a manager to have the ability to communicate than a knowledge of baseball.'"[7]

The other concern expressed by club officials was a more romantic and emotional issue. They claimed that players would be happy with the current situation were it not for prodding by Miller. Bob Short, the owner of the Texas Rangers, phrased this best when he explained why he was opposed to salary arbitration: "'I've never had a player complain that I've treated him unfairly. I've never had a player who delivered who wasn't paid well.'" Short may also have had financial reasons to distrust the effects of salary arbitration, if there was any validity in the comments he had made to a reporter earlier. At that time, Short said he had lost so much money that he might be forced to sell the team at any time.[8]

The idea of salary arbitration was completely novel for baseball. It could have serious economic consequences, and it could force important changes in how the clubs conducted their affairs. It could create a whole new relationship between the individual player and his club. There was another huge stumbling block preventing Gaherin and Miller from reaching a compromise over the issue of salary arbitration. They had to overcome one of baseball's most cherished myths—that the commissioner was a neutral party in the relationship between the players and the owners.

The belief in a fair-minded, impartial commissioner who protected everyone's interests had currency with reporters, fans, owners, and especially with Commissioner Kuhn.[9] Miller rejected this claim from the start of his tenure in office. By 1972 it would have been difficult to find many players who did not share his opinion that the commissioner, whoever he might be, was an employee of the owners and was therefore, by definition, not impartial.

Even most critics of Bowie Kuhn's performance as commissioner are convinced that he believed sincerely his own rhetoric about the independence of the office of commissioner. It is necessary to understand how the relationship between Kuhn and the Players Association developed between his appointment in 1969 and the negotiations that resulted in the 1973 Basic Agreement. He had been shocked at the 1969 Puerto Rico meeting with the Executive Board of the association when, "for the first time, we [players] told the commissioner, 'you're not *our* representative, Marvin Miller is.'"[10] Curt Flood's appearance had been the dramatic highlight of that meeting, but the interaction between Kuhn and the player reps was an equally important indication of the changes taking place in baseball.

Kuhn had started his presentation in San Juan by telling the players that he was sorry they were not meeting at the same time and place as the owners, because "we are more likely to pull together on things" if they met together. He hoped that the power of the commissioner would be increased "so *all of us* can work more effectively together. . . . I think it is important that I attend all your meetings in future, *even if I have nothing to say*" (emphasis added).[11]

Miller immediately challenged Kuhn's assertions, especially the idea that the commissioner had a role to play in the affairs of the Players Association. He told Kuhn that he would be glad to ask the Executive Board to vote on Kuhn's idea that he should be present at the association's winter meeting, but "frankly, [I] don't think if you have nothing to say, you should be here, almost as a member of the board."[12]

Kuhn might have written off Miller's comments as part of his antagonism toward the owners and the commissioner they employed. What followed Miller's remarks was something that should have alerted Kuhn about the new attitude of the players. Individual players stood up and raised troubling questions about subjects including astroturf, stadium design, and bargaining for a Basic Agreement. Their tone was aggressive and angry. They showed no deference to the office of the commissioner. When Phil Regan asked whether the players had been consulted about astroturf, the commissioner replied, "I believe they [the members of the committee looking into the subject] have talked to players."[13] The committee was made up of an owner, Clark Griffith, two general managers, Bob Howsam and Bing Devine, and one other management employee. One player after another returned to the same theme—that the committee was one more example of the owners and the commissioner ignoring the players. The point was summed up by Steve Hamilton: "But we have had no say about what clearly involves our cause. . . . Our considerations [are] not taken into account."[14]

At San Juan, almost all of the players had addressed Kuhn as "you" and described the union as "us" when talking about negotiations for the next Basic Agreement. The long-time veteran Mike McCormick summarized the bargaining: "[it] will take great strength on your side and on ours."[15] This concept of opposing sides was not the way the commissioner saw his role or the way he thought baseball should be. He believed that everyone was in it together and that an impartial commissioner adjudicated whatever rare problems might arise.

In his 1987 autobiography, Kuhn's position remains essentially the same. His is convinced there never was the need for impartial arbitration for grievances or salaries because "There had never been a commissioner whose fairness in disputes between clubs and players could be questioned, and if anything they had probably been more sympathetic to the players' side of disputes."[16]

In the early years of Gaherin's tenure, Kuhn made it a point to leave the room when Gaherin gave his reports to the owners. This was his way of showing that he was not involved directly with the PRC and that he was an advocate for the players as well as the owners. At his 1969 meeting with the players, Kuhn told them, "I can look at [bargaining] problems more dispassionately than anyone else in baseball. It is important [for me] to be available to players." According to Gaherin, Kuhn described himself as the paterfamilias of baseball.

Gaherin was disappointed that Kuhn could not accept Gaherin's view of reality: "To a guy like Marvin Miller, you're the president of a trade association. . . . You're the same kind of sonofabitch as I am."[17] In one important respect, Gaherin was wrong; Miller had very different feelings about Gaherin and Kuhn. Gaherin was an opponent who knew he was an employee of the owners, just as Miller knew he worked for the players. Miller seemed to regard the commissioner as a hypocrite, a naive employee of the owners, or their willing tool in an effort to maintain a system that Miller was trying to end. However valid these opinions might have been, there is no question that Miller was sincere in his dislike of Kuhn and what he represented. No one fit Miller's stereotype of a romantic baseball man using tradition to mask self-interest more than Kuhn.

The enmity was reciprocal. Kuhn never believed that the players needed Miller or someone with views like his. Kuhn thought Miller was motivated by "a deep hatred and suspicion of the American right and American capitalism. And what could be more the prototype of what he hated than professional baseball with its rich, lordly owners and its players shackled by the reserve system?"[18]

In 1973 the union's leadership put everyone on notice that it not only intended to protect the gains it had made, it intended to obtain more changes. Miller's choice of phrases often seemed determined to provoke and insult long-time owners. One blatant example is his comment that any future modifications in the reserve system "could easily be negated if, by a 'gentlemen's agreement,' no other club would sign him."[19] The last time the phrase "gentlemen's agreement" had been part of the vocabulary of baseball was to describe how owners had worked in unison to bar blacks from "America's national pastime" until 1947.

It became clear that if the two sides were going to conclude a Basic Agreement in 1973 without a work stoppage, some form of salary arbitration would have to be a part of it. That meant recognizing that the status of the commissioner had already changed. It also meant that Gaherin had to convince a majority of the owners that the possibility of another strike was real, that the union would remain solid, and that salary arbitration would not do irreparable harm to the ability of the owners to run their teams.

While the negotiations dragged on, the owners talked about the need to lock out the players during spring training. The players became even more determined to make no concessions. The owners used Kuhn as their spokesman. This gave Miller the opportunity to label Kuhn as "the Coordinator of the owners' negotiating committee, whose job it was to dress up the inadequate proposals made by the owners." Miller then accused Kuhn, along with Cronin and Feeney, the two league presidents, of acting in bad faith by sending letters to players that "conveniently" omitted the fact that the owners were trying to cut jobs by reducing the size of rosters. At the same time, the union said it was willing to modify efforts to end the reserve system in return for "a bona fide salary arbitration procedure so that a player could obtain an impartial review of an unfair salary dictated by an owner."[20]

A lockout was a real possibility. Miller and Moss had to prepare the players for that and other eventualities. In this instance, Miller used the press to communicate with the players and to remind them what was at stake. He complained to writers that most of them talked about a strike, but they never seemed to mention a lockout, even though the latter was a more plausible eventuality. In at least one statement, Miller pointed out that the players had a potent ally in the law: "A lockout is an extremely serious matter . . . [and] there are legal lockouts and illegal lockouts . . . where an employer has threatened a lockout to pressure and coerce the employees and avoid collective bargaining, as is the inescapable conclusion in this case, then the lockout is clearly illegal and can be enjoined."[21] This was his not-very-subtle way of telling the owners something Gaherin had tried to show them. It also reminded the players that they had potential weapons in the National Labor Relations Board and the courts.

Miller's remark about "the misinformation which has been fed to them [reporters and players] out of Mr. Gaherin's and Mr. Kuhn's offices" was another effort to link the commissioner with the enemy.[22] Within a day, Kuhn took the bait by issuing a press release to present his version of the negotiations. He gave credit to Miller for "persuading" the clubs to put salary arbitration on the table, especially since so many clubs had "strong and sincerely held reservations" about the concept. Then he accused Miller of having "abandoned the bargaining table . . . [and] resorted to a deliberate effort to create confusion in the minds of the clubs, players, and the public." There were no details given about what Miller had done. Kuhn sounded offended by Miller's "questioning of my judgment because in this instance, I am supporting the clubs' position." Kuhn accused Miller of using history selectively, and he wanted to know why Miller didn't credit him for stopping a threatened 1969 spring stoppage of baseball "by urging the clubs to increase their offer on player pension proposals they had rejected."[23]

Kuhn warned that fans were "fed up with this disruptive annual exercise of the players and the clubs rending at each other. . . . Neither Baseball or any sport is an indispensable part of American life."[24] He certainly was right in recognizing that baseball could cause problems for itself if its labor relations were mismanaged. But the immediate problem was how to convince the owners to make concessions that would persuade the players that cooperation was a viable alternative to confrontation.

Threats of a lockout were not going to accomplish that. The bargaining table was the only sensible course.

The union had not abandoned its antipathy to the reserve system, but it had decided to concentrate on more modest changes. Salary arbitration was the new priority. But it was never meant as a substitute for changes in the reserve system. It was the union's way to ameliorate the worst excesses of the reserve system.

Players had always been involved in the negotiating sessions, so much so that representatives of the owners often complained about too many players being at the table. In 1973, some of them, including Jim Perry, Tom Seaver, and Joe Torre, played an increasingly important part in the talks. Along with Miller and Moss, they made sure to keep the other player reps fully informed about the tone and substance of the negotiations. Torre played a special role in many of the meetings. He had acquired a background in finance, and he had stood up to management in Atlanta, two qualities that served him well during the negotiations. In the tedious, often grim parts of the talks, he often served another function, "by being [openly] optimistic . . . [I] didn't have much choice, since everybody else was so pessimistic."[25] Gaherin remembered Torre as "the original godfather, talking out of a cloud of cigar smoke," but always ready to bring the discussion back to an important point when it wandered and always aware of both the economic realities and the vital interests of the players.[26]

The pace of negotiations intensified as spring training came closer. The final days of bargaining were almost a classic study of the sides coming closer on the issues that could be compromised. Among these were the number of years a player needed before he was eligible for salary arbitration, the minimum salary, and the details of what became known popularly as "the ten and five rule" or "the Curt Flood Provision." It is easy to forget that Flood's suit was triggered by the trade of a veteran player. The new provision meant that a player with ten years of major-league service and the last five with one club had some control over his future. From the union's standpoint, this was progress.[27]

The owners' proposal for salary arbitration called for three full years of major-league service as the basis for eligibility. It excluded evidence concerning the financial position of the player and the club, previous offers, and press evaluation as criteria for arbitration. The Players Association got eligibility cut to two years. It convinced the owners to drop a proposal that would have ended limits on annual salary cuts and another that would bar the introduction of "other baseball players' salaries" as one of the criteria for the arbitrator.[28]

Another issue threatened to scuttle the talks during the discussions about salary arbitration, something that was very much a part of the traditions of baseball. This was how much, or how little, the players would know about one another's salaries. The owners were opposed to allowing the union to receive salary data. Miller and Moss were adamant that the information was essential to the process. This was a straightforward issue for the union. If a player or his representative did not have the most relevant data, they could not make the best possible case to an arbitrator.

It was common that "players never talked about with one another in the '60s [about] their salaries."[29] Ed Roebuck's description of life on an earlier Dodgers team is typical: "'If you talked about a union it was like being a communist, so nobody talked about unions or other players' contracts.'"[30] Dick Ellsworth's experience with the Cubs was in stark contrast to other players: "'Players didn't discuss their salaries openly, but we talked privately amongst ourselves. We trusted each other.'"[31] Possibly players were embarrassed at how low their salaries were, or they did not want their teammates to be jealous. Even though management encouraged players not to share the information, for years executives had exchanged much of the same information among themselves. Players knew that some of them could make a little more money if "they were willing to bitch enough," but everyone's salary was at the mercy of the club and its general manager.[32]

General managers told players not to talk with one another about salaries because it would cause dissension in the clubhouse and hurt the team's performance. The monopoly of salary information was useful to the clubs. Buzzie Bavasi was proud of using false salary data to convince players what they were worth. It was all part of the game, as far as he was concerned. Some general managers became famous, or notorious, for the negotiating ploys they used to keep down salaries, often delighting in their ability to con players about salaries. Many players suspected what was happening, but there was little they could do about it.

Gaherin convinced the owners that they had to concede the point about sharing salary information. He was certain that if the players chose to file an unfair labor practice on the issue, they would win. That would cost time and money and would cause public embarrassment. It was not worth the fight.[33] The Basic Agreement contained some restrictions on the usage and dissemination of salary data provided by the clubs, but the wording that "the names and clubs of the Players concerned will appear on the tabulations" was an enormous victory for the union and a huge break with baseball's historical unwillingness to provide information to the players.[34]

The distribution of "confidential Major League salary data" as a result of salary arbitration meant that it was no longer confidential. Players began to talk about salaries and to share their frustrations. The union justified its insistence on disclosure by saying it was needed to make arbitration work, but its leadership knew that the importance of the data went far beyond arbitration. Once players had a chance to look at salaries, it might harden their attitudes about the need to make further changes.

The reserve system cast a shadow over everything in the negotiations. Salary arbitration and the "ten and five rule" clearly were reactions to it. During negotiations for the Basic Agreement, Miller constantly brought up the reserve system and made clear that the association "would continue to try to change it."[35] The Basic Agreement stated simply, "The parties have differing views as to the legality and as to the merits of such system as presently constituted. . . . Except as adjusted or modified hereby, this Agreement does not deal with the reserve system."[36] From the association's point of view, this was more than cosmetic phrasing. In the unlikely possibility that the courts overturned the reserve system, the union did not want to be in the position of having to uphold it.

There had been almost a year of negotiations leading up to the conclusion of the Basic Agreement, but it took less than six weeks to get from "salary arbitration is a must" to "We got a deal." Miller and Gaherin agreed on basic principles and the need to improve the overall relationship between the two parties. Gaherin brought enough owners over to his point of view and was aided enormously by the fact that Walter O'Malley wanted to conclude an arrangement. O'Malley did not like the idea of the players having an aggressive, unified bargaining unit, but he was pragmatic enough to understand the need to deal with the union once it was clear that the players supported it. He had demonstrated that in the aftermath of the 1972 strike, when he had indicated that he thought the Dodgers would be better off as a team if the few players who had voted against the strike ended up with other organizations.

The union continued to seek out ways to challenge the reserve system. Miller pointed out many times that "under the Reserve System [the] only procedure left to the player [is] to refuse to sign and play under owners' option for a year."[37] This was a commentary on the limited options available to a player, but it was also a preview of where the next battle might be fought. Miller and Moss were looking at a path that had been contemplated by Al Downing a few years earlier and that Ted Simmons had taken the previous year.

DIFFERENT ROADS TO FREE AGENCY

FREE AGENCY WAS THE ULTIMATE GOAL for the players. Curt Flood's action had shown the players the need for it and reminded them of the difficulties that might stand in the way of achieving it. In the years immediately following the decision in *Flood v. Kuhn*, a number of players took different steps to achieve the goal Flood had sought for himself. Unlike Flood, each of these players contacted the union before they took any steps, and they chose a course of action that had nothing to do with baseball's historic exemption from antitrust provisions.

On October 8, 1976, future Hall of Famers such as Willie McCovey, Reggie Jackson, and Rollie Fingers, journeymen Royce Stillman, Paul Dade, and Tim Nordbrook, and twenty-two other players received a letter from Dick Moss that included the simple statement, "Most of you became free agents on October 4, 1976."[1] A revolution in baseball had taken place. Its direct causes were the grievances filed by Andy Messersmith and Dave McNally, carried forward by the union, and concluded by a decision of the arbitrator, Peter Seitz, on December 23, 1975. The actions taken by Messersmith and McNally had roots that went far beyond the two pitchers and their grievance hearing. Miller was correct when he observed in 1976 that "from 1967 on, . . . there was scarcely a [spring training] meeting that did not include a discussion of the reserve rules."[2]

Messersmith and McNally were not the first players to start down this path. They were following in the footsteps of others like Al Downing, Ted Simmons, and Bobby Tolan. All of them worked within a structure that was the product of the collective bargaining efforts of the Players Association. The union was involved at every stage in the actions contemplated by the individual players. The grievance procedure that was incorporated into the 1968 Basic Agreement made free agency possible. It was inconceivable that the players could have received a favorable ruling in the system where the commissioner ruled in disputes between a player and his club. It is just as difficult to imagine that any player would have thought to bring such a grievance under those circumstances.[3]

The standard players contract included Clause 10(a), which said that if the club and player could not agree on terms for the following season, the club had the right to "renew this contract for a period of *one year* on the same terms" (emphasis added) except for the agreed-upon allowable cut in salary. Players paid little attention to 10(a). It was a commonplace part of their reality. Every player returned a signed contract, since clubs would not allow an unsigned player to participate in a major league contest.

Al Downing, a left-handed pitcher with the Yankees, had returned every contract with his signature from the time when he arrived in the major leagues in 1961 until 1969, when for the first time he gave serious second thoughts to what he was doing. At that time, he mentioned 10(a) to Miller. Downing had suffered from injuries in 1968, and the Yankees wanted to cut his salary for the following season. He was upset when he remembered that when his teammate, Tom Tresh, had been injured a few years earlier, he had not taken a pay cut. Downing thought it was unfair and a personal slap, but there wasn't much he could do about it. He did start thinking about how the Yankees had dealt with players who no longer seemed to matter. Downing remembered Elston Howard's warning to him when Downing had been a young player: "they [management] lie, and someday it will happen to you." When Downing refused to sign the 1969 contract, the Yankees told him that until he signed he would not be able to play.

Downing had shown little interest in the union until 1968, when he began to think that "stars would protect the little guys [and] Miller looked like he had credibility."[4] When Downing decided he did not want to accept the terms the Yankess offered, he contacted Miller to see if there was a way to play out his option and become a free agent. Downing was not interested in 10(a) for theoretical reasons; he wanted to do something about his career. His reliance on the union to help him showed how much things had changed since 1966.

Miller and Downing thought that if the Yankees renewed the option unilaterally, a player could test the validity of the contract the following year and get a legally binding definition of "one year." The initial reaction by the Yankees to Downing's situation made Miller realize for the first time that lawyers working for baseball might have doubts about using the renewal clause as the basis for perpetual renewals of the contract. Neither Downing nor the union knew exactly how concerned baseball officials were about 10(a). According to John Helyar, Gaherin had been worried about 10(a) since the first time he had read it, and the National League counsel, Lou Carroll, had even cautioned Gaherin, "Don't ever let them try that renewal clause."[5]

Downing and the union had to confront a difficult reality of a career in baseball before they could bring 10(a) to an arbitrator. In order for Downing to test anything, the Yankees had to renew the contract. The team could decide to release him. He would be free, but he would also be unemployed with no certainty that another club would offer him a contract, let alone one that was as good as the Yankees'. Downing was not important enough to the New York pitching staff to warrant any special attention. The Yankees would do what was best for them. Downing had to look out for himself. Near the end of spring training, he and his agent came to an agreement with the Yankees that was supposed to satisfy both sides, but in his words, "I was in the dog house the rest of the year."[6] During negotiations, management told him he was not one of the ten pitchers that mattered, but he became the fifth starter and had a good season.

Downing reflected later, "[my] dealings with the Yankees opened [my] eyes . . . and [I] took a more realistic approach in the future. . . . [It was] so callous. . . . I had seen it happen to other players, [but I] never thought it would happen to [me]."[7] His brief rebellion against the system collapsed amid the realities of his performance. He was traded the next year to the Dodgers.

After the trade, he resurrected his career. He became part of baseball history as the pitcher against whom Henry Aaron hit home run number 715 rather than the man who tested the reserve system. A test case on 10(a) would have to wait for a player as determined as Downing, but who was either in the prime of an established career or on the verge of stardom.

Ted Simmons, the twenty-two-year-old catcher for the Cardinals in 1972, was a star in the making. He had hit over .300 and driven in close to eighty runs in 1971, his first full season in the major leagues. These were remarkable totals for a catcher, let along one so young. In the winter of 1971, he had a problem that was causing him more trouble than major league pitching: the salary offer he received from the club.

The Cardinals were in transition, having broken up a veteran team. The owner complained about the ingratitude of his players, and his anger caused the 1972 trade of the future Hall of Fame pitcher Steve Carlton. That probably cost the Cardinals a number of division championships and pennants. Carlton's problem was his refusal to back off from his salary demands. The team contained some of the toughest-minded veterans in baseball. Men like Bob Gibson, Dal Maxvill, and Joe Torre would not be pushed around off the field any more than they would be on it. That was the climate in which Ted Simmons learned what it meant to be a major leaguer.

Simmons refused to sign the contract that was sent to him by the Cardinals for the 1972 season. He replied by telling the general manager what he thought he deserved to be paid based on what he had accomplished the previous season and his estimate of what he meant to the Cardinals. He had gotten some sense of what other players were making. He wanted a raise from his salary of fourteen thousand dollars to something approaching the major league average of thirty-four thousand dollars. The Cardinals told him that young players were supposed to wait for rewards. Simmons is a thoughtful, often introspective man. He worked out his numbers in a dispassionate, analytical fashion, something that was not expected from a young player. His decision to reject the contract and challenge the club might have been influenced by his inexperience. He did not know how futile his situation was supposed to be. He had the arrogance of youth, what he described later as thinking he was "bulletproof."[8] He also had the advantage of being on a team with many veterans who were involved deeply in the union.

Simmons's refusal to sign his 1972 contract put him in a difficult position and the Cardinals in an uncomfortable one. He could damage a potentially brilliant career by inactivity and being branded as a troublemaker. The team had all the contractual leverage except for the fact that it couldn't force him to play. The club gave in. The Cardinals brought Simmons to spring training, and when he started the season, he was the first unsigned player to do so in this century. This unparalleled situation received some attention in the press, but the baseball public had other, more dramatic off-the-field issues to consider. The strike was the main event at the opening of the season. Even in St. Louis the fans were too busy being angry about the new militancy of the players and booing Joe Torre to think about what their young star catcher might be doing to baseball.

His older teammates admired how Simmons held up under pressure that was huge for anyone, even more so for someone of his age. This included episodes like the club delaying the start of a home game for a few minutes while Gussie Busch talked to Simmons about the error of his

Ted Simmons, a young star with the Cardinals, played half of the 1972 season without a signed contract and was prepared to test the renewal clause of the reserve system.

ways. In Torre's words, "You knew he [Simmons] was goofy sometimes and that he was a rebel, but you had to respect him for doing what he believed."[9] Subsequently, during his long career as a player and club executive, Simmons showed he did not conform to stereotypes.

Despite the stresses of the strike, Miller and Moss paid attention to what was happening in St. Louis. Miller was the first person Simmons contacted after making the decision not to sign his contract. They talked about the consequences of playing without a contract and the possibility of "playing out his option."[10]

There were obvious differences between Downing and Simmons. The former was old by baseball standards, black, and coming off of bad seasons with a team that operated with businesslike efficiency toward its players. The latter was young, white, had put up astounding batting numbers for a catcher, and could be the foundation for years of a team that was trying to regain respectability in a town where baseball was very important. There were also some striking similarities. They were both men who made up their own minds. No one was going to manipulate them. Their decision to do something took place when they were frustrated in their careers and thought the system was the cause of what they saw as an injustice.

Simmons did not set out to become a test case or a standard bearer for the association, but he did not back off from that role or from encouraging anyone to think about it in those terms. He was making a statement about his worth and was using the only leverage that was available to him. There were countless stories of how different Simmons was from the supposedly typical major leaguer. Many of these articles attempted to trivialize what he was doing or to fit him into the ideas that writers had about how antiestablishment attitudes of some young people were damaging baseball. Simmons did have shoulder-length hair, and by the prevailing standards of baseball, he did hold radical political and social views.

Simmons was much more complex than the University of Michigan radical "Simba" that became almost a caricature in the press. He had strong feelings of professionalism about his job. He also did not like to be pushed around by anyone, including management. Sam Rayburn's supposed dictum of "get ahead by going along" was as good a description of baseball tradition as it was of congressional politics. But the atmosphere was changing by 1972, and Simmons was symptomatic of those changes. Paternalism and quietly accepting authority were not part of Simmons's makeup.

All too often labels are substituted for analysis in discussions about the motives of players who challenge the status quo. Some writers and executives tried to ignore what Simmons was doing by dismissing him as an impulsive and thoughtless rebel or a young impressionable tool used by Miller, just as Flood supposedly had been a moody troublemaker and Downing an aging failure trying to blackmail baseball into a better contract. Charges were leveled that Simmons had no sense of responsibility, either to his team or to his sport. On the contrary, he was taking his responsibilities to himself, his family, and his profession very seriously. In his mind, his performance showed what he was worth. Not to fight for that meant he was not providing what he could for his wife and children and that his accomplishments on the field were discounted by the Cardinals.

It is important to note that Simmons thought immediately of contacting the union. This was based on having heard Miller a few times and talking to other Cardinal players. A few years earlier it would have been even more unimaginable for a young player to expect the association to help him than it would have been for him to challenge the system.

Simmons might have been McNally and Messersmith three years earlier, but his situation was not hypothetical. Just before the All-Star Game, the Cardinals met his salary demands and offered him a multiyear contract, something that was very rare. It doesn't matter whether the club took the decision to avoid the embarrassment of having a young star who wouldn't sign a contract or if it was a shrewd baseball decision. Whatever thoughts Simmons had about changing the system, his decision about signing the contract was clear-cut. The Cardinals were giving him what he had demanded and offering him a lot of money.

Simmons had made his point, had not caved in to the pressure, and had remained true to his word. He had told the Cardinals what it would take to sign him. When they agreed to it, he felt that he had no choice but to accept the contract. He contacted Miller and told him what he intended to do. Miller raised no objections about either Simmons's proposed actions or his motives. The young catcher was taking care of his career and his family. He had not done anything to compromise the union or the prospects of any other player. In the future, he remembered what the union had done for him and what it might be able to do for other players. He became one of its most actively involved members.

In 1973 Bobby Tolan was an outfielder with the Reds. During that season, he and the union won a victory that showed how much the power relationship in baseball had changed. No organization was a more determined opponent of the union than the Reds, and no executive was more hostile to it than their general manager, Bob Howsam. The team had a well-deserved reputation for extremely conservative policies concerning dress and deportment of the players. The Reds had placed Tolan on the disabled list, fined him for failure to keep a medical appointment and "insubordination and abusive language," and suspended him for alleged lack of interest in batting and fielding practice. The union filed a grievance on his behalf to overturn the punishment exacted by the club. Since the two sides agreed about the facts in the Tolan grievance, the issue at stake was the limits that could be placed upon the actions of a club.

Tolan had been involved in an obscenity-laced shouting match with Sheldon Bender, a Reds official. The Reds fined him for that and again later for his refusal to shave off his mustache after being instructed to do so by the manager, Sparky Anderson. When the grievance was heard, the club took the position that Tolan had been insubordinate by yelling at club officials and asserted that "Bender and Stowe [two club officials] are . . . more credible [than Tolan]" in describing what had happened.[11]

The union took the position that a club official had no greater credibility than a player. It asserted that the actions of players had to be judged against the standards of people involved in any other line of work and that players had to be informed in writing of the causes for disciplinary actions. Since Tolan's suspension had been the culmination of a series of offenses against club policy, he should have been informed of his earlier offenses and been given the right to challenge them at the time.

In previous grievances, the union had usually tried to show that the player had not violated club rules. In the Tolan case, the association put the rules and their enforcement on trial. It argued that the Reds did not have the right to make rules unless they had been agreed upon with the bargaining agent for the players or an individual club could demonstrate a rational purpose for them. It must have been particularly bitter for Howsam to see that his warnings about the possible effects of allowing an impartial grievance procedure were coming true and that his team was one of its first casualties.

The union introduced a new element by attacking the judgment and trustworthiness of a club official, in this case, Bender, who was Howsam's right-hand man. When Miller stated that "Bender was not forgiving, would not go out of his way to perform courtesies, and had as his purpose the establishment of dominance over Tolan,"[12] it showed again that the union's officials were unwilling to go along with the accepted norms of baseball. Romantic notions about tough-guy managers and executives answerable to no one collided with the realities of the Basic Agreement.

When the union won a grievance filed by Bobby Tolan (with Reds' executive Sheldon Bender), it was clear to all the players that the union could limit the power of ownership.

Commentators portrayed this situation as "the inmates running the asylum" and compared it to university administrators who didn't have the guts to invite the police on campus to arrest student demonstrators. Baseball purists wanted a version of Frank Rizzo, the no-nonsense chief of police of Philadelphia, someone who would shape up the players. What they got was an arbitration hearing where the Reds had to defend power that had been taken for granted by all sides for years. During the arbitration hearing, Miller pulled no punches. His sarcasm was evident when he said that "Tolan just didn't understand that Bender was being courteous" when he called Tolan a bastard and made threats to his wife. These remarks must have struck a special chord with players who were used to taking sarcasm and abuse silently.[13]

The decision of the "impartial chairman" of the grievance hearing recognized the need for discipline and "for the imposition of reasonable penalties" but concluded that "Mr. Bender was at fault in his behavior and utterances" and rescinded the suspension and remitted the fines.[14] The arbitrator's refusal to order the Reds to apologize to Tolan provided little comfort to the team. If the Reds were accountable for how they treated players, could any owner, official, or manager feel safe from the reach of the union? If the right to control players' conduct was challenged successfully in 1973, was it any more far-fetched to believe that the control over the movement of players might be just as vulnerable? As it turned out, Tolan was not finished causing trouble for management or providing a cause for the union.

In November 1973 Tolan was traded along with Dave Tomlin to the San Diego Padres for Clay Kirby. The same month, in a totally unrelated incident, Buzzie Bavasi, the president of the Padres, wrote to Miller, "I feel slighted. During the past year, you and I have had no correspondence re: player grievances."[15] Thanks to Bobby Tolan, that quickly changed more dramatically than Bavasi could have imagined.

Tolan refused to accept the contract offered to him by the Padres for the 1974 season and played the entire season under the club-imposed 10(a) renewal. At the end of the season, the Players Association filed a formal grievance on Tolan's behalf that contended that he was no longer under contract to the Padres and should be declared a free agent.

The latest Tolan grievance was the nightmare Gaherin had been fearing. He had worried that his employers did not understand how close they had come to a test case with Simmons, which Gaherin thought they would have lost. He was apprehensive about how much the owners were relying on their supposed invincibility to legal challenges. In 1974 he continued to hope that he might be able to convince men like Bud Selig, Ed Fitzgerald, and Dick Meyer (a labor relations expert with Anheuser-Busch, a top official with the Cardinals, and a confidant of Gussie Busch) to persuade the hard-liners to make concessions before "they lost everything they thought they had."[16]

Ironically, in the Tolan case Gaherin was dependent on Bavasi, whom Gaherin thought represented the attitude that had done so much to make the players turn to Miller. Bavasi hated having to meet Tolan's demands, but the alternative was potentially worse. Shortly before the arbitration hearing was scheduled, Tolan accepted a contract from the Padres that paid him very well both for the season recently completed and the season to come. The union then withdrew the grievance filed on Tolan's behalf. Like Simmons, Tolan had gotten what he wanted.

Miller might have been disappointed at losing another opportunity to test 10(a), but he certainly did not show it. His job was to create a situation where every player had the maximum possible freedom to get what was best for himself as long as it did not diminish the collective rights of the membership.

The end of the Tolan grievance was a reprieve for Gaherin and the owners, but it only delayed the crisis. There was little question that another Downing, Simmons, or Tolan would come along soon. Gaherin wanted the owners to give him the flexibility to work out an agreement with Miller before then, while the union would be in a mood to accept such arrangements. Gaherin was more convinced of the union's intentions to find a way to change the reserve system than he was in the willingness of his employers to negotiate some modifications. He was right on both counts. The result was the Messersmith-McNally grievances at the end of the 1975 season that finally brought 10(a) and its implications into open confrontation before an impartial arbitrator, the case that turned Peter Seitz into what one reporter labeled with bitter irony as the "man who freed the slaves."

In 1974 Dick Moss might have been exercising his well-known talent for humorous hyperbole when he wrote to Seitz that "the parties in the baseball industry, in their collective wisdom or lack thereof," were offering him the position of permanent arbitrator "for the settlement of disputes in the national pastime." Moss said that the arbitrator could be "the Thomas Jefferson" of baseball. After 1975 others would invoke the name of Abraham Lincoln in referring to Seitz. When Moss told Seitz that he might gain "enormous prestige" and deal with "various unique and challenging intellectual problems," he probably did not foresee that the "prestige"[17] would come from writing a decision in 1975 that revolved around the definition of the words "one year" in 10(a). When Seitz accepted the appointment as chairman of the Arbitration Panel, no one could have predicted that he would receive entries in *The Biographical History of Baseball* and *Baseball: The Biographical Encyclopedia*, let alone that they would be longer than those of some Most Valuable Players and members of the Hall of Fame.[18]

Seitz participated in a number of arbitration hearings, but in 1974 and 1975 he ruled in the two cases that changed the way baseball had conducted its business for almost a century. In the first case he upheld a grievance filed by the star pitcher Jim "Catfish" Hunter against the Oakland Athletics. Seitz's remedy had been to declare Hunter a free agent, but specific circumstances were the basis for this ruling. There had been a contractual agreement between Hunter and Charlie Finley, the owner of the A's, and Seitz's ruling made it clear that both sides had to live up to their obligations.[19] Seitz's ruling in the Hunter case was based on his reading of a specific contract between an employee and a club, not on some abstract notion of the relationship between a player and his team.

The special covenant in Hunter's contract for 1974 stipulated that the A's would pay him deferred compensation by a specified date. The payment was not made on time or in the manner set out in the contract. As far as Hunter was concerned, there was both money and principle involved. Without the deferred compensation, he would have held out for more money, "because I want to get at least as much as Reggie Jackson got. Like Gaylord Perry, I like to have as much as anybody else on my team . . . the other players said [I] could have signed for a lot more money. They didn't know I had this clause in my contract."[20]

On September 16, 1974, Hunter's lawyer, J. Carlton Cherry, wrote to Finley about his "refusal" to return an amended contract and pay the fifty thousand dollars due to Hunter, adding, "we do contend most seriously that you have breached the contract, and we believe the Commissioner will so hold, giving Mr. Hunter due right to sign with any other club he desires, and surely the Court will construe the same as a breach of contract."[21] It was fortunate for Cherry and his client that the decision was rendered by an impartial arbitrator rather than the commissioner. Less than a month after he wrote Finley, Cherry received notification from the commissioner's office that Kuhn would "not go along with Hunter's request . . . for a declaration of free agency."[22] Years later, Kuhn wrote that granting free agency to Hunter "over a few days' delay in paying the $50,000 was like giving a life sentence to a pickpocket."[23]

Jim "Catfish" Hunter was the first major leaguer to win free agency through a grievance procedure. The contract he received from the Yankees showed how the reserve system distorted the market value for salaries.

The disagreement between Hunter and Finley played out against the background of Oakland's participation in the playoffs and the World Series. Finley asked his star pitcher, "Why the hell do you want to become a free agent now instead of after the World Series?"[24] Disputes had been common in the past between players and Finley, and they never seemed to hurt the team's performance on the field. It was the same in 1974. The A's beat the Orioles in the playoffs and the Dodgers in the Series to win their third consecutive World Championship. Hunter capped off a great season by winning the Cy Young Award on October 30. Twenty-seven days later, Hunter and Finley testified before an arbitration panel in New York composed of Marvin Miller, John Gaherin, and Peter Seitz. The purpose was to determine whether Hunter had a contract binding him to the A's or if he was a free agent.

One of the few light moments at the hearing came when Seitz asked the A's owner, "isn't it true that Mr. Hunter has a good year every year?" to which Finley replied "yes" and added, "I am very proud of him." Seitz turned to Hunter, saying, "If you would like that in writing suitable for framing, Mr. Hunter, we can arrange it for you."[25] There is no mention that Hunter replied to the offer, but it is clear that he was after something of much greater consequence from Seitz. Hunter wanted the freedom to market his services to other clubs.

In the days leading up to the arbitration Hunter had been unsure of exactly what might happen, which was reasonable, since no player had gotten free agency when his club had been opposed to it. In one conversation between Hunter and Miller, Hunter said that if he became a free agent that would also mean that he was not under contract and was therefore unemployed. That concern, however fleeting, was at the heart of what was at stake in the arbitration hearing. The union wanted the arbitrator to declare that a player was a free agent and then to have the power to ensure that the clubs did not conspire among themselves to negate the effect of free agency.

At one point in the proceedings, Miller rejected out of hand the claims made by the commissioner's office that baseball rules would allow him to negate a possible declaration of free agency for Hunter. Kuhn's position might have been based on his sincere belief that the A's were guilty of nothing more than a minor bookkeeping error. He certainly believed that free agency would destroy the integrity and the competitive nature of the game.[26] In his view, solving problems like these without damaging baseball was the reason why the office of commissioner had been created under Judge Landis.

The position of the union was equally clear. The commissioner had no right to interfere in a process that had been created by collective bargaining, and the union was not going to let him exercise the powers he claimed to have. These two views of the office of the commissioner could not have been more diametrically opposed. The one was based on tradition, the other on recent contractual arrangements. Miller presented the union's version of recent history: "The Commissioner does not have any authority to rule on contract disputes involving a player. As you know, he has had no such authority since 1970, the year the clubs and the Association agreed that all such matters would be resolved by impartial arbitration." Miller went on to claim that any Major League rule that was inconsistent with the Basic Agreement "is void."[27]

The way the executive director of the players union lectured the commissioner of baseball on how the rules of baseball had been altered showed what was at stake in the Hunter case. If Peter Seitz upheld Hunter's complaint and the commissioner could not do anything about that decision, Miller's point and the new power of the association would be validated for everyone to see.

Barry Rona, who represented the A's at the hearing, summed up the case as "a good faith dispute" about the interpretation of the wording in a contract. Finley had not been trying to take advantage of Hunter or to avoid responsibility for carrying out his part of the contract. Rona contended that even if Hunter were right, he deserved compensation, but the panel should not penalize the club "by terminating the contract of one of the most valuable players in Major League Baseball."[28] Dick Moss, arguing for Hunter, was more brief and more direct—to him it was a "simple question" of whether a contract means what it says, and if contracts truly were reciprocal, then one side did not have the right to change it without voiding the contract.[29]

Seitz's ruling made it clear that contractual obligations between players and clubs were mutually binding and that there was an impartial body ready to enforce the contracts and to level penalties that it deemed appropriate. The decision stated that "his [Hunter's] contract no longer binds him and he is a *free agent* . . . [because] the Panel found that the contract between Mr. Hunter and the Oakland Club was clear and free from ambiguity" (emphasis added).[30] The Hunter decision showed that free agency was obtainable. The union reacted immediately to the decision, saying it was "a forthright affirmation of the sanctity of contracts" and claiming that the only proper remedy was to allow Hunter to sign his next contract with any team of his choice.[31]

The Hunter decision forced everyone in baseball to see the importance of impartial arbitration. The commissioner and attorneys employed by baseball made it quite clear that they thought the decision was a serious blow to the stability of the game and a threat to the integrity of the game. But the commissioner did not prevail in either his desire to take the matter away from arbitration or to change the remedy imposed by Seitz. The Basic Agreement gave a new definition to the powers of the commissioner, which were circumscribed now by terms agreed upon by the union and the PRC.[32]

The implications of the decision went far beyond Hunter's personal situation. When he signed a lucrative contract with the Yankees, everyone could see the direct benefits of free agency for a player. It also showed how much players' salaries were restrained by the reserve system. Other players saw the connection between free agency and big money, even if most of them did not think of themselves in the same category as Catfish Hunter. The situation was just as clear to the owners, and it strengthened their resolve to hold the line against further weakening of the reserve system. His success showed the players what they were worth in a free market and how they could enter into it. The Hunter case made it clear that it would not be long until a prominent player went to arbitration to test 10(a) in hopes of becoming a free agent.

Some observers have argued that the Hunter decision made it inevitable that some player would test the reserve system through arbitration. Actually, it accelerated the process that had been started earlier by Downing, Simmons, and Tolan. Hunter used the mechanisms of impartial arbitration that they had been ready to employ. The following year, the same process with the same arbitrator would yield results that changed baseball forever.

MESSERSMITH AND McNALLY
Two Pitchers and One Big Win

THERE WAS GENERAL AGREEMENT among baseball executives that the Dodgers were the best-run franchise and that its owner, Walter O'Malley, was the sport's most savvy and most powerful executive. Gaherin was convinced that if baseball had more O'Malleys, there would have been a way to craft a series of mutually beneficial compromises with the union, avoiding the confrontations that led to work stoppages and other problems. That made O'Malley an unlikely target for the ruling that changed baseball forever. Nevertheless, actions taken by the Dodgers provided the case the union needed to pick up where Downing, Simmons, and Tolan had left off in their challenges to 10(a).

Andy Messersmith had started his major league career in 1968 with the California Angels. He had a 20 and 13 record in 1971, but slipped to 8 and 11 the following year. In November 1972 he was traded to the Dodgers as part of a seven-player deal. As the alternate player rep for the Angels, Messersmith probably was aware of what Simmons and Tolan had contemplated. He certainly had seen how the union used the power of an arbitrator during the grievance filed by his teammate, Alex Johnson.

Johnson was a talented player who had disciplinary problems with many of the seven major league teams he played for during his twelve-year career. He had fights with other players and physical altercations with writers. A teammate pulled a gun on him. He was fined twenty-nine times by the Angels during spring training and finally was placed on the restricted list, without pay, by the club. The union filed a grievance on his behalf, claiming that Johnson was suffering from acute mental distress, an illness that should be regarded contractually in the same way as a physical problem that would prevent a player from performing to his capabilities. The issue went to arbitration, and the union prevailed. It got disability with full pay for Johnson, and the fines were rescinded.

The decision outraged management and reporters, both of whom argued that the inability to punish Johnson would render management incapable of maintaining any kind of discipline. That would lead more players into making bogus claims for payment. The union's argument was just as simple; it was the responsibility of both parties to live up to the terms of a contract, and the purpose of impartial arbitration was to enforce that. Even those players who distrusted and disliked Johnson and were aghast at his actions recognized that the union would protect its members.

Messersmith had experienced a difficult reality of baseball when he was traded. After that, he became the ace of the Dodgers' pitching staff and led the league in wins and winning percentage in 1974. At the end of that season he asked for a no-trade clause in his contract for the next year. The club refused his request and responded that it did not believe in such restrictions. It would not abandon this point of principle to satisfy Messersmith's apprehensions about the possibility of a trade. The club wanted the freedom to deal with its personnel. The player wanted assurances that he either would not be traded or would have some control over where he went. The two positions seemed mutually exclusive.

Another pitcher on the Dodgers took a special interest in the proceedings. Mike Marshall had outspoken ideas about many things, including physical conditioning, pitching, and the union. His activities as a player representative probably caused some of his trades and entailed other costs for him both during his career and after his retirement. In 1975 Marshall was a strong supporter of Miller, Moss, and the Players Association. During negotiations, he often ended up in what he described as his "role as outrageous point man . . . [who] had a flair . . . to say outlandish things . . . and was [sometimes] amazed that so many people took me seriously."[1]

Marshall might have wanted to test the renewal clause himself, but his physical condition, age, and his reputation as a troublemaker made him an unlikely candidate. However much Marshall might have been involved with his teammates' decision to play out his option, it was Messersmith who made the decision. He did it for his own reasons and with the support and assistance of the union.

In retrospect it is easy to criticize the Dodgers for not coming to terms with the demands of a talented pitcher whom they wanted to keep.

Ownership already had accepted some restrictions on the right to trade players with the ten and five rule. Years later, Gaherin commented on the black humor of the situation: "O'Malley [was the] smartest man in baseball [and] Bavasi was the kind of executive who hardened the players' attachment to the Association."[2] Yet Bavasi had been willing to satisfy Tolan to avoid a confrontation, while O'Malley went down the path that Gaherin was certain would mean the end of the reserve system as it had existed for a century. The Dodgers made their decisions about Messersmith on the same grounds as they had made others, including the decision to leave Brooklyn—Walter O'Malley's considered opinion of what was necessary to produce a profitable and stable organization. That put the team on a collision course with Messersmith and the union.

Messersmith must have pitched under enormous pressure during the 1975 season. He responded brilliantly, ranking first in the league in starts, complete games, shutouts, and innings pitched, third in strikeouts, and second in earned run average. No executive in baseball truthfully could say that Messersmith would not be a valuable asset to his club. This point became central to the arguments of both sides during the arbitration hearing and its aftermath in court. The Dodgers claimed that they would be losing an almost irreplaceable commodity if Messersmith became a free agent. After the ruling was made, the union argued that if multiple clubs did not try to sign Messersmith, that would be prima facie evidence that they were acting in collusion to negate the decision reached by the arbitrator.

The "Messersmith Case" is the common shorthand for the decision that ended the reserve system. He was a glamorous pitcher who was able to take advantage of the benefits of free agency, but another pitcher, Dave McNally, was also a party to the arbitration. More than twenty years after the case, many people still can't understand why he was involved. There was no personal gain for him. His decision to remain a party to the case cost him a great deal of money. The simplest explanation is that he wanted to help break a system that he thought was wrong. It is hard to disagree with the opening sentence of his entry in *The Biographical Encyclopedia of Baseball:* "McNally really did it for principle in associating himself with Andy Messersmith in the 1975 challenge that ended baseball's reserve clause and opened the way for free agency."[3]

McNally had a distinguished fourteen-year career as a major league pitcher, all but the last year (1975) with the Orioles. He won at least twenty games in four consecutive seasons (1968–1971) and won nine World Series games. Friends describe him as "quiet, a private guy with strong beliefs" who had been a dependable starter and a good teammate.[4] According to one of his former general managers, Harry Dalton, McNally was "the staunchest holdout . . . someone who was willing to lose time and money rather than take less than he thought he deserved."[5] A teammate described him as someone "who was upset with things over the years and felt that someone had to change it. . . . He might have been laid back, but when he'd had it up to eyeballs, he just exploded."[6] McNally's "explosion" in 1975 was the somewhat quiet step of saying no to a contract. He played out his option during 1975, the one unsuccessful season he spent with the Montreal Expos. He intended to retire but was still an active player in contractual terms. That gave McNally the right to file a grievance demanding that he be declared a free agent, since he had played out the one year specified in 10(a). If Messersmith had gotten his no-trade provision and signed with the Dodgers, McNally would have been there to file the grievance that the union needed to test 10(a) in an arbitration setting.

The owners were aware of the situation, and because of this the Expos were prepared to go to great lengths and expense to sign McNally. They

Andy Messersmith (with teammate Steve Garvey) became a free agent as a result of Seitz's ruling, setting the pattern for future free agency.

Even though Dave McNally (shown during his one season as an Expo) was planning to retire, he turned down a substantial offer from the club in order to continue as part of the grievance.

offered him a significant signing bonus. He could just sign a contract, show up for spring training, retire, and keep the bonus. Clubs generally did not like to give away money for nonproductive players, and John McHale, the veteran general manager of the Expos, was willing to make a charade offer to McNally. The pitcher even received a phone call from McHale when he just happened to be passing through the airport in McNally's home town on a winter's day. Billings, Montana, is not a place that baseball executives normally visit without a purpose. McHale's interest in McNally had nothing to do with baseball on the field and everything to do with the business of baseball.

Years later, McNally explained his actions: "The main reason . . . was what happened to me in Montreal [where he felt that the club had broken promises it had made to him]. . . . Another thing that kept me going was what happened to younger players. A lot of them were being held in reserve instead of being let go to places they could further their careers."[7]

Since 1969 there has been a lot of criticism levelled at the motives of players who tried to change the system in baseball. The most common complaint has been that players are selfish and that greed has been their only reason for their self-proclaimed fights on "principle." Even when judged against the most rigid standard of self-interest, no one can question McNally's motives. He turned down a lot of money to pursue arbitration to win benefits for other players knowing there was no way he would benefit financially himself. Ironically, the fact that Messersmith became a highly paid free agent and set the example for others made most people forget about McNally's importance.

McNally is another example of how the Players Association changed the relationships in baseball. He was raised in the Orioles organization, which prided itself on bringing young players up through its minor league system and teaching them standards. There was something special about being an Oriole. Veterans were supposed to set an example, and younger players were supposed to learn what it meant to be a major leaguer and a teammate. The team had a lot of thoughtful, articulate player reps who took leadership roles in the association. Brooks Robinson took abuse from the fans for his role in the association, but in the clubhouse he was part of the Orioles tradition of standing up for other players. McNally had been a player rep for a short period when the union was gaining its new, more assertive character. It was no coincidence that many Orioles, including Dick Hall, Milt Pappas, and Moe Drabowsy, became player reps with their new teams after being traded and that others like Don Baylor, Doug DeCinces, and Mark Belanger were involved deeply with the association.

The lawyers for baseball filed an action in federal court in Kansas City to stop the Messersmith and McNally arbitration hearing from moving forward. The brief claimed that free agency was not amenable to arbitration because it would do irreparable damage to the structure of baseball and harm every club. Since that involved the integrity of the sport, the commissioner should rule on the issues raised by Messersmith and McNally. His office had been entrusted by the owners with that responsibility, and it could not be ceded to an arbitrator. The brief further asserted that arbitration did not apply because the language of the Basic Agreement did not deal specifically with the reserve system or the option clause. The lawyers for baseball presented the same argument to the arbitrator and asked him not to go forward with the hearing. Neither federal Judge John Oliver or Peter Seitz saw merit in their claims.

Before the arbitration hearing took place, there was a serious discussion among the baseball hierarchy about dismissing Seitz. There was a lingering distrust of him as a result of his ruling in the Hunter case. Their decision to retain him was a combination of public relations considerations and advice from Gaherin, who also assured them that Seitz would rule in accordance with the wording of the players' contract, which was exactly what any replacement would do. Twenty-five years after the ruling, Bowie Kuhn still thinks the owners made a mistake in allowing Seitz to rule in Messersmith-McNally: "he was a nice guy; I liked him. I didn't think he was the right man to be handling a decision of this magnitude"; "I was not surprised. I had people examine his record. I thought there was a tilt to the players' side."[8]

The problem facing the owners was not so much which arbitrator would decide the case as the fact that an arbitrator would be involved at all. The owners were correct in their assumption that the best solution for them would be to have the issue decided by Commissioner Kuhn. His stated views in the Flood and Hunter cases had made clear that he would have ruled in favor of the clubs in both cases and would not allow the reserve system to be dismantled.

It is possible that the aftereffects of the Hunter decision had shown Seitz how the reserve system artificially limited salaries. There is also no question that Seitz felt strongly that salary arbitration had played a positive role in baseball. In private correspondence, he reacted sharply to the question, "what the hell does a labor arbitrator know about baseball?" As far as Seitz was concerned, if an arbitrator who made a good income could "be ideally impartial in disputes [concerning] those who labor for a paltry wage," why should baseball be any different? The core of his philosophy was that "the choice of arbitrators in salary arbitration in baseball is not dictated from Olympus: it is the result of agreement between the parties."[9]

Seitz often used literary and classical allusions and had a fine touch for sarcasm, but he took a pragmatic approach toward his professional responsibilities. He understood fully that the reserve system was an integral part of baseball's history and its current business operations. He also knew that it was part of a broader set of contractual relationships between the union and the owners and individual players and their clubs. A significant change in any part of that would reverberate throughout the structure of the sport. It was his regard for the importance of the collective bargaining process that led him to hope that he could convince both parties to deal with the issues raised in Messersmith-McNally as part of a broader settlement of outstanding concerns. Nine months earlier, Seitz had reflected privately that arbitration might "have the effect of persuading clubs and players to abandon their utterly unrealistic bargaining of yesteryear, with gross damaging results to both, and to bargain realistically under hazard of having a neutral decide."[10]

When Seitz was forced to make a decision in Messersmith-McNally, he placed the case in a historical perspective. He pointed out that the players had tried for decades to use litigation to temper the reserve system "without resolving much" and had reached "a dead end" with the Flood decision. "But for the developments in collective bargaining and the proliferation of arbitration clauses in collective agreements," the players would have had no chance to change the reserve system without resorting to "a struggle that would wreak great damage to all concerned in the sport." Seitz was correct on both counts. Arbitration gave the players the weapon they needed to force concessions that the owners resisted. In Seitz's words, "The Players Association then decided to play what, in the jargon of foreign affairs, may be called the 'arbitration card,' and that was how the stalemate that existed for generations was broken in the Messersmith-McNally case."[11]

What Gaherin had warned about in the aftermath of the Supreme Court's ruling in *Flood v. Kuhn* came true in 1975. The owners chose to fight to retain the reserve system in its entirety rather than making concessions. There were understandable reasons for their conduct. They were wedded to the reserve system, and it had weathered previous challenges. They had reason to believe that they could continue to prevail, and they were not alone in that belief.

In 1974 the economist James Scoville presented a perceptive analysis of the history of labor relations in sports in which he showed an understanding of the position of the owners and a belief that they might be able to prevail. He pointed to the difficulties faced by players in various sports in using the courts to attack the reserve systems, and he claimed that collective bargaining might be the most useful approach for the players to employ, "but here the players must overcome the objections of the owners who thus far have been extremely reluctant to allow the issue to be subject to negotiations."[12] If Scoville was correct, there were good reasons for the owners not to change their stance.

Scoville's analysis did not take into account the fact that the grievance procedure had already changed the relationship between the players and the teams to the point where it could impinge on the reserve system. He concluded with a reasonable prediction about the future of labor relations in baseball: "unless the reserve system is dismantled by the courts, these negotiations [for the 1976 Basic Agreement] will be the definitive test of whether player associations have the strength to force significant changes in the institutional structure of the sports labor market."[13] His prediction happened to be incorrect.

Scoville was correct about the importance of the 1976 negotiations, but for reasons that had little to do with his argument. He could not foresee that the two parties would be operating from positions of relative power that were the opposite of what they had been in the past. Scoville did not take into account the fact that it might not be the courts that "forced significant changes" but an arbitrator whose decision was upheld by the courts. If this economist working with a wealth of knowledge and not hindered by either self-interest or attachment to the reserve system could not predict that someone like Peter Seitz could alter everything, surely the owners should not be criticized too strongly for a similar oversight. In any case, if Scoville or other outside observers did not see what was coming, their futures were not at stake.

The hearing on the Messersmith-McNally grievance did not bring out any issues that had not been involved in previous informal discussions about 10(a). The positions of both sides were clear. The Dodgers, supported by Major League Baseball, argued that they had the right to renew the entirety of the contract, including the right to renew the renewal provision. They also contended that the reserve system was integral to the protection of the sport and the investments that all teams had made in their players. Clearly, something that was essential to the foundation of the reserve system could not be destroyed as part of a grievance brought by individual players who wanted to negate their obligations. If the owners had wanted arbitration to deal with the reserve system, they would have specified that in the Basic Agreement.

Moss argued the case for Messersmith and McNally on the most narrow possible interpretation of the Basic Agreement and the individual players' contracts. The Basic Agreement called for impartial arbitration of grievances concerning contractual issues. This was all the players were asking of Seitz. The fact that the owners had entered into a collective bargaining agreement that might have unintended consequences for them was not grounds for claiming that the arbitrator had to protect them from themselves. At the heart of Moss's case was the simple hypothesis that the word "one," when used in 10(a), meant a single year rather than a rolling number of one-year renewals stretching into perpetuity.

Before the hearing started, Seitz made it clear to both sides that he thought everyone would be better off if they found a way to fashion a compromise and did not go forward with the grievance. Once the hearing was concluded, Seitz could not tell either of his fellow panelists precisely how he intended to rule, but he gave them strong indications of where he was heading. Miller "was sure we had won," and Gaherin said that part of his job was "to be able to read the tea leaves . . . [and] Seitz made it pretty easy." When Seitz indicated that one side was going to get hurt by the decision and then said, "John, you're going to get your head cut off," one didn't need an advanced degree in linguistics or labor law to guess at what was coming.[14] Seitz had possibly gone further than any arbitrator should in trying to engineer a compromise. Years later, he described his frustration and bewilderment in a private letter to Kuhn:

> I shall go to eternal rest wondering why the Leagues gave a negative response to my suggestion (forwarded in written form through John Gaherin) to seize the opportunity to bargain for a less rigid reserve system in advance of the date when I should have to wield the surgical knife of arbitration. That suggestion, although not supported by John when I first mentioned making it at a board meeting [of the arbitration panel], was not opposed by him: and I thought he recognized its value to his constituents. Had he actively opposed the suggestion, as a member of the board, I would not have made it. I believe he was already seeing "Mene, Mene, Tekel, Upharsin" (or something ominous) on the wall of the room where we were working.[15]

Armed with a belief that "Seitz would rule against us," Gaherin tried to convince the owners to allow him to negotiate a compromise in Messersmith-McNally that would retain at least part of 10(a). He did not have a chance. The owners were still convinced that they could never lose in court. Their lawyers assumed that the unique status of baseball protected them from the consequences of whatever Seitz might do. Gaherin made a presentation to the owners, and he got the response that he expected and feared. When Charlie Finley got up and told Gaherin, "What do you want to do, give it away?" the latter replied that "there comes a time when you have to recognize the obvious."[16]

But Gaherin should have recognized something equally obvious. The owners were not going to accept meaningful changes in the reserve system unless they were forced to do so. They weren't in a mood to take advice from their own chief negotiator, the only man in the room who appeared to know what Seitz would do. Gussie Busch accused Gaherin of "destroying this business." No one at the meeting did anything to support Gaherin's views. All Gaherin could do was shrug and ask once again for the authority to salvage something for his employers. Nothing changed, and Gaherin phoned Seitz with a brief message: "Turn the Crank."[17] Seitz, Gaherin, and Miller all knew that in a few days they would see what Gaherin understood to be "the end of the reserve structure."

Years later there is still disagreement among baseball officials about the wisdom of forcing Seitz to issue a ruling rather than accepting his suggestion that the two parties should agree on a compromise. On the twenty-fifth anniversary of the ruling, Kuhn reflected, "in that setting, probably something better could have been negotiated than was. But the difference could be tweedldee tweedledum."[18]

The essence of Seitz's ruling was that clause 10(a) gave the club the right to renew a contract for one year, and he took a simple definition of the word "one." Renewing the contract did not include a renewal of the right to renew. Seitz addressed the potential impact of the decision: "It would be a mistake to read this opinion as a statement of the views of the writer either for or against *a* reserve system, or for that matter, the Reserve System presently in force. It is not my function to do so!"[19]

The PRC fired Seitz as soon as he made his ruling public. The owners could be excused for not wanting to accept Seitz's conclusion. He had ruled that "as a matter of contract construction, the position of the Players Association in the dispute has merit and deserves to be sustained." Seitz went on to summarize, "It deserves emphasis that this decision strikes no blow emancipating players from claimed serfdom or involuntary servitude such as was alleged in the *Flood Case.* . . . It does not counsel or require that the System be changed to suit the predilections or preference of an arbitrator . . . intent upon imposing his own brand of industrial justice on the parties."[20] No matter how Seitz explained his decision, the fact was that Messersmith and McNally were free agents. That was exactly what Flood had sought.

Seitz pointed to "a fortuitous coincidence": the clubs and the union were negotiating a new Basic Agreement that gave them "the unique opportunity" to resolve the problems surrounding the reserve system. Seitz's decision concluded, "The clubs and the players have a mutual interest in the health and integrity of the sport and in its financial returns. With a will to do so, they are competent to fashion a reserve system to suit their requirements."[21] This was another effort to do what he had attempted before the decision—to get the parties to work out their problems on their own as part of the collective bargaining process. He was still convinced that Miller and Gaherin could resolve the Messersmith-McNally grievance in a way that would be satisfactory to both parties. Seitz was right about the two negotiators but wrong in thinking that Gaherin had the authority to fashion a compromise that would be acceptable to the union.

When Seitz consistently refused to comment for publication on the reasons and the impact of his decisions, he cited the canons of his profession to justify his reluctance to discuss the ruling. He reminded journalists that "the place for that was in the decision where I spread my views at considerable length" and encouraged them to look at the decision. He refused either to take credit for "freeing the slaves" or for presiding over a revolution in baseball. He maintained that he had dealt with a single grievance, but there was no doubt that he understood fully the ramifications of his actions on December 23, 1975.[22]

Baseball authorities and a number of writers claimed that Seitz had overstepped his authority. The most novel explanation came from Dick Young. He based it on recent baseball history and found a way to resurrect his own long-standing animus toward Walter O'Malley for having moved the Dodgers out of Brooklyn. Years earlier, Young had written that Miller desired to ruin baseball because he was an embittered Brooklyn Dodgers fan. Now, Young coupled Seitz with Miller and pointed out that the Messersmith decision was "events finally catch[ing] up with O'Malley because Seitz also had rooted for the Dodgers when he had been a young man." Seitz had gotten even with "a decision particularly damaging to Walter O'Malley." Young also provided legal advice to the owners, suggesting that they could "upset the ruling of Peter Seitz, former Brooklyn fan . . . [because] bias on the part of an arbitrator is grounds for overturning a decision."[23] Baseball's officials were attempting to formulate their own rationale to overturn the ruling, but their strategy ignored the Brooklyn connection. Instead, they focused on efforts to discredit Seitz and claimed he had overstepped his authority.

Twenty-five years after the decision, Lou Hoynes, an attorney for baseball, analyzed it as "a goofy decision that doesn't make any sense. . . . Basically, he [Seitz] says [the reserve system is] un-American, and that's not what arbitrators are supposed to do." Hoynes also thought that "he was hostile to ownership and the rules of the game. He was looking for a loophole to make the players free."[24]

After firing Seitz, baseball's hierarchy began to think about the next step. There was no consideration given to accepting Seitz's ruling and using it as the basis for bargaining a compromise with the union. The owners decided to appeal the decision in federal court. That gave a judge the opportunity to do what Gaherin thought was a certainty, to turn the arbitrator's ruling on two players into something of greater scope. Baseball would have been better off finding ways to cope with the ruling rather than continuing a rearguard action that was costly in time and money, expanded the scope of the ruling, and led to further bitterness in relations with the union. Gaherin assured the PRC that he "could get a deal." However, he was powerless to stop the march into Judge Oliver's court in an atmosphere that Gaherin characterized as "reeking with legalisms" and dominated by lawyers who were convinced that since baseball had prevailed in other courts, it would do so in Kansas City.[25]

The owners had to choose a venue where there was a major league club. According to Ewing Kauffman, in whose name the suit was filed, "they felt a judge in New York would be too liberal and thought judges in Kansas City would be more conservative and more inclined towards their cause."[26] Bowie Kuhn asked the Kansas City owner to be the standard bearer for baseball. Kauffman was convinced by baseball's hierarchy and their advisers that they would win in court what they had lost in arbitration.

Gaherin argued vehemently against the decision to appeal. He recalls, "I told the law firm and owners [that] it would be futile. . . . The only thing [that would come out of the appeal] was lawyers would put another couple of kids through college." Gaherin described the decision to appeal as "using the Flood case as an applause meter for the legal sagacity of the legal establishment in baseball."[27] This 1991 assessment was certainly influenced by the fact that the owners fired him in the wake of their failure to overturn the Seitz ruling and to use a brief lockout to pressure the union into accepting severe restrictions on free agency. That does not change the fact that Gaherin did try to stop the appeal and that his prediction about further losses came true.

The lawyers and advisors to the owners misread the atmosphere in the Eighth Circuit. New York and Washington lawyers might have thought that the judges in Kansas City were not sophisticated and would be amenable to arguments that hearkened back to the pastoral heartland of America and the national pastime image that baseball ownership liked to project when it wanted to claim special privileges. After all, that approach had worked with Supreme Court justices ranging from Oliver Wendell Holmes to Harry Blackmun. The judges of the Eighth Circuit had impressive credentials. Each of them had been members of the honor society as law students, and most of them had graduated near the top of their class. Furthermore, important decisions upholding the power of arbitrators had come out of the Eighth Circuit.

The fact that the trial was held in Kansas City had unforeseen, long-term consequences for the union. It employed local counsel to assist Moss, a young labor lawyer, Donald M. Fehr, who had clerked for another federal judge in Kansas City. Fehr's familiarity with the situation in the Eighth Circuit and the characteristics of its judges proved useful to Moss and Miller during the trial. A short while after the trial, Moss resigned his

Don Fehr (with Brian Harvey at the 1993 All-Star Game) succeeded Dick Moss in 1977 as the Player Association's counsel and became executive director in 1984.

position with the union, and Fehr succeeded him. After a series of changes in the union, Fehr went on to become its executive director in 1986.

"This is simply another case on this Court's docket, which must be processed and decided in accordance with the applicable laws of the United States"[28] sounds like an unnecessary statement of the obvious by a federal judge. But when John Oliver opened *Kansas City Royals v. Major League Baseball Players Association* with that remark, he was spotlighting the strange legal and emotional world in which baseball had operated for almost a century. The way Oliver framed the problem was reminiscent of the explanations offered by Seitz. They both were dealing with a single labor relations case that had to be decided within the framework of an existing collective bargaining agreement. The fact that the industry involved in the dispute was baseball made little difference to either of them. The biggest problem facing Major League Baseball in court was the necessity of meeting the simple test laid out in Judge Oliver's opening remarks.

If anyone thought Oliver was going to rhapsodize about the virtues of baseball, à la Blackmun, the start of the trial should have ended that fantasy. He singled out a passage in the owners' brief that might be described as their doomsday scenario, an assertion that the only way to avoid destruction of baseball was a favorable ruling from Oliver. They claimed that it might be necessary to protect the game "by resort[ing] to industrial strife." He pointed out that they were claiming to protect baseball from the alien influences of the labor movement while, at the same time, they were threatening to use the tactics employed by embattled employers. Oliver made it clear that he was in no mood for hyperbole of any kind.[29]

The judge had more unpleasant surprises for the owners. He put them on notice that the Flood decision would have no influence in his court. The issues were different, and he intended to regard the Messersmith case in the same way as "it [the court] has been processing many labor controversies over the years it has been on the bench." In case anyone missed his absence of romanticism, Oliver stated for the record that, in his opinion, Congress had not vested any court in the land with either the power or responsibility "to act as some sort of guardian of what the Club Owners refer to in their brief as the national pastime."[30] Oliver's efforts to separate the romantic history of baseball from the realities of its labor relations sounded like what Seitz had attempted to do in his role as the impartial arbitrator. They were reminiscent of the arguments made by Gaherin when he had tried to head off the rush to judgment in Kansas City. The owners could dismiss an arbitrator or ignore an employee, but not John Oliver, the federal judge who was going to put an exclamation point on the Messersmith-McNally decision.

The January 1976 trial was the second time Oliver had dealt with Messersmith-McNally. Before the arbitration hearing had begun, the owners had asked him to rule that Seitz had no jurisdiction as an arbitrator to deal with the issues raised in the grievance. Oliver ruled that the hearing should go forward and that the owners were free to appeal the decision if they so desired. The case law made it clear that it would take a major error by Seitz for Oliver or any judge to reverse the decision.

Once the trial began, Oliver made good on his promise to take a narrow approach toward his responsibilities. The questions Oliver raised highlighted the inconsistencies in the positions management had taken over a period of years. Neither Seitz nor Oliver were charged with protecting the owners from any damage that resulted from their unwillingness to compromise. Oliver's function was to rule whether Seitz had operated within the guidelines laid down by the Basic Agreement. The judge seemed surprised "that everyone showed up at the arbitration ball park when the proceeding was scheduled [since both sides had the power] . . . to fire the umpire [Seitz]."[31]

The testimony on both sides demonstrated the huge difference in their views of what the arbitration had decided. The commissioner and his general counsel, Sandy Hadden, raised the specter of something that would endanger the very foundations of the game, clubs tampering with players of another team. Implicitly, Kuhn and Hadden were arguing that a system that penalized the players was necessary to protect owners from their own potential dishonesty. They appealed to history, pointing out that since players like Ed Roush had not been allowed to play without a contract and wartime players were not under contract, baseball had established both the precedent and the necessity for player control. They ignored the more recent examples of Simmons and Tolan, who had played at least part of a season without signed contracts. Baseball had not suffered in either situation.

In the union's reply, Miller virtually dismissed the historical arguments, except to assert, "There was no discussion whatever [in the negotiations for the Basic Agreements] which would remotely suggest that this language was in any way intended to have reference to the Reserve System or any of its components."[32] Miller underlined that passage and added a marginal expletive. Throughout the legal proceedings that followed in the wake of the Seitz ruling, Moss hammered at the point that the owners could not ask for relief by claiming they were ignorant of the possible consequences of the provisions they had accepted in the Basic Agreement.

Kuhn used the Flood decision in an attempt to challenge the honesty of the union and the judgment of the arbitrator. According to Kuhn, since the union had not suggested during the Flood case that the reserve system depended on the one-year option in 10(a), the players were being unfair in resorting to the grievance procedure.[33] They should have accepted that the ruling in *Flood v. Kuhn* was the end of the matter. Kuhn did not consider that once the union failed in one approach, it had the responsibility to its members to find another one that might work. Did the commissioner of America's national pastime really expect the players and their union to act like English gentlemen amateurs and willingly accept the decision of an official, no matter how unfair and illogical it might seem to them?

Hadden was uniquely qualified to comment on previous discussions about possible changes to the reserve system. He had been part of the 1969 Joint Study Committee. In Kansas City he quoted at length from his notes from the committee. He drew the conclusion that since the players had recognized the need at that time for some version of the reserve system, the owners had the right to retain the system in its entirety. After all, in 1969 the counsel for the National League, Louis Carroll, had rejected the proposal to have players "free of reservation at age 65 . . . [because] that would open the door to relaxation of complete player control."[34]

Judge Oliver thought it was appropriate and important to question both sides about the context in which Seitz's decision was made. Oliver did take notice of one significantly unique attribute of baseball: a commissioner who was entrusted with sweeping powers to protect the integrity of the sport and to ensure the public respect for it. Even the arbitration provisions allowed some role for the commissioner. Before the arbitration hearing took place, the owners had tried to get Judge Oliver to intervene. He had refused, but he discussed the role of the commissioner in terms that resembled Sherlock Holmes's dog that did not bark. Why Kuhn had chosen to do nothing if he thought that free agency was a direct threat to the continued integrity of the game puzzled the judge. Oliver did not produce an answer, but neither did the commissioner or his lawyers.

At the trial after Seitz's ruling, Lou Hoynes told Judge Oliver that the commissioner had considered removing the matter from arbitration and deciding it himself. He would have taken that step under the commissioner's interpretation of the "integrity of the sport," the powers that he thought were the basis for the office of commissioner since Judge Landis. If the commissioner had attempted to limit the powers of the arbitrator to rule under the terms of the Basic Agreement, it would have made for a dramatic confrontation in federal court. But that did not happen.

A few months later, Kuhn discussed the powers of his office when testifying before Congress. He pointed out that since Judge Landis, the owners had given the commissioner the right "to decide what is in the 'best interests' of baseball."[35] While true, this ignored how much had changed since the conclusion of the first Basic Agreement. The confrontation between Kuhn and the player reps in San Juan in 1969 was testimony to that. It was clear that the union would challenge any effort he might make to substitute his judgment for that of an impartial arbitrator who had ended the reserve system. Miller had enunciated clearly the union's position on the status of the commissioner during the Hunter arbitration, namely that the Basic Agreement between the clubs and the union superceded any powers the commissioner might derive from his employers. Perhaps Miller had further arbitration cases in mind. Perhaps it was a warning to Kuhn not to interfere in the relationship between the players and the clubs. Perhaps Miller had said it so strongly as a means of impressing the same point upon Seitz.

Another insight into what took place in 1975 came years later in an exchange of letters between Kuhn and Seitz. In 1982 Seitz reminded Kuhn that when they agreed in 1975 that arbitration "was the wrong way to resolve disputes concerning the Reserve System," Seitz had asked for guidance on how to get the subject to the bargaining table, since "the clubs you represented had *already* refused to do so at my suggestion. You were unable to provide me with any guidance."[36] Kuhn recognized that he had not answered Seitz in 1975 and replied, "I did not do so because I felt the clubs' case was overwhelming as a matter of law, *and indeed still do*. Alas you felt otherwise" (emphasis added).[37]

Kuhn's role in Kansas City highlighted the problems of baseball's responses to the union since 1966. Oliver wondered aloud what Judge Landis might have done in similar circumstances, but he followed that immediately by asking how the union would have reacted and what the federal courts would have done to limit the powers of a Landis-like commissioner. Oliver was reminding everyone that labor relations, baseball, and labor relations in baseball had changed a lot since 1922.[38]

The owners and their commissioner had an understandable desire to retain the established system, which was more comfortable and profitable for them. An active union and an impartial arbitrator were elements that did not exist in that world. However, Oliver had no inclination to be part of the owners' version of baseball.[39]

When Oliver rendered a decision, he took pains to point out that the owners "seemed preoccupied" with how baseball had operated before the first Basic Agreement and wanted to run baseball as "though the Basic Agreement were not relevant." He saw no reason to allow them to retain "the unilateral practices of the owners from 1878 to the signing of the 1968 Basic agreement."[40] Oliver gave the same message to the owners that Gaherin had preached for years: the Basic Agreement(s) meant that there was a new relationship with the players, and any changes had to take place within that context.[41]

In their brief and in testimony, the owners staged a frontal attack on the integrity and the judgment of Peter Seitz. Since none of the facts in the Messersmith case were at issue, they claimed that Seitz had "arrogated to himself jurisdiction of a purported grievance" where no real grievance existed. He was wrong when he "determined that the historic reserve system was something different from what everyone thought it was and with the stroke of a pen . . . he adopted the baseless and disingenuous theory of the Association." His decision was a "sham attempt . . . [because he] did not like the Reserve System and wanted to change it."[42] These charges flew in the face of Seitz's reputation. It was the equivalent of charging him with unprofessional conduct. Seitz was enraged at the charge that he was acting as a "philosopher-king," a phrase the owners used in their brief. Judge Oliver pointed out that the brief "lifted the 'philosopher king' words out of context" from another decision. Seitz never forgot the ill grace with which the owners treated him, writing later to Kuhn, "I was dismissed unceremoniously with the conventional pink slip without a word of kindness except from John Gaherin, who, being a gentleman, could not act otherwise."[43]

Judge Oliver was unambiguous in his comments about Seitz's conduct and the decision he had rendered. Oliver said it "draws its essence from the collective bargaining agreement. . . . [Seitz did nothing] other than discharge the duties imposed upon him by Article X of the 1973 Basic Agreement with the highest sense of fidelity, responsibility and intelligence." Seitz could also take comfort in Oliver's remarks that he had acted "conscientiously in the achievement of [his] designated mission."[44]

Years later, Seitz described the circumstances of his dismissal as "ignominious and shameless in character and took no account of my professional career and general acceptance as an arbitrator. Perhaps the manner of the dismissal told the public more of the character of those who ran the Major Leagues of Baseball than it told them of my competence and integrity. . . . Professional baseball is regarded as the quintessential American sport. . . . However I doubt that there was anything essentially American in the mean and vindictive manner of my dismissal as arbitrator."[45] He wrote these comments in a private letter to Kuhn shortly after the latter had lost his job as commissioner in 1982. Kuhn replied, "I certainly am not surprised to learn of your feelings. . . . Baseball people like their brethren in other business often act in a graceless way. . . . I am truly sorry that you were subjected to that, at least on the part of some of our people."[46]

The ghost of the abortive Joint Study Committee came back to haunt the owners during the trial. According to Lou Hoynes, the owners' representatives on the committee had approached the reserve system with a "very pragmatic focus," which meant not doing "anything to gut the reserve system."[47] Oliver pointed out that there was no evidence in anyone's notes to show that the owners "would do anything to change the status quo."[48] Hoynes reinforced this by saying that he and his colleagues on the committee were "on a short tether . . . [in considering] the immutable core of the right to reserve the Player and *control his destiny throughout the career*" (emphasis added).[49] These ground rules were set by the owners and not shared by the players. The men who represented the owners had reached their conclusion before the Study Committee had its first meeting. Therefore, it was no surprise that the Players Association felt compelled to find other ways to achieve the purpose for which the committee had been established.

Oliver made the point repeatedly that it was not his job to ensure either the profitability of baseball or its traditions. He gave some advice to the owners about how they could salvage something. He reminded both sides that "Courts cannot force the parties to be reasonable." He showed them how their reading of the history of baseball had led them to their uncomfortable situation and that it had been virtually impossible for Seitz to come to any other decision. Oliver gave the owners one more chance to reconsider by reminding them that he found it impossible "to cite one [instance] where a labor dispute had ever been settled by any court decision." In an aside about Judge Cannon, Oliver mentioned that baseball had more than its share of judges and lawyers and that merely being in his court was doing damage to all the interested parties. Why didn't the owners sit down and negotiate in an industry that he praised for having "adopted the most innovative system of salary arbitration and advanced arbitration"?[50] Why not build on that foundation and create a workable modified reserve system? Over the course of the trial, Oliver came to understand that the owners had turned the reserve system into a kind of holy writ that had to be protected against any and all questions and challenges. Oliver's actual ruling in the case was almost an anticlimax: "No contractual bond existed between Messersmith and McNally" and their clubs.

The owners took Oliver's decision to the Court of Appeals, where they lost on a two-to-one ruling. The fundamental problem, as phrased by the Court of Appeals, was that "the disagreement lies over the degree of control necessary [by the owners] if these goals are to be achieved." Gaherin, Seitz, Oliver, and the Court of Appeals all agreed that "some form of the reserve system is needed" for the integrity of the game and for public confidence to be maintained.[51] Outsiders like Oliver had no trouble accepting the idea that the players as well as the owners had a vested interest in the future of baseball.

The proceedings in Judge Oliver's court did exactly the opposite of what the owners had wanted. Their own attorney had characterized their earlier actions toward reforming the reserve system as a sham. Their comments about Seitz portrayed them as poor losers. Their decision to take the ruling to court and to choose Kansas City called into question the legal skills of the men who represented the owners. Years later, Judge Oliver remarked that it seemed to him that one member of baseball's legal team had a solid grasp of where matters were heading, and "the more the trial went on, the more they pushed him into the background."[52] He was referring to Barry Rona, who had worked closely with Gaherin before and during the arbitration hearing.

PROTECTING FREE AGENCY

NEGOTIATIONS FOR THE 1976 BASIC AGREEMENT started in June 1975. Since they continued long after the Messersmith-McNally rulings, it is easy to forget that Peter Seitz handed down his ruling after negotiations had been going on for six months. Throughout the talks, the union focused on the reserve system as never before. It made a series of proposals for specific changes. The PRC representatives listened but did not respond. Miller and Gaherin recognized that whatever the outcome of Messersmith-McNally, it would have an impact on the structure of the next Basic Agreement. Their participation on the arbitration panel gave them a good idea of where Seitz might be heading.

In the summer of 1975 almost every baseball executive would have agreed with the view that Gaherin expressed to the union: "continuing and extensive changes" had been made to the reserve system, and "we have reached equity for all."[1] The union certainly did not see things in a similar light. Whatever changes might have taken place did not come close to satisfying the players. Miller's response to Gaherin's analysis reflected the union's dissatisfaction with the pace of change and what it saw as the efforts of the owners to fool the players into thinking that there had been progress. In Miller's words, "[there] never had been any negotiations on the Reserve System. The matter of salary arbitration had nothing to do with [changes]. The ten and five hardly affects anyone." He asked that bargaining take place on "an important and basic matter," and if the owners were not prepared to do that, there was "no point in joining a pretense" that the reserve system had been modified to anywhere near what the players found acceptable.[2]

From the start of the negotiations, both sides had talked about the need to "demonstrate good will." They discussed detailed concerns like the expense involved in various proposals. But it was clear that little would be accomplished until there was a resolution of Messersmith-McNally, either by Seitz or by negotiation. The union was willing to bargain, but Gaherin had little latitude to work on that front. In a conversation with Miller during a bargaining session, Gaherin interjected, "Our problem is monumental—on the threshold of a whole new relationship" and appealed to the union to understand what "is doable in this industry."[3]

At the first negotiating session in June 1975, Miller had stated that problems had occurred in the past because "one side read the other incorrectly."[4] That was his not-too-subtle warning to the owners that they had been wrong in 1972 to think that the players would not strike and could not maintain it if they did. The union made it clear that it did not want a similar misunderstanding to be the cause of another work stoppage. The sooner both sides got down to bargaining on the tough issues involved in the next Basic Agreement, the better chances were that they could conclude it without the need for a strike. Gaherin and Miller agreed that publicity about the negotiations was a problem, since the press was more interested in writing about conflict than in dealing with the issues. Both sides agreed to try to keep their discussion private. Over weeks of negotiations, difficult problems were raised, discussed, and resolved. The position of the union was clear: "all rules with which players are expected to comply are bargainable . . . [and] we want to bargain on all rules including proposed club rules for 1976."[5]

Early in the negotiations, Gaherin talked about a "wish" to discuss the reserve system. Before 1975 no discussion, let alone compromise, had been thinkable. Why did Gaherin now want to clutter up the Basic Agreement negotiations with it? Andy Messersmith and Dave McNally were the reasons. Despite Miller and Gaherin's effort to keep the negotiations private, two of the most influential executives decided to negotiate through the press. Frank Cashen of the Orioles warned that there was "'just no way we can exist under these conditions. We have troubled franchises now,'" and Ed Fitzgerald of the Brewers went even further, stating that if "'you gave him [Miller] everything he wanted, you'd put a franchise like this out of business. . . . Maybe all you'd have left would be one league with four or six clubs remaining in it. . . . There would be four major league franchises left and 100 ball players. The other 400 would be out of work.'"[6]

Cashen and Fitzgerald gave Miller a new set of targets, and he leveled his fire at both of them. He contacted Gaherin and reminded him that if any of the claims made by "authorized spokesmen of the Major League Clubs are true then the whole basis for the negotiations had changed and the [Players Association was entitled] to obtain the factual basis for the owners' allegations . . . [about] the financial ruin of existing franchises."[7] Miller demanded that the union be given detailed financial information for all of the twenty-four clubs, including their income, expenses, profit or loss, and cash flow. He knew he had no chance of getting the data. But he made the point that if the owners wanted to run a high-stakes bluff on the association, they should be prepared to see their hand called. Miller might not have been especially interested in public opinion, but he was not going to give the owners a free ride to claim that they alone were concerned with events that might "cripple the business" of baseball. He would accept some hyperbole from Gaherin behind closed doors, but not from any club officials in the press.

Cashen and Fitzgerald provided the union with the equivalent of the 1967 Buzzie Bavasi magazine articles. Miller used their remarks to tell the players that crying wolf was a bargaining tactic employed by the owners and that the players should put little trust in any of their claims. He sent all the players a summary of what Fitzgerald and Cashen had said along with a commentary that portrayed them in the worst possible light. They were accused of "using the shop worn tactic of downgrading the players by implying that the [association's] proposals were not those of the players. [Cashen and Fitzgerald] stuck to the traditional owners' line that *any* change would result in chaos." When Miller pointed out that there were "indications" that the owners were refusing to bargain in good faith for anything that would "bring balance to the reserve rules," he was setting the stage for possible future legal challenges as well as reminding the players of the long history of the inability to obtain any compromises in the reserve system.[8]

The union's officials spent a lot of time keeping the players informed. But they certainly were much more than a transmission device for information. Their job was to analyze situations and make recommendations. The players had faith in them because they had a track record of success and they seemed able to anticipate the actions of the owners and the consequences of these actions. The latter was clear in the "observations" that Miller sent out to all the players when the negotiations for the Basic Agreement heated up. His memo opened with the assertion that the owners were "following the same tired procedure of the past—draw the talks out through the winter, pretend to negotiate, refuse to work out their most basic matters, confuse the public with their distorted versions of the issues, and once again try their game of 'chicken' with the players to see if they can divide the players through an owner-manufactured 'crisis.' Such a policy, if it can be called that, is an exercise in futility."[9] The events that unfolded over the next nine months proved that Miller was as good a prophet as he was a negotiator.

Miller decided to put the baseball situation into a broader context, one that was calculated to give the players cause for pride in their own accomplishments and fear for the future.[10] The National Football League Players Association (NFLPA) had just ended a disastrous strike. The NFL owners and the league executives had come up with an ingenious method to limit the freedom of players to move between clubs. A player could move after playing out his option, but only under the limitations of the so-called Rozelle Rule, a regulation named after Commissioner Pete Rozelle. A club that lost a player to free agency had the right to receive compensation from the player's new club. The compensation was a player of equal status, to be determined by the commissioner. In effect, the Rozelle Rule turned free agency into a form of trades, but one that held great risks for any club that pursued a free agent, since it would have no control over the player that it would lose. General managers were not willing to play a form of personnel roulette and take the chance of losing players that might be irreplaceable. The application of the Rozelle Rule meant that free agency did not exist in the NFL.[11]

The NFLPA mounted a legal challenge to the Rozelle Rule while also trying to modify it as part of its collective bargaining strategy for a new basic agreement. The Rozelle Rule was the major concern for both sides. The union used the slogan, "Players demand freedom." The owners contended that "the league could not survive without it." The rhetoric was reminiscent of what had been going on in baseball since the Flood suit.

The NFL players struck starting July 1 and told their members not to attend the preseason training camps. By July 21, the union reported 108 defections, and by July 29 it had reached 248, almost 20 percent of the membership. The owners remained united in their refusal to grant any concessions, and more players continued to return. By August 10 the owners threatened to end negotiations unless the union dropped the "freedom issue," and the next day, Ed Garvey, the director of the union, announced that the strike was over, although the union would continue to press legal action against the Rozelle Rule. Later, Garvey described the situation: "'The strike had collapsed and we lost. . . . It was time for plan B.'"[12]

Miller and the baseball players liked to remind people how their union had fared in comparison to those in other sports. Miller had taken the time to write a CBS correspondent to object to his comments that the NFLPA was the first sports union "not in the nature of a joke." Miller pointed out that by 1972, the MLBPA was the first sports union that had negotiated a collective bargaining agreement, arbitration for grievances, and used "concerted action in withholding services."[13]

The complete victory for the NFL owners might have influenced some baseball owners to think they could emulate the success of their counterparts in football. The baseball players saw lessons in the fiasco of the NFLPA. When Miller reminded his members that the failure of baseball owners "to recognize the vast differences between our organization and that of the football players displays incredibly poor judgement," he probably was thinking along the same lines as Garvey had been when he explained the failure of the strike to one of the teams. He told the players on the Atlanta Falcons, "'We didn't stick together . . . so we lost.'"[14]

It is easy to see the quality of the leadership of the MLBPA as the sole reason for its success compared to the problems of the NFLPA. Miller and Moss did play a huge role, but the differences between the sports, the players, executives, and the owners were even more critical. Pete Rozelle was famous for having convinced the owners to adopt his slogan, "Think League," as the basis for many of their decisions. His ability to persuade the owners to accept his vision created the structure of the sport. The short war between two established leagues had graphically shown the owners the cost of competition and the value of giving up much of their autonomy to a strong commissioner. The owners in football created a form of corporate socialism as the basis for their economic success. Sharing television money, the primary source of their revenue, was a conscious decision by the owners not to compete with one another.

Rozelle was employed by the owners, but he had gained virtual autonomy from them. He exercised far more authority in his sport than any other commissioner. His success in negotiating lucrative television contracts, attracting favorable media attention for the league, and enforcing measures that added to the prosperity of every team convinced the owners to accept his authority. The new popularity of the sport and the quest for franchises enabled Rozelle to gain concessions from Congress that allowed the league to protect the attributes it thought it needed to prosper—the common draft and the division of television revenues. The NFL owners expected their commissioner to deal with problems facing them. Most baseball owners and their commissioner talked about the ambiguous powers that had been granted to Commissioner Landis to deal with the aftermath of the 1919 Black Sox scandal. Since 1946 the owners had kept the commissioner on a short leash. Instead of talking about the traditions of the sport, the football owners dealt with a new reality, stayed out of policy issues, and followed a commissioner who was doing the job they wanted him to do.

A crucial distinction between the two sports lay in the attitudes of the players, which were shaped by their individual experiences and the differences between the two sports. Football players came directly from college. Most of them had spent their high school and college years being reminded how important they were and receiving special treatment. Baseball players had the experience of the minor leagues to toughen them and to give them a more cynical view of the business side of the sport. This created an antagonistic attitude toward management.

The football draft had a further negative impact on the players. It destroyed whatever contract leverage a player might have had at the start of his career. For many of them, the weeks before they joined their professional teams was the apex of their career. This was when they were completing highly publicized careers as college players. They should have been in a position to capitalize on that. A rookie in the NFL should have had the same power to negotiate for terms as when a baseball player achieved free agent status, but the results were very different.

From the start of their time in the NFL, the players knew that the owners had the power. The relatively small difference in the skill level between top-quality college players and many NFL players meant that there was a steady supply of potential NFL players arriving every year. With the exception of a few star performers, most NFL players lived with the insecurity of knowing before each season that someone who was paid less and was younger could take their job. The possibility of career-ending injuries was part of the everyday life of pro football players and added to their insecurity. Getting involved with the union or pushing it to make demands that might antagonize the owners meant taking a risk that seemed too high for most players.

The games themselves bred different attitudes. One might think that because football is more of a team activity than baseball it might have fostered a strong sense of unity among the players that would translate into solid support for their union. Just the opposite was the case. Football is a game of discipline and set plays where an authoritarian coach and his staff set the standards and do much of the thinking for their players. Football players are conditioned to take orders and to accept the status quo. That is part of what makes them successful at the job of winning games.

The biggest difference between the membership of the two unions was the unwillingness of stars to get involved in the NFLPA, let alone to push it to challenge the existing business structure of the sport.[15] After 1966, the members of the MLBPA convinced themselves that they had grievances and that they had a mechanism to force changes. From then on, they needed unity and leadership. That was when the stars assumed an indispensable role. Players like Joe Torre, Brooks Robinson, Bob Boone, and Sal Bando took responsibility on themselves. Established major leaguers were willing to take chances with their own careers to provide the leadership that the union needed. Lesser players grew to depend on them and trust them. Football players looked to their coaches for direction; baseball players looked to their teammates.

In the fall of 1975 the staff and Executive Board of the MLBPA was preparing its members for a fight that could be more difficult and disruptive than the strike of 1972. Red Smith presented an analysis that went to the heart of what was happening. A decade earlier, he had been a firm supporter of the need for baseball to retain its traditional structure and had seen little need for an active players' union. Since the Flood suit, Smith had been one of the most active supporters of the union in the press. In an article written days before a crucial negotiating session between the union and the PRC, he talked about the need to "modify the reserve systems to take most of the curse off that feudal institution." The prose was distinctively Smith, but the sentiments echoed Miller.

Smith was supporting the players' proposal that would have allowed anyone to become a free agent after five years in organized baseball. He wanted to address "the bugaboo always raised to defend the reserve system," the danger that all the star players would race one another to play in glamour spots with high-profile teams. Smith pointed out that the players' proposal established a free agent pool and that the players were suggesting something other than total free agency. They understood the possibility of the competitive nature of the sport being damaged. Smith used baseball history to make a telling point. Under the current system the Yankees had dominated baseball for years, but they were "never the richest club nor the wildest spenders." They were a championship organization because men like Ed Barrow and George Weiss "did their jobs better than anybody else."

Smith tried to lay to rest the decade-old misconception that was shared by a majority of the owners and the public: that Miller told the players what to think. Smith pointed out, in an almost matter-of-fact fashion, *"incidentally, this is the players' plan, not Marvin Miller's"* (emphasis added). His analysis, that "in baseball, as in other industries, the bosses tend to blame the union leader for everything the union does," described a reality that few executives in baseball wanted to recognize.[16]

Smith echoed John Gaherin's sentiments. Baseball was an industry, and the owners were bosses. The players were workers who were willing and capable of analyzing their own situation and deciding how the executive director of their union should work on their behalf. It was hard for owners, writers, and fans to understand this, despite the fact they'd had almost a decade to become accustomed to the idea. The decisions and the tactics involved in 1975 and 1976 would be a further test of the involvement of the players in determining the future of their industry and their own careers.

In 1976 the players were facing the strong possibility of a strike. Much had changed since 1972. That strike had contained an element of bravado on the part of many players and the need to show themselves and the owners that they could remain solid and not be pushed around any longer. In many ways, the most important issue involved in the strike had been the strike itself. If a strike took place in 1976, it would be because the players were concerned enough about the newly won free agency to take the risks involved in a work stoppage.

Miller and Gaherin were trying to bargain while they were waiting for Seitz's decision. Tempers were shorter than usual at the bargaining table, and the tone was more antagonistic than at any time in the past. Miller talked about the "exasperation, frustration, and sorrow" in the negotiations and the "highly destructive acts" of the owners in trying to overturn the Hunter decision and trying to use the courts to block a ruling in Messersmith-McNally, which "raised questions of the motives you [ownership] have."[17]

Gaherin talked about "deception," "obfuscation," and "no-win positions." He reminded everyone that "we [the owners] have been dealing with the Reserve System since the inception of your [Miller's] tenure." That led to a brief exchange that showed that both of them knew what was at stake at the end of November 1975. When Miller asked, "Was there anything in your [current] proposals which would liberalize Reserve System?" Gaherin's answer was, "No. Wanted to discuss." Miller concluded this exchange, "Same thing you've been saying for ten years."[18]

One public spokesman for the owners went further and declared, "Any change in the reserve system would hurt them, the average player, much more than the owners. . . . [That would] hurt baseball. . . . End the reserve clause and you drive the wealthy owners out of baseball and fly by nighters take over the ballclubs."[19]

The tone and substance of the negotiations for the Basic Agreement changed after Seitz's ruling on December 23, 1975. When the owners used their clear legal right to try to get the ruling overturned in court, Miller tried to assume the moral high ground by chiding the owners for going to court "with ill-conceived and frivolous litigation."[20] This was not the first time that Miller accused the owners of something like "several layers of bad faith." He urged them to end a process that was "counterproductive and extremely destructive to any mutual effort to find solutions to problems through mature collective bargaining." In his remarks, Miller combined his faith in collective bargaining with the pragmatic consideration based on the union's victory in Messersmith-McNally. He was correct that the owners were wasting time and money trying to undermine a decision imposed by a process that they had accepted and an arbitrator whom they had approved. But that was their decision to make.

Despite Miller's rhetoric, there was no moral difference between the tactics of the owners after Messersmith-McNally and the union after the Flood decision. The goals clearly were different. The union had been trying for years to get some changes in the system, and the owners had refused to talk about it. There was also a practical difference. The players had nothing to lose by adopting new tactics after the Flood case. That was not true for the owners in 1976. When Miller objected to Gaherin's comment that there was a "'pall' on the negotiations," he was ignoring the obvious.[21] Gaherin reminded him that "it is unrealistic for either of us to *pretend* that the Messersmith and McNally cases have not cast a pall over the Basic Agreement and Benefit Plan negotiations" (emphasis added).[22]

Gaherin complained about "the anger" that was now present in the talks. Miller criticized the commissioner for an "attitude after the Hunter decision [that was] arrogant" and for trying to negate the impact of an arbitration decision, when "he knows damn well he has no such authority."[23] Until 1976 the focus of the negotiations for every Basic Agreement had been efforts by the union to gain concessions and achieve some kind of parity in their relationship with the owners. The Seitz ruling altered that equation. The power relationship had changed, the issues had changed, and the expectations of both sides had changed. For the first time in its history, the leadership of the Players Association was faced with the prospect of being asked to make concessions, not from its bargaining position, but from what it had already gained.

Messersmith's personal situation introduced another issue that had the potential to poison the negotiating atmosphere and derail the process that was needed for the new Basic Agreement. One way for the owners to sabotage the impact of Seitz's ruling was to present a united front in refusing to sign Messersmith to a contract. He was free to negotiate with any team, but was anyone obligated to deal with him? Since one of the oldest clichés of baseball and the moan of all general managers was "we never have enough pitching," it would have looked peculiar if a star pitcher was available and no one tried to sign him.

Miller made it a point not to get involved in public discussions about a specific player's performance. Messersmith was different. When Miller accused a prominent reporter of writing two articles "of which you can not be proud," he was complaining about stories that claimed that Messersmith might be a sore-armed pitcher who would not be worth much money to a new club. The purpose of this letter was to warn the writer that "you have been used [by anonymous scouts] in a most unprincipled way for an obvious purpose," to depress the market for Messersmith and to attempt to kill free agency at birth.[24]

The relative positions of the parties had changed dramatically. Even Bob Feller, a consistent critic of Miller and the union, remarked on the differences. In a newspaper article, he said that the owners had been warned thirty years earlier but had not paid attention. Feller was worried because "'now the garbage has hit the fan'" and salaries were going out of sight. He sounded like Frank Cashen or the commissioner when he warned that he was "'afraid half the clubs won't be able to make it.'" But he did recognize that some fault lay with the owners, "'who thought they could go on with their slaves rules forever. They felt they were untouchable [and] they fell apart in a hurry.'"[25]

It was noticeable to everyone just how much had changed in a decade. When Miller had toured spring training camps in 1966, he was regarded by many of the players with a combination of curiosity and apathy. They had little idea of what to expect or what to ask him. They had a general feeling that something should be done to improve their situation, but even those players who were interested in the association had no specifics in mind. A decade later, when spring training camps were supposed to open, the reality of baseball was different. In negotiations for the 1976 Basic Agreement, the union was trying to deal with the fruits of its most important victory and cope with circumstances that no one could have foreseen even a few years earlier. No one involved in baseball—owners, players, writers, or fans—could ignore the impact of Messersmith-McNally, least of all Gaherin, who now had to get some modified form of free agency.

Less than a month before the spring training camps were supposed to open, Gaherin told Miller and Moss that "[there is] nobody sitting on this side of the table with authority to make an Agreement which includes the Seitz decision. . . . [it] is not something we can live with as a factor in our reserve system." The union assumed that Seitz's ruling would be maintained and was trying to figure out how much, if anything, it should concede back to the owners. Miller's distrust was apparent at the negotiations: "The approach you have used so far has been—Messersmith decision does not exist. [This is] not acceptable. . . . In view of what happened, I shudder to think of what you would have proposed if you had won."[26] Miller could vent his feelings, but he still had to fashion a new Basic Agreement.

Each side made proposals about possible limits on total free agency. The owners proposed ten years' service in the major leagues as the basis for free agency plus restrictions on salary arbitration. They were acting as if they had won in Messersmith-McNally. Miller also had a potential problem within the ranks of the union. The Seitz ruling meant that every player had the possibility of becoming a free agent within a year. Some players might object to giving up those rights. That could lead to a split if the union had to face a lockout. There also was the possibility that a player might sue his union. In February Miller responded to a reporter's question about the "concessions" the players wanted from the owners by reminding him that there was no need for any: "They [the owners] don't have to do anything . . . because the players aren't asking for anything. They already have gotten what they want from arbitrator Peter Seitz, and Judge Oliver."[27]

The union had to figure out how to compromise. Miller made it clear that "the concept of compensation [for losing a free agent], if it is limited . . . is acceptable. . . . The concept that we ought to do what we can in the interest of competitive balance is also acceptable."[28] What stood in the way of compromise was the owners' unwillingness to recognize that the union had already made a major concession in accepting that there would be some limits on free agency. Any further bargaining would have to be on terms acceptable to the players.

Until a new Basic Agreement was negotiated, "free agency" meant that players had the ability to move between clubs with no restrictions. As noted earlier, one of the features about baseball that attracted potential owners was a sense of certainty and a knowledge that they could run their businesses with a minimum of interference. Even competing clubs were part of a shared enterprise in which they all needed one another. Control was more than just an abstraction to management. It enabled the owners to get the most out of their investment, whether that meant cash or emotional satisfaction. The activities of the union had chipped away at the freedom of the owners, and the Seitz ruling had delivered a body blow to what the owners thought was the basis for their power. In the aftermath of Messersmith-McNally, the owners found themselves in a position analogous to what the players had faced when Curt Flood told them he was going to file suit. He had forced the players to take a stand on one side or the other. In 1976 each owner had to decide how much it was worth to take a stand to force the players to give up some benefits of the recent arbitration decision. The negotiations for the next Basic Agreement gave them the chance to regain some of their lost control.

Bob Howsam was one of the leading advocates of the "No Agreement, No Camps" approach toward the players. He explained that drastic measures were needed because "'as a result of arbitration, the entire reserve system has changed. We have virtually no control at all. This undermines the foundation of the game.'" The lockout was necessary because the owners were "'seeking only to carry on in the traditions of the game as it was.'"[29] Howsam summarized all the conflicts of the past ten years when he concluded that the current struggle over the new Basic Agreement was about control. There is little doubt that Miller and the players agreed with him on that.

Howsam's description of what had disappeared was not just romantic hyperbole. He was describing a former reality that no owner wanted to lose and few wanted to modify. There was no question that the recent activities of the union had altered the "traditions of the game." For the first time, Howsam recognized that "there is some room for modification in some ways." He stepped back from any realistic concessions when he added, "we must have an agreement that allows us to do the job."[30] Minor concessions like what Howsam suggested were not going to have any influence on the union. It was willing to negotiate about the specifics of free agency, but it would not allow team executives to define anything unilaterally.

The issue facing baseball executives in 1976 was how to cope with a new system that had some version of free agency at its core. The immediate reaction of the owners that spring was to play what they thought was their trump card and to deprive the players of a chance to gain whatever benefits free agency might have for them. The owners decided not to open the spring training camps and lock out the players. When it began, Miller observed correctly that the owners "have miscalculated completely in terms of pressure the lockout will cause. . . . Clear to players. [They're] getting pissed off."[31]

In mid-March, an unlikely third party entered the negotiations, Commissioner Kuhn. A few days earlier, Miller had publicly talked about the possibility of the commissioner ordering the camps to be opened. Kuhn had replied privately to Miller and Gaherin, "I would be willing to get that done [open the camps] if there were sufficient progress towards a solution, particularly on the reserve system."[32]

An increasingly large number of players came to the negotiating sessions, a minimum of twelve, as opposed to the normal three or four. Gaherin presented "our last final offer" on March 15. A player could become a free agent after seven years in the major leagues plus an option year. The owners' earlier version had required ten years before free agency. There would be no salary arbitration for the next two years, limits on it for the next two years, and thereafter it would exist only by mutual consent. The owners would have the right to reopen the Basic Agreement for negotiations after two years. This would give them a chance to see its impact on the clubs. Gaherin told the assembled players, Miller, and Moss that the agreement "must be ratified on or before April 1, 1976, and . . . we do not intend to open spring training until the [association's] board acts affirmatively."[33]

Twenty-three players attended the meeting. They included veterans like Joe Torre and Jim Kaat, who had seen the union when it was a supplicant, stars like Johnny Bench and Willie Stargell, who had not been very involved in the union, and younger activists like Bob Boone and Ted Simmons. After Gaherin had presented the "final offer," Miller asked Gaherin to affirm what he had said the day before about the proposal and what the alternative would be if the players rejected the proposal. Gaherin was not sure, but he assumed it would be withdrawn and the status quo would be in effect. Miller responded for the union, "if it is take it or leave it, they will leave it."[34] It was a short meeting.

On March 15, the Player Relations Committee met with the commissioner. The PRC was responsible for maintaining the lockout and for negotiating the terms of a new Basic Agreement. The PRC misjudged both sides of the lockout. It underestimated the resolve of the players to defend their newly won free agency and overestimated the unity of the owners. Bill Veeck, newly returned to baseball, once again acted as a maverick and made clear his desire to open the camps. Behind the scenes, a much more powerful force was talking about the need to start the season and to negotiate in a less confrontational atmosphere: Walter O'Malley of the Dodgers. Veeck and O'Malley might have represented opposite poles of respectability among the owners, but they shared a streak of independent pragmatism and an understanding of the necessity to deal with the union. The difference was how much influence O'Malley had with the commissioner.

Kuhn also talked with Jim Kaat, a veteran player who was respected by both sides. Kaat pointed out forcefully to Kuhn that the lockout was damaging any prospects for a settlement. Kuhn was in the uncomfortable position of disagreeing with a powerful faction among the owners, including his good friend and confidant, Ed Fitzgerald, the chairman of the PRC. The commissioner returned to New York, and after talking with Gaherin and Sandy Hadden, he made the decision to order the camps opened on March 17.[35] It was a decision guaranteed to distress some owners. Kuhn had another problem. He was unable to contact either Howsam or Fitzgerald before the decision to open the camps appeared in the press. Kuhn gained public plaudits for his action. However, some owners believed that if Kuhn had not opened the camps, the association would have been starved into capitulation, and the owners would have been able to restore a reserve system little different from pre-Messersmith.

Kuhn took an independent, courageous stance based on his sense that opening the camps was the only way to salvage the situation. The owners had to find someone to blame for their loss of power. Gaherin was released in the aftermath of the 1976 negotiations. A few years later, Kuhn's efforts to retain his position were destroyed by owners who still objected to what he had done in the spring of 1976.

The lockout and the negotiations for the Basic Agreement almost obscured the fact that Andy Messersmith took advantage of free agency to sign a lucrative contract with the Atlanta Braves. This relationship between freedom and money was not lost on the other players. It made them even more determined to limit what they would bargain away. Catfish Hunter's contract demonstrated how much money might flow out of free agency. But his situation was exceptional in two respects. He got his freedom from the A's because of the peculiarities of his contract. In addition, other players understood the magnitude of his talent. He was a great pitcher, the most consistent in the American League, and was headed for the Hall of Fame. Every major league player had a significant ego, or they would not have gotten that far, but they were also realistic judges of talent, their own and other players'. Even a good pitcher would have problems realistically thinking of himself in Catfish Hunter's class, but comparing himself to Andy Messersmith was not that far out of the question.[36] That reinforced the need for the players not to give up the chance to be the next Messersmith. The owners had talked about equity for years, and now the players had their own working definition. It meant staying in baseball long enough and being good enough to follow in the footsteps of Andy Messersmith.

Once the lockout ended, the tough work of hammering out the details of a Basic Agreement remained. Gaherin faced divisions among the owners, ranging from Howsam and Busch, who were determined to keep the old system entirely in place, to newer owners like Ted Turner of the Braves and George Steinbrenner of the Yankees, who saw free agency as a way to bring their teams back to respectability. Miller and Moss had to take into account a broad range of views among the players, from those who rejected any restrictions to those who feared that the new system would bring chaos.

The negotiators had to come up with restrictions on free agency that were acceptable to the players. One proposed method was to limit the number of free agents that any club could sign. This was based on the number of free agents that were available. The thorniest issue was how many years of major league experience a player should have before he could become eligible for free agency. When the owners came down to eight years, the players responded with six years. Some of the players wondered why there should be any restrictions at all. The most vocal of that group was Mike Marshall, who thought that "a player should for any reason he wanted be a free agent. . . . It would have brought higher salaries sooner, but the best players would have been happier."[37] What Marshall wanted was a system that emphasized absolute freedom and what he thought was best, in the short term, for lower-paid players.

A sizeable majority of the members of the association was disposed to take a different approach. They reckoned that salaries paid for the top free agents determined the contours of the market for other players. There were important pragmatic concerns that led them to accept some restrictions. They wanted to end the stalemate. The six-year arrangement seemed to be the best the union could expect at the time without the possibility of a protracted work stoppage.

There were also market concerns that influenced the willingness of the players to accept the six-year restriction. Hunter and Messersmith were special, and clubs could be expected to compete against one another to employ them. But what about the average ballplayer who became a free agent? What would be the market for him, and what would happen to the overall market if there were dozens of free agents competing with one another? There were different views of how the market would operate. One version assumed that every player who became a free agent opened up a job for someone, and therefore there could never be an oversupply of free agents. The other idea was that by establishing an artificially restricted market for free agents in any given year, the bargaining power of a free agent was increased. The best player available that year at a given position became, in bargaining terms, the best player at that position.

The owners made a decision based on tradition and realistic concerns about talent. Control and the ability to plan for a few years in the future were enormously important to most owners. There were solid baseball and economic reasons for wanting to retain younger players for a significant period of time, and the new proposal allowed that. A majority of the owners lined up to support the proposal.

The most uncomfortable moments for Miller came from an unlikely source, Charlie Finley, the always outspoken owner of the Oakland A's. "Make 'em all free agents" was his approach to handling Messersmith-McNally. Finley understood the dynamics of free-market capitalism, but he had never learned much about the history of baseball or what concerned his fellow owners. Most owners responded predictably and reflexively to Finley's idea.[38] Something that came from him was bound to bring opposition. As Ewing Kauffman described it years later, "If Finley pointed out the window at noon and said the sun was shining, many of the owners would have said it was dark."[39] In 2000, Kuhn thought, "'Maybe Charlie was right. . . . I don't say that too often.'"[40] In 1976, anything that lessened the owners' control was bad; something eliminating it was catastrophic. Harry Dalton realized that there might be some merit in the proposal, but he "was worried about the rich clubs . . . and needed to put restrictions on what they could do."[41] Kauffman certainly understood market concerns, but he was also sure "that teams with the most money would have all the best players soon . . . every owner seemed opposed to Finley's crazy suggestion."[42]

From Miller's perspective, a dangerous idea could not have come from a better source than Charlie Finley. When Miller tried to put himself in the position of an owner, Finley's idea made sense. That was why it disturbed Miller so much. It was one of the few times he was genuinely worried by a proposal put forward by the other side ("Marvin was scared to death by Finley's idea," Mike Marshall claimed),[43] and his ability to show no emotions and seemingly ignore events served Miller well. He did not respond to the proposal for total free agency and continued to work with Gaherin to fashion a compromise. Miller hoped the owners would not shed their views about the importance of control or drop their prejudices against anything Finley said.

Miller also had the potentially uncomfortable task of finding a way to phrase the union's rejection of a proposal for freedom. That was, after all, exactly what players had been talking about for years. He asked himself, "How do you turn down 'freedom'?"[44] Luckily for him and the Executive Board, they were never forced into a position of having to answer that question. Gaherin was relieved by the way the compromise worked and thought, "I got something from Miller because he knew that the players needed something for their own stability."[45]

Miller recalls that "no one knew then or now [1989] what was the magic figure."[46] In any case, he got a deal for the players that did not include major league compensation for free agency and gave them the added economic benefit of selling their talent in a restricted market. For decades, the owners had enjoyed the advantages of being part of a cartel. In the 1976 Basic Agreement the players used a similar power to set the standards for their future contracts. The negotiations for the adjustments to free agency showed that the classic attributes of free bargaining, compromise, concessions, self-interest, and a recognition that the other side had interests could work even in baseball. It had taken a work stoppage, lots of angry rhetoric, and the plausible threat of another stoppage to pave the way for the agreement, but those were qualities that were common in labor bargaining in the world outside of baseball.

The tentative agreement that was reached on July 11, 1976, was the product of thirteen months of negotiations and the unusual circumstances created by the Messersmith-McNally decision. It still had to be ratified by a majority of the members of the Players Association and the owners. Every change made in the proposals had been in response to the objections raised by the union. In April the owners had offered what they thought were serious concessions, including eight years toward free agency, financial compensation for the loss of a free agent, and no salary arbitration except by mutual consent. The union replied that the first was unrealistic and the latter two were totally unacceptable.

Before the players voted on whether to accept the Basic Agreement, they received a memorandum from Miller describing the tentative agreement and what had been involved in obtaining it. Given where the association had been ten years earlier, it was an exercise in hyperbolic understatement when Miller wrote, "I think you will agree that they [the provisions] represent the greatest improvements made to date by the Players Association and its members. . . . They incorporate a number of new important rights which guarantee greater democracy and dignity for players, as well as significantly improved benefits." The statement that prefaced the text of the proposed agreement showed how much things had changed: "The right of players, *under their present contracts,* to become free agents ('1' and '1') [one-year renewal] have been preserved."[47]

If any powerful owner or members of the PRC had been wise enough to take seriously Miller's summation of the events of 1976, the destructive strike of 1981 might have been avoided. In 1976 he pointed out how the players responded to threats and made it clear that they would not accept any form of compensation that placed significant limits on free agency. In 1976 the union preserved something that until recently had been only a bizarre dream. Miller chose to remind the players that it had been their "refusal to be panicked . . . by such tactics as an unjustified lockout . . . and their ability to remain unified in the face of an organized attempt to divide them" that had made the victory possible. He gave them a chance to gloat when he talked about the many "final best offers" made by the owners and asked the players to "compare them with the proposed new Agreement before you."[48]

1980-THE STRIKE THAT DIDN'T HAPPEN

THE 1976 BASIC AGREEMENT allowed baseball to go forward while it adjusted to the new world of free agency. No one could be sure what would be the impact of breaking with a century-old regimen. For years the owners had based their strategy and their public relations on the assumption that free agency would not happen, and if it did, it would damage the sport, both on and off the field.

The union's position about free agency had been slightly more complicated. It claimed that the existing system had to be changed because it was fundamentally unfair and one-sided. The players might not have had a firm idea about what the future might bring, but they were convinced that anything the owners put forward as a defense of the reserve system was a self-serving exaggeration.

The two sides had to negotiate a new Basic Agreement before the start of the 1980 season. By that time, there had been four seasons to see how free agency worked for the players, the owners, and baseball. In the National League, the Pirates and the Phillies dominated the Eastern Division and the Reds and the Dodgers traded titles in the West. In the American League East, the Orioles and the Yankees shared championships. For the former it was business as usual; for the latter it was a return to the glories that had disappeared when an aging team had not been rebuilt after the mid-1960s. In the West, the title run of the A's ended in 1976. The Kansas City Royals won four of the next five division championships, and their string of successes was broken in 1979 when the California Angels won their first division title.

The owners of the Yankees, Angels, and A's reacted dramatically to the advent of free agency. George Steinbrenner had gained control of the Yankees in 1973 and quickly became the personification of the publicity-seeking owner who interfered directly in the management of his team. After serving a one-year suspension resulting from his involvement with illegal political contributions, Steinbrenner threw himself into changing the Yankees. The team outbid other clubs for Catfish Hunter and got to the World Series in 1976, where it was swept by the Reds. At the end of that season, the Yankees signed the most high-profile free agent available, Reggie Jackson. In 1977 he was the star of the Yankees' first championship team since 1963. Gene Autry, the owner of the Angels, opened the checkbook in response to free agency, and the Angels brought in a number of highly paid players.

Arbitration and free agency were the prices of success, and both took a toll on Charlie Finley. The owner of the A's had the best and most flamboyant team in baseball. Finley always operated on a shoestring, and after a while he had to pay the market rate for his players. Great teams are the product of special players. Once arbitration came into effect, the players who made the A's the best team in baseball were among the most successful in the new system. Jackson and Bando won big awards in 1974, and the next season many of the A's stars did not sign their contracts and played out their options. In 1976 Finley traded Jackson and Ken Holtzman. In June he sold Vida Blue to the Yankees for $1.5 million and Joe Rudi and Rollie Fingers to the Red Sox for $1.5 million each. That was one owner's solution to the new market. The money might have given Finley the breathing spell he needed to create another winning club, but Commissioner Kuhn never gave him the opportunity. In an unprecedented step, the commissioner voided the sales, acting in the "best interest of baseball."

There was a serious question about whether Kuhn had the power to stop an owner from selling players. The A's owner decided to test it in federal court. Finley's suit placed his fellow owners in an uncomfortable position. They did not want a situation where a commissioner could exercise real power over the owners. After all, he was their employee. If Finley prevailed, however, whatever damages he was awarded would have to be paid by the other owners. The commissioner's office had no funds of its own. The personal hostility of many owners toward Finley made it easier for them to support Kuhn, at least in this instance.

The way the owners rallied to the support of the commissioner had its roots in the new relationship between the owners and the players. Finley had taken extreme measures as a way to cope with the results of salary arbitration and free agency. But how much did it differ from what Connie Mack had done immediately after World War I and in the 1930s when he had sold players from two championship teams in order to cut salaries and make a profit?

The owners talked publicly about the need to restore stability to baseball. One possible approach was to resurrect the idea of a "strong commissioner." This was nothing more than talk. The owners did not want a commissioner who could exercise independent power, and many of them still thought Kuhn had acted against their interests when he opened the spring training camps at the start of the 1976 season. Nevertheless, it was a useful public relations device to support the commissioner. In the short term, that could have the joint benefits of getting rid of Charlie Finley and making it appear that baseball was going back to Landis-like probity. There was always time to rein in the commissioner if he tried to limit the autonomy and power of the owners in the future.

It is easy to look at some post-1976 developments in statistical terms. Throughout the 1970s there was a steady rise in overall attendance at major league games. At the start of the decade, clubs averaged 1.20 million fans per season. By 1980 that had risen to 1.93 million, an increase of 60 percent. Gross revenues for the sport went up by 144 percent, and television revenues increased by 355 percent. The values of the individual clubs appeared to appreciate during the period. In 1970 the top sale price for a club had been $10.8 million. In 1980 it was $21.1 million, an increase that exceeded the rate of inflation.

It would be hard for even a dedicated supporter of free agency to prove that there were direct correlations between free agency and the economic prosperity that baseball was enjoying. It would be impossible for the men who had opposed free agency on the grounds that it would destroy competition and would bankrupt clubs to show how the events since 1976 supported their fears.

It was clear that baseball was going through a transitional period. Despite, or perhaps because of, the lack of hard evidence about the impact of free agency, players and owners clung to their previous views. The players saw individual gains, renewed competition on the field, and greater popularity. The owners saw the end of a system that had worked for a century and the start of something that was both unfamiliar and dangerous. One set of figures was plain for both sides to see. These were the average salaries for major league baseball players between 1975 and 1979. They had risen from $44,676 to $113,558. The biggest increases had been between

1976 and 1977 (from $51,501 to $76,066, a rise of almost 48 percent) and between 1977 and 1978 (from $76,066 to $99,876, a rise of 31 percent).[1]

The two sides were worlds apart in their interpretation of what those numbers said about the past and the future of baseball. The players concluded that the new salary structure showed that there was a lot of money coming into baseball, and more of it was making its way into the pockets of the players than had been the case in the past. The new salaries were proof to the players that the old system had placed an artificial and unfair cap on salaries. The owners saw the new salaries as the road marker on the path to the financial ruin of baseball, the sign of a system out of control. Neither baseball nor the continued stewardship of the owners could survive if the trend continued. The owners probably agreed with one conclusion drawn by the players: the cause of these changes had been the union and the way in which Marvin Miller had won time and again against the PRC and its chief negotiator.

By 1980 the owners were determined not to repeat the mistakes of the past. They would enforce unity among themselves and cushion any economic losses a strike might cause them. They would employ a bargainer who would not demonstrate what so many influential owners thought was John Gaherin's willingness to appease the union in order to avoid conflict. The negotiations for the 1980 Basic Agreement were going to be the time when the owners finally stood up to Miller and the union and restored the proper balance of power within baseball. The owners' sense of loss and desire to make up for past defeats played an important role in how the negotiations unfolded.[2]

When the two sides started the bargaining process in 1979 for the 1980 Basic Agreement, almost all the circumstances had changed drastically since 1976. In the aftermath of Messersmith-McNally, the players had higher salaries and more freedom than any of them would have imagined possible even a few years earlier. Now it was the union that talked about the need to protect the game and ensure its prosperity. They equated the improvements with the advent of free agency and set themselves up as the guarantors of the gains made by both sides. The union was attempting to turn a decade of owners' rhetoric on its head and claim that it was the players who were trying to protect the "good of the game" against the owners, who wanted to make changes just to advance their selfish interests.

There was also a level of personal animosity that had not been present in earlier negotiations. Some of the owners and Miller had a genuine personal dislike for one another, but they were not usually involved in the face-to-face negotiations. Gaherin had spent more than a decade sparring against Miller, but the two men respected one another. Gaherin's replacement was Ray Grebey, who came to the job with a reputation as a tough bargainer with a hostile attitude toward workers. He was best known for his career at General Electric, where he had been the point man in a series of bitter labor disputes. He immediately antagonized the players who dealt with him.

In *Lords of the Realm*, John Helyar asserts that Grebey tried to convince the owners that the "take it or leave it" approach toward labor relation no longer was the norm at General Electric and that he intended to treat baseball as a "win-win" situation between the players and the owners. If that were the case, it was not the message that the players received from him. They were convinced that the owners had hired him precisely because of his take-it-or-leave-it successes at General Electric. The members of the PRC who spoke to the press gave the impression that Grebey's job was to stand tough in the face of the union and force it to make concessions. That meant new restrictions on the modified free agency that was part of the current Basic Agreement.[3]

All of the different constituencies involved in baseball had expectations about Grebey, and he lived up to most of them. Executives saw him as the long-overdue antidote to past miscalculations. They were tired of losing to the players. The time had come to reassert their control and to bring order and business sense back to baseball. Many owners were convinced that the problems were simple—salaries were too high, and players were too free. Their analysis of the cause of the problem was equally clear. Miller and the union had won too often at too little cost. The solution was obvious. The owners had to beat the union at its own game. Across baseball, the general feeling was that the owners had finally brought in their guy to challenge Miller. The man who had seemed to go from victory to victory was finally going to meet his match. With the possible exception of Miller and Grebey and their confidants, almost everyone seemed to get caught up in the mentality of the one-on-one fight. It certainly made for more exciting and easier-to-understand press coverage than writing about the details involved in the bargaining. It also seemed to reflect the emphasis on winning and one-on-one confrontations that were the essence of baseball on the field, and it was a more familiar situation to most sportswriters and fans than the subtleties of labor bargaining.

On October 30, 1979, the Player Relations Committee presented the union with formal notice of its intention to terminate the Basic Agreement on December 31. There was no question that the owners were acting in accordance with their contractual obligations in taking this step.

It showed everyone, especially the players, that the owners were serious in their efforts to make changes. This step was the labor-relations equivalent of Dr. Johnson's remark about how the construction of the gallows focuses the mind of the condemned man. It got the undivided attention of the union. But the union was not a captive and had powerful weapons with which to defend itself.

The owners ensured that if there were a work stoppage, it would be different from any previous one. They enforced a new unity among themselves and had a forceful advocate heading their team. A self-imposed gag order gave the PRC the power to fine anyone in management who made unauthorized public statements. Harry Dalton discovered the reality of this rule when it cost him fifty thousand dollars for an innocuous public remark that gave the impression that the players might be more interested than the owners in reaching an agreement quickly. Most important, the owners had taken the fiscally prudent precaution of buying strike insurance. This provided them with a sense of financial security. It might have emboldened them to take a more rigid stance in the negotiations. There is little doubt that it helped to convince many players to suspect that the owners welcomed a strike as a way to break the union.

There were complicated proposals and counterproposals exchanged between the two sides over a period of almost eighteen months, but the essential parameters and concerns were clear from the beginning. The arbitrator and the courts had stripped the owners of the control they had exercised over the players. Concessions by the union had restored some of this control, and that was as far as the union was prepared to go. As the new counsel for the Players Association, Donald Fehr, said, "free market should be the only way to set value." A note he wrote to himself indicating that the owners' proposal "appears to be nothing more than a simple attempt to cut salaries" reflected precisely what the players thought. In five years the players had seen the market give them freedom and economic independence. When Grebey and baseball executives reminded them how well they were doing, it only reinforced their determination to make no concessions.

The journalist Leonard Koppett summed up the situation: "From Commissioner Bowie Kuhn on down, baseball authorities are obsessed with the craving for a 'victory,' however pointless and symbolic, over the ogre, Marvin Miller."[4] He was right. Miller was still the visible target, since he represented what had gone so wrong in baseball over the past decade. Veteran owners loathed him for having broken their power, and newer owners saw him as the force that held the union together. But if the owners felt they finally had to win in 1980, they should have taken into account that they were facing men across the table whose whole careers were based on winning.

Miller's convictions and his style clashed head-on with Grebey. Even some of Miller's admirers have the impression that he spoke in a moralistic tone. From his first day at the union, he was faced with a system that he was convinced was intrinsically unfair. The moral high ground had belonged to the players. That had changed significantly thanks to Peter Seitz. In 1980 it was hard for Grebey to accept being preached at by someone protecting the increased salaries of his membership. Grebey saw no reason to be held responsible for the sins of a system that predated his arrival in baseball and, in any case, no longer existed. However, he was handicapped by his inability to appreciate just how much the players who had lived under the reserve system were willing to do to ensure it did not return and how much they enjoyed having turned the tables on the owners. Grebey had no sense of how deeply the players distrusted the tactics and the motives of the owners. There was no one involved with the PRC who made him aware of that.

Grebey's demeanor and reputation reinforced the distrust the players harbored for the proposals the PRC made. He consistently brought up the point that the owners had given up something in the free agency provisions of the 1976 Basic Agreement, a version of history that made the players even more suspicious. Their memory of recent negotiations was simple and very different—"they [players] made all the concessions on Reserve Rules . . . [and the] view that owners made concessions is wrong." One veteran player told Grebey at an early meeting in 1980, "We gave last time," to which Grebey replied, "That was last time."[5]

Grebey told the players that he could understand the negative reaction "if baseball said we want an NFL system," but since that was not the case, why were the players so adamantly opposed to changes? It was a bad choice of comparisons. To the players, the plan did not appear "very much different than hockey and basketball." Baseball players took a special pride in the fact that they had done better for themselves than other professional athletes. Grebey stressed that compensation would affect few players, but the union still saw it as a threat and an unacceptable giveback.[6] It was the union that adopted the rhetoric of free-market capitalism. The only thing that should determine where, how, and if a player moved and what he was paid should be the market and freely negotiated contracts. The heart of the players' argument was that any club could keep any player if it was willing to pay the price and he wanted to play there.

The players were convinced that Grebey had been hired to end the longest winning streak in baseball history, the victories of their union. The owners believed that their losses had been the result of bad tactical decisions rather than the weakness of their case. This was going to change. Grebey would provide steel at the table, strike insurance would stop weaker owners from panicking, and the gag rule would ensure a unified bargaining position. The influential owners seemed to share the belief that players were unwilling to sacrifice much to support the association.

In the 1972 strike and the 1976 lockout, ownership had assumed that since the players did not make that much money they would feel the financial pinch of a long strike and could be forced into making concessions. In 1980 the assumption was that because the players were now making so much money, they would not support a strike because they had too much to lose. The owners aimed their appeal at star players who had the most to lose. One history lesson that Grebey never learned was that the strength of the union had always been based on the willingness of star players to put their popularity and salaries on the line.

In 1980 it was the veteran players who knew from experience that all their gains had been made through the efforts of the union. The need to protect the association had become an article of faith among the players that management had identified as the weak link in the union. The PRC's original proposal to the union included two features that were significant departures from the past Basic Agreements, a salary scale and direct compensation to a club that lost a free agent.

The lack of trust between the parties was evident in an early bargaining meeting when the owners submitted a proposal for a salary scale and direct compensation for the loss of a "quality" free agent. Grebey added that there was no connection between compensation and salaries. Miller replied, "Bullshit."[7] That set the tone for the rest of the negotiations. Much of the correspondence between Miller and Grebey bordered on open hostility.

The 1976 Basic Agreement had contained a form of compensation. Once a club signed a free agent it must "compensate the Player's former Club by assigning to it a draft choice in the Regular Phase of the next June Major League Rule 4 Amateur Player Draft."[8] What the owners were demanding in 1979 was direct compensation: if a team signed a player defined as a "quality free agent," it would have to provide the team he left with another major league player.

Miller stressed the point that it was up to the owners to provide the data to prove that free agency had harmed baseball. If that were true, they had to show how the compensation they proposed was the most equitable way to solve the problem. The players pointed to the continued rise in attendance and the competitive pennant races that had taken place since 1976 and asked how the owners could claim that free agency had caused either an imbalance on the field or a decline of interest among the fans. Grebey explained that the owners were trying to end "the negative imbalance created by inadequate compensation . . . [and to rectify] the imbalance in player personnel for players lost."[9]

The players were troubled by the PRC's refusal to consider any of the counterproposals, and they were convinced that compensated free agency was, by definition, no longer free agency. This version of compensation looked suspiciously like a trade or baseball's version of the Rozelle Rule, albeit without the direct participation of the commissioner. This limitation would make it difficult for a player to be free to leave on his own terms. The players assumed that any new system that would hinder the ability of a player to market himself would also result in lower salaries for free agents. Since the union worked on the premise that salaries at the top set the market for those below them, any restrictions would depress salaries across the board. Issues of freedom aside, the economics of the situation were enough to unify the players in their opposition to Grebey's proposals.

The PRC dropped the idea of a salary structure early in the negotiations. Perhaps it had been meant as a sacrificial offering from the beginning, but the action did nothing to change the union's stance about direct compensation. The only circumstances under which the players would even talk about direct compensation was if the PRC made a case that convinced the players that the problems with the new system were grave enough to warrant changing it radically. That was going to be a tough sell for Grebey and his colleagues.

In a January 1980 negotiating meeting, Barry Rona, a lawyer for the PRC, alluded to the possibility that some clubs might not be able to compete in the new system. He phrased his remarks with the extreme caution of a good attorney who knew he was approaching dangerous ground: "Hypothetically it's conceivable a club can't pay what the player is worth."[10] He knew that if management introduced claims of financial hardships into negotiations, the union would ask to see the evidence to prove it. This could force owners to open their books or admit that supposed losses were nothing more than a public relations device. Miller, Fehr, and the players present at that session understood that Rona had not given them enough of an opening to make a formal request to see the books. At a later stage, the union was prepared to do so if it was a useful negotiating tactic and the owners or their representatives opened the way for it.

Nine days after the session in which Rona had talked about the financial implications of free agency, the Executive Board of the Players Association held a no-holds-barred meeting to discuss the proposals made by the PRC and to formulate their own response. It would have amazed writers and executives that the comments ranged from complimenting Miller on keeping his cool to accusing him of being "too soft." The reaction to direct compensation and a salary scale was simple and unanimous—they were out of the question. In this closed meeting, players showed how strongly they felt. Two remarks summed up the attitude toward compensation: "they [the owners] want to raise the Titanic—we sunk that fucker—we won't sell out any player," and "This [compensation] is the main issue. Let's make sure this information gets passed along to players—so they understand the facts. This is the battle line. All players must know why we have to hold this line."[11] It was particularly significant that the latter point was made by Bob Boone, one of the players whom baseball executives regarded as a "reasonable person" who would make solutions possible.

The union might appear solid to outsiders, but there were issues that had the potential to fracture the unity needed for the tough bargaining ahead. Different players had different concerns. The minimum wage was important to some, while others thought that the point at which a player was eligible for salary arbitration or free agency was much more important. However, every player knew that free agency was the most important issue at stake. Its impact went far beyond players who might become free agents. It set the comparative salaries for arbitration-eligible players. The dramatic rise in salaries was a product of free agency, and it was in every player's interest to keep it as free as possible. The proposal for direct compensation affected very few players personally, but the players were determined to strike if that was the only way to force the owners to drop the issue. This was collective self-interest at work. There were extended, sometimes contentious discussions about issues and tactics. Players talked among themselves about the differences between actions that would harm the owners and those that might "hurt baseball."

The attitude of the players was also a referendum on the union and how much current players were willing to sacrifice for it. Few remarks seemed to bother the players more than the oft-repeated query in the press, "What do the players want this time?" The question completely misinterpreted the situation. The most militant players were fighting the hardest to protect the new status quo. Board members expressed concern about how owners were "working on" individual players and trying to convince younger players that neither salary arbitration nor compensation mattered. "We need more players at the negotiations" became the strategy of the board. One player rep's call, "Let's lead them," was followed by "Let's educate them." The two ideas were complementary.[12]

In the midst of heated discussions about an impending strike vote, the player reps began to discuss the history of the union. One veteran player talked about what had been strike issues in the past. His characterization of compensation as "the battle line" was not a wild metaphor. He wanted a "handle on the membership [and] strengthening our weaknesses before drawing battle lines." He also stressed the "need to educate those who feel that compensation may be fair." No one on the board thought it was likely that the owners would drop their compensation plan, at least not until the association proved to the owners that talk of a strike was more than just rhetoric. The board members were not even sure if the players would "settle for no improvements and just get compensation off the table," since this would be the first Basic Agreement in which the union could not point to some significant gains.[13]

The discussion turned quickly to practical concerns, such as ensuring that all the players were informed and when would be the best time to strike should it become necessary. The latter point revolved around one concern—how to inflict maximum pain upon the owners while hurting the players as little as possible. What they discussed around the table was the same thing they talked about thousands of times in clubhouse meetings and pitching-mound conferences: how to beat the other guy.

Despite Grebey, strike insurance, and the publicly stated resolve of the owners, the members of the Executive Board of the Players Association were convinced that there would be no movement until the owners thought there was a crisis. Everything had to be done to make sure the owners did not think they could "con them [the players] into playing without a Basic Agreement. . . . [The owners] underestimated the players the last 13+ years . . . they think players are patsies. . . . It promotes foot dragging."[14]

Playing without a Basic Agreement posed real dangers for the players. Although arbitration would continue in force until or unless there was a legally declared "impasse" in negotiations, the players feared that in the future there might be no mechanism of impartial arbitration for players to enforce their rights. That meant they either could go to court or "appeal to Ayatollah Kuhn." Neither of these possibilities was acceptable to the board. Players showed concern that there could be a "gradual stripping away of rights and benefits . . . [that could] lead to the dissolution of the Players Association [and] the danger that the owners kid themselves about the situation."[15]

If the players decided to start the season without an agreement, that could give the owners an opportunity to seize the initiative and set up a defensive lockout. The specter of the NFL loomed in the minds of the Executive Board. They assumed that baseball owners admired the NFL approach toward labor relations. What would the players do if the season was completed without an agreement and then the owners decided in the autumn to eliminate free agency or to cut back on benefits? These might look like doomsday scenarios, but the players had to prepare for them. There was always the possibility of striking the World Series, which would enable all the players to collect their season salaries. This certainly would make an impression on ownership and the public. It would mean an unequal sacrifice among the players, but the board was sure that "players would do it."[16] The board finally rejected a boycott of spring training or striking during the World Series. What remained was to plan for a strike during the season.

During spring training the negotiations went from deadlock to overt hostility. Players who participated showed an increasing distrust of Grebey. They accused him of not wanting to discuss compensation in front of them. Miller began to believe that the owners were trying to provoke a strike. A subcommittee of players met on April 1, 1980, to set a date for a strike. The eight players who were present had a deep involvement with the union, even though Don Baylor, Mark Belanger, Bob Boone, Doug DeCinces, Phil Garner, Reggie Jackson, Randy Jones, and Mike Marshall were at very different stages in their careers.

They agreed that no more spring training games should be played. There were only a few left, but canceling the Freeway Series in Los Angeles meant that the action got attention. There was some support expressed at the meeting for striking opening day to dramatize how strongly players felt. "Opening day" for all of the clubs, however, stretched out over two weeks. One opponent of the idea described it as an emotional reaction that could backfire, possibly leading to a season-long strike, something that no one wanted. The board made its decision on the basis of what one member characterized as the need "to hurt them the most and benefit us the most."[17] That meant May, when the players would be in better shape financially and the strike probably would be shorter, since the owners would feel its effects quickly. Earlier in the season there were more scheduled off-days and more rain-outs. From May onward, there were more games scheduled, and attendance was higher because of the improved weather and the fact that school was over. One committee member said that his teammates probably wanted an early strike, but he would vote for May. Miller's only comment was that it would take "great discipline." The players responded that they had no doubts that the discipline was there.

This was uncharted territory for the players. There was no certainty about how they would react to a strike that took place in the midst of a season. There was no way to predict the effectiveness of the communications network the Executive Board was trying to set up to keep the players involved after they scattered across the country. Later that day, the full Executive Board met to consider the recommendations of the subcommittee. Considering what was at stake, the discussion was almost dispassionate. The recommendation was made to start the regular season and then to strike after May 22, because at that time "players are strongest financially, owners weakest financially."[18] No mention was made of pennant races, travel arrangements, or other concerns. The players' intentions were clear: management must back away from its idea of compensation or face a unified union out on strike. The board unanimously passed a motion to strike the remaining exhibition games, open the season, and set May 23 as a strike date.

Opening games in the 1980 season had a surreal quality about them. Everyone involved in Major League Baseball was looking back at canceled exhibition games and forward to the possibility of an abrupt end to the season. In 1972, once the strike ended, the season had started and carried on to its completion. In 1980 the season started with a strike on deck.

As the strike date approached, both sides came closer on a number of unresolved issues. It became clear that most issues other than compensation could be resolved. In the closed meetings of the union, it was the same player who had described the 1976 agreement as a sell-out who reminded everyone of the need for pragmatism in the current negotiations.

A few days before a strike was scheduled and after months of dealing with the players, Grebey wrote an article in *The Sporting News* addressed to them. The headline, "Grebey: Pay Averaging $149,000, Why Strike?" might have appealed to the sentiments of fans who had trouble understanding why players should make so much. But if his purpose was to win over any players, he had chosen the wrong method and the wrong tone. According to Grebey, there was no justification for a strike to protect the high salaries that players were receiving. He asked rhetorically, how could players not be contented when salaries had risen 23 percent over last season and "a whopping 191 percent over the 1976 average of $51,500? . . . It is difficult to understand why there should be a player strike. . . . What would the players be striking to gain? . . . There is no reason for an interruption in the baseball season."[19]

The answer to Grebey was deceptively simple from the players' point of view. They were not trying to gain anything; they were not willing to give up what they had gained; they would strike rather than accept the owners' proposals for compensation. Every player harbored the belief that someday he might be able to cash in on the bonanza of free agency. The article in *The Sporting News* showed how Grebey seemed to have acquired one of the owners' failings, a predisposition to tell the players what the players should think was best for them.

Grebey's article reinforced the players' belief that it was his job to break the union as the first step toward getting the players to go back to the conditions before Messersmith-McNally. He appeared to be asking players to turn their backs on the leadership of the union, the very men that the players credited with creating the high salaries. This infuriated many players, who thought that Grebey should talk to his employers since it was their intransigence that was forcing a strike.

Two highly respected sportswriters, Red Smith and Jim Murray, showed the range of opinion about the possible strike. Both wrote columns that appeared when it looked like the strike would take place in May. Smith described baseball as an industry that "invests 2 percent of its revenues in a strike fund and buys strike insurance worth $1 million a day" and then asked rhetorically, "Which side seems to be trying the harder to avoid a strike?" He went through a brief history of baseball's labor relations, when a "ballplayer was owned outright by the first club that signed him to a contract" and the prevailing attitude of management was to dictate to a player on "take it or leave it terms [and] 'Let him sit home and rot' was the stock comment about a player who held out." He emphasized that the players had made all the compromises after the Messersmith-McNally ruling and that the public was being deceived into thinking that the players now were asking for additional gains.

Smith chastised the owners for complaining about "greedy players driving them to the poorhouse" and was upset about a gullible public that "buys the 'greedy player' argument blindly." He pointed out that owners offered salaries for a variety of reasons and asked why players should be pilloried by the press and fans for accepting what was being offered to them. It was the owners who were "unable to control their own impulsive generosity . . . [and] are demanding that the players control it for them. Maybe a nice long strike would starve the players into coopera- tion." Smith offered a simple explanation for those who could not un- derstand why highly paid athletes would be willing to strike: "All ball- players have to strike for is the limited freedom, the self respect and the money they have fought for and won in recent years. The employers have made no secret of their determination to diminish these gains."[20]

Jim Murray presented an equally unambiguous explanation of the sit- uation: "What is at stake is whether or not baseball is entitled to extract indemnity for an aggrieved club when one of its stars is signed as a free agent by another club. This is not a proper subject for a strike. It's a court decision, as Marvin Miller must well know. The swollen-salary free-agent market, which has made millionaires out of right fielders, *is not a labor triumph* anyway. It was brought about by a legal decision by a man the owners themselves had hired as an arbitrator" (emphasis added).

According to Murray, the association was not really a union because baseball was not work. In his phrase, the association's members were "highly paid parts of an activity which contributes nothing to the gross national product except popcorn sales, whose skills were not transferra- ble to anything that mattered. Some guys make more money than they can count to. . . . million dollar a year players . . . can even turn Samuel Gompers into a company man. They will give new meaning to Jean Jacques Rousseau's [sic] war cry 'Workers of the world unite! You have nothing to lose but your chains!' which will now become, 'Baseball play- ers of the world unite! You have nothing to lose but a half a million dol- lars—or your wife's new Rolls.'" Murray continued:

> The craven way baseball players have gone about their strike is hardly in the best traditions of the United Mine Workers, anyway. They struck during the exhibition season, a period in which the players receive only meal money and expenses. They propose to stage the real strike some- time at the end of May, at which time I expect the vote will be some- what less unanimous than a 767-1 announced for March. . . . [Players] were lucky baseball is around to keep them in minks and Rolls. . . . They should be grateful for the spadework done by generations of promoters, reporters, announcers, technicians, contractors and so forth who made it all possible. They're grateful to a man who had nothing to do with it, Marvin Miller, the only labor leader in history to represent a company of millionaires.[21]

The players had a very different version of history than Murray. They knew how much they had gained in the past few years and assumed it had been the product of the ability of their leadership to bargain and from the willingness of the individual players to support the union. Their private conversations as well as their public statements made it clear that they were not going to return to a previous version of baseball. They might be dogmatic in believing that if they made any major concessions the owners would attempt to strip away all the gains made by the union. In any case, the perceptions of the players shaped the reality of the negotiations. There was no question that any significant changes to free agency were not negotiable.

Murray emphasized the new prosperity of the players. He found time to give credit for it to virtually everyone and everything other than the players, Miller, Moss, or the union. The players probably ignored Murray, but a columnist with his reputation and popularity might have convinced wavering owners of the popularity of their position and emboldened the majority of them to stand fast in negotiations. This would ensure that a strike would result.

Murray was right in many respects. The Players Association was not the mineworkers union or even the steelworkers, but it aspired to be neither. It was not even a union of all professional baseball players. It represented its members, who were Major League Baseball players. It had no desire to expand its scope. Its members made a lot of money and were not the least bit apologetic about it. The union made no pretense to be a debating society, a think tank, or a role model for other organizations. Its leaders were not romantics. They were baseball players and union officials who discussed whether to strike, when to do it, and how to have the best results for their cause. "Craven" was not a word, or a concept, that applied to the discussions about when to strike. A strike was one possible weapon to be utilized, and it had to be used in a way that would hurt the owners more than the players. Murray did not understand that the MLBPA was not in the business of scoring moral points but of winning and protecting tangible gains for its members.

The proposed strike ended with an almost comic-opera abruptness. When league officials and those of some clubs inquired why players were not heading to the airport to board planes to go to the sites of their next games, they were informed that there was no reason to go since the games would not be played. The season was coming to an abrupt halt. The reality of players not getting set to play the next games brought home the fact that the strike was not an abstraction. There was an all-night and early-morning bargaining session on May 22 between principals for both sides. Miller was "shuttling in and out of our [the association's] caucus room [and] a strike was averted." What followed were negotiations to end a strike before it started. The agreement that allowed the 1980 season to continue contained an important provision that the owners wanted, the establishment of the Joint Study Committee to look at possible changes in the current system. On all the other provisions of the agreement, the association got what it wanted.

After the strike was averted on May 23, 1980, Miller took time to catch up on his correspondence. As in the past, he spent most of that time countering arguments he thought were incorrect. He supported his criticisms meticulously. But he took a different approach with Murray, sending him a short letter with a lighter tone: "I am told that you are known for pulling people's legs. If that is accurate, your reputation is intact. Whether the absurd statements in those columns were written tongue in cheek or straight, your errors surely exceed the total that most scoreboards could handle.* I prefer to think you were aiming at humor. Although your aim was somewhat off the mark, you succeeded, you are funny." Miller used the asterisk to tell Murray, "Documentation supplied upon request."[22]

Grebey issued a public statement shortly after the agreement: "In 1981, the Clubs' proposal for compensation becomes a part of the Basic Agreement and *it cannot be removed without agreement of the two sides*" (emphasis added). This interpretation was what the hard-line owners wanted to hear, since it appeared that Grebey had finally beaten the union. To Miller and the players, it was one more sign of the problems in dealing with Grebey. Miller replied in a memo to the players, "In summary, then, *there can be no change in compensation for free agents without the agreement of the Players Association*. In the event the Clubs determine unilaterally to announce changes, the Association retains the right to strike in response thereto." He characterized Grebey's conclusions as "erroneous; evidence of an intent to ignore the Agreement; evidence of bad faith; and notice of the intent on the owners' part to make a mockery of the joint study and the negotiations to follow." In case anyone doubted what he meant, Miller concluded that "this continuation of such propaganda by the owners' representative, which tips off the owners' aggressive intent against the Players' rights, will be a matter of record for all to see and thereby determine the root cause of any future dispute which may arise on this matter of compensation."[23]

The owners seemed to assume they had gotten their version of compensation by default. The players saw this as proof of Grebey's duplicity, which meant that the prognosis for the Joint Study Committee was not very good. During the season, Miller reminded the players that they should have no illusions and that they should be proud of how they had "refused to be panicked or conned by the owner propaganda or by threats 'to shut down the entire season.'" A little later, he wrote to all the players, "The strength of the Players Association is the firm unity of the players; and when that exists, it is sufficient to do the job." In case anyone outside of the Players Association did not understand the implications, Miller concluded, "Only a foolish man would believe that the Players will show less determination and unity in 1981, or thereafter, than they demonstrated this year."[24]

Miller's rhetoric was not only for effect. The players firmly believed that direct compensation was an effort to destroy free agency and to weaken the union. They saw Grebey as the device chosen by the owners to accomplish both of those tasks. The players became increasingly suspicious of every step taken by the PRC. For years Miller's critics had complained that the combative relations between the union and the owners would end when players started to think for themselves rather than being led by Miller and Moss. In 1980 the players were setting the tone, and what resulted was a nightmare for the owners. It would be counterproductive for the owners to formulate their policies on the belief that the players were controlled by Miller and Fehr.

The owners' new strategy was based on their belief that the majority of the players were not willing to strike over compensation that affected so few players directly. Grebey appealed to the rank and file of the union and launched this effort with a widely circulated question-and-answer session with himself, "Answers to Your Questions." A few of Grebey's "answers" demonstrate why he became an asset to the union leadership. He started his remarks with the comment, "The players union has been helpful and useful in the past and will, I'm sure, continue to be."[25] This approach was almost guaranteed to get a reaction of disbelief or to confirm that Grebey had little respect for the ability of the players to understand the situation. By this time, the players had been dealing with Grebey for months. Don Baylor's later assessment is typical of their feelings: "I got to see Grebey close up and personal. I can only speak for myself, but my dislike of Grebey was instant and complete. Grebey was a labor gunslinger with a history of overseeing protracted strikes."[26]

Grebey continued, "No changes are being sought in the principles of the Free Agency system." It was going to be a tough sell to convince players who had lived through the pre-Messersmith era that the owners had no desire to limit free agency. It would be even tougher to get them to think that direct compensation was "no change." When Grebey stressed that compensation in baseball was not like the plan used in any other sport, since "in baseball, the clubs are only seeking an equity return," he reminded the players of what the NFL had done. When Grebey characterized the pension fund as "a gift from the clubs, the players don't pay a cent," he came as close as possible to destroying what credibility he might have had with any player. The pension fund was sacrosanct. Players were convinced that it belonged to them and that its improvements had been the product of collective bargaining by their union. There weren't many players left who believed that an owner "gave" his players anything. Grebey would have made a better impression if he had continued to sound like a tough-talking labor negotiator rather than the new incarnation of a paternalistic owner. That might have worked in the days of Judge Cannon, but the idea of a benevolent ownership had disappeared from the vocabulary of the players on the way to the sinking of the "Titanic" of the reserve system.[27]

Grebey asked, "if the players walk out, what would they be striking for?" He answered it with a rhetorical question, "What is there to strike for?" From his perspective, the answer clearly was "nothing," a view that Grebey hoped would be echoed by both the press and the public.[28] For the players, the answer was just as clear. They wanted to avoid a strike, but not at all costs. A strike was preferable to allowing the owners to dictate terms that meant giving up the advantages they had gained. Less than a week after the strike was avoided, battle lines were drawn again. The agreement to establish a Joint Study Committee contained a restatement of the owners' intention to "unilaterally adopt and put into effect [their plan for compensation] as part of the Basic Agreement," a phrase that Miller highlighted in his copy of the notice. Harry Dalton, one of the management representatives on the committee, commented years later that Miller "always had his guns pointed at the owners and took any shots he could."[29] If this was true in 1980, Grebey's public statements were an easy target.

In 1980 the Executive Board appeared somewhat more concerned than in the past about its public image. As one member described it, "we've always been silent. Always defensive. The clubs spend lots of money on p.r." Miller and most veteran players thought it was a losing battle to convince the public to have any sympathy for either individual players or the Players Association. There had been little support in the past, even when the reserve system was intact and the minimum wage was six thousand dollars. Why should players expect any more support now, after they had been portrayed for years as greedy ingrates who cared nothing about the game, their teams, or the fans? No player liked to be booed or to read articles that disparaged his character, although most of them had grown accustomed to it. Many of them wore the scorn of the press as a badge of honor. The owners had done an effective job of turning public opinion against the players. Now the union talked briefly about trying to capitalize on the public-spirited efforts of some of the players, in this case by using the good works of the Dave Winfield Foundation as "a vehicle for public relations and positive image. For future negotiations [to get] public attitude on players' side."[30] The board decided to have further discussions about the proposal. Those did not take place because the need to plan for a probable strike became the all-consuming issue.

One provision of the agreement that kept the season going was a proposal to establish a new joint study committee to examine free agency. The players and the owners had different ideas about what the committee might do, but the owners should not have assumed that the players were going to let management set the agenda or use the committee as the basis for cutting back free agency. There was a striking difference between this committee and the other one that had existed less than a decade earlier. The previous committee had considered (however futilely) the reserve system, this one was discussing free agency. Nothing could have shown more dramatically how much things had changed.

There were many details to handle before the committee could begin its work. The players had long discussions before choosing their members. The Executive Board wanted to make sure that its representatives were not predisposed to accept the owners' previous position that compensation was a necessity. The union wanted the committee to discuss the whole range of issues concerning free agency, not only varieties of compensation. The men who composed the committee, Frank Cashen and Harry Dalton for the PRC and Sal Bando and Bob Boone for the union, represented years of experience in baseball. All of them had the respect of both sides, as well as strong feelings about the cause they represented. Neither Cashen nor Dalton were identified with efforts to criticize the union in public and they had not questioned the integrity of its leadership. Although Boone and Bando had been active in the Players Association, no one in management regarded either as a firebrand. Barry Rona and Don Fehr attended meetings and took notes of the proceedings. Grebey, Miller, and others were present at some of the meetings.

Boone was probably the most influential player in the union at that time. He was thoughtful and well-educated. He was not loud or flamboyant but was rock-solid in his beliefs and his demeanor. He had made it clear in closed-door meetings of the players that he was determined to ensure that no agreement would be concluded that would weaken free agency. The realities of baseball intruded on the committee when an early October meeting had to be postponed due to Bob Boone's "understandable preoccupation with his team's pennant race."[31]

The 1980 season ended in an implausible, albeit dramatic fashion, with the Phillies winning their first and only World Series. The team had been owned by the Carpenter family, who personified the "sportsmen owners." They had shown some of the deepest hostility toward the union and Miller. A few years later the Carpenters sold the team, claiming that baseball was no longer enjoyable. They found a buyer willing to pay millions of dollars to invest in what was supposedly a losing enterprise. The stars of the 1980 team were Mike Schmidt, the product of a farm system in the best traditions of the sport, Steve Carlton, acquired when the owner of the Cardinals traded him for asking for more money, and Pete Rose, who had left his hometown team to join the Phillies as a free agent.

Ownership was demanding compensation for the effort and money put into developing players like Schmidt. The players were contending that six years of major league service was more than enough compensation and that veterans had earned the right to be like Rose. The 1980 season, with the Phillies winning their first championship, the Royals their first pennant, and the Astros making a rare appearance in the playoffs, was tangible evidence of something the players had insisted upon for years—that post-1976 free agency had increased the competitive nature of baseball, on as well as off the field.

No matter how much goodwill might be present or how insightful the members of the committee might be, they were facing an almost impossible task. The two sides came to the table with very different expectations. The owners were convinced they would be talking about what form direct compensation would take. The players demanded to be shown that there was a compelling case for any compensation. When Cashen and Dalton talked about compensation, Bando and Boone talked about free agency. At an early meeting, the difficulties of the task became obvious. Boone asked for a point-by-point analysis of how free agency had worked since the Messersmith ruling, and Cashen replied that "historical stuff [is] not important." What was "historical stuff" to an executive was also the most important positive change any of the players had experienced. The association's leadership claimed that even if the players made concessions, "the Clubs will still feel free to seek still more compensation in 1984 [and] if no agreement can be reached, the Players Association is prepared to live with the status quo." The rhetoric of the players coincided with their prosperity: "there is a serious matter of principle involved here . . . [blocking] an involuntary transfer of another player. We sometimes lose sight of how feudal this type of arrangement really is. Players are not slaves, serfs, or indentured servants."[32]

If writers and fans had ridiculed Curt Flood for being a "ninety-thousand-dollar slave," what would be their reaction at a time when the average salary of major league players had risen to more than $143,000 a season? In any case, that mattered as little to the players in 1980 as it had in 1970. There had been enormous changes since Curt Flood had challenged the system. Players had real control over their lives, at least those who were able to survive for six years in the major leagues.

At the first meeting of the Joint Study Committee, Boone stated simply that he wanted a solution that was *"in the best interest of the game"* (emphasis added), and then he proceeded to define that phrase "from a player's standpoint." It was an article of faith among the players that the 1976 Basic Agreement had created a balanced reserve system with gains and losses for both sides because the association "had agreed to limitations . . . in order to assist in the creation of a balanced system in the best interests of Players and Clubs." Players who read this must have remembered how, prior to 1976, the owners and their supporters had countered every suggestion for reform made by the association with the rejoinder that actions must be taken in the best interests of baseball.

It was quite clear that before the association was even going to consider any new limitations on free agency, it was going to demand solid evidence that the change was needed and that it would benefit the players. It was going to be a hard sell to the players, who asserted that "experience under the new system reveals that it is basically sound and has brought significant gains to all concerned."[33] That meant change was acceptable only if it did not limit player mobility or adversely affect salaries.

Since the 1976 Basic Agreement, salaries were up, attendance was up, and competition for pennants and world championships had reached a hitherto unthinkable level. But this was not enough to convince the owners that the system was working. They continued to contend that free agency was ruining baseball. The expense of running a team was certainly higher, but management did not produce any evidence that any clubs were in financial difficulties. Earlier in the year, Barry Rona had been very careful when he came close to talking about financial problems as the reason the owners needed more restrictions on free agency. In December 1980, Commissioner Kuhn raised the same issue, albeit with less caution and in a public setting.

When the Commissioner presided over the seventy-ninth annual convention of professional baseball, he addressed the more than eighteen-hundred guests with a note of pessimism: "You cannot avoid the fact that our game has some exceedingly tough problems—salaries were rising too fast for revenues for the seasons 1974 through 1979. Baseball's operating statements have reflected a combined loss before income taxes amounting to many millions of dollars." He singled out the Atlanta Braves for a 1979 loss of $3.4 million. There's no telling how Ted Turner felt about being used as an example of irresponsible management. It might not have been a coincidence that the commissioner focused on the club that had signed Andy Messersmith.[34]

If free agency was the cause of baseball's financial problems, it followed that restrictions on it could save the game. Kuhn predicted that operating losses would continue to mount, ticket prices would have to rise, franchises would go out of business, and the competitive balance of baseball would be destroyed. He pointed out that "happily there is a player–general manager study committee at work on the subject on compensation for clubs losing free agents. . . . Certainly it is hard for *any reasonable person* to quarrel with the proposition that compensation is needed and fair. . . . Everyone in the game, both clubs and players, is going to have to recognize that there is a problem. . . . But there will be no solution until the players along with the clubs recognize that corrections in the system must be made. If that light doesn't begin to shine pretty soon, a lot of players along with the clubs are going to be among the financial losers"[35]

Kuhn's remarks probably were intended for an audience much wider than the one in the hall listening to him. He was going to be disappointed if he hoped to influence the players. They already thought they were being "reasonable" in trying to maintain the current system, and they had little regard for any proposals made by someone they thought of as a mouthpiece for the owners.

The Joint Study Committee held eight meetings during which it discussed a number of detailed issues, including definitions of ranking players and the impact of free agency on various classes of players and clubs. At one time in the proceedings, Grebey or Rona replied angrily to comments made by the union and asserted that the players were more interested in making a record for future review than they were in solving the immediate problem. There was some truth in that assertion. The union staff had concluded that the PRC would not support any recommendation from the committee that did not include direct compensation and felt that the committee was going nowhere. Fehr and others were looking toward the next step in the process, possible action by the National Labor Relations Board (NLRB) or the courts.

Both sides stepped back from the temptation to negotiate in the press, realizing that the angry language of the past spring had not helped. They kept various drafts of the proposals confidential. But outward civility or intelligent discussion should not be mistaken for either cooperation or the probability of an agreement. In this case, the devil was not in the details, the crisis was in the principles. Rona and Fehr wrote the drafts for their respective principals, and these drafts reinforced the idea that the differences could not be compromised. The PRC's summation was that the "need for additional compensation was firmly established during the course of the eight meetings."[36] This must have come as a great surprise to Bando and Boone, who countered, "The study was hampered by the inability or unwillingness of the management members to provide any factual support for the proposition that increased manpower compensation is needed for a club which loses a free agent."[37]

At the end of the process, everyone was back where they had started. The final reply from management was that it was a matter of "equity," since clubs were "entitled to someone who might help very soon" if they lost a free agent.[38] The concepts of "equity" and "loss" showed the gap between the parties. "Equity" could only be part of the equation if one accepted the idea that a six-year veteran with no contract was the property of his most recent club. This went counter to everything the players assumed Messersmith-McNally had accomplished. The days of owning players was gone, having been replaced by a limited contractual relationship freely entered into by both parties. The owners showed no interest in countering any objections by the players, although they did admit that direct compensation might have an incidentally negative effect on the growth in players' salaries. When the committee's report was issued, it was a monument to the obvious—no solution was possible as long as the Players Association would not accept the owners' stated principle that baseball could survive only with direct compensation.

THE UNION'S STERNEST TEST

THE STRIKE OF 1981 TESTED whether the gains the union made in the past fifteen years would survive intact. Since that time, the participants have provided almost completely different interpretations of the events. Miller described it in his 1991 autobiography as follows: "Top to bottom, star to sub, liberal to conservative, the players stood firm. . . . Rereading the press clippings ten years later, I'm reminded of how strong and effective and militant the Players Association had become. I'll say it again: It was the most principled strike I'd ever been associated with: it was the Association's finest hour."[1] Bowie Kuhn analyzed it in his autobiography in this way:

> Miller's folly had cost the players nearly $30 million. . . . [Players had the] spirit of thoroughbreds [and] led by Miller as a trusting light brigade into the valley of death. . . . [Miller] turned insincerity into an art form. Guided by an ego that was the North Star of his life, he followed it wherever it led. Fortunately for the players, the path of that star sometimes coincided with the path of their own destiny. In 1981, it did not. He left a legacy of hatred and bitterness between the clubs and the players that would destructively sour labor relations in baseball for years to come. If he was not the only cause [of the strike] he was the preponderant one.[2]

In the battle of memoirs, Miller's main theme is that the "players' willingness to go on strike and their ability to maintain the strike was the deciding factor."[3] Kuhn's contention is that Miller had planned this kind of strike for almost fifteen years. The longer the two men had been away from baseball, the more they seemed to share a mutual disrespect for one another.

Kuhn probably would concede the accuracy of the title of Miller's book, *A Whole Different Ball Game*, while ruing the changes. Miller probably would scoff at the subtitle of Kuhn's book, *The Education of a Baseball Commissioner*. They might agree that the events of 1981 ended one stage of baseball, as well as shaping its future. There was a whole new level of bitterness within baseball and an even greater sense of anger from fans and journalists.

The 1981 season started against the backdrop of failed negotiations. The strike that interrupted the season had many issues, but direct compensation for the loss of a free agent was the unbridgeable divide. A decade later, Sal Bando, one of the members of the Joint Study Committee that had been unable to craft a proposal to avoid the strike, was convinced that "Free agency and compensation were worth striking over because [free agency] gave you some control over your life. [What] if you never had a chance because you played behind someone, or didn't get along with ownership, or had personal reasons for wanting to live someplace else? . . . Eighty-one was worth it because you kept what you had. You made your point. That's why we have the right to strike in this country."[4]

Bando had put those principles into practice when he used free agency to get away from Charlie Finley. He then chose to accept a contract for less money than was offered by some teams in return for playing in the city of his choice. There is a certain irony in his 1991 reflections about the strike. He made them after he had started a new career as the assistant general manager of the Milwaukee Brewers. He was sitting in an office next to the general manager who had hired him, the same Harry Dalton who had been on the Joint Study Committee. Bando's employer was the owner of the Brewers, Bud Selig, who in 1994 and 1995, as acting commissioner of baseball, presided over the longest work stoppage in the history of American professional sports.

Kuhn was correct that the players' decision cost them dearly, both financially and emotionally. But the financial blow was short-term, and the players made it up over the next couple of years. The owners never recouped the lost revenue from the games that were canceled. Most players learned how to cope with disapproval as one of the risks of the profession, like bad hops on the infield or brush-back pitches at the plate. The real damage caused by the hostile attitude toward the players was at the gate, and the losers there were the clubs.

The members of the Executive Board who made the decision to strike and the players who voted to support it by a tally of 587 to 1 (the one negative vote was based on religious scruples) could have been wrong in their evaluation of the issues or misjudged the reaction of the owners. But they certainly did not take the step lightly, nor were they maneuvered into it by Miller. The votes took place after months of discussions among the players.

The strike that did not happen in 1980 and the strike that did take place in 1981 were two stages of a long series of negotiations. The players agreed not to strike in May 1980, with the hope if not the expectation that a future strike could be avoided. There was little question that the players would sanction a strike in 1981 if the owners insisted on direct major league compensation for the signing of a free agent. It appears that the PRC was willing to push its compensation plan even if that meant taking the risk of a strike. On February 9, 1981, the Players Association received a hand-delivered letter from Grebey in which the owners exercised their right to unilaterally implement their plan for compensation. Miller immediately used this action to assert that the owners could not be trusted.

The owners then sent letters to every player that stressed that the compensation plan was not like the NFL and "is not a salary cutting effort, regardless of what some have said . . . salaries [are] at an all time high . . . the benefits of being a Major League player are at an all time high."[5] The latter point was a double-edged sword for the owners. It could show the players how much they stood to lose in a strike. It also could remind the players how much they had gained because of their willingness to support the union. When spring training opened, the players were convinced that the owners were once again testing them. Grebey was absolutely correct when he complained publicly that some of the players were "constantly accusing [ownership] of surreptitious motives."[6]

On May 11, 1981, one of the players involved in the negotiations summarized the situation: "[We] reported back to players . . . [these are] same proposals on table for eighteen months. Was strike issue last year . . . nothing's changed. There will be a strike."[7] Battle lines were drawn when the union officials sent out a letter to all player reps giving them instructions on how to handle arrangements for the strike that would take place the next day. The logistics were almost as nightmarish as Miller and Moss had predicted years earlier. After the players scattered it would be extremely difficult to keep them informed; therefore the player reps were instructed to set up a telephone network. The owners had fewer problems, since they delegated strategy decisions and negotiations to the Player Relations Committee.

When the negotiations seemed stalled and the strike date came closer, the union played another card. For years, Miller, Moss, and Fehr had been frustrated at the way the owners and their representatives spoke public-ly about the economic hardships they were undergoing, but they were careful not to use that approach at the bargaining table. In 1981 Miller and Fehr decided to press the issue and applied to the NLRB for an in-junction against the owners claiming they had not bargained in good faith. A day before the strike deadline, the NLRB agreed to seek a restraining order to allow a hearing before a district court judge.

If the union's position were upheld, it could have a major impact on the situation. The plan of the owners to unilaterally implement their version of free agency would be postponed, as would the date set by the players to strike. The owners might be forced to open up their books to scrutiny. If they were found guilty of not bargaining in good faith, there was the possibility that the players could recover the wages lost during a strike. Lloyds of London, the company that carried the owners' strike insurance, might have a justification to cancel the insurance just when the owners were counting on it to sustain them. The union had little to lose by filing the charges. Even if its position did not prevail in court, it gained some time to prepare for the strike, both logistically and finan-cially. It was another opportunity to remind players that they were in-volved in a union-management struggle. On June 10, Judge Henry Werk-er found no cause to support the call for an injunction. Two days later, the strike began.[8]

A few days before the strike deadline, the Players Association proposed that a pool of major league players be used for compensation. The pool concept was supposed to ensure that free agency was not transformed into a type of trade, especially one where the club that signed a free agent would labor under the uncertainty of not knowing which player it might lose as compensation. In the union's plan, a club losing a free agent would receive another major league player selected from a pool of players that was established by the clubs before the process to pursue free agents start-ed each year.

The day before the strike started, a large number of players attended the negotiations. Many of them had not previously been active in the process. It was a situation calculated to bring out the worst in Grebey. He had lit-tle enthusiasm for any players being involved. Possibly he thought they got in the way of the professionals doing their job or that Miller was play-ing to the crowd. Players like Joe Niekro, Don Sutton, and George Foster said little, but there was no way to ignore the fact that high-priced veterans were showing their support for the union. At the end of the meeting, Miller commented, "[I] gather from Ray's comments [that they] don't like our proposals. . . . Strike begins tomorrow." He followed that with something that took virtually everyone by surprise: "further meetings will take place. This will be my last—starting tomorrow, players only—hope you jointly do better than [we] were able to with me here."[9]

Miller's withdrawal has been the source of controversy ever since he took the step. His version is that personal feelings between him and Grebey were getting in the way of the give-and-take necessary to create the framework for a workable Basic Agreement. Some management representatives thought Miller's action was a combination of grandstanding and trying to show he was indispensable. Many players who were not involved in the negotiations did not understand it. Miller did not take this action without serious thought, and it was not done out of pique or annoyance. The players involved in the negotiations knew what he intended to do. Earlier in the negotiations, Grebey had remarked to one of the players that Miller was the impediment in the way of an early settlement of the outstanding differences and that reasonable men like Grebey and this player could sit at the table and work out their problems. Miller and the players decided to challenge this assertion in a dramatic fashion.

Rumors had circulated through the press that the players were ready to make concessions, but Miller was stopping them. It does not matter if Grebey and some of the owners believed this to be the case or if it was just wishful thinking. The union decided to capitalize on it. Miller's withdrawal showed everyone, in a most dramatic fashion, that it was the players who were driving the position of the union. The players at the table knew what Miller was doing and why.[10]

In any case, Fehr and other attorneys were there, and the negotiating team would keep in touch with Miller. But would that be enough to replace his active participation or the confidence that the players across the country might derive from his presence at the table? Bowie Kuhn certainly seemed to think Miller's withdrawal was a good idea, and he later commented, "however clever he [Miller] was at tactical maneuvering, he was not good at the bargaining table, where he had little sense of timing and virtually no idea how to close a deal. This weakness was compounded by his hatred—with all its emotional baggage—of the owners and Grebey."[11]

The strike began in June, while negotiations continued. Miller was away from the bargaining table, and the PRC came face-to-face with players' determination and ability to set the tone for negotiations. There were no concessions forthcoming. The pace and the content of the talks showed little change without Miller. In discussions among themselves, the players shared a feeling that once the strike insurance began to pay the clubs, the owners would be willing to sacrifice as many games as they thought necessary to force the union to submit. Both sides showed little inclination to change the positions that had brought on the strike. Two weeks after the strike started, the dialogue around the table sounded familiar and pessimistic. The players seemed to feel they were wasting their time. They impressed upon Grebey that the idea of a player pool for compensation was a major concern. He replied, "Pool [is] no more palatable today than [it was] yesterday or 6/11."[12]

Miller returned to the negotiations a couple of weeks later at the behest of the Executive Board. His absence had done nothing to improve the relationship between him and Grebey. However, some of the players involved in the negotiations had increased their dislike for the opposition's chief bargainer. Steve Rogers, a star pitcher with the Expos, was part of the meetings. His impression, that Grebey "condescended to us and made us feel that we didn't know anything. . . . When he laid out the figures for us, he made it seem that we couldn't understand any of it. We could handle some numbers," is common among other players. There's more than a tinge of anger and sarcasm in Rogers's comments. Since he had a degree in petroleum engineering and later would help develop computer programs used by players in salary arbitration, he probably is right in thinking he could "handle numbers" as well as Grebey.[13]

Even in the midst of the strike, the Players Association took time to handle everyday activities. In what might have been the closest thing to a light moment during the strike, with millions of dollars and the 1981 season on the line, Fehr filed Grievance 81–7 on June 23, 1981, by sending an official letter to Grebey and Howard Fox, the executive vice president of the Twins, with copies to Jerry Koosman, the Twins' player rep, and Barry Rona. The fact that twelve players and one coach had to pay $27.50 for drinks on a flight because they did not get "first class meals" while seated in coach had to be addressed.[14] Maybe the scale of the grievance just appealed to Fehr's sense of the absurd, but it was a reminder that the union was playing its role of holding the owners accountable for even the smallest infraction of their contractual obligations.

It appears that the owners assumed that once the players stopped getting checks and had the normal rhythm of their lives disrupted, they would doubt the wisdom of striking. The owners repeatedly asked publicly why baseball should come to a halt just to protect the current rights of eight or nine potential free agents. Conversely, players wondered aloud that if so few players really were affected, why should the owners continue to insist on direct compensation? Both sides could reply to the other that there were principles involved. Just as correctly, they could reply that there was a lot of self-interest, ego, and money involved. The majority of the players and virtually every player rep was convinced that they were in a test of wills with the owners and that the future of the union and free agency were at stake. As far as they were concerned, the owners had defined the issues, and now the players were going to beat them on a field of their choosing. When the player reps discussed the attitudes of their teammates, the rhetoric was revealing and straightforward: "we've given as much as we can," "no more, we made too many concessions in 1976," "everybody said no back down," "preserve 1976 rights," "they're fucking us, we'll fuck them," "a settlement only if it doesn't hurt us," and "if we offer anything, we'll get no solution."[15]

The player reps knew that some players were hurting financially. They discussed the fact that some players might be wavering, but they were pleased at how few there were. The reps noted at their July 7 meeting that the strike had garnered the public support of some of the marquee players who had been critical of the union in the past. By that time, there were new pressures on some of the owners. Cities were threatening to sue, the strike insurance was coming to an end, and some clubs appeared unwilling to sacrifice the most profitable part of the season. Some players thought the owners would break for the same reason that owners thought the players would capitulate—no one wanted to see the 1981 season disappear. Both sides believed that the other had compelling reasons to start playing soon. The players might have been overly optimistic in their views about how much the owners were hurting and definitely underestimated how much the owners thought they were involved in a last-ditch battle to overturn some of the measures that were destroying baseball.

There were also external pressures being applied on the union and the individual players. The mayors of Pittsburgh and Cincinnati were among the elected officials who wrote Miller about their concern for the economic impacts of the strike on their communities. They urged him and the association to do whatever was necessary to end the strike quickly.

Ken Moffett, the deputy director of the Federal Mediation and Conciliation Service, had gotten involved in the negotiations in March. After a few meetings, it appeared to him that his presence served no useful purpose. When negotiations began after the strike started, he reentered the scene. Moffett offered a compromise proposal, which the players accepted and the owners rejected. The owners had an amended version, which stipulated, "If a ranking player becomes a free agent, *compensation shall be made from the signing club to the former club*" (emphasis added).[16] This was the "poison pill" as far as the players were concerned.

The seriousness of the situation was underlined when there were no games played on the Fourth of July, the traditional midway point of the season, and the All-Star Game was canceled. Secretary of Labor Ray Donovan entered the negotiations in an effort to use public pressure, his office, and the popularity of a newly elected president with an affinity for baseball to end the strike. In the midst of these efforts another issue emerged that had the potential of sabotaging any possible agreement. This was the question of whether players should receive service credit for the time they were out on strike. Service time was the accumulation of the days that a player served in the major leagues. A specified minimum was necessary to be eligible for salary arbitration and free agency. In the past, there had been little objection to granting service credit for time involved in work stoppages. Gaherin and Miller had treated service time in baseball as the equivalent of time toward seniority in other industries. But everything was different in 1981. The owners were determined not to make the same kind of concessions they had made in the past. In the matter of service time, they found allies in the press and the fans, who derided the thought that the players should have the effrontery to even ask for it. After all, if players did not play, why should they get credit?

But the issue was a potential deal-breaker. It had direct impact on virtually every player. The refusal of the owners to treat service time as they had in the past gave the impression that they were trying to find ways to hold up a settlement. The owners' view was based on their feeling that this strike was more costly and that the players should not expect the same free ride they had received in the past. The player reps saw it as another sign that the owners wanted to turn back the clock and to inflict a humiliating defeat on Miller and the union. The players thought that the owners would not be satisfied until they had taken back rights from the players and instituted limits on movement and salaries.

The attitudes of the players varied greatly from club to club. At a July board meeting, one team was described as "all but two very militant," while another as "the veterans were ready to sit financially, the young players worried about money, but everyone supports the union," and a third club had nine standing fast, two considering compensation, and "three to four whatever Marvin thinks."[17] Just before the talks moved to Washington, Bob Howsam used an interview to state that the latest proposal by the owners was different from "the original plan [which] was not nearly so liberal, . . . [now] we tried to cover the whole waterfront . . . we were trying to get a quick settlement. We feel this proposal is fair and should be accepted." Howsam was a co-author of the new proposal. The writer who interviewed Howsam reminded the readers that service credit would not have been a problem if the players had accepted earlier management proposals. The players were going to have to pay the price of their recalcitrance. In the same article, an agent who supposedly was close to both Miller and Grebey said that there was room for compromise, but everyone should take the union at its word "that there will be no settlement unless the credited service is settled in favor of the players."[18]

The Washington meeting was more like a series of monologues than a negotiating session. The union decided to let the owners "know why and how players feel." The presentation was made not by Miller but by one of the most respected and experienced players. He presented an account of why baseball had ended up in its present situation. He claimed that since 1976, the players were convinced that a compensation plan was coming, and they had tried to get it on the negotiating table because it was certain to become a strike issue. When the owners insisted on compensation, a strike was inevitable. What frustrated the players was the feeling that while they had made concessions, the owners had stood back and waited for more. The union had been willing to accept the mediator's proposal, although it contained elements that were anathema to it. In every instance, the answer from the owners had been "no."

Miller followed with a summary of the substance and tone of what had been discussed behind closed doors by the Executive Board. The union would not accept any compensation plan that "punishes or taxes a club signing a free agent." If the owners really wanted "equity," then a player pool should be enough. The players thought that any effort to present compensation as a noneconomic issue was "comical, outrageous, and unreal." This sense of indignation was not one-sided. One executive told the players that the owners had given up so many things over the years that they needed and deserved something back. That meant that direct compensation was necessary and fair for both sides.[19]

At the end of the meeting, both sides agreed on a couple of things. They were drawing close to a time when they might not be able to salvage the season, and everyone was tired. Miller introduced another concern. It might be impossible to keep their lack of progress from the public much longer. The players had to know what was going on in Washington, and the association intended to inform its members the next day. After that, there was no telling how much information would be made public.

The potentially public nature of the negotiations became more apparent when a group of powerfully placed congressmen sent a long letter to Miller and Grebey, writing "both as baseball fans and as representatives of large numbers of baseball fans." The letter spoke of the "irreparable harm to our national pastime" and the economic damage being done to cities and businesses. The congressmen said that the "glare of publicity" was not helping and that "a precedent for such a solution can be found in the successful Camp David talks between the leaders of Egypt and Israel."

The letter concluded that congressional intervention in baseball is not appropriate or desirable, but as long as people are suffering because of the strike, "the greater the pressure that will build up to have someone, anyone, bring an end to the strike."[20] It is fascinating to picture Marvin Miller, Ray Grebey, Gussie Busch, Mike Marshall, and others gathering at the presidential retreat to be greeted by an honest broker.

Wyche Fowler from Georgia, the author of the letter, stated, "As you may know, last month a number of us wrote a letter to Commissioner Kuhn urging him to intervene to bring a quick end to the strike." This was one more example of the inability of people, especially baseball fans, to distance themselves from the Judge Landis myth and to understand that any belief in an all-powerful, impartial commissioner was both illusory and irrelevant. The letter unintentionally raised the ongoing problem of the distrust that existed between the union and baseball officials.

After the strike was over, Miller wrote to Fowler saying that the union had only learned on July 23 that the congressmen had written to Kuhn on June 26. Miller chose to put a sinister explanation on events by saying that the first letter was probably "consigned to the trash can of discarded ideas by the Commissioner" because management was not interested in using arbitration to resolve the dispute.[21]

The Executive Board meeting a few days after the Washington negotiating session showed how much the players distrusted the proposals, tactics, and motives of the owners. The general sense of the meeting was that as early as 1977 the owners had decided to test the players in 1980 and hoped to finish the process of destroying free agency by 1983. The players had done all the suffering caused thus far by the strike, and any further burdens should be on the owners. They wanted "to rescue the season [with] an honorable settlement," but the players were going to define what was "honorable."[22] The acceptable minimum would be service credit and no direct compensation. Having gone this far, the players intended to win the strike, not only to survive it. When the board surveyed the attitudes on every club, little had changed from previous discussions. The union appeared solid. The biggest difference was that some players were talking about next season and wondering if the union might be weaker after a long off-season.

The union had created a fairly effective mechanism for keeping players informed, by using the player reps and a few designated players as conduits. Some of the players met to have informal workouts among themselves. This gave them another way to share information as well as to keep their spirits high. The key to Miller's strategy always had been to get as much information as possible out to the players. Now the players wanted more details. Many of them "wanted to see Marvin." One possible solution was to hold a series of regional meetings. The reaction of the board showed that little about this strike was as simple as it might appear. When Miller pointed out that the regional meetings "could present problems," and attempts would be made to say it "was a show of weakness," a veteran player responded that "anything we do is seen as weakness." There were also questions about the structure of the meetings. The most serious concerns were about how detailed the presentations should be and what should be included. Would they be open forums for questions from players, or should they deal with the issues that Miller and the negotiators thought were most important?

At the same time that the board was talking about where and when to hold open meetings, they also were trying to figure out if the owners could afford "to sit it out" and whether the "season [is] over if we don't take the last offer." Finally, the board voted on "DOC MILLER'S TRAVELING ROAD SHOW." The motion passed 26 to 5 and was put into a formal resolution that passed unanimously. The final few minutes of the meeting were devoted to "miscellaneous Bullshit."[23] When the players walked out of the meeting, they knew that the next few days would show them just how solid the union remained.

The regional meetings were supposed to serve two purposes for the union. They were the most direct way to bring players up to date on what had happened in the negotiations and the prognosis for the future. The meetings also provided a visible setting where the press and management could see lots of players together in circumstances where they were energized and even more motivated to win the strike. There was a real danger that the local press might use the meetings to question the resolve of the players. In one instance, a writer with good connections to the union ran a story headlined, "Strike Shows Cracks." The extent of the "crack" was an admission by Miller that one or two clubs might be "iffy" about the strike.[24] There was no question about the truthfulness of either the story or the facts involved. Players on two clubs were divided roughly fifty-fifty about whether to accept the last PRC proposal in return for ending the strike. The reactions among other clubs ranged from eight or nine waverers to unanimity. A number of clubs felt that even talking about accepting the current proposal was a "sell-out."[25]

The regional meetings turned out better than the board had expected. Players who missed the comradeship of the clubhouse and were left to worry about their future in isolation were part of a team again. A few days after the last regional meeting, the dynamics of the negotiations changed radically. As the strike approached its fiftieth day, the strike insurance payments to the owners were going to run out soon.

The PRC decided to make changes in how it conducted the negotiations and showed this to the union in a very direct way. It was Lee MacPhail, the president of the American League, a man who literally had grown up in baseball, who contacted Miller about setting up new meetings. Grebey was relegated to the sidelines while Miller and MacPhail handled the details that led to the agreement that ended the strike. In the view of the player reps, when the owners jettisoned Grebey, they were giving a signal that they were willing to make concessions in order to end the strike.

Once negotiations resumed, the position of the owners moved closer to what the players had proposed. How much of this was because strike insurance was ending and how much was the realization that the union would not crack are matters of speculation to the present day.

The new agreement awarded a player from a free agency compensation pool to a team losing a free agent. Clubs who signed free agents could protect twenty-four players on their major league roster. Other clubs could protect twenty-six. There was some minor monetary compensation if a club lost a player from the pool. There was little similarity between the outcome and what the owners had demanded as "equity." The players even got full-service credit for the games that were canceled because of the strike.

In the aftermath of the settlement, the so-called gag rule among the owners no longer operated. Some of them, like Edward Chiles of the Rangers, tried to make the best of the situation, pointing out, "'They [players] hung tight, they hung tough, they're made of strong stuff. You gotta be proud of them.'" Others, such as Edward Bennett Williams of the Orioles and Roy Eisenhardt of the A's, stressed the importance of never allowing a strike to occur again, claiming, "'we need the additional time to reorient our thinking and out structure so these earthquakes don't have to occur again.'"[26]

No one was more forthright in his comments about the outcome of the strike than Gussie Busch. While Miller talked about a "feeling of great pride; pride in the solidarity of the players," Busch said that he was "never more disgusted, angry, and ashamed of a situation in which I was involved. Once again we [the owners] are being ridiculed by everyone—inside and outside of sports." Busch waged a lonely rearguard action, trying to convince the owners to reject the draft settlement. He was frustrated that "a horrible contract has been extended for one year" and that the players had won on every issue. According to him, in an act of self-defeating folly the owners "have made the union our partner," and a senior partner at that. Busch said his fellow owners had "sold us out in New York . . . because of their individual problems and egos . . . owners who undermined the P.R.C. and shamefully cheated and deceived all of us."[27]

After almost two years of negotiations, the union had prevailed on almost every issue. The new agreement enshrined free agency and even increased the minimum salary. Miller and Busch might have shared a common view about the ego of the owners and the gains made by the players, but that's where the agreement ended. To Busch, the future of baseball was in the hands of men with no vision and even less courage to do what was needed to bring the sport to its senses. For Miller, there was at least the hope that some of the new guard in baseball had recognized two essential truths—that the union could not be broken and that long-term cooperation was the only way to ensure that 1981 would not be the first of many drawn-out work stoppages.

In the aftermath of the 1981 strike, the dire predictions of journalists and owners did not materialize. Fans grumbled but returned to the ballparks. It was hard for anyone in management to deny that the union had been strengthened and that its strategy had worked. There had been times when the strike could have been settled sooner and with less rancor, but that decision had always been up to the owners. The union had made clear what it was willing to accept to end the strike, but the PRC had refused to believe it. Miller had every reason to exult in the victory of the union, but he did little in the way of public celebrating. That was not his style, and, in any case, he was more concerned with driving home the lessons to be learned from the strike than talking about victory.

Miller was encouraged by the remarks made by some of the owners. He singled out one of them for favorable comment in an article for the *New York Times*. Miller described him as someone who had learned the valuable lesson that free agent compensation had not been important enough to be the cause for a strike. The owner in question had written, "'I don't think there was any point, *from the owners' standpoint*, to this strike. . . . There's a small minority of us who have been pushing . . . to get this settled. This is an instance where the majority doesn't know what's good for it.'"[28] This was Jerry Reinsdorf of the White Sox, who in 1981 had pushed for creating a cooperative relationship with the players based on the realities of the new situation. Ironically, in 1994 Reinsdorf was the driving force behind the new "hard-line" owners who tried to force a salary cap on the players and, in so doing, brought on the work stoppage that killed the World Series in 1994 and part of the 1995 season.

The association's Executive Board showed its appreciation for the efforts of Miller, Fehr, and the other staff attorney, Peter Rose, in a direct way. All three of them had "voluntarily relinquished any monetary payment for the period of the strike," and the board decided to pay Fehr and Rose their retainers and to "provide Mr. Miller (and Mrs. Miller) with a one-month all expense paid vacation at a place(s) of his choosing."[29] In the aftermath of the strike settlement, Miller received congratulations from many former players who had been involved in building the union. His responses to them in private letters echoed his public statements, namely, that the unity of the players had made all the difference.

Miller and Fehr also spent a lot of time catching up on the reporting concerning the strike. Fehr thought that one article by John Schulian "should reside in the permanent files relating to this particular dispute" and sent a copy of it to Ken Moffett. The article paralleled Fehr's reactions to the recently concluded strike.

> The owners, spoiled children in rich men's togs, were only too happy to let the strike drag on and on, for they had the insurance and the alternate sources of income and the support of media lap dogs around the country. . . . The players won, and though you may have to look twice to believe it, the fans did too. . . . All the fat cat treachery in the world failed to force the hired hands to give their egomaniacal bosses a tool for controlling the foolish way they throw dollars around. They [the players] knew what baseball was like when their predecessors had to take what was offered or go pump gas for a living. . . . Yet the owners thought they could win the war with outdated bullying tactics. . . . The players refused to crack. . . . In the big leagues, the owners' tyranny is dead, a dragon that has breathed its last. Surely, the players must realize that, whether they care to admit it or not. The fans, of course, are another story. Too many of them have been brainwashed into believing that the strike was a dagger thrust into their collective chest. What they should realize

is that, given the temper of the '80s, labor and management had to go to war some time in some sport and now it is over.[30]

Schulian proved to be a better analyst than prophet, as the events of 1994 showed. More typical than Schulian's opinion in 1981 were those of widely read writers like Bill Conlin of the *Philadelphia Daily News* and Hal Bock of the Associated Press, both of whom stressed that past gains made by the players had been gifts from the owners rather than a result of the players' willingness to fight. Bock and Conlin reflected the views of most journalists that the players did not deserve or need more gains in 1981 and that a strike was not necessary. That meant that Miller must have sold the players on a strike. Conlin placed his analysis in a historical context: "Not even Josef Goebbels, who had a controlled press and a vast propaganda apparatus behind him, could have accomplished what Marvin Miller has accomplished. . . . Miller, who must borrow his technique of persuasion from the Moonies (or maybe they borrowed them from him), has somehow convinced the men who pay his salary that life for a 1981 baseball player is the pits."[31]

When Miller wrote to Bock and Conlin, he emphasized the same point he made to opponents and supporters of the union's actions—the strike had been almost wholly defensive, and it was the unity of the players and their willingness to take risks with their income and career that had made the owners drop their original demands. Miller wrote a number of letters to men with whom he had disagreed over the years. But the situation in 1981 had been so bitter that he took greater care than usual in the way he phrased his letters. He consistently made the case that the players saw the actions of the owners as a concentrated and conscious effort to turn back the clock and to break the union.

Two sets of letters with nonjournalists reflect the depth of Miller's feelings. One exchange of letters brought him into contact with someone from an unexpected place, an Ivy League university. It showed the sarcasm that Miller reserved for people whose motives he distrusted or who he thought were being hypocritical or disingenuous. The other was to an old friend, a former player and Players Association activist. Miller wrote this letter with a sense of sorrow rather than anger.

Bart Giamatti achieved an almost mythic reputation during his brief tenure as president of the National League and commissioner of baseball. It even made its way across the Atlantic, where the British columnist and periodic U.S. resident Hugo Young described him as "reputed to have been the best of all commissioners."[32]

One of Giamatti's first public forays into the world of baseball was an article entitled "Men of Baseball, Lend an Ear," which appeared in the *New York Times* only four days after the strike started. Giamatti directed the article to "Sovereign Owners and Princely Players" who were the "temporary custodians of an enduring public trust," a treasure bequeathed to the nation by Alexander Cartwright and his successors. Baseball, in Giamatti's phrase, was "not simply an essential part of this country, it is a living memory of what American culture at its best wants to be." How could any fan not be moved by the power of the poet-president's appeal to the purity of the sport of baseball? Many would have joined in his condemnation of the "Princelings and Sovereign of baseball [who] speak of the game as an industry . . . [who] play the game for whatever mercenary motives you wish."[33]

Giamatti often talked about his love of Fenway Park in Boston, which symbolized his enjoyment of the special nature of baseball. Somehow, he never took into account that it was a place built to give professionals a chance to perform for a living and the business that employed them an opportunity to increase its profits. That was the reality of the history of Major League Baseball, instead of the pastoral origins that Giamatti summoned up in his appeal to return to a yesterday that existed only in legend. He might have had a deep emotional attachment to the romantic version of baseball's past, but he chose to ignore the realities of its history and economic structure. Given the way Giamatti handled a nasty labor situation at Yale and his relationship with some of the baseball owners, it's hard not to see his *New York Times* article as a virtual job application. Despite the seeming impartiality of its introduction, the article was passionate advocacy that came down firmly on one side. Giamatti wanted readers to think the article was a plague on both houses that proposed a straightforward solution to a complicated problem: "Men of baseball, you try our patience. Enough is enough. *Go back to work"* (emphasis added).[34]

In the circumstances of 1981, Gaiamatti's stricture could apply only to the players, at the price of giving in to the owners. He did not appeal to the owners to drop their demands or even to accept the reality of Messersmith-McNally. There's no way of knowing whether Giamatti believed that the principle of free agency was wrong, but there is no doubt that his remedy was strikingly similar to that of the owners and most of the sports press. Everything would be fine if only the players would go back to playing the game and trust in the good faith and generosity of the owners to do the right thing.

Months after the article appeared, Miller responded to Giamatti in a letter that accused him of being antiunion and misleading in a way that was expected not of an educator but one of "the owners' hand picked flacks masquerading as sportswriters." In case Giamatti was unsure of Miller's opinion, the letter concluded with "concerns about the future of education—at least in one section of the ivy league."[35]

An exchange of correspondence followed in which Giamatti repeated that he was interested only in helping to rescue baseball from its current mess. This reinforced Miller's interest in hammering home his case for the union. He treated a world-renowned scholar as a naive, pompous meddler making proclamations based on ignorance, malevolence, or self-interest. Miller sarcastically dismissed Giamatti's "professed innocence" as "mind boggling." Miller gave Giamatti a simplified history of the excesses of the reserve system, and then accused the "unbiased educator" (Giamatti's self-description) of having "lent his pen to a strike breaking effort which, if successful, would have returned the players to, or close to, their former status as pieces of property."[36]

Giamatti's article and letter personified much of what bothered Miller about attitudes toward the union. The idea that baseball was "in such a mess" drew withering fire from Miller, since phrases of this type had been used for years as a way to attack the need for the union and the tactics it employed. Miller replied that "major league baseball has never been in a better condition—attendance, gate receipts, television revenue, number of teams, huge increase in value of franchises, closeness of pennant races, number of contending teams, and all time record rate for season tickets sales in 1982." In Miller's view, this was evidence of "your [Giamatti's] ignorance of the facts."[37]

It's intriguing to speculate about what would have been the relationship between Miller and Giamatti had Miller been involved actively with the Players Association when Giamatti was employed by the owners. After Giamatti became the president of the National League, a mutual acquaintance made arrangements for the two men to meet. It would have been an interesting time for both men, given their intellect, the strength of their feelings, and the width of the division between them on so many issues. Unfortunately, nothing came of those plans. Miller and Giamatti never met.

Miller probably enjoyed lecturing Giamatti, but another set of letters he wrote at the same time were difficult for him. They present insights into Miller's view of what had happened since 1966 as well as the events of 1981. They were addressed to Robin Roberts, one of the creators of the union and a man who probably destroyed his future in organized baseball because of his involvement with Miller. The 1981 strike and its aftermath was supposed to be the culmination of Miller's fifteen-year involvement with the union. At that time, "a highly placed baseball official" said, "'You can blame Robin Roberts for this strike. He's the one who hired Marvin Miller.'"[38]

Roberts had commented publicly about why he thought the strike had been the wrong step for the union. Miller wrote to Roberts and made no effort to disguise the differences that existed between them concerning both the factual and philosophical aspects of the strike. Roberts was a link between the worlds of Judge Cannon and Marvin Miller. He knew first-hand how much had been wrong in the power relationship between the owners and the players. He knew that change was important, but he had mixed feelings about tampering too much with the traditions of the sport. Since 1966 he had expressed reservations about the association using a strike as a weapon.

In the aftermath of the Messersmith decision, Roberts had contacted Miller to voice his concerns and to offer advice. Roberts was "worried about the route you are taking" and thought that Judge Oliver's ruling had "created a need for some stability," which could only come if the two sides cooperated. He thought it would be a mistake to oppose efforts by the clubs to get some compensation for the loss of free agents.[39]

The 1981 strike deeply troubled Roberts. He reflected back to 1966, when "We weren't even thinking of such things as compensation or arbitration. Our greatest concern was the pension plan." While the strike was going on, his old friend and teammate, the Phillies announcer Richie Ashburn, quoted Roberts in a newspaper column: "'there is no room in baseball for a strike. . . . I think the players are right in their stand. In fact, they are so right they should never have put themselves in a position where they were committed to a strike. That was Marvin Miller's mistake. . . . I don't think Marvin or the players ever thought they would have to strike.'"[40]

It was hard for anyone, especially Miller, to ignore Roberts's remarks. They represented the views of a thoughtful person who had grown up in the traditions of baseball and had sacrificed for the union. Roberts was convinced that the union had improved the situation of the players, and that was long overdue. He applauded the way the balance of power was redressed between the two parties, but he was bothered that the most elusive commodity, "the good of the game," might have been lost in the struggle between two parties, each acting in their self-interest.

Roberts said that he understood that the union had to protect what had been won. He admired what Miller had accomplished for the players, but he was sorry that Miller would be remembered more for the strikes than for the gains. Roberts was convinced that "the players were right in principle, but wrong when the fans' interest wasn't given priority." He thought the strike showed that the union had "let the owners bring you to that level . . . some hard nosed owners wanted to show that they could break your hold on the players. You showed how tough you could be and nobody won." Roberts wanted to remind Miller that when they had met in 1966, "I said strikes had no place in baseball. I think the latest episode has proven that to be true."[41]

Miller took the time and care to answer Roberts in some detail. The former player had raised the complicated, ambiguous issues that had been the cause of so much trouble for the union in the public arena. Miller could not accept the assertion that "strikes have no place in baseball," since that "is completely at odds with the very idea of the existence of a collective bargaining organization of players." Whether or not the players had wanted a real union in 1966, there was no way that the players of 1981 were going to return to an earlier period and give up their new-found wealth, freedom, and power. Miller tried to convince Roberts that any concession on compensation would have been a return to the pre–collective bargaining days, a time when "a premier pitcher with almost 300 wins [a reference to Roberts's own career] was exploited by being paid, in his peak years, a fraction of his true value and worth."[42]

The critical difference of opinion between Miller and Roberts was over the latter's assertion that "nobody won." That ran counter to Miller's philosophy of labor relations and his whole career at the union. Miller tried to convince Roberts that both sides might emerge from a strike with some losses, but that was different from saying that no one won a strike.

For the players in 1981, the result of the strike was a major victory that came with a price tag. They lost thousands of dollars in salaries, but they could make that up in future contracts. They were subjected to massive criticism in the media both as individuals and as part of the Players Association. They were targets of personal abuse from fans and the public. They were accused of being ungrateful and selfish and of trying to tear down the very sport that had made them rich, famous, and special. Some supposed supporters of the union in the press compared what the union had done in 1981 to a famous quote from the Vietnam War about the necessity to burn the village down in order to save it.

Before 1966 many players had talked about what they had been given by the owners, starting with the pension and extending to other issues

like meal money, better schedules, and improvements in playing conditions. After 1966 players assumed that all of the gains made by them and
their union had prices, both real and emotional. The players in a sport
where one-on-one confrontations were more apparent than in any team
game had accepted that they were involved in a one-on-one fight between
the association and the owners: It would be called labor-versus-manage-
ment in virtually any other industry. Before 1966, the members of the
association had not recognized the existence of competing interests. That
meant that the players lost by default and never realized what they might
have won. It was the job of Miller, Moss, and Fehr and the role of the
Executive Board to convince the membership of the need to fight and to
help in defining the issues. At no time did Miller or the union stage a fight
to show how tough they were. That certainly was true in 1981. The union
was not in the business of posturing or of playing macho games. It did
not take long for the players to accept Miller's proposition "that within
reason, you're the game . . . players are irreplaceable."[43] Unlike the situation in other players' unions, remarks like those were not for public
consumption and not intended to be used as slogans. They were presented
as a quiet, simple statement of fact to remind the players of the reality
of baseball.

A strike had never been a goal in itself. In 1972 the union did everything possible, short of surrender, to avoid a strike. But once the union
had decided that a strike was necessary, it wanted to make sure that the
losses were on the other side and that it emerged from a strike with the
status of its members either enhanced or damaged as little as possible.
The 1981 strike was the union doing business as usual, even if the tactics were more dramatic and the potential losses more severe. The stakes
in 1981 were much higher because the union was convinced that it was
protecting the concrete, lucrative benefits that the players had derived
from the outcome of Messersmith-McNally.

People who criticized the union for forcing a supposedly needless strike
in 1981 fell into two broad categories—those who felt that the union
should never have been in a position to challenge management, and those
who were convinced that the players had gained too many concessions
and should be willing to give up something. Players and former players
who had been involved with the union in the years between 1966 and
Messersmith-McNally knew first-hand how much the players had gained
because of the union. Unlike many of the pre-1966 players, they did not
begrudge the newfound riches and freedom of the players of 1981. Many
of the players who had weathered the strike of 1972 and suffered intense

criticism at that time did not benefit from Messersmith-McNally. Yet they were among the first to write Miller with their support and praise for how the players had reacted. They talked about how the union "was terrific as usual," and they took special pleasure in telling him, "you brought us out of the woods and into the sun. . . . You gave the players the respect and credibility they deserved. Because of you they are where they are today."[44] Miller replied by giving the credit to the players, who "were simply magnificent throughout. . . . The owners gambled that the players could be forced to their knees—and lost the gamble."[45]

In fifteen years the players had transformed themselves from supplicants in a company union to a united force with its own agenda that prevailed in a bitter fight against the men who paid their salaries. The 1981 strike put an exclamation point to Miller's tenure at the union. It proved that the union was there to stay and had the resolve and the power to protect its gains.

CONCLUSION

BEGINNING IN THE LATE 1960S, there emerged a body of literature about a potential "revolution" in sports. It focused on why athletes should take greater control over their own lives. Antiestablishment attitudes and questions about long-held assumptions permeated much of it.

Baseball was wedded to tradition and history more than any other major American sport. It was run by owners who knew their power and played by men with little apparent interest in change. It was surprising that the "revolution" that actually transformed a major sport and the structure of all professional sports and changed the attitudes and rhetoric of participants and fans was carried out by baseball players acting through a union. They were men in the most individualistic of team sports. They were at the top of their profession, were politically and socially conservative, and were making a very good living.

The actions of the baseball players fit the classic historic, as opposed to the romantic or ideological, model of a revolution. It was a revolution of the relatively successful who wanted to protect their success and build upon it rather than an uprising of the downtrodden. Within that scenario, the owners played almost to perfection the role of an ancien régime that was too caught up in its own traditions and rhetoric to think that there could be any meaningful discontent.[1]

Jim Bunning was representative of a strongly pragmatic sense of self-interest that motivated players. In his case, pushing for new power for the union was the equivalent of a pitcher throwing close to batters to protect his right to the inside corner of the plate.[2] Rather than talking about the problems caused by the traditional paternalism of baseball, players like him decided to do something about it. They decided to think and act for themselves. This type of conduct did not fit the stereotype of players held by owners, writers, and fans, which accounts in part for the ease with which so many people accepted the idea that Miller was calling the tune for the players. Miller's great contribution was not that he told the players what to think but that he showed them they had the responsibility to think for themselves and the collective power to do something for themselves.

Free agency was the crown jewel of the union's accomplishments, and as such it has received the most attention. It is easy to look at the changes made before 1975 as a prelude to Messersmith-McNally or building blocks toward destroying the reserve system. That would be a bad case of reading the future into events that were important in their own right. The tactics of the union were to fight for specific gains that appeared obtainable at the time and to establish an atmosphere and framework for making further changes that could alter the fundamental relationship between the players and ownership. If the union had any kind of master plan, it was to gain for itself the same rights that labor unions had in other industries and to tailor them to fit the situations that were unique to major league baseball players

The impartial grievance procedure was the key to all future successes of the union, as well as an important victory in its own right. It showed the players that they had a chance to challenge management on matters that affected the everyday lives of the players, like fines, discipline, accommodations, transportation, and playing conditions. Again, the union was not dealing with abstract philosophical questions. It got something for its members. The arbitrator was there to ensure a fair fight if a player chose to challenge his club. This led players to realize that the existing structure might not be the only possible one.

Salary arbitration received a lot more attention in the press than the grievance procedure because it was public and it dealt with lots of money. It combined the principles of the impartial grievance with a recognition that the reserve system needed some adjustment. Salary arbitration has become the all-purpose whipping boy for executives, writers, and fans who feel that baseball has been damaged permanently by escalating salaries, especially those paid to marginal performers. The supposed villains in this version are the players who want too much and the arbitrators who have no idea of what a player really is worth. Buzzie Bavasi summed up this attitude: "arbitration is what has caused the problem." But when it was pointed out that a club could avoid the supposed problems of arbitration by simply not offering a contract to a player, he responded incredulously, "but then we would lose control of the player, and we wouldn't get anything for him."[3] That is the quintessential view of an experienced executive. Control was what mattered, even if it cost the club money in the short term.

Baseball was a business for the owners and an occupation for the players. There was a steady growth in salaries after arbitration and a dramatic rise after free agency took hold. Experience and performance made a difference in salaries, but arbitration and free agency (or the possibility of them) meant that market rates would apply. The money that the clubs used for the post-1976 salary structure came from many sources. Among them were the new money that came into the game from television, increased attendance, and a reallocation of money within clubs. The game prospered. In simple terms, more money for the players meant less for the owners.

After 1974 the players continued to get an increasingly larger share of the club revenue, but compared to what? Again, the history of baseball and conventional wisdom were in conflict. If fans and owners wanted to return to some golden age of baseball salaries, would they like to go back to 1929 when salaries were 35.3 percent of team revenues or even 1939 when they were 32.4 percent of revenues? Salaries as a percentage of team revenues had declined consistently after 1935, reaching 17.6 percent in 1974.[4] In 1977, the year after free agency, the salaries for players crept to over 20 percent of gross revenue. The symbolic value of this figure probably was lost on all the participants. That was the figure that some players had discussed in the late 1950s, when owners such as Tom Yawkey warned about the dangers of a militant union approach and the possibility that owners would get out of baseball because of it.

Before the 1968 Basic Agreement, it was fanciful to talk about a player negotiating with his general manager. All the power, other than the decision not to play and not to get paid, resided with the management. Buzzie Bavasi made that clear in his *Sports Illustrated* articles, which were published shortly after Miller and Moss came to the Players Association. Bavasi described the tricks of his trade and enjoyed the various ways he had been able to deceive players. One of the first accomplishments of the union was to deny this kind of power to general managers. A provision in the Basic Agreement gave a player the right to an attorney or advisor of his choice to handle contract negotiations for him. The urging by the player reps that players should talk among themselves about their salaries and the insistence by the union that salary data be made available as part of the salary arbitration process further eroded the ability of a general manager to play according to his own rules.

As early as the start of the 1967 season, the players knew Miller's philosophy about baseball and labor relations. They had seen him deal with the owners and their representatives, and they supported him. There was no place in Miller's vocabulary for a "generous owner." Tom Yawkey of the Red Sox personified so much of what Miller thought was wrong about the way baseball operated. The feeling became mutual. In 1973 Yawkey commented to a reporter, "'if this [union] stuff is going to continue every spring, I have to ask myself if it's all worthwhile.'" Yawkey was particularly "disturbed" about Miller's activities, adding, "'I've never met the man personally so I don't know him or what his aims are . . . but he keeps saying all the owners are s.o.b.'s and that really bothers me.'"[5]

Rising salaries were a visible consequence of free agency, but the freedom involved was even more important. A player could decide where to play based on a number of factors, including how much playing time he would get, what position he would play, the style of the manager, the reputation of the front office, the attitude of the fans, the shape of the stadium, the attractiveness of the city, and any other reason that might appeal to him.

The essence of free agency was that the player had the freedom to make choices. Free agency had impacts on player movement that often went unrecognized. Some players got a lot of money not to move. Free agency was a bargaining tool used by players, who stayed or left as they wished.

What happened to the oft-cited "loyalty to the fans" as a consequence of the changes forced on baseball by the union? Loyalty never seemed to have been a major consideration for the owners when they decided to trade a player, however much he might be a fan favorite. Can any baseball fan forget the photograph of a weeping Enos Slaughter, when he learned he had been traded from the Cardinals to the Yankees? The chance of World Series fame and riches mattered much less to him than his feelings about his team and his fans. But he had no control over whether his loyalty was reciprocated. The Cardinals traded Slaughter for the same reason that players had been traded for decades: any reason the club thought was important. It could be to decrease a payroll, make room for a promising minor leaguer, to obtain a player they wanted, or for no discernable reason at all. In any case, the clubs were never under any obligation to tell anyone why they made a trade. If a team chose to talk publicly about why a deal was made, the explanation was always a version of "for the good of the club."

Fans were supposed to assume that ownership was doing everything in its power to build the best team possible. Fans might idolize a player, but their primary attachment was to a uniform and a team. In the era before free agency, fans assumed that any player on their team wanted to play for it. A holdout was a selfish malcontent. Anyone who asked to be traded was a traitor. Free agency changed everything. Players could choose where they played and made no pretense about debts they owed to a team or its fans.

The number of players who changed teams in the fifteen years after free agency was no greater than the number who had moved in the years preceding that, although there was a slight rise in the number of star players who changed teams.[6] How many moved mattered much less to the fans and the writers than the circumstances under which they moved. Fans had an unstated assumption that players were not supposed to think or act for themselves, a belief held openly by managers, coaches, and general managers. Players certainly were not supposed to spurn a team or to be courted by others.

Opponents of free agency claimed that a free market for players would destroy the competitive nature of baseball and create dynasties. This misreads the history of baseball before 1976 by assuming that competitive pennant races had been the norm. Dynasties had been the fact of baseball life, and a significant number of teams had never been competitive. From 1901 to 1969, the pennant races in the American League were dominated by four teams. The Yankees, Red Sox, A's, and Tigers won fifty-four out of sixty-eight pennants. In the National League, the Cardinals, Dodgers, Giants, and Cubs won fifty-two. During the post–World War II period and in the decade after 1969 (the start of divisional play), the domination of a few teams was as great. It took a few years for the effects of free agency to take hold. The competitive map after 1981 is an interesting commentary on free agency. Between 1981 and 1993, all twelve National League teams finished first at least once in their division, and eleven of the fourteen American League teams finished first. From 1901 to 1968, 36 percent of pennant races were won by the defending champion; from 1969 to 1980 it was 36 percent, and from 1981 to 1992 it was 17 percent.

Another feature of the new system that attracted negative comment from executives, writers, and fans was multiyear guaranteed contracts. But this was a choice made by owners and general managers. The essence of negotiating a contract in virtually every circumstance other than baseball before 1976 was that both sides had to decide what commitments to make and what risks to assume. After 1976 the general manager had to decide what he was prepared to pay to attract a player. This often meant something besides money. A multiyear contract was a calculated risk taken equally by both sides. The clubs had to live up to the contractual obligations, and players were locked into its terms.

Free agency placed a new premium on executive competence, judgment of talent, the ability to relate to players, and an ability to deal with the new economics of the sport. Mistakes and successes of management were visible in a way that they had never been before. In the past, only the most dedicated fan was interested in following the intricacies of the farm system, and there weren't many heated disputes in the press about player development. Major league free agents were a totally different story. In order to qualify for free agency, a player had to have been in the major leagues for six years and to have established a reputation for himself. There were no "dark horse" free agents, analogous to diamonds in the rough buried in the farm system of another team or in islands off the coast of the continental United States. Anyone with even a casual interest in baseball knew who the free agents were and knew something about them.

Fans looked at the front offices in new ways. The inability to re-sign a valuable free agent gave the impression that the club did not care about being a contender or that the general manager didn't have the skill to deal with a player or his agent. Signing a high-priced free agent was good for public relations and might help ticket sales, but it also left the club open to the accusation of throwing money in the direction of worthless players. Fans took it for granted when a new player succeeded. The only thing that was worse than not signing a free agent was signing one that became a flop. Free agency made executives publicly responsible for their supposed failures, either of omission or commission.

When a free agent moved, fans in one city appreciated the wisdom of his decision. But that meant that fans elsewhere felt rejected, and they took out their annoyance on the individual player and the system that allowed him to disappoint them. The level of fan and journalistic annoyance with players increased with the advent of the union, the work stoppages caused by both sides, and the dramatic increase in salaries to a level that seemed beyond the imagination of fans and writers alike. Miller had recognized the probability that any union worth having would alienate many people who were devoted to the sport. At the start of his tenure, he addressed this:

Even among dedicated baseball fans and veteran observers there is a feeling that players live the best of all possible lives—affluent, relaxed, se-

cure and famous. Except for fame, and except for the relatively good salaries of the outstanding stars of the game, affluence, relaxation, and security are not in evidence. Because of these myths, however, there was
considerable puzzlement when the players moved to strengthen their
Players Association. . . . The average baseball fan views baseball solely
as a sport. His own experience with the game involved pleasure and rec-
reation. Small wonder that his reaction to getting paid for playing is that
the professional baseball player "has it made."[7]

It did not take Miller and Moss long to understand that they could court
popularity for themselves and the union or try to alter the relationship
between the players and their employers. They could not do both. Despite the fact that Miller and Moss were fans of the sport, their approach
was the antithesis of the uncritical romanticism about baseball that was
present in so many quarters. They were hired by the players to improve
their situation, not to be cheerleaders for baseball. There is no question
that Miller and Moss hardened divisions between the players and the
owners, but neither man created the problems. If the players had not
thought something was wrong in 1966, they would have had no reason
to hire Miller, no reason to support him, and no reason to show admira-
tion for how he went out of his way to confront the owners and their
representatives.

Miller's periodic displays of outrage were much more than a bargaining technique. He represented a whole new attitude within the union and
among the players. He believed what he said about the unfairness of the
relationship between the players and the owners and the necessity for a
system that respected the "dignity" (a phrase he used often) of the individual player. But he never gave any evidence of allowing his personal
dislike to get in the way of his role as tactician and negotiator. Being
unpopular or being seen as a threat to baseball were not high prices to be
paid in return for having a legitimate shot at forcing the system to reform.

A recent biographer of Bart Giamatti describes Miller as having "a
narrow mind," and a biographer of Bowie Kuhn states that "the calcu-
lating Miller was no baseball fan, but the players loved him." Both of these
contain elements of truth. Miller did have a "narrow," or focused, view
of baseball's traditions and the need for the union to change them. The
players loved and respected him because he changed their lives.[8]

Miller and Moss were convinced that the players had been victimized
as the result of an unequal relationship, and they had been hired to change
that. They drew a sharp distinction between playing baseball and being
a part of the industry that was the business of baseball. The players must

have accepted this distinction, or the union could not have succeeded in changing the way baseball conducted its business. In 1999 Bill Werber, a player who retired in 1942, presented an interesting summation of Miller's career: "He assaulted a system which worked solely in favor of the club owner. This assault on the system was absolutely necessary to the welfare of the sport and the people who play it."[9]

The actions of the union and individual players within it created a new relationship between them and the writers and the fans. Players did not appear to have the same reverence for authority or for the traditions of the game. A new vocabulary came into baseball and the reporting about it. Players talked about the "industry," and they were concerned about heretofore arcane issues like length of contract, incentive arrangements, and no-trade clauses. These were not the type of comments that the public expected from their ballplaying heroes. The player who would say, "aw, shucks, gee-whiz, I'm so glad to be a major leaguer that I would pay to put on the uniform," had always been a small minority and was possibly even the product of the imagination of sportswriters and novelists. The stereotype did have a hold on the public imagination. After 1966 the players and their union demonstrated little of the modesty and appreciation that was supposed to be a part of this professional persona. The sense that players had seized some power to control their careers bothered many fans and sportswriters. It was not baseball as it was supposed to be. The players not only were determining their own futures, they made no pretense or apologies about it.[10]

The phrases "selfish player" or "greedy player" became a standard part of sports journalism and fan conversation in the wake of salary arbitration and free agency. Annoyance with players was not a new phenomenon, but the level increased as the union became more active. In 1927 a baseball writer had noted, "Today the players regard the game in a different light. . . . It has become a business with the boys, who play for the income." In 1915 the complaint had been, "The sordid element of baseball as a business has cast a shadow over the sport. Players make too much money and become spoiled," and in 1888 it was, "Somehow or other they don't play ball now as they used to do some eight or ten years ago. . . . They don't play with the same kinds of feeling or for the same object as they used to."[11]

Don Fehr has pointed to two phrases that have been part of the vocabulary of baseball executives since the sport started: "we don't have enough pitching" and "the team is losing money." Perhaps he should have added a third: the "overpaid, selfish, not-as-good-as-they-used-to-be-in-the-old-days ballplayers." Complaints about the players increased by almost exponential proportions in the 1980s. Some of this was a result of the off-the-field behavior of some players—drug problems, violence against fans, and the like. But the basis for the condemnation of players was a belief by fans that players were too wealthy and that they did not respect either the sport or the fans. This was another way of saying that players did not demonstrate the kind of humility that fans wanted to associate with their idols.

The most visible sign of this supposed arrogance, some would argue the cause of it, was the freedom the players had gained and the power of their union to protect their rights and to shield them from some of the consequences of their actions. It is hard to say which of the aspects of the union bothered fans and journalists more—that it assisted its members in obtaining multimillion-dollar contracts, or that it supported them in appeals and grievances against disciplinary actions. This new attitude toward players coincided with the enormous growth in the broadcast coverage of sports, both on cable television and sports talk radio. What was wrong with players and why the union was ruining baseball became the staples of many broadcasters and their fans.

In the late 1960s some writers, like Red Smith, "became convinced that baseball writing must reflect society's concerns." Smith was a minority within the profession, whose majority still came closer to what David Voigt described as the "Gee whizzers."[12] Writers did not seem to believe that young, inexperienced players thought about much other than the next game. The players were making good money and were treated well for playing baseball, while the reporters had to do a "real job" and did not get the kind of fame and adulation that the players received. Who were the players to complain and organize a union, as if they were real workers? An extreme, but not isolated, version of this approach appeared in a 1962 column in *The Sporting News*, "Pity Poor Ball Players!" which concluded, "Our opinion has always been that ball players ought to pay to get into the park, and pay double to get into the game. Some of the old timers have told us they secretly agree with that."[13]

In the 1960s, increasing radio and television coverage of games meant that beat writers had to do something more than tell the reader what had happened on the field. Many writers had grown up in the system where players knew their place, and that place certainly did not include setting the terms of their contracts, choosing where to play, or telling reporters about baseball. For their part, players increasingly saw no reason to seek either the advice or the approval of the writers who, in turn, thought they still knew what was best for both the sport and the players.

This attitude of journalists toward players was not unique to baseball or to the United States. A parallel set of circumstances developed in English football when young players became rich celebrities. Their predecessors had incomes that were similar to the reporters who covered them. The new generation of star players were younger and seemed to have little respect for either the knowledge or power of the reporters. As the sports sociologist Richard Giulianotti describes it, "questions of trust bedevil their relationship where players were wary of the reporters' motives and journalists assumed that the players wanted to be un-cooperative."[14] The prevailing attitude of journalists toward players was a combination of condescension and distrust.

For most baseball writers, there was no reason to examine, let alone criticize, the relationship between players and their clubs. If there were any problems, the players should trust in the fairness and integrity of the owners to address them. It was not until long after the players had exerted their collective power that stories began to emerge about how management had acted in the past.

One noteworthy example was the experience of Mickey Mantle, the great center fielder for the Yankees. As a twenty-five-year-old, he won the American League Triple Crown (batting average, runs batted in, and home runs) in 1956. When he asked for a significant raise, George Weiss, the general manager, told him he was too young and said that if Mantle did not accept the club's offer and keep his mouth shut, Weiss might have to show Mantle's wife reports from a private detective hired by the club to follow him and Billy Martin. Years later Mantle commented, "He [Weiss] threatened to trade me to Cleveland for Herb Score and Rocky Colavito."[15] Mantle had no choice but to accept the contract offered to him by the Yankees. If those were the circumstances of the brightest young star playing for the most profitable and famous team, what were the experiences of lesser players? It is interesting to conjecture how the union would have responded if this had happened after 1968. Would even the general manager of the Yankees have been willing to try something like that after 1968?

Ironically, an important factor in creating the negative attitudes toward the players was the continued efforts of the owners to criticize their prime asset. They were using a labor-war tactic against the players by emphasizing publicly all that was wrong with them. This was a strange way to market the unique skills of the attraction of baseball, its players. In 1976 a recently retired player, Jim Northrup, pointed out the foolishness of this approach in a letter to the president of the American League: "It is in this light that I feel you could be most helpful by reminding Management that the players they condemn and blame today are the same players they will be promoting and attempting to sell tomorrow."[16]

There is no evidence that anyone in a position of authority in baseball ever attempted to put a brake on the continued efforts of baseball's hierarchy to demonize what the players were doing. The more attention the owners directed toward the injustice of how much money players made and how aggressive the union had become, the more they encouraged the fans to look at the least attractive aspects of the sport at the expense of the drama of the game and the talent of its performers.

Many owners and executives did foolish things concerning the union, often in the glare of publicity. But even the most belligerent of them were not stupid. Many of them were very successful in other businesses and ran equally successful franchises. Their behavior often was a combination of thoughtlessness and the arrogance bred by years of unchecked control. Almost a century of the reserve system had shaped their reality, and the 1922 Supreme Court decision had given them a feeling of invulnerability. They spent too much time talking among themselves, reinforcing a sense of their power and creating a comfortable version of history and the present. Decades of supportive press coverage had added to their conviction that they alone knew what was best for baseball and that anyone who challenged it was trying to destroy the game and fighting a hopeless battle.

Gussie Busch was a prime example of the kind of owner that Bill Veeck described as an unwitting ally of Miller's. This was the same man who had built Anheuser-Busch into the world's largest brewery and had transformed a declining franchise into one that won three pennants in the 1960s. The Cardinals were one of the most progressive teams in dealing with racial matters. Many of Busch's players, including those who were active in the union, genuinely liked him. He dealt with unions as an everyday reality in the beer business, but he could not abide the existence of the Players Association and made those feelings public in a condescending, often antagonistic manner at crucial times. No owner contradicted him publicly or appeared to try privately to silence him.

Roger Angell described the actions of the owners toward the union as "'a total distaste for self-discipline—a flaw that anarchizes the entire body and repeatedly renders it victim to its loudest and least responsible minority . . . any kind of retributive forced return to an older and simpler time that were voiced by their least restrained and most vocal members.'"[17] Vocal owners continued to talk about all that was wrong and getting worse with baseball. This was a bad strategy, both as a market-ing tool and as the basis for labor decisions.

In 1958, long before the Players Association had any direction or agen-da, Frank Lane, a highly successful general manager, warned the players to remember all the "ghost towns" that were in New England because of unions and to make sure that did not happen to baseball. He did not draw the parallels between the abandoned mills and the abandoned Polo Grounds and Ebbets Field, homes of the recently transplanted Giants and Dodgers, respectively. No one challenged either his view of American history or baseball's future. He told the players they did not need a union because he was "'your general manager, as well as for the clubs. You have to have confidence in me.'"[18] It's hard to think that many men involved with baseball would have disagreed with Lane.

Bowie Kuhn probably would have described himself as employed not by the owners, but "by baseball." He asserted, "it was never my job to side with the players or the owners, but rather to bring the two together."[19] That sentiment was part of the unbridgeable gulf between him and the union. Kuhn worked for the owners, something that was very different from base-ball. This was much more than a semantic quibble. The players made it clear that they thought that the proper role for the commissioner was to enforce the rules of baseball as defined in agreements between the union and the owners. That was the message that the Executive Board of the union gave Kuhn when he appeared at its meeting in 1969. The commis-sioner could not accept it, since it contradicted his lifelong experience in baseball, as well as his concept of how baseball should operate.

One of Kuhn's admirers described him as "the last true commissioner of baseball in the Judge Kenesaw Landis tradition."[20] If true, that was all the more reason for the union to deny any employee of the owners the kind of power that Landis supposedly had exercised. At least one base-ball fan, Judge John Oliver, pointed out in 1976 that a lot had happened to labor law and baseball since the time of Judge Landis. The responsi-bility of the executive director of the Players Association was to make sure that Kuhn did not interfere in labor-management relations.

In one interview, Curt Flood spoke about the professed values of base-ball: "They say baseball is the all-American sport. When you think of all-American, you would think of something democratic, something free."[21] This echoed the sentiments but not the later actions of one of the men who created professional baseball and helped to make it part of Ameri-can folk mythology, A. G. Spalding. As a player he had been forthright in pointing out that it was honorable to be paid to play and that no reasonable American would believe that a talented ballplayer would not be want to be paid. This was Spalding's way of rejecting the hypocrisy of the "gentleman amateur" in favor of real American values of free market capitalism and being rewarded for talent and hard work. As an owner, Spalding helped refine the reserve system and became one of its most articulate defenders. He popularized the notion that the sport could not exist if players determined their futures and teams could not be secure in their ability to keep players.[22]

The reaction of the owners to the newly assertive union took a variety of forms. During the early years of Miller's tenure, some veteran executives believed that he was a momentary annoyance and that the players would recognize that he was destroying the game. Others thought it might be enough to offer what Buzzie Bavasai described as "a few concessions to placate Marvin."[23] When both approaches failed, the owners took a tough bargaining stance. They equated compromise with surrender.

The owners started from a position of complete control and could not recognize that diminished power was not the same thing as impotence. The most important way in which the owners were self-destructive was in their unwillingness to negotiate about the reserve system. They refused to bargain even when their chief negotiator told them it was in their best interest. The first Joint Study Committee on the reserve system was a charade because the owners refused to discuss proposals for any changes. They seemed to think that merely sending someone to show up for a meeting would satisfy the players. This approach misread the changes that had taken place in the Players Association. The players came to the meetings because they were interested in what happened to them and thought there might be a chance of change.

Various factors contributed to the relative speed with which the power of the owners was broken. Some were of their own making, however understandable they might have been. They were not used to being questioned about their actions, let alone to facing opposition. They were ill-prepared to even consider making compromises. Finally, we should not underestimate the important weapon the union had in a settled body of labor law. The players and their union had not chosen previously to take advantage of their legal position. That changed dramatically after 1966. In a strange way, the inactivity of the union before 1966 lulled the owners into what became a false sense of security.

Early efforts of the union to get modifications in the conditions faced by the players were met with condescension and dismissal. After that, the union became aggressively pragmatic in pursuing changes in the reserve system. When Curt Flood's efforts to overturn the reserve system failed in court, the union had no compunctions about choosing the arbitration route. Some executives, including Commissioner Kuhn, regarded that as an unfair effort to change the rules, but the union responded that it was playing to win. The union was prepared to negotiate for modifications in the reserve system from the time Flood decided to take legal action until Peter Seitz rendered his decision. After 1976 the roles were reversed, and it was the owners who were asking for concessions.

Many players who were active in the union went on to have distinguished careers. Among them, Sal Bando, Ted Simmons, Tom Haller, Woody Woodward, Bill Stoneman, and Dal Maxvill became general managers. Joe Torre, Don Baylor, Jim Fregosi, Davey Johnson, Bob Boone, Phil Garner, Buck Martinez, Bob Rodgers, and Harvey Kuenn were managers. Brooks Robinson, Rusty Staub, Jim Kaat, Don Sutton, and Tim McCarver became successful broadcasters. Steve Rogers and Mark Belanger had leadership roles in the Players Association. Jim Bunning became a minor league manager and player's agent before being elected to Congress and, in 1998, to the Senate from Kentucky. Robin Roberts had a long career as a college baseball coach. Many of his contemporaries felt that he never got the job he merited in the major leagues because he was labeled as the man who brought Marvin Miller to the union. In 1977 someone who had retired after a few years as a bench player and was completing law school asked Miller if there might be a position at the union for someone with his "baseball and legal background." Miller informed him that "we are not planning any further staff additions," leaving the path open for Tony LaRussa to begin his long career as a highly successful major league manager.[24]

In his influential 1986 book *The Sports Industry and Collective Bargaining,* the labor economist Paul Staudohar commented that "the accomplishments by the MLBPA established the modern era in labor relations that has affected all professional team sports. Miller took a weak owner-dominated union and fused its membership into a united front. He not only excelled in winning unprecedented gains at the bargaining table, but managed to protect those gains from later attacks by management."[25] Eleven years later, in an article analyzing the 1994–95 work stoppage, Staudohar noted, "Marvin Miller set the tone when he refused to accept the paternalism between owners and players that had existed for so long in the game. Instead, he determined to establish an adversarial relationship that continues to the present."[26]

Miller's privately expressed views on the subject parallel Staudohar's assessment. In his first year as executive director, Miller had made some notes about changes that were needed to bring some equity to the relationship between players and ownership. A decade later, in a court deposition, he was asked to list what he thought were the most important positive accomplishments of the union during his tenure. The two lists are remarkably similar—the understanding by the players that they needed to participate in the union, the creation of the idea that an employer-employee relationship was based on contract and collective bargaining, the establishment of a formal grievance procedure with impartial arbitration, and economic changes favorable to the players. Miller's primary concern was to establish a relationship where the players had rights that would be considered normal in virtually every other industry. This meant dealing with more than economic or legal issues. Miller concluded his deposition with a phrase that he used often: "There was—sometimes it is an over used word, but there was no dignity to that relationship. And that has all been changed."[27]

In less than thirty years, the MLBPA had gone from a classic company union that appealed to the owners for trivial concessions to an aggressive union that many observers thought had become the senior partner in a relationship with the owners. There was a temptation by some fans and talk-show hosts to label Donald Fehr, the executive director of the union, as "the real Commissioner" and the most powerful single man in baseball. These comments were never meant as compliments, but they do indicate that a new reality had entered baseball.

The MLBPA was the engine for the changes that transformed baseball and all other professional sports. Staudohar's comment, "the modern era in baseball labor relations undeniably began with Miller,"[28] is an accurate description of the importance of what happened between 1966 and 1981. I would modify this analysis slightly—the modern era of labor relations in baseball began with the decision of the Executive Board to hire someone like Miller.

A number of factors and events shaped the relationship between the players and the owners and caused the changes occasioned by the union. But there were three defining moments for the union whereby, had events unfolded in another way, the history of labor relations in baseball would have been markedly different.

The first step in the transformation of the union was when enough players decided they had to challenge the owners in order to gain things that they thought they deserved as basic rights of their profession. This ran counter to the views of their employers, who regarded the players as transient visitors to baseball who had no real stake in the future of the sport. The new vision of the players led them to take the decision to hire a labor veteran as the first executive director of the Players Association. This set the course for collective bargaining in baseball. Miller's most important visible characteristics were that he came from a union and from outside of baseball. Throughout his tenure at the association, he placed a priority on what was called "consciousness raising" in the 1960s and "paradigm shifting" in the 1990s. Shorn of the jargon, it meant assuming that the players had the right to determine their own future and trusting in the intelligence of the players to know what was best for them and the sport.

Miller acted as a teacher in the nondidactic sense of the word. He was there to help players see that there were alternative views to what they had grown up with in their lives in baseball. Once the players were determined on a set of goals, it was the responsibility of Miller, Moss, and Fehr to lay out the alternatives and come up with a set of strategies. Then it was up to the players and their union to decide how and when to push matters to a conclusion.

The second event was the signing of the 1968 Basic Agreement and the inclusion of a grievance procedure. The agreement demonstrated that the association had the rights and powers to act as a union. The grievance procedure was the foundation for the gains made by the association. It enabled the players to deal on an equal basis with their employers, broadened their horizons about what might be accomplished, and provided the mechanism that led to free agency.

The third event was the 1972 strike. It established the credibility of the union and showed the players that a solid union could prevail in a battle against the owners. After 1972 the policy of the union became to press for further changes and to protect what it had gained. This was noticeable in the wake of the Messersmith-McNally decision and in the willingness of the union to strike in 1981 to ensure that the owners could not place any meaningful restrictions on free agency. That tradition and policy carried over into the events of 1994.

The owners repeatedly appealed to history to show how Miller and the union were trying to subvert the nature of baseball and undermine what made it special.[29] The owners' concept of a "golden age" had a quasi-religious appeal about it. They made it appear that after 1966, or 1972, or 1976, or 1981, baseball had been expelled from its Garden of Eden. If that were the case, Miller was cast in the role of the serpent bringing the apple of knowledge to the supposedly innocent players.

A view from an outside observer presents an interesting perspective on the events since 1966. Hugo Young is one of the most respected political journalists in Britain and has spent time living in this country, writing about its social and political trends. He realized that he "couldn't dismiss baseball's connection with the country that came to enthral me" and became "an obsessive student" of baseball and its history. In 2000 he tried to explain the sport to his British readers and pointed out, "In every financial or social struggle in baseball's history, the owners have sought to hold the line. Essentially, the postwar history of the game is one of player power, at first slow to work, but now aptly evidenced by the fact that no regular major-league pitcher earns less than a million bucks a year."[30] I might disagree slightly with his chronology or his salary figures, but Young's essential point is correct.

Closer to home, another writer made the same point, but with greater authority and with his customary eloquence. Tom Boswell is one of the most articulate, insightful observers of baseball. He has shown a special ability to convey the unique charm, tradition, and romance of the sport. One of his book titles, *Why Time Begins on Opening Day*, has become almost an anthem to the qualities that make baseball special. When he was asked to evaluate Miller's role, he put it into a broader context: "As to whether or not he's been good for the National Pastime, I think a larger issue is whether or not what he did was right or wrong, and it was right, and so baseball has to take its lumps."[31] The "lumps" Boswell described were the changes in the fundamental structure of baseball that the union forced on a business that had operated by its own rules and standards for almost a century. By 1981 no one could deny that the union had been the driving force in bringing an end to baseball as it had existed before 1966.

EPILOGUE

1990s–Parallels Abroad and Problems at Home

IN THE MID-1990s, events on both sides of the Atlantic provided a perspective on what the MLBPA had accomplished by 1981. Shortly after Miller arrived at the MLBPA, he discussed how unionism among professional athletes in Europe had produced some tangible gains for soccer players. What he probably had in mind was a recent court victory by the Professional Footballers Association (PFA) in England. The system that had operated there was even more restrictive than the reserve system. It included a "retain and transfer" provision that gave the clubs lifetime control and a *maximum* wage provision that applied to all players. Clubs could consign players to its reserve team, the equivalent of the minor leagues, even if other clubs wanted to obtain him.

By the late 1950s trade unions in England exercised considerable power, and their members had significant job rights. The one area in which that was not the case was the most popular professional sport, football. In 1958 an English footballer wrote about his problems to the secretary of his union. The letter sounded much like the one written in 1970 by Dave Leonhard to Marvin Miller. The footballer had been offered the minimum wage by his club, and he refused it, since "the wages they offered me are not enough to live on . . . and I know I can get more money at another club if I were free. . . . I know technically they are in their rights, but it is wrong to stop me from making a living." The head of the union replied that the only course open was to appeal to the head of the league, but he held out little hope that that would accomplish anything.

A couple of months later, the player made his peace with the club, accepted their offer, and signed a contract.[1]

In 1961 a star English player, George Eastham, decided to fight the system. With the active support of the PFA, he brought a court action, claiming that the league and the clubs were acting in illegal restraint of trade by denying him the right to market his services. The case went to the High Court and resulted in a victory for Eastham and the players. The maximum wage was dead. The PFA negotiated a system that allowed the clubs to keep some aspects of the retain and transfer system but secured new rights and economic gains for many players.[2]

In 1972 Mike Brearley, the Cambridge-educated captain of Middlesex County cricket club (and a future captain of England), was visiting the United States. He wrote a series of articles for *The Guardian* that dealt with baseball. He had the advantage of being an outsider who could take a detached look at both the sport and the business of baseball. He had to explain some things to his English audience that American readers would take for granted. The most important of these were the facts that "baseball is clearly run as a business with large profits to be made" and that owners had been quite successful in using moves, or the threat of them, to get economic concessions.[3]

Brearley's second article, entitled "The Slave Trade with a Pension Scheme," focused on the MLBPA. Brearley understood the arguments in favor of the reserve system, but he was convinced that the doomsday version was overdone: "even if competition would to some extent be lessened, it seems to me that this does not outweigh the denial of basic rights to the players." He admitted that baseball players, at least major leaguers, were well paid, but every player was "in short, a well-fed, well-housed chattel."[4] A few years after Brearley's trip to the United States, major league players were much better fed and housed and were not chattel, unless an apprenticeship in the minor leagues and six years in the majors before free agency could be considered the equivalent of slavery.

If Miller had compared the situation of his members with professional footballers in England after 1968, he would have had many reasons to be proud of what the MLBPA had accomplished. In the quarter-century after the Eastham decision, wages went up for footballers, but they had little control over either their freedom of movement or their ability to bargain with their employers. The situation was comparable in the other important football nations in Europe. By the 1980s football authorities throughout Europe looked at the U.S. situation (at least in baseball) as a portent of what dangers faced football if they did not exercise control and maintain traditional standards. The MLBPA represented what many European football officials and journalists described as "player power." The term was not meant as a compliment. The leadership involved in football used their understanding of what had happened in baseball as a warning about what could go wrong if traditional standards were discarded.

There are important parallels between the evolution of labor relations in baseball and the situation in European football. Both sports had a special place in their respective societies and existed as combinations of businesses, sports, and cultural activities. The authorities in charge of both sports reacted similarly when faced with challenges to their continued ability to control their respective sports without interference. They tried to avoid all changes and warned constantly that the sport could not exist with new rules.

By the end of the 1980s the structure of European football faced a radically changed set of circumstances. The commercialization of the sport and the influx of new revenues from television and other forms of sponsorship led the players to question what they were getting and the restraints that were placed on their ability to get better terms for themselves. The internationalization of the sport gave players a new market for their services. It introduced a new factor into the equation between football clubs and their employees: the rules of the European Community, which had created a new set of legal standards for all workers. The MLBPA had taken the fullest possible advantage of labor law, and a similar scenario played out in European football, with one significant difference. In baseball, the players had challenged the system through their union. In Europe, the important attack on the system came from one player, and he received little support, or notice, from the unions.

In 1989 a meeting of high-ranking politicians, football officials, journalists, and academics took place in Florence to discuss the relationship between football and the European Community. Much of the conversation sounded like what had taken place in baseball more than a decade earlier. David Will, the vice president of the Union of European Football Associations (UEFA), the governing body for professional football throughout Europe pointed out that the rules that restricted the free movement of players were necessary and were "totally misunderstood by many individuals outside the game." He hoped that the European Commission would "realize that the present structure of football in Europe did not come about by accident . . . [and should] be maintained."

Will asserted that it was the responsibility of the football authorities to enforce a system whose purpose was "the specific good of football" and that interference from "outsiders" was an effort to damage the sport.[5] He found support in the person of Brian Glanville, the widely read sports columnist, who described the necessity of "working against the arrogant bullying of the ghastly Dutch woman [elsewhere he described her as an 'egregious Dutch MEP'] Mme. Larive [who was] threatening UEFA on behalf of the European Parliament."[6]

Mme. Larive's "threats" consisted of pointing out that as far back as 1974, the European Commission had raised concerns about how the contractual system in European football operated and had repeatedly asked the governing bodies of football to make changes. She reminded everyone present, especially David Will, that the leadership of football had made no effort to modify their rules or to reply to entreaties of the European Court and the European Parliament. In her words, "The sports world has to be open like any other world. . . . It is high time the high and mighty in the soccer world accept that discrimination [in matters concerning movement of players] has been abolished a long time ago. The European Parliament will continue to tell them so."[7]

Football officials and journalists saw no need for change, nor did the various footballers unions. The leadership of the leagues and the clubs used the same arguments that baseball had used before 1976—competition would end, all the best players would move, and the sport was too special to be governed by the normal standards of society. They fought a rearguard action reminiscent of baseball.[8]

The impetus for sweeping change came from an unlikely source, a relatively unknown Belgian footballer, Jean-Marc Bosman. When his contract with his club, RC Liege, expired, it offered him a contract for the following year that would have cut his wages by between 50 percent and 75 percent. He sought employment elsewhere and received an offer from a French club. RC Liege then exercised its right to demand a transfer fee to allow him to move, even though he no longer had a valid contract with that club. It had that power under the operating rules of the Belgian Football Association. The French club was not prepared to pay this additional amount and withdrew its offer. Bosman claimed that the league's regulations denied him the opportunity to earn a living at his chosen profession and thus violated provisions of the European Union's rules that guaranteed the free movement of capital, goods, and labor within the boundaries of the community. The traditions of football and the prevailing legal opinion within the sport supported the right and need of the clubs and football administrators to determine what was best for the sport and its individual participants.[9] When Bosman maintained his right to take legal action, that meant that two sets of standards were on a legal collision course.

Bosman's suit finally made its way to the Court of Justice of the European Community, where a decision was delivered on September 20, 1995. The basis of the suit against RC Liege and the organizations that enforced its actions was that the existing rules governing football were in direct violation of the first two paragraphs of Article 48 of the EC Treaty:

1. Freedom of movement for workers shall be secured within the Community by the end of the transitional period at the latest.
2. Such freedom of movement shall entail the abolition of any discrimination based on nationality between workers of the Member States as regards employment, remuneration and other conditions of work and employment.[10]

The international nature of the dispute gave it a dimension that was not present in baseball. But the most important aspects of the Bosman case— the right of a player to determine where he played, the role of impartial judges, the power of the sports authorities to enforce their rules, and the way in which vested interests attempted to defend the status quo—had striking parallels to both the Flood and Messersmith-McNally cases.

Peter Seitz would have empathized with the position taken by Advocate General Lenz that it was his responsibility only to define whether the wording in Article 48 meant that freedom of movement was a "fundamental right."[11] Lenz noted at some length that the football authorities had defended the need for the existing rules on the grounds that the "abolition of existing rules on transfers would lead to dramatic changes in football or even to expropriation." Lenz concluded that clubs would have to reorganize themselves and change the way they operated, which might even "entail some hardships and reminded them that these were the normal risks of business."[12]

In their brief, the football authorities pointed out that the sport had a special place in people's lives. This was the equivalent to baseball's appeal to itself as the "national pastime," a tactic that had resonated with Justice Holmes in 1922 and Justice Blackmun in 1972. Judge Oliver would have appreciated Advocate Lenz's argument, which stressed two points: the fears that football would cease to exist were overstated, and it was the responsibility of a judge to uphold the law, not to protect a cultural institution. He noted that the men who controlled football had been given repeated warnings about the necessity for change.

A number of people, including those representing Bosman, had made suggestions for modifications in the transfer system that could have brought it into harmony with the laws and regulations of the European Community. The leadership of football had worked under the twin assumptions that no one was capable of mounting an effective challenge to the traditions of the sport, and if that did take place the courts and governments would protect the status quo.[13]

There are many interesting comparisons between the Bosman and Flood cases. In professional terms, the two men could not have been more different. Jean-Marc Bosman had been a great young player, the captain of his country's youth team at a time when Belgian football was reaching new heights, but his career stalled after that promising start. Flood's first three years with the Cardinals were nothing special, but in the fourth year, 1961, he blossomed. Like so many "overnight stars," his success was a combination of years of hard work, natural development, and finding himself in the right place.

Bosman undertook his legal action because he wanted the right to move from the club that had been his home for years. Flood filed his suit to stop the Cardinals from trading him. Both men went to court because the regulations in their sport gave them no control over their own futures. In Bosman's case, if RC Liege did not want him at anything other than the minimum wage, he wanted the right to seek his own future elsewhere. In Flood's case, if the Cardinals did not want him, he wanted the right to choose where he would play. Both men rejected the proposition that a club could exercise virtually unlimited control over the career of a player just because he happened to sign a contract with them at one time.

There were important difference between the two cases. Flood had the aggressive support of the players union, and Bosman waged a lonely fight. Flood's case was newsworthy in the United States, and Bosman's case worked its way to Advocate Lenz in virtual obscurity through the Belgian courts and finally to the European Court of Justice.

Thus far, this discussion has ignored the most obvious comparison between Curt Flood and Jean-Marc Bosman—the former lost his court case, and the latter won. Since the creation of free agency through Messersmith-McNally, many seem to assume that Flood had prevailed. Flood energized the union and reminded individual players of the restrictions placed on them by the reserve system. He brought the issue of the reserve system into the open after decades of players had either ignored it or thought of it as one price to pay for being a major leaguer. But Flood did not win his case, nor did he benefit personally from the victory of the players who followed in his footsteps. Likewise, Bosman did not benefit noticeably from his victory in court. During the years his case went through the courts, his career was nonexistent, his marriage broke up, and he became bankrupt. He was thirty years old when the decision was rendered, and he no longer had a future as a top-level footballer.

In the immediate aftermath of the Bosman ruling, the chief executive of the PFA, Gordon Taylor, had reacted with dismay. Taylor pointed out that it was unfair that English football should have to change because of the Bosman ruling, since the transfer system in England had been reformed when the PFA had negotiated a series of compromise arrangements with the league that enabled players to have a limited degree of free agency and additional benefits. Taylor remarked, "'This system has the support of the employers and the employees and there is little reason to abandon it. If it ain't broke, why should we mend it? I have never had a complaint from any of our members since 1978 when at regional meetings players chose the present system as opposed to pushing for a literal freedom of contract.'"[14]

Five years after the Supreme Court ruled against Flood, the union had its victory in Messersmith-McNally. Five years after the ruling in the Bosman case, the various constituencies in football—unions, leagues, national associations, and international governing bodies—were still unable to come up with a system that would satisfy the minimal requirements set forth by the European Court. In September 2000 a spokeswoman for the European Commission issued a statement about the actions taken or not taken by FIFA (the governing body of international football) and UEFA: "We're extremely disappointed that they haven't come back to us with proposals . . . we don't want to bring chaos to football, but the commission has bent over backwards to meet the legitimate needs of the game."[15]

The aftermath of the Bosman ruling became a political issue in England and part of the ongoing political debate about England's place in Europe. *The Times* (London) used the Bosman ruling to explain the supposed unpopularity of the European Union:

> This whole saga speaks volumes for the real reasons why the EU is often less popular not only in Britain but in many other member nations. The European Commission has demonstrated an itch for intervention even though none is warranted. It has displayed a truly comical sense of priorities, proclaiming that transfer fees 'illegally prevent the free movement of players in the EU.' . . . It reveals a depressing desire for conformity if the same rules set out for postman or journalists are to be imposed on sportsmen, despite the many distinctive and unconventional features of this career.[16]

In 1997 Gordon Taylor looked at the potential downside of something like Messersmith-McNally when he discussed the dire economic consequences that free agency could cause for football. He reminded his readers that "there are signs that the situation is coming to an end as industrial unrest at owners' attempts to cap salaries has caused disillusionment to fans and attendances have fallen making the large wages even more difficult to sustain."[17] Clearly, he was referring to the events of 1994–95 in baseball, the longest work stoppage in the history of American sports.

In the winter of 1998–99, there was widespread joy about the glories of the recently concluded baseball season. In books describing the season, there was some hyperbole and more than a little of the romance that had become a standard aspect of baseball writing, but there was a lot to celebrate. Mark McGwire set a new home run record after a season-long battle between him and Sammy Sosa. The Yankees had a record win total, David Wells pitched a perfect game, and there was a host of attractive new young stars. Some of the exultation had a kind of whistling-while-walking-past-the-graveyard atmosphere about it, celebrating against the background of recent crises, which a few years earlier had the same writers wondering if major league baseball had a future. This is what Mike Lupica had in mind when he ended *The Season of '98* with a reminder that baseball had to confront what he described as the "imperfections in the perfect game."[18]

The cloud over the euphoria of 1998 were the events of 1994 and 1995. The final weeks of the 1994 season, the World Series, and the opening weeks of the next season were canceled as a result of a work stoppage forced on the players by the actions of the owners. No matter how many home runs McGwire hit or highlight catches Ken Griffey Jr. made in 1998, there remained the apprehension that the next time a labor agreement had to be negotiated, there would be another debacle.

The 1994–95 work stoppage was the longest in baseball history, but it was not the first to affect pennant races. It damaged the emotional relationship between fans and the sport in ways that no similar event had done. It took place in a season when four players had a legitimate chance to break Roger Maris's home run record, which had stood since 1961. Most of all, it caused the decision in September 1994 to cancel the World Series. Neither previous labor problems or wars had done that. Leonard Koppett put it into perspective: "This was the defining moment. This is what 'ends' the story [the history of baseball] that began in 1876."[19] His chronology about the World Series might have some problems, but his conclusions are correct. The World Series embodied, in the minds of many fans, traditions of the game that preceded 1903. The labor stoppage broke the continuity of baseball for many of its fans. They did not care about the details, whether it was a strike or an employer-induced work stoppage. The players refused to play, thus it was their fault. A sport that is so dependent on romance and history is particularly vulnerable when those aspects are ignored by the very men who run it and claim to be protecting it.

In the 1990s the men running baseball had difficulty recognizing what was special about the sport. They seemed to make changes based upon what appeared to work for professional football and basketball rather than looking at their own sport. The respected broadcaster Bob Costas described these innovations as the equivalent of "a highly successful steak restaurant that sees a pizza parlor making a good profit, and since it has tomato sauce on the pizza, the steak house decides to cover every steak with tomato sauce."[20]

The 1994–95 strike was the result of a set of miscalculations on the part of the owners, the most serious of which was to repeat mistakes they had made in dealing with the players union for almost twenty-five years. They ignored how strongly the players felt about the union and underestimated their repeated willingness to make individual sacrifices to remain solid in their opposition to what they perceived as efforts to scale back free agency. Management seemed averse to taking seriously the recent history of its industry. In the 1980–81 Joint Study Committee, a general manager dismissed a player's concern about the need to consider the background of the reserve system as "just history,"[21] and in 1994 one club executive told Koppett that anything that took place before 1990 was "ancient history."[22]

The all-important issue in 1994 was the efforts of the owners to ameliorate what they saw as the destructive long-term effects of free agency—rising salaries, lack of control over players, and economic uncertainty for the clubs. Variations of these issues had been present in virtually all of the previous labor disputes. One economist summed up the process that led to the strike: "the first shot leading to the 1994–95 strike was the owners' decision in December 1992 to reopen negotiations on salaries and the free agency system."[23]

Both sides were working from a set of absolutes that led to siege mentalities. The owners were convinced that they had to put a system in place that would enable them to exercise collective control over players' salaries. They said that if they did not have this power losses would mount, clubs might fold, and the competitive balance of baseball would be destroyed. After the owners decided to reopen the contract, they waited almost eighteen months before they submitted their collective bargaining proposal to the players. The proposal included revenue sharing with the players, the elimination of salary arbitration, an escalating scale of minimum salaries for players with less than four years in the major leagues, free agency in four years rather than six, albeit with some restrictions, and a salary cap.

From the players' point of view, the situation in 1994 was as serious a challenge as they had faced since 1981. They found many problems with the owners' proposals. The share of revenue for the players would drop from 56 to 50 percent. In addition, the union would have to share its licensing revenues with the owners. Salary arbitration would disappear, and clubs would have the right of first refusal on free agents who wanted to leave. The restrictions on free agency were completely unacceptable. In the minds of the players, the salary cap was at the heart of the owners' proposals. It became the visible sign to players, especially veterans, of how much the owners were trying to test the union and roll back the gains it had made.

Players were convinced that the owners were presenting proposals that they knew the union would reject in order to force a strike. This hardened the players' resolve not to accept anything that looked like the owners' proposal and added another level of suspicion and bitterness to the negotiations. The players wondered why any reasonable businessmen would want to endanger their product, especially when it seemed to be thriving. Their answer was that the owners were trying to break the union. There was no way to prove that this interpretation was accurate, but it was impossible to dismiss it. What mattered was that the players believed it. The more the negotiators for the owners talked about the need for equity and the necessity to bring the system back into balance, the more it sounded like a thinly veiled effort to overturn the gains made since 1976. The basis for those successes had been the union, and the players assumed that what ownership really wanted to do was to end the union as an effective force.

The atmosphere within the negotiations was acrimonious. The players knew that the owners had violated the 1985 Basic Agreement by colluding to deny free agents a market for their services. That called into question whether they could trust the owners to live up to any future commitments. The players also had serious doubts about the economic woes described by the owners and had no faith in the numbers presented to support claims of the imminent economic crisis in baseball.[24]

Defenders of collusion claimed that it was necessary to correct the imbalance between players and owners or asserted that "it's their money; they can decide not to spend their money, can't they?" This ignored the fact that the players and the owners had a contractual relationship that spelled out what both sides could not do. The most damaging impact of collusion was that it convinced many players that they could not trust the owners to honor their contractual obligations. This was scarcely the basis for a harmonious long-term working relationship.[25]

The decision by the owners to employ Richard Ravitch, someone who "admits to having been 'characterized as a union buster' in his pre–baseball jobs," as their chief negotiator brought back memories of 1981.[26] The relationship between Fehr and Ravitch seemed to be as antagonistic as that between Miller and Grebey. Just before the scheduled strike date, the owners took an ill-advised step that damaged the bargaining atmosphere. They decided to withhold a scheduled payment of $7.8 million to the pension fund, money that was due to the players from their participation in the All-Star Game. This action had a symbolic value that was not lost on the union. Any restrictions the owners introduced would damage freedom of movement and depress (or at least stop the increase of) salaries. The players were sure any concession to the owners would be only the first step.[27]

Any thought the players had that their fears about "union busting" were paranoid ended when the owners introduced the concept of "replacement players," a euphemism for strikebreakers or scabs. One former union activist, who was a baseball executive in 1994, noted wryly, "since the owners had never been able to beat Marvin [Miller] at the bargaining table, they decided they would finally beat him more than a decade after he had retired."[28]

Five years earlier, during another work stoppage, Marvin Miller had addressed meetings of players to discuss how a solid union had forced changes on the owners. Miller had been away from the union for almost a decade, but most of the players were familiar with him and his style. In the midst of the 1994–95 strike, the leadership of the union decided to use living history to remind the players what was at stake. The atmosphere surrounding a guest at a meeting in 1995 was electric. Curt Flood met with a group of almost one hundred players. When he walked into the room, there was a standing ovation.

The players who listened to him might not have known much about the detailed history of their union, but they did know that Flood had challenged the system and had put his own career on the line. Their response to him was a recognition of Flood's own courage and how much things had changed since 1970. The players in 1995 understood how much they had to lose and how little power the players had possessed only a few years earlier.

Veteran players and former players had to remind younger players about the history of baseball and what had taken place since 1966. Popular history, conventional wisdom, and baseball journalism would not provide that. The owners' version of the history of baseball, especially its labor relations, was the received wisdom among the press and the public. After the strike ended, two literature professors, Mick Cochrane and William Wright, made this point in an insightful article that discussed how versions of history had been used in previous labor negotiations; 1994 showed the cumulative effect of years of the public and the press accepting what the scholars described as "The Owners as Teachers."[29] This version portrayed events like the Hunter and Messersmith-McNally ruling as aberrations that went against the fabric of baseball and laid the basis for its future problems.

In 1994 Bud Selig asserted that the purpose of the owners' bargaining position was "'to preserve and protect the long-term future of the sport. All along, our goal has been to reach an agreement that would keep Major League Baseball affordable for the fans, accessible to the fans, and competitive for the fans.'"[30] The players and union officials have a different version of history. Don Fehr phrased it succinctly: "'All the players have ever wanted in a collective bargaining agreement is to have a relatively free market for their services.'"[31] Few outside of their ranks were interested in that at any time, and was more true than ever in 1994.

Pete Harnish, a pitcher for the Astros in 1994, gave a player's perspective: "'The players understand that we've come this far from some really bad days, and we don't want to take steps back. People are amazed at how united we've been. That's because we've had strong leadership, and because most of the players, no matter how much they're making now, have struggled in the minor leagues as I did.'"[32]

When Don Baylor was a player, he had a reputation as a no-nonsense, tough competitor and a thoughtful student of the game. After he retired, he became a successful manager. In his later years as a player, he was active in the union and was one of the negotiators during the 1981 strike. A few years after that, he gave his version of what was involved in the strike:

> The owners wanted to water down free agency. . . . The union, represented by Marvin Miller, viewed significant direct compensation at such levels as an absolutely nonnegotiable issue. . . . The owners underestimated the players' resolve. The owners figured the players would miss one paycheck and come crawling back. . . . The owners settled for what they

could have had several weeks before. . . . The players had preserved free agency and the direct result was significantly higher salaries. . . . Perhaps most significantly, the game lost a certain innocence . . . players, management, and fans alike were left with a tremendous sense of loss. I thought it would take a long, long time to heal the wounds. I was wrong.[33]

Baylor's comments about 1981 sound much like what Harnisch said about 1994. Harnish's remarks would have been just as accurate in 1972, 1976, or 1981 as they were in 1994. That showed how much the most recent strike was part of a continual process in the relationship between the union and the owners.

After the strike began in 1994, compromise was almost impossible. The strike itself was almost an anticlimax. The public saw the gravity of the situation on September 14, 1994, when the owners announced that the World Series was canceled. The scheduled start of the 1995 season was uncharted territory for everyone. Many owners pushed the idea of playing a regular season without the major league players, replacing them with so-called replacement players. This radical break with the past was forestalled on March 31, 1995, when Federal District Judge Sonia Sotomayor granted the NLRB's request for a preliminary injunction against the owners. The union called off the strike, and the new season, shortened to 144 games, began at the end of April.[34]

The fact that the strike lasted so long and that the World Series was canceled created an aura around it, making it the most important such event in the history of baseball. That might be understandable among owners, journalists, and fans, but it extended further. One description by an academic is typical of other opinions, albeit a bit hyperbolic: "the monumental strike of 1994–94 . . . was not only the most important strike action taken by the union, but also was the catalyst for far-ranging changes in the baseball industry."[35] This seems to overestimate both the novelty of what happened in 1994 and the seriousness of its consequences. It was noteworthy because it was the most recent strike as well as the longest and because the World Series was canceled. There was nothing new in the reasons for the strike, and the results were all-too-familiar to the owners. The players emerged from the strike with all their previous gains intact and with the union as solid as ever.

The dynamics involved in 1994–95 had an almost eerie resemblance to the strikes of 1972 and 1981. In 1972 the issue was a small amount of money in the pension fund. In 1981 it was direct major league compensation for a handful of players. In 1994 it was millions of dollars involved in a salary cap that might affect only a few players. In all cases, the players thought the future of the union and the benefits they had gotten from it were at stake. If the players were willing to strike in 1981, when restrictions on free agency affected only a few players, why should it come as a surprise to anyone in 1994, when they struck to make sure that free agency for most players had no limits imposed on it? The union organized itself around two slogans that were familiar to anyone who understood the previous strikes—that the owners were challenging the ability and willingness of the players to fight and that the contract offer made by the owners was an effort to take back something that the players had won through the efforts of their union.

The two parties reached a new agreement through collective bargaining in November 1996. It contained many of the features of the previous Basic Agreement, especially those dealing with salary arbitration and free agency. This was what the union had been trying to accomplish since the start of negotiations. There were some provisions that dealt with revenue sharing among the clubs that had a minimal impact on the economics of the sport. For the fans, the most visible result of the agreement was the players' willingness to accept interleague play, which was a break with the traditions and history of the sport.

One familiar aspect of the 1994 strike was the way in which fans and journalists rallied to the cause of the owners and condemned the players for having brought on the work stoppage. Comments like, "I don't really care anymore. . . . They deserve each other" and "I promised myself that if they canceled the season I'd never go to another game" were common. But the scope of this strike led to something new in the analysis of it. Some commentators, on various sides of the issue, tried to place the strike in a historical context and to draw lessons from it. On one side were the views of David Cone, a player-negotiator for the union, who justified the union's position by pointing out, "'the past makes a difference, absolutely.'"[36] His version of the past probably started in 1966. An editorial in the *Boston Globe* took the view that the strike was simply the culmination of "'the currently commercialized version of baseball [which] has been diluted, disfigured, degraded.'"[37] Somehow, the editorial writer ignored the simple historical reality that baseball had been a commercial enterprise for more than a century, and Boston was one of the first places where the profit motive had been important to the owners. There was a great deal of discussion about how much baseball had changed and whether it any longer could claim to represent the values of American society.

The discussion after the strike brought another issue to the forefront: how much the future success of baseball might be dependent on the existence of a strong, insightful commissioner. Many fans and journalists looked for another Judge Landis to bring the factions together and to take control of the sport. Scholars who have produced some of the best work dealing with baseball combined a condemnation of the recent history of the sport with an appeal to the office of the commissioner for future guidance. In his prize-winning baseball book, William Marshall wrote:

> baseball has become even more selfish. The 1994–95 strike and the loss of the 1994 World Series was an unmitigated disaster. . . . [It] polarized baseball into three groups—the owners, the players, and the fans. Though the strike is over, the same issues that divided management and the players (salary caps, salary arbitration, revenue sharing to assist small-market teams, and free agency) remain unresolved. . . . Fortunately, after a five-year hiatus, baseball finally selected a permanent commissioner in former Milwaukee Brewers owner Alan H. Selig. He will be carefully observed to see if he can provide baseball with the leadership it requires.[38]

Paul Staudohar concluded an article on the strike as follows: "A big remaining problem was the absence of a commissioner. Interim commissioner Bud Selig, the Milwaukee owner, tried to be impartial, but it was difficult for him to avoid charges of conflict of interest (however unfair they might have been) and to function successfully in all facets of the job. This problem was resolved when Selig put the Brewers into a trust (administered by his daughter) and he was named permanent commissioner by the owners in 1998."[39] No one has done more than Staudohar to enable us to understand the dynamics of labor relations in sports and the special role played by the MLBPA. However, on the issue of the commissioner, I find myself in disagreement with him and William Marshall, and many others who share their view.

There are serious questions about how much power and independence even Judge Landis had when he was commissioner and how often he ever acted against the fundamental interests of the owners. Although succeeding commissioners might have acted independently in a few instances, they were employees of the owners, and their basic job was to let their employers get on with their business. Marshall asserts that commissioners from Bowie Kuhn through Fay Vincent "proved to be far more influential and powerful than most owners liked."[40] If that were the case, it is probably more of a comment on the sensibilities of some owners than it is on the actions of either commissioner. Kuhn and Vincent did provide convenient scapegoats for the owners. The more the owners lost control and failed to beat the union, the more they had to find someone to blame. That was easier than trying to recognize the new legal realities of baseball's labor relations or giving credit to the ability of the players to stand together. When the commissioners took any independent actions that owners thought endangered how they ran baseball, the commissioners lost their jobs.

Whatever independence and power the commissioner might have had concerning the players' status as employees was challenged by the union after April 1966 and virtually disappeared after the signing of the 1968 Basic Agreement. The hostility of Miller, Moss, and the players toward the commissioner had little to do with who happened to be the commissioner at any given moment. They knew that the commissioner was an employee of the owners, and they expected him to live up to his responsibilities to his employers. The players had no reason to entrust their futures into the hands of the commissioner. In 1981 one of the player reps spoke about how the union had "sunk the *Titanic* of the reserve system" and were not going to let it rise to the surface again.[41] He could just as easily have been talking about their willingness to allow the commissioner to play a significant role in baseball's labor-management relations.

The first Basic Agreement regularized the structure of labor relations between the owners and the players, bringing it into the mainstream of American industry. There was no place in that scheme of things for a supposedly impartial figure, especially when he was chosen and paid by one side. There might be a romantic appeal about a commissioner who could lead baseball and heal its divisions, but that does not fit the realities after 1966. The dismantling of the role of the commissioner might not have been apparent outside of baseball, but it was one of the significant results of the revolution undertaken by the union.

In the aftermath of the strike, the commissioner established the Blue Ribbon Commission, which analyzed the current economic structure of baseball. The commission comprised men who had achieved significant reputations outside of baseball—the president of Yale University, the former majority leader of the United States Senate, the former chairman of the Federal Reserve Board, and a Pulitzer Prize–winning political columnist who had written widely on baseball. All of them had personal ties to Major League Baseball and were named to the Blue Ribbon Commission by the commissioner. There were also a number of men on the commission who represented individual clubs.[42]

Its report focused on what baseball officials saw as the biggest problem facing the sport—what it described as the "economic imbalance between teams" that had led to a competitive imbalance, which foredoomed many teams to have no chance at World Series glory. The report made two significant, however brief, mentions of the union. It recognized that "the concurrence of the MLBPA is necessary, and we encourage the MLBPA to collaborate with the implementation of our recommendations."[43]

Throughout the 2000 season, it seemed that there was almost as much interest in the economic future of baseball as there was in the pennant races and the individual performances on the field. Most of the questions raised about the problems facing baseball presupposed there were problems. Underlying these doubts and fears were concerns that had been present over the previous thirty years. There is no doubt that the changes that the union accomplished had created the circumstances that were at the root of what so many people regarded as an ongoing crisis in baseball.

In the months immediately after the end of the 2000 season, two stories dominated the media coverage of baseball. The first was the signing of free agents. The salaries of quality free agents had risen consistently (with the exception of the collusion period) over the years. What happened leading up to the 2001 season appeared to be a quantum leap in salaries, in emotional terms if not in absolute dollars. Alex Rodriguez, a young shortstop and possibly the best player in baseball, had completed six years with the Seattle Mariners and became a free agent. A number of clubs pursued him, and he ended the process by signing a ten-year contract with the Texas Rangers for more than $252 million. The signing took place shortly before the twenty-fifth anniversary of Messersmith-McNally, and many articles on the case pointed to how much players like Rodriguez had benefitted from what the union had accomplished in 1975 and protected ever since that time.[44]

The second issue was the possibility of another work stoppage after the 2001 season. At that time, the owners would have the option to cancel the Basic Agreement and to reopen negotiations. Long before the 2001 season began, many people were trying to predict what would happen to baseball. In this case, they were not talking about potential pennant or World Series winners; discussion centered on whether the owners might try to use a lockout to accomplish in 2002 what they had not been able to do in 1995. Whatever might be the plans or motives of the owners and however the negotiations might play out for the next Basic Agreement, it is obvious that the issues at the forefront of baseball's concerns are those that derived from the actions undertaken by the union between 1966 and 1981.

The *Report of the Blue Ribbon Commission* stated, "Players have recognized that unlimited free agency is unacceptable because too much player movement could destroy the fabric of the game."[45] This is an accurate version of what happened in 1976, 1981, and 1995. It is equally

clear that what the union accepted was on its terms and with its definitions. If the past is any guide to future behavior, it is probable that the
union will be willing to stage a battle to ensure that it defines what is
meant by "too much" and by "the fabric of the game." The efforts of the
owners and the commissioner to reform baseball make it clear that by
1981, the union not only brought to an end one era in the history of baseball, but it also provided the agenda for the succeeding two decades.

Notes

Introduction

1. Quoted in Milton Richmond, *Atlanta Journal,* December 1, 1967.
2. Press release, Major League Baseball Players Association, April 16, 1966.
3. Warren Goldstein, *Playing for Keeps: A History of Early Baseball* (Ithaca, N.Y., 1989).
4. Frank Scott, typescript of summary of his proposed autobiography (ca. 1990) that he sent to Marty Appel for submission to potential publishers. I want to thank Mr. Appel for giving me a copy.
5. Robert F. Burk, *Much More Than a Game: Players, Owners, and American Baseball since 1922* (Chapel Hill, N.C., 2001), 123; Marvin Miller, *A Whole Different Ball Game: The Sport and Business of Baseball* (New York, 1991), 338.
6. Interview with Joe Torre, March 25, 1991.
7. Paul Staudohar in conversation with the author, October 1999.
8. "Average Salaries in Major League Baseball, 1967–1992" (MLBPA).
9. For a good discussion of the reserve system, see Lee Lowenfish, *The Imperfect Diamond: A History of Baseball's Labor Wars,* rev. ed. (New York, 1991).
10. John Gaherin, negotiating session for Basic Agreement, November 13, 1975.
11. Marvin Miller, policy statement of the MLBPA, January 11, 1969.
12. Written text of radio broadcast editorial.
13. Speech by Harry Walker reported in *Birmingham News,* February 3, 1971.
14. Interview with Dixie Walker in *The Sporting News,* April 18, 1951.
15. Leonard Shecter, *Baseball Digest,* December 1967.
16. Quoted in Bob Hertzel, *Cincinnati Enquirer,* March 3, 1973.
17. Quoted in Bob Hertzel, *Cincinnati Enquirer,* April 30, 1975.

18. *Cincinnati Reds-Letter: Official Publication of Cincinnati Reds, Inc.*, February 1976.

19. Quoted in Thomas Boswell, *Inside Sports*, July 1980.

20. Marvin Miller quoted in ibid.

21. Jack Fisher, Minutes of Negotiating Session, December 14, 1967.

22. Quoted in Thomas Boswell, *Inside Sports*, July 1980.

23. Leonard Shecter, *Baseball Digest*, December 1967.

24. Interviews with John Gaherin, March 27, 1991, Marvin Miller, July 1, 1991, Bud Selig, August 17, 1991, and Buzzie Bavasi, November 17, 1989.

25. Interview with Selig, August 17, 1991.

26. Quoted in "Sports' Golden Age Over?" *Cincinnati Enquirer*, April 30, 1975.

27. Jackie Robinson at the "Sport and American Society" conference, February 1972, University of Missouri–St. Louis; Bob Hertzel to Marvin Miller, July 3, 1972.

28. Quoted in *The Waiting Room*, May 1984. *The Waiting Room* is an important source for a much-neglected aspect of the social history of baseball—the role of spouses. The magazine, which ran for three years, was created and largely written by Maryanne Ellison Simmons (the wife of Ted Simmons), a talented artist and writer. The magazine handled issues as diverse as finances, trades, retirement, racial attitudes and problems, and the players union. Marvin Miller to Bob Hertzel, August 8, 1972.

29. Tom Callahan, *Cincinnati Enquirer*, February 28, 1976.

30. Paul Staudohar, report to University of Illinois Press, October 1999.

31. Quoted in Frederick Klein, *The Sporting News*, March 23, 1974.

32. Quoted in "Baseball's Transfer of Power," *New York Times*, December 23, 2000.

33. These are some of the terms popularized by Dick Young, the widely read columnist for the *New York Daily News*.

34. Larry Claflin, *Boston Herald Advertiser*, February 11, 1973.

35. Interview with Torre, March 25, 1991.

36. Quoted in "Miller-Led Players Show Huge Economic Gain," *The Sporting News*, March 23, 1974. Bunning's view has remained consistent over the years. See Frank Dolson, *Jim Bunning: Baseball and Beyond* (Philadelphia, 1998), 100–114. When I interviewed Bunning on June 30, 1987, he made it a point to say that if he ever was elected to the Baseball Hall of Fame, he wanted recognition for the role he had played in bringing Miller into the union.

37. Quoted in Richard Giulianotti, *Football: A Sociology of the Global Game* (Oxford, 1999), xv.

Chapter 1: A "House Union"

1. Editorial, *The Sporting News*, August 28, 1946. The editorial went on to point out that "knowledgeable baseball men" had told Murphy that play-

ers would not trust their fate to anyone, especially an outsider, and predicted that the "burial" of the new guild would take place the following week when the owners "will grant virtually all the demands made by the players." For years after this, *The Sporting News* reported consistently about "demands" made by the players and "concessions" made by the owners. These reports usually dealt with the pension fund or small increases in meal money. In the 1960s the paper devoted a lot of space to the historical background of the Players Association and to the 1946 effort to unionize. The lesson to be drawn from all of this was that it was a bad idea for the players to consider a union, and it was foredoomed to failure. See also the issues of April 25 and June 19, 1946, February 4, 1948, and March 30, 1949, for a sample of the attitude of "The Bible of Baseball."

2. Interview with Ralph Kiner, November 15, 1989. For a discussion of the 1946 efforts to unionize the players, see Lowenfish, *The Imperfect Diamond*, 139–53.

3. Interview with Kiner, November 15, 1989.

4. Lowenfish, *The Imperfect Diamond*, 149.

5. Miller, *A Whole Different Ball Game*, 338.

6. Press release, MLBPA (written by Scott), May 1959. On May 1, 1959, a newspaper announced that Scott would head up the central office and would fulfill many of the functions of "dismissed attorney, J. Norman Lewis." Scott would be paid ten thousand dollars plus five thousand in expenses. Early Wynn, a White Sox pitcher who was active in the Players Association, objected to hiring Scott, saying he was "unequal to the task . . . nothing but a ten per center . . . a players' agent, unqualified and overpaid for the job we need done" and that Roberts had railroaded him into the job. Roberts replied that Scott was "best qualified for the job" and that he was "really glad to see Early take such an interest in this thing. I hope the other players feel the same way." Scott was elected by a vote of ten to six. "Baseball Notes," *New York Daily News*, May 4, 1959.

7. Interview with Kiner, November 15, 1989.

8. "Moguls Listen, but Make No Promises over Player Gripes," *The Sporting News*, July 22, 1953.

9. "Allie Answers Terry, Denies Plan for Union," *The Sporting News*, September 1, 1954.

10. Shirley Povich, *Baseball Digest*, August 1954. The following year, Dan Daniels, a widely circulated New York writer who was friendly with many of the owners, wrote, "On the surface, the points the players are fighting for, appear to lack great importance. . . . Why are the owners so obstinate?" *The Sporting News*, December 25, 1955.

11. *The Sporting News*, August 18, 1954. Kiner described the situation in 1951: "Actually, the owners were as much responsible for our hiring a lawyer as anyone else." "My Job as Player Representative," *Sport*, May 1951.

12. Text of song courtesy of Leonard Koppett.

13. Interview with Kiner, November 15, 1989.

14. "Players' Demands Exorbitant," *The Sporting News*, December 10, 1958.

15. Ibid.

16. Letter sent by Scott to all members of the MLBPA, August 1959. The response is from a member of the Chicago Cubs whose off-season residence was in New York. One example of what he meant was Young's reaction to the idea that the players (through Scott) should have some role in changes affecting baseball. "The players never had it so good . . . living at fantastic Fontainebleau [hotel]" and exercising a veto over scheduling of games. Dick Young, *New York Daily News*, December 5, 1959.

17. Completed questionnaire to Frank Scott from H. Harold Brown, February 1960.

18. "The Immediate and Urgent Need for a Central Office," Minutes of the Player Representatives Meeting, July 12, 1960.

19. Ibid.

20. Memo prepared by Roberts for player representatives, July 1960.

21. The decision was noted in the Minutes of Player Representatives Meeting, September 1, 1959.

22. The material about the applicants in "Summaries of Candidates for Counsel," distributed by Scott to the player representatives, September 1959. Scott had written to Edward Bennett Williams "through our mutual acquaintance, Joe DiMaggio," and told Williams "that more than one player has suggested" that he might be interested in the position. Frank Scott to Edward Bennett Williams, July 1959.

23. Bob Friend to Frank Scott, August 24, 1959.

24. Robert C. Cannon to Frank Scott, August 28, 1959.

25. Robert C. Cannon to Frank Scott, January 18, 1960. This letter was written on stationery of the Major League Baseball Players Association, as was all his subsequent correspondence dealing with the association.

26. Robert C. Cannon to Frank Scott, April 25, 1960.

27. Robert C. Cannon to Frank Scott, May 12, 1960.

28. "Help Players and Magnates—Judge Cannon's Chief Aim," *The Sporting News*, March 30, 1960.

29. Minutes of Meeting of Player Representatives, May 20, 1960.

30. Robert C. Cannon to Frank Scott, August 18, 1960.

31. Robert C. Cannon to Billy Martin, August 11, 1960, Robert C. Cannon to Jim Brewer, August 11, 1960.

32. Roberts and Kuenn attended the October 20, 1959, meeting of the Major League Executive Council. Also in attendance were the commissioner, the two league presidents, two owners, and a general manager. "Various proposals . . . submitted by the players" were discussed. They dealt with ticket policies, scheduling, and exhibition games. The scheduling issues were the most complicated, and a proposal about days off after night games when traveling

to the West Coast, get-away days, and rescheduling games "without consent of the players" took most of the meeting. The position of the owners and the officials was that it would be impossible to eliminate all of the disputed arrangements "without a great loss in revenue." The players accepted that there could be no hard and fast rule but "would appreciate clubs advising the players whenever a change in the schedule is made." Most of the other proposals made by the players were withdrawn during the course of the meeting. One of them was withdrawn without any discussion, but the issue returned years later in a much more serious fashion. It was to discuss the possibility that "a player should be allowed to work out in spring training, even though he is unsigned and still negotiating for contract." Minutes of the Major League Executive Council Meeting, October 20, 1959. The agenda for meetings of player reps shows how they were dominated by concerns over scheduling, bull pens, stadium lighting, the possibility of sixty days severance pay rather than thirty days, the possibility of changing time for infield practice, the possibility of a doctor being available for visiting clubs, and like matters. For a sample of these issues, see Agenda for Player Representative Meetings, July 12, 1960, July 9, 1962, July 6, 1964.

33. Interview with Steve Boros, March 26, 1991. According to Steve Hamilton (the Yankees player rep), his teammates showed their first real interest in the union when they discovered that their general manager kept a percentage of the difference between what the owner had budgeted for salaries and what he could convince the players to accept. Baseball writers covering the Yankees had been aware of this system for years. Interviews with Red Foley, March 25, 1991, and Leonard Koppett, February 14, 1990.

34. Interview with Judge Robert Cannon, August 16, 1991.

35. Ibid.

36. Frank Scott to Ken Boyer, July 26, 1962.

37. Minutes of Player Representatives Meetings, July 12 and November 30, 1965. The application is in Robert C. Cannon to Robin Roberts, December 30, 1965.

38. Interview with Cannon, August 16, 1991. In 1990, Robin Roberts said that the pension fund was uppermost in his mind when he suggested Miller's name, and "the rest developed later." Robin Roberts to the author, August 6, 1988. "The rest" refers to the fact that the union employed strikes as a tactic, something that troubled Roberts. There is no doubting the sincerity of Roberts's feelings in the letter, but it is also true that he knew Miller's background and attitudes toward labor negotiations in 1966.

39. Dolson, *Jim Bunning*, 100–144.

40. Quoted in "Player Rep Friend Raps Proposal That Athletes Form Labor Union," *The Sporting News*, August 3, 1963. In September 1961 *Sport* magazine had an article about Friend as a "Symbol of the New Ballplayer." The author pointed out that Friend had a B.S. in economics from Purdue University and was "a polished gentleman-businessman-ballplayer."

41. Interview with Cannon, August 16, 1991.

42. *New York Journal-American*, March 12, 1966.

43. Interview with Jim Bunning, June 30, 1987.

44. Interview with Cannon, August 16, 1991.

45. Ibid.

46. Interview with Milt Pappas, June 29, 1987. Although the quote is from Pappas, the vast majority of the former player reps I interviewed volunteered the same sentiments.

47. Interview with Cannon, August 16, 1991.

48. Ibid.

49. Ibid.

50. Ibid.

51. Dick Young, *New York Daily News*, July 7, 1964.

52. Furman Bisher, *Atlanta Journal*, March 25, 1976.

Chapter 2: The Association Chooses Change

1. Robin Roberts, quoting a letter he wrote to Commissioner Eckert, *Sports Illustrated*, February 24, 1969. According to Miller, the fact that the players consulted with management representatives was one of the features of the union that indicated to him how different labor relations in baseball were from any other industry.

2. Minutes of Player Representatives Meeting, March 5, 1966.

3. Ibid.

4. John Helyar, *Lords of the Realm*, rev. ed. (New York, 1995), 17–22. Interviews with Miller, March 17, 1988, and July 1, 1991, Dick Moss, May 7, 1992, Tim McCarver, August 23, 1989, Steve Hamilton, March 10, 1990, and Bunning, June 30, 1987. Facial hair was an important social issue in the 1960s, and it is remarkable how many times Miller's mustache was featured in articles about the union. Moss put a different spin on the discussion when he responded to a question from an attorney about the rules of the Chicago White Sox concerning goatees worn by black players: "the Commissioner of Baseball . . . often was photographed sporting sideburns and Marvin Miller has a mustache." Dick Moss to Laurence E. Seibel, November 15, 1968.

5. Interview with Bunning, June 30, 1987.

6. Interview with Hamilton, March 10, 1990.

7. Interview with Koppett, February 14, 1990.

8. Interviews with Bob Barton, November 16, 1989, and Bavasi, November 17, 1989.

9. Interview with McCarver, August 23, 1989.

10. Ibid.

11. Goldstein, *Playing for Keeps*, 3.

12. Interview with Miller, October 19, 1988, and Miller, *A Whole Different Ball Game*, 45–46.

13. Paul MacFarlane to Marvin Miller, ca. August 1975.

14. Interview with Reggie Smith, March 26, 1991.

15. Interview with Hamilton, March 10, 1990.

16. Ballot summary submitted by San Francisco Giants.

17. Interview with Hamilton, March 10, 1990.

18. Interview with Bunning, June 30, 1987.

19. Interview with Sal Bando, August 17, 1991.

20. Interview with Bunning, June 30, 1987.

21. Interview with Torre, March 25, 1991.

22. Interview with Boros, March 26, 1991.

23. Memorandum by Bing Devine, attached to letter to Frank Scott, August 17, 1961. The cover letter said, "Certainly, I believe it is evident we are cognizant of the undesirable conditions which have prevailed at spring training and we are making an effort to bring about an improvement for our Club." For a discussion of the Cardinals' policies in Florida, see David Halberstam, *October 1964* (New York, 1994), 58–63.

24. Dick Young, *New York Daily News*, March 22, 1972, and "Young Ideas," *The Sporting News*, November 22, 1980. There were different reasons for disliking and distrusting Miller. For some writers, it was his background and his personality, even his mustache and choice of clothing. Other writers believed that virtually any changes for baseball, especially those heading toward unionism, would be bad for the sport. The most important national sportswriter, Red Smith, came to be a supporter of the union, but as late as 1967 he wrote sarcastically about "Underprivileged Athletes Wooed by Union Bigwig." The subject of this article was a proposed effort by the Teamsters to organize players in other sports. *New York Times*, January 9, 1967.

25. Rick Cullen, *Salisbury (Maryland) Times*, February 14, 1973.

26. Furman Bisher, *Atlanta Journal*, December 3, 1967.

27. Ibid.

28. Furman Bisher, *Atlanta Journal*, March 25, 1976.

29. Furman Bisher, *Atlanta Journal Constitution*, January 13, 2000.

30. Tom Callahan, *Cincinnati Enquirer*, March 18, 1973.

31. Robert Lipsyte, *New York Times*, January 18, 1968.

32. Interview with Bob Hunter, March 26, 1991.

33. Interview with Joe McGuff, November 16, 1990. Bob Hertzel was a young writer in 1972 with the *Cincinnati Enquirer*, a paper whose management and senior sportswriters were among the most adamant opponents of Miller and the union. Hertzel suggested to Miller that the union should hire a public relations firm "because while you are virtually always factually right, it is often presented in such a way as to cause dislike from reporters and the public." Bob Hertzel to Marvin Miller, July 3, 1972.

34. Interview with Koppett, February 14, 1990.

35. Minutes of Player Representatives Meeting, July 11, 1966.

36. Marvin Miller to the editor, *The Sporting News*, June 20, 1967.

37. Bob Addie, *Washington Post*, July 20, 1966.

38. Minutes of Player Representatives Meeting, July 11, 1966.

39. Deposition of Marvin J. Miller, *Fleer Corporation v. Topps Chewing Gum, Inc., and Major League Baseball Players Association*, October 6, 1976, pp. 11–12 (hereafter cited as Miller deposition, 1976).

40. Interview with Cannon, August 16, 1991.

41. Stenographic Transcript of Proceedings: Meeting of the Executive Council of the Pension Fund with the Player Representatives, June 6, 1966.

42. Ibid.

43. Minutes of Special Meeting of the Player Representatives, June 6, 1966.

44. Meeting of the Executive Council of the Pension Fund with the Player Representatives, June 6, 1966.

45. Ibid.

46. Ibid.

47. Minutes of Player Representatives Meeting, November 29–30, 1966.

48. Richard Moss to Warren Giles, May 2, 1967.

49. Minutes of Player Representatives Meeting, November 29–30, 1966. On December 30, 1959, Frank Scott had sent a letter to Moss that concluded, "I regret very much the Major League Baseball Players Association could not take advantage of your gracious offer to serve as advisor in respect to legal matters."

50. Elliot Bredhoff (Bredhoff and Gottesman) to Marvin J. Miller, October 12, 1966.

51. At least one baseball person, Bowie Kuhn, had a different view of the Moss-Miller pairing. The former commissioner described Moss as "a counterbalance [to Miller] . . . he [Moss] was a real baseball fan. . . . He really cared about baseball. He was neither a philosopher nor a zealot, as was Miller. Practical, irreverent, and sassy. . . . He was also a personality you could touch." Bowie Kuhn with Martin Appel, *Hardball: The Education of a Baseball Commissioner* (New York, 1987), 78.

52. Richard Moss to Dick Young, August 9, 1967.

53. Richard Moss to Alexander Hadden Esq., May 21, 1976.

54. Richard Moss to the Hon. Joseph M. Barr, June 28, 1967. Moss wrote this eleven days after he had sent a similar letter to David M. Craig, the director of the Department of Public Safety.

55. Richard Moss to Bob Broeg, Sports Editor, *St. Louis Post-Dispatch*, April 22, 1969.

56. Bob Hertzel to Marvin Miller, July 3, 1972.

57. Dick Moss to Bob Hertzel, July 11, 1972.

Chapter 3: A New Focus for the Association

1. Miller, *A Whole Different Ball Game*, 147–48; Miller deposition, 1976.

2. Marvin Miller to Bob Addie, August 2, 1966.

3. Marvin Miller to Executive Board, November 27, 1967.

4. Financial statements of Major League Baseball Players Association, April 30, 1967, January 1968.

5. Constitution and By-Laws of the Major League Baseball Players Association, July 21, 1967, and "Summary of Major Substantive Changes in Constitution and By-Laws."

6. Ibid.

7. Interview with McGuff, November 16, 1990.

8. Meeting of the Executive Council of the Pension Fund and Player Representatives, June 6, 1966.

9. George Baer quoted in Nell Irvin Painter, *Standing at Armageddon: The United States, 1877–1919* (New York, 1989), 182. I want to thank Joseph Losos for bringing this to my attention. In *Hard Ball: The Abuse of Power in Team Sports* (Princeton, N.J., 1999), James Quirk and Rodney Fort use the same quote to characterize the views of the owners in the 1960s. They add, "Actually, even as late as 1970, you might have found a sizeable number of players who agree with old George Baer and the owners, which gives some idea of just how far we have come from those not-so-distant days" (52).

10. Kuhn, *Hardball*, 158.

11. Minutes of Joint Meeting (owners and player representatives), December 3, 1963.

12. Marvin Miller to Arthur Allyn, May 3, 1967.

13. Marvin Miller to the Player Representatives, May 4, 1967.

14. Interview with Gaherin, March 27, 1991.

15. Memorandum from Marvin Miller, July 7, 1966. This document took the form of a long historical analysis of the association. He repeated his views about the nature of the Players Association as a legal union at every opportunity. A later statement of this view was contained in Miller deposition, 1976: "The Players Association was a labor association within the meaning of the law. The fact that it had not functioned effectively before [1966] that didn't change that" (p. 20).

16. Interview with Miller, October 19, 1988. Another version of this episode is in Miller, *A Whole Different Ball Game*, 81–82.

17. Interview with Gaherin, March 27, 1991.

18. For slightly different versions of the details, see Helyar, *Lords of the Realm*, 23–24, and David Voigt, *American Baseball*, vol. 3 (University Park, Pa., 1983), 224. Bavasi's version is in his autobiography, Buzzie Bavasi with John Strege, *Off the Record* (Chicago, 1987), 101–12.

19. Buzzie Bavasi, *Sports Illustrated*, May 15, 1967. His recollection had not changed more than twenty years later. Interview with Buzzie Bavasi, November 17, 1989.

20. Buzzie Bavasi, *Sports Illustrated*, May 22, 1967.

21. Ibid.

22. Ibid.

23. Interviews with Hamilton, March 10, 1990, and Pappas, June 29, 1987.

24. Walter O'Malley to Frank Scott, August 8, 1961, and Buzzie Bavasi to Frank Scott, August 9, 1961.

25. Interview with Bavasi, November 17, 1989.

26. Interview with Hamilton, March 10, 1990.

27. "Baseball—Developments Off the Field," a talk by Marvin Miller to the City Club of Cleveland, February 6, 1972.

28. Ibid.

29. Interview with Mike Marshall, March 28, 1991.

30. Interview with Torre, March 25, 1991.

Chapter 4: The Union Asserts Itself

1. Joe Cronin to Marvin Miller, February 25, 1968.

2. Marvin Miller to Joe Cronin, April 19, 1968.

3. Ibid.

4. Ibid.

5. Interview with Gaherin, March 27, 1991.

6. Interview with Torre, March 25, 1991.

7. "Richards had a few words for Joe Torre. They, too, were short and to the point. They, too, matched the color [scarlet] of Paul Richards' jacket." Milton Richmond, *Atlanta Journal*, December 1, 1967. Torre became an involved player rep. His first experience with the association showed the casual nature of the organization. When he was a rookie, he made some complaints about the shower heads. Joe Adcock heard him and suggested that Torre become the player rep, and "from then on I took it seriously." Interview with Torre, March 25, 1991.

Torre proved to be one of the most forceful and articulate leaders of the Players Association. He played a crucial role in the most difficult negotiations, including the 1972 strike. His legacy to the union was important. In 1976, when Torre decided not to run for reelection as the National League representative, he wrote Miller that he would like to nominate Bob Boone because of his interest and activity during "the recent problems." Torre ended his letter with the rhetorical question, "Do I hear a second?" Joe Torre to Marvin Miller, November 26, 1976. Boone assumed the position and went on to become one of the most respected men in the union and the leader during the 1980–81 negotiations, Joint Study Committee, and strike.

8. Marvin Miller to the Atlanta Braves players, January 1968 (not sent).

9. Minutes of Player Representatives Meeting, February 28, 1967.

10. Interview with Hamilton, March 10, 1990.

11. Basic Agreement, February 19, 1968, p. 3, and Schedule C, pp. 18–19.

12. Minutes of Negotiating Session, December 14, 1967.

13. Interview with Gaherin, March 27, 1991.

14. Kuhn's 1987 comments about arbitration reflect the size of the gulf

between him and the association on this subject: "I thought the change [arbitration] was neither necessary or beneficial." Kuhn, *Hardball*, 141.

15. Basic Agreement, February 19, 1968, p. 18.

16. Remarks of Richard M. Moss at the 26th Annual Meeting of the National Academy of Arbitrators, April 5, 1973, pp. 3–4.

17. Basic Agreement, February 19, 1968, p. 4.

18. Minutes of Executive Board Meeting, July 21, 1969.

19. Memorandum from Marvin J. Miller to All Major League Players, August 1969.

20. Helyar, *Lords of the Realm*, 89–92.

21. Minutes of Executive Board, December 13–14, 1969, and Memorandum from Marvin J. Miller to All Major League Players, December 26, 1969.

22. Basic Agreement, February 19, 1968, p. 4.

23. Kuhn, *Hardball*, 74–78.

24. Minutes of Meeting of Study Committee on the Reserve System, April 24, 1969.

25. Ibid.

26. Ibid.

27. Ibid.

28. Ibid.

29. The memory of the effort of the owners to deny the $150,000 to the Players Association was not allowed to fade by Miller or the players involved. It was used by the player reps to remind other players about the supposed vindictiveness of the owners and how much they wanted to stop the union from employing Miller. He made effective use of it quite often, including his deposition in the Fleer suit. He stated bluntly that the owners would not allow the association to be funded with All-Star Game funds "with me as executive director." Miller deposition, 1976, pp. 17–19.

30. Meeting of Study Committee on the Reserve System, June 4, 1969.

31. Ibid.

32. Ibid.

33. Meeting of Study Committee on the Reserve System, July 31, 1969.

34. Meeting of Study Committee on the Reserve System, October 10, 1969.

35. Meeting of Study Committee on the Reserve System, February 19, 1970.

36. Memorandum from Marvin Miller to Members of the Players Association, February 1970.

Chapter 5: Curt Flood and the American Dream

1. "Statement of Curtis C. Flood," p. 1. The public version of the statement contained a few revisions made in conjunction with Miller, but the fundamental issues were raised by Flood, and the rhetorical devices were his and remained largely unchanged.

2. Curt Flood to Bowie Kuhn, December 24, 1969.

3. *St. Louis Post-Dispatch Weekend Magazine,* April 16, 1969. Gussie Busch supposedly showered favors and special treatment on Flood, including buying some of his paintings. The press in St. Louis had a lot to say about the lack of gratitude the players showed to Busch. The Cardinals owner had been particularly upset at the union's successful effort to get the players to refuse to sign their contracts before the 1969 season. During spring training, he delivered a long, profanity-laced lecture to the players about their responsibility to the game and to the owners. It made quite an impression on many of the players, including Flood, but not in the way Busch intended. He hardened pro-union attitudes and helped to lay the emotional and intellectual basis for Flood's actions. See Curt Flood with Richard Carter, *The Way It Is* (New York, 1972), 143–49, and appendix, 195–204. Busch was so pleased with the speech that he had it published and sent to all the shareholders of Anheuser-Busch (the brewery owned the team) with the comment, "the philosophy he [Busch] expressed has even wider significance and application than to baseball players," to which Flood added in his book, "I agree." Certainly Flood, Miller, and many players did think that Busch's comments should be taken seriously, if only to show what the union had to oppose. This was the most flagrant, although far from the only, instance where Busch became an enormous asset to Miller in his efforts to remind players why they needed a strong and united Players Association.

4. "Curt Flood in the Midnight League," *Sport Magazine,* March 1965, "Cynical Flood Bathes Prose in Acid," *St. Louis Post-Dispatch,* March 27, 1971, and Dick Young, *New York Daily News,* August 30, 1971. This is only a brief selection of the articles that called into question Flood's motives and his character.

5. Interview with Hamilton, March 10, 1990.

6. Minutes of Executive Board Meeting, December 13–14, 1969, p. 2. The union's memory of the abortive study committee had been reinforced by a statement made by the owners (after their meeting on May 15, 1969) that "the players have the mistaken impression that the owners were willing to ponder a change in the reserve clause." This was quoted in a press release by Miller, issued on May 23, 1969. The owners were wrong. By 1969 few if any players thought the owners would consider any changes in the reserve system. That was precisely why the Flood case was as timely as it was important.

7. Minutes of the Executive Board meeting, December 13–14, 1969, p. 3.

8. Interview with McCarver, August 23, 1989.

9. Interview with Dal Maxvill, March 15, 2000.

10. Interview with Torre, March 25, 1991.

11. Interview with Hamilton, March 10, 1990. In an interview with Maury Allen, Hamilton was quoted as saying, "We're not interested in helping Curt Flood make more money . . . we're interested in modifying the reserve clause. . . . One thing is for sure. The commissioner will not settle this. He works for the owners. . . . That's why if we don't get it settled in a new agree-

ment, it will be settled in court. We know the court is impartial." Maury Allen, *New York Post,* January 2, 1970.

12. Interview with Gary Peters, March 27, 1991.

13. Interview with Pappas, June 29, 1987.

14. Handwritten notes of Executive Board meeting, December 13–14, 1969 (not meant for public distrbution). An accurate version of these notes was published as appendix A in Flood and Carter, *The Way It Is,* 185–94. The "Discussion with Commissioner Kuhn" has attracted little interest from researchers.

15. Handwritten notes of Executive Board meeting, December 13–14, 1969.

16. Ibid.

17. Ibid.

18. Minutes of Executive Board Meeting, December 13–14, 1969, p. 4.

19. Bowie M. Kuhn to Curt Flood, December 30, 1969. Copies were sent to Miller, Bing Devine, the general manager of the Cardinals, and John Quinn, the general manager of the Phillies. In the previous year, two major league players, Donn Clendenon and Ken "Hawk" Harrelson, had rejected trades and used that to get better contracts. Neither player even talked about the reserve system or the control exercised over players by their clubs. In both cases, Commissioner Kuhn intervened. Clendenon had refused to report to the Astros after being traded there by the Expos. Harrelson finally accepted the trade to the Indians from the Red Sox and got an almost unheard of two-year contract. I want to thank Professor Larry Gerlach for bringing this situation to my attention. For details, see Leonard Koppett, *Koppett's Concise History of Major League Baseball* (Philadelphia, 1998), 331, and Kuhn, *Hardball,* 45–50. Koppett notes that after Clendenon received a large raise as a result of his actions, "The players got the point immediately. 'Great, if I'm traded, I'll retire before I report,' declared Kranepool." Koppett, *Koppett's Concise History,* 331. After all the players gained free agency, Ed Kranepool wrote to Miller and asked about Flood's welfare and suggested that the union should make a significant financial contribution to Flood.

20. Bing Devine to Curt Flood, October 8, 1969. There is every reason to believe that Devine's closing in the letter, "Best of luck," was heartfelt. The two men retained a mutually respectful and cordial relationship, a point attested to by both of them and many former teammates of Flood.

21. Interviews with Gaherin, March 27, 1991, Bob Broeg, August 27, 1989, and McGuff, November 16, 1990.

22. Press Statement of Major League Presidents Joseph E. Cronin and Charles S. Feeney, January 17, 1970. Two days later, Miller issued a response. He emphasized how the owners had ignored the Study Committee and referred to a comment by one of the lawyers for the owners in which he "admitted that they . . . never did intend to change one comma in any of the restrictions which comprise the reserve system." Press release, Marvin Miller, January 19, 1970.

23. Press Statement of Major League Presidents Joseph E. Cronin and Charles S. Feeney, January 17, 1970.

24. Ibid.

25. Ibid.

26. Veeck, the free-thinking owner of three teams, testified on Flood's behalf at the trial. Shortly after the Supreme Court rejected Flood's appeal, Veeck wrote, "Thirty years ago, I asked Judge Landis to try the reserve clause. It seemed then, as now, indefensible, legally and morally. The Supreme Court's majority does not change my view." Bill Veeck, *Chicago Sun-Times*, January 25, 1972. The owners made it a point to ignore Veeck in most instances. It would have been useful to pay attention to the title of his article: "Reserve Clause Battle Still Not Over."

27. Dave Leonhard to Marvin Miller, April 13, 1971.

28. Quoted in *Baseball: The Biographical Encyclopedia*, ed. David Petrusza, Matthew Silverman, and Michael Gershman (New York, 2000), 764.

29. Marvin Miller to Dave Leonhard, May 24, 1971. The letter was addressed c/o Rochester Red Wings, the top minor league team of the Orioles. Leonhard was pitching for them at the time.

30. Dave Leonhard to Marvin Miller, April 13, 1971.

31. Quoted in "Flood's Threat to Sue 'Surprises Phils,'" *The Sporting News*, January 24, 1970.

32. Quoted in "Miller Pointed Out Pitfalls, but Flood Refused to Back Off," *The Sporting News*, January 24, 1970. Roberts said that he suggested to Miller that the players should try to get something like the NFL, and Miller replied, "In practice, a football player isn't free. It's semi-fraudulent."

33. Editorial, *Wall Street Journal*, January 13, 1970. The story opened with a phrase that was unusual in the reporting about the case: "Flood adds distinction to his cause."

34. Editorial, "A Threat to Baseball," *Houston Chronicle*, February 7, 1970. One of the few papers that editorially supported Flood was the *Lansing [Kans.] Leader*, May 12, 1971, which said that the issue of the size of Flood's salary was "a bad rap . . . [having] nothing to do with the issues involved" and went on to point out that the "shabby interests" of baseball were shown by owners like O'Malley who moved teams. More representative of the press coverage was an editorial in the *Washington Post*, August 13, 1970, which pointed out that Flood was "not compelled by law or statute to play baseball for Philadelphia" and that he always had "the right to retire."

35. Bob Broeg, *St. Louis Post-Dispatch*, January 25, 1970. Miller and Broeg both emphasized a similar point, the willingness of the union to accept a modified reserve system. They drew completely different conclusions. Miller thought the union needed someone like Flood to force the owners to deal with the issue, while Broeg still had faith in the goodwill and generosity of the owners and their willingness to make compromises. He was joined in that view by many of his contemporaries. In the years since 1972, Broeg and many

other writers of his generation have become convinced that the owners were not willing to make any substantive changes in the reserve system. Interviews with Broeg, August 27, 1989, Hunter, March 26, 1991, Foley, March 25, 1991, and David Lipman, August 27, 1989.

36. Quoted in Dick Young, *New York Daily News*, May 23, 1970.

37. Ibid. Young dismissed the fact that Jackie Robinson supported Flood by saying that Williams felt that "Robinson thinks baseball has gone straight down hill since he stopped playing it." Neither Young nor Williams offered any reason why Hank Greenberg, a great player and later a successful baseball executive, also supported Flood.

38. Bob Broeg, *St. Louis Post-Dispatch*, January 25, 1970. The headline was not written by the author of the column.

39. Red Smith and Milton Richmond, *The Sporting News*, June 15, 1970.

40. Interview with Al Downing, March 26, 1991.

41. Handwritten notes of Executive Board meeting, December 13–14, 1969.

42. Interviews with Bunning, June 30, 1987, and Miller, October 19, 1988.

43. Interview with Hamilton, March 10, 1990.

44. Interview with Downing, March 26, 1991.

45. Interview with Hunter, March 26, 1991.

46. Dick Young, *New York Daily News*, May 23, 1970. This part of Flood's statement drew the most criticism. Typical were Milton Richmond's comments: "When Flood said he 'was bought and sold like cattle' he lost all sympathy." Milton Richmond, *The Sporting News*, June 15, 1970.

47. Quoted in "'Mistreated' Flood Draws Walker's Ire," *Birmingham News*, February 3, 1970. Walker was angered by a recent *Sports Illustrated* article in which Flood had said that he did not want to go to Philadelphia, which was "the nation's northernmost southern city . . . [and] the scene of Richie Allen's ordeals." Harry Walker had been a member of the Phillies in 1947, when its players, executives, and fans became infamous for their treatment of Jackie Robinson.

48. Richard Moss to Gloria Steinem, January 29, 1970.

49. Bill Nunn Jr., *Pittsburgh Courier*, May 30, 1970. I want to thank Professor Gerald Early of Washington University in St. Louis for bringing to my attention these quotes from the black press. Gerald Early, "Curt Flood, Gratitude, and the Image of Baseball," paper presented to the annual meeting of the Organization of American Historians, St. Louis, April 1, 2000.

50. Bill Nunn Jr., *Pittsburgh Courier*, March 21, 1970, and Bayard Rustin, *Philadelphia Tribune*, February 17, 1970.

51. Jess Peters Jr., *Pittsburgh Courier*, April 22, 1972.

52. "Found—An 'Abe Lincoln' of Baseball," *Ebony*, March 1970.

53. Press Statement by Cronin and Feeney, January 17, 1970.

54. Press release, Marvin Miller, January 19, 1970.

55. Interview with Torre, March 25, 1991.

56. Handwritten notes of Meeting of Executive Board, December 13–14, 1969.

57. Carl Yastrzemski to Marvin Miller, January 15, 1970.

58. Marvin Miller to Carl Yastrzemski, January 22, 1970.

59. Business Research Services to Marvin Miller, January 29, 1970.

60. Interview with McCarver, August 23, 1989.

61. Interview with Downing, March 26, 1991.

62. Interview with Smith, March 26, 1991.

63. Interview with Peters, March 27, 1991.

64. Jim Kaat to Marvin Miller, November 27, 1970.

65. H. Zane Robbins, president of SL&H-Robbins, Inc., to Marvin Miller, July 21, 1971.

66. "Average Salaries in Major League Baseball, 1967–1992" (MLBPA).

67. Some examples of how opinions and memories about Flood had changed are Dan O'Neill, *St. Louis Post-Dispatch*, January 24, 1997, Sam Donnellon, *Philadelphia Daily News*, January 22, 1997, and Bill Conlin, *Philadelphia Daily News*, January 22, 1997. Conlin used his column to complain about the current "vintage ballplayer whining" and the "Brain Dead Generation" of ballplayers who didn't know anything about Curt Flood. Conlin asserts that if Flood had been traded to a number of teams besides the Phillies, he would have gone, but he presents no evidence to support this. He also points out that Flood was wary of being traded to "a racist organization . . . in a town that treated [Dick] Allen with the hatred of a lynch mob." Later, although "owner Bob Carpenter and general manager John Quinn . . . said all the right things a black man wanted to hear . . . [Flood] rejected the concept of a man, any man, in any profession, being treated as property." Gerald Early presented an insightful analysis of the how the racial climate in Philadelphia affected Allen's life and Flood's reaction to the trade in "Curt Flood, Gratitude, and the Image of Baseball." Given Flood's pride in the freedom obtained by the next generation of players, it is hard to imagine him regarding them as selfish whiners. The *St. Louis Post-Dispatch* commemorated Flood in an editorial in which it criticized free agency, "lack of loyalty" by the players, and "too much business" in baseball relationships, showing that the writer misinterprets almost completely the principles involved in Flood's battle against the reserve system. Editorial, *St. Louis Post-Dispatch*, January 22, 1997.

Chapter 6: Only One Chance at a First Strike

1. John Roberston, *Montreal Star*, April 20, 1972.

2. Interviews with Torre, March 25, 1991, and Brooks Robinson, August 17, 1991.

3. Marvin Miller to Charles P. Korr, December 10, 1971.

4. Bob Hertzel, *Cincinnati Enquirer*, April 7, 1972.

5. Quoted in Helyar, *Lords of the Realm*, 119. The St. Louis sports press responded vigorously in support of Busch and the hard-line owners. In the *Post-Dispatch*, April 2, 1972, the columnist John Sondereggar asked fans to

make their views known about "baseball players who are dedicated to driving up the price of that ticket next season," and the sports editor, Bob Broeg, headlined his column, "Players' Goal? To Have Cake and Eat It, Too." The other daily newspaper, the *St. Louis Globe Democrat*, April 5, 1972, editorialized, "Marvin Miller, Get Lost!" The editorial took the position that since the owners contributed all of the money to the pension fund, the players had no right to ask for an increase. The strike was the result of Miller's "bad advice," and he was leading the players into a disaster. "Marvin Miller has struck out. He would do the game of baseball a great favor if he disappeared, got lost or found the nearest hole and jumped into it." This type of comment was almost guaranteed to build greater unity among the players.

6. Interview with McGuff, November 16, 1990.

7. Interviews with Pappas, June 29, 1987, Peters, March 27, 1991, Miller, March 17, 1988, and Moss, May 7, 1992.

8. Interview with Downing, March 26, 1991.

9. Interview with Marshall, March 28, 1991.

10. Interview with Barton, November 16, 1989.

11. Interviews with Miller, July 1, 1991, Moss, May 7, 1992, and Terry Miller, July 1, 1991.

12. Interview with McCarver, August 23, 1989.

13. Interview with Miller, March 29, 1989.

14. Interview with Peters, March 27, 1991.

15. Interviews with Barton, November 16, 1989, and Pappas, June 29, 1987. John Helyar has interesting comments on Jackson's role in *Lords of the Realm*, 119–21. For Miller's version, see *A Whole Different Ball Game*, 203–23.

16. Interview with Hamilton, March 10, 1990.

17. Interview with Pappas, June 29, 1987.

18. Miller, *A Whole Different Ball Game*, 212.

19. Interview with Downing, March 26, 1991.

20. Interviews with Pappas, June 29, 1987, and Hamilton, March 10, 1990.

21. Interview with Peters, March 27, 1991.

22. Interview with Torre, March 25, 1991. Dal Maxvill was the Cardinals player rep, and Torre was the alternate. Both of them were involved deeply in the union, and Torre was on most of its negotiating committees. He went out of his way to assume a public stance, despite knowing that it would be taken badly by the fans in St. Louis.

23. Interview with Peters, March 27, 1991.

24. Ibid.

25. Interview with Smith, March 26, 1991.

26. Interview with Hamilton, March 10, 1990.

27. Interviews with Barton, November 16, 1989, and Hamilton, March 10, 1990.

28. Larry Claflin, *Boston Herald American*, February 11, 1973.

29. Interview with Bavasi, November 17, 1989.

30. Interview with Koppett, February 14, 1990.

31. Interview with Gaherin, March 27, 1991.

32. Interview with Ewing Kauffman, November 16, 1990.

33. Dick Forbes, *Cincinnati Enquirer*, April 15, 1972.

34. John Robertson, *Montreal Star*, April 20, 1972. Robertson was particularly vehement in his comments about Gussie Busch, "[who] found out during the strike that his money had bought him a major league franchise, it didn't give him the right to 'own' the human beings who played for him. He found out that the players weren't just family pets—like his prized team of horses—who could be jerked into line with one tug of the reins from on high."

35. Phil Pepe, *New York Daily News*, February 25, 1972, and Leonard Koppett, *The Sporting News*, February 1972.

36. Dick Young, *New York Daily News*, April 2, 1972. Young took the opportunity to repeat as fact the assertion that "all added costs are being passed on to their [the fans'] ticket prices, prices already out of hand." This "fact" was one of the claims that distressed Miller and the players more than almost any of the conventional wisdom about baseball. It ignored the fact that salaries were a smaller percentage of club revenues than they had been in the 1930s. Most sports economists have pointed out that ticket prices are driven by what the market will pay for them, but it was easier for writers like Young to blame the players than to examine the facts. He was far from alone in accepting this version of reality.

37. Interview with Gaherin, March 27, 1991.

38. Interview with Harry Dalton, August 17, 1991.

39. Interview with Gaherin, March 27, 1991.

40. Marvin Miller to Daniel Galbreath, May 16, 1972.

41. The vast majority of these letters were written to newspaper reporters, but for the first time he replied to people who described themselves as fans. They had written to the union to express their anger at the strike. The points that Miller stressed in his letters (both in reply to articles and/or editorials and to fans) was that the strike had been forced on the players by the owners, the pension fund was not a "gift" from the owners, and that he had not "convinced the players to strike." He reminded a professor of business administration that comments about how much players make in comparison to other wage earners "is completely irrelevant. Salaries were not involved."

Miller expressed his feelings in a letter to an old friend, John Carmichael, the executive secretary of the Newspaper Guild of the Twin Cities: "Just as you were appalled at the reporting of the strike in Minneapolis and St. Paul, I found the reporting throughout the country, with some notable exceptions, was shameful." Marvin Miller to John Carmichael, May 2, 1972.

Miller made the same point to members of the working press. He wrote to Bob Hertzel of the *Cincinnati Enquirer*, "I have reviewed several thousand news clippings and columns on the baseball strike. Without exception, those stories and columns which were the most biased and distorted were by writers who made no effort whatsoever—not even one telephone call throughout the entire period—to attempt to get some facts and views which would have given balance to their coverage of the strike." Marvin Miller to Bob Hertzel, August 8, 1972.

42. Marvin Miller to Jim Murray, April 24, 1972. Murray was consistent in his opposition to the union throughout his career as a sports reporter. The tone of Miller's letters might have been light, but the disagreement between the men was real and profound.

43. Marvin Miller to Reverend William R. McGeary Jr., D.D., June 8, 1972. Miller's first letter to him, April 25, 1972, was in response to a letter McGeary wrote to the editor of the *Pittsburgh Gazette* on April 2, 1972. McGeary replied to Miller on June 5.

44. Reverend William R. McGeary Jr., D.D., to Marvin Miller, June 5, 1972.

45. Marvin Miller to Reverend William R. McGeary Jr., June 10, 1972.

46. Charles P. Korr, "Two Cheers for the Professional: Some Anglo-American Comparisons," *The British Journal of Sports History* 2.3 (December 1985): 291.

47. Interview with Hamilton, March 10, 1990.

48. Interview with McGuff, November 16, 1990.

49. Interview with Hunter, March 26, 1991.

50. Leonard Koppett, *The Sporting News*, April 1972.

51. Ibid.

52. Interview with Dalton, August 17, 1991.

53. Dick Forbes, *Cincinnati Enquirer*, April 15, 1972. In his autobiography, Miller asserted, "The press in Cincinnati was particularly virulent—no surprise considering that Reds owner Francis Dale also owned the *Cincinnati Enquirer*." Miller, *A Whole Different Ball Game*, 216.

Chapter 7: A Loss in Court and a Gain at the Bargaining Table

1. Negotiating Notes for Basic Agreement, February 25, 1973.

2. The Executive Board put the best face on the loss in court, but nevertheless its members were correct when they pointed out that "the lawsuit had resulted in a successful educational campaign concerning the inequities and unnecessary restrictions of the reserve system as presently constituted." Minutes of Executive Board Meeting, November 28–29, 1972.

3. Interview with Gaherin, March 27, 1991.

4. Policy Statement of the Executive Board, July 24, 1972, appended to the Minutes of Executive Board Meeting.

5. Negotiating notes for Basic Agreement, January 5, 1973.

6. Ibid. Miller made the point more forcefully in a press release issued on January 9, 1973, and a Report on Negotiations sent to all players on January 10, 1973. He pointed out, "we have concluded that meaningful changes can-

not at the present time be made in the free agency area without a lengthy strike." The players proposed a joint study committee and the creation of salary arbitration.

7. Quoted in Earl Lawson, *Cincinnati Post,* February 12, 1973.

8. Quoted in Merle Heryford, *Dallas News,* January 14, 1973, and Milton Richmond, *San Francisco Chronicle,* November 30, 1972.

9. Kuhn, *Hardball,* 24–25, 139–43.

10. Interview with Hamilton, March 10, 1990.

11. Handwritten notes of appearance of Commissioner Kuhn at meeting of Executive Board, December 13–14, 1969.

12. Ibid.

13. Ibid.

14. Ibid.

15. Ibid.

16. Kuhn, *Hardball,* 141.

17. Interview with Gaherin, March 27, 1991.

18. Kuhn, *Hardball,* 77. As early as December 5, 1972, Miller accused Kuhn of potentially having "poisoned the negotiations irrevocably" by statements he made at the owners' meeting. Throughout the negotiations Miller used Kuhn as a convenient scapegoat for what was wrong with the relationship between players and management and why the system had to be altered radically. Miller was consistent. His condemnations of Kuhn were just as strident behind closed doors as they were for the public. Kuhn was aware of what Miller was doing and accused him of "questioning my judgment because in this instance I am supporting the clubs' position." He reminded Miller that four years ago, Kuhn had resolved a threatened spring training by convincing the owners to increase their pension offer.

19. Report on Negotiations, sent to all the players by the Executive Board, January 10, 1973.

20. Proposal by Players Association, January 5, 1973, part of Negotiating Notes.

21. Statement of the MLBPA (for immediate release), February 12, 1973.

22. Press release, Marvin Miller, February 12, 1973.

23. Statement by Baseball Commissioner Bowie Kuhn (for immediate release), February 13, 1973.

24. Ibid. Kuhn also made the point that he had "succeeded in persuading the club representatives to put salary arbitration on the table . . . [although] there are strong and sincerely held reservations on the part of most clubs in respect to it."

25. Interview with Torre, March 25, 1991.

26. Interview with Gaherin, March 27, 1991.

27. Basic Agreement, January 1, 1973, Article 14 A(1), p. 26.

28. This was contained originally in the proposal made by the association on February 20, 1973, in response to a proposal made by the owners a day

earlier. The former included no mention of the use of comparative salary data. The original proposals concerning arbitration were made on February 8, 1973, and were discussed at meetings from February 17 to February 25, 1973.

29. Interview with Hamilton, March 10, 1990. This sentiment was echoed in interviews with Boros, March 26, 1991, Smith, March 26, 1991, Downing, March 26, 1991, and Torre, March 25, 1991.

30. Ed Roebuck, in Danny Peary, ed., *We Played the Game: Sixty-Five Players Remember Baseball's Greatest Era, 1947–1964* (New York, 1994), 325.

31. Dick Ellsworth, in Peary, ed., *We Played the Game*, 505.

32. Interview with Hamilton, March 10, 1990. The theme that there was no such thing as salary negotiations, that the players were at the mercy of management, and that players refused to talk about salaries among themselves shows up repeatedly in interviews in Peary, ed., *We Played the Game*, a book whose subtitle identifies 1947–64 as "baseball's greatest era." In his introduction, Lawrence Ritter laments the changes since 1964, "quarrelsome players' strikes" and "spoiled millionaires with .240 batting averages" among them. Ritter also points out that "almost every player interviewed admits he felt grossly underpaid and underappreciated by management, yet felt incredibly lucky just the same" (ix).

33. Interview with Gaherin, March 27, 1991.

34. Basic Agreement, February 25, 1973.

35. Negotiating Notes, Marvin Miller, February 6, 1973.

36. Basic Agreement, February 25, 1973. This came as the result of extended discussions concerning what each party viewed as the status of the reserve system in the wake of the Flood decision.

37. The union made it clear that it wanted a side letter clarifying the status of the reserve system and the right of the union to challenge it. A week earlier Miller said that the Executive Board had authorized the negotiators (Miller, Moss, Torre, and Perry) to enter into a three-year agreement but specified that there should be no reference to the Flood case. Miller also told the negotiators for the owners (Feeney, Cronin, Gaherin, Garner, Hoynes, and Rona) that if there was no agreement within a few days, "we do not want to say publicly that we have offered you an agreement with no changes in the reserve system or length of service." Negotiating Notes, February 17, 1973.

Chapter 8: Different Roads to Free Agency

1. Richard Moss to major league baseball players, October 8, 1976. Among the other players to whom the letter was addressed were Dick Allen, Bobby Grich, Doyle Alexander, Sal Bando, Don Baylor, and Gene Tenace.

2. Statement by Marvin Miller, February 16, 1976.

3. In his autobiography, Kuhn makes clear his views on the inappropriateness of arbitration as a remedy for Hunter, Messersmith, and McNally. Kuhn, *Hardball*, 139–42, 155–59.

4. Interview with Downing, March 26, 1991.

5. Helyar, *Lords of the Realm*, 36.

6. Interview with Downing, March 26, 1991.

7. Ibid.

8. Interview with Ted Simmons, December 4, 1991.

9. Interview with Torre, March 25, 1991.

10. Interviews with Miller, March 29, 1991, Moss, May 7, 1992, and Simmons, December 4, 1991. Even after Simmons became involved in management, including being the general manager of the Pirates, he retained close ties with Miller and other staff members of the Players Association.

11. Arbitration before Impartial Arbitrator Gabriel N. Alexander and Arbitration Panel, Grievance Nos. 73-16, 73-18, Brief on Behalf of Cincinnati Reds, Inc., February 6, 1974, p. 7.

12. Marvin J. Miller to Gabriel N. Alexander, Re: Grievance Nos. 73-16, 73-18, March 4, 1974.

13. Ibid.

14. Opinion by Gabriel N. Alexander, Impartial Chairman, Decision No. 19, Grievances No. 73-16, 73-18, April 19, 1974. Some Reds players appeared unclear about the ruling, and Miller went to some length to explain to them that "it does *not* mean that a Club is unable to discipline a player for just cause. . . . Bender was the first one to swear; Bender testified that he called Tolan 'a no good bastard.' . . . It [the Reds] tried everything including character assassination at the hearings." Marvin Miller to Johnny Bench, May 14, 1974.

15. E. J. Bavasi to Marvin Miller, September 7, 1973.

16. Interview with Gaherin, March 27, 1991.

17. Richard Moss to Peter Seitz, August 12, 1974.

18. Donald Dewey and Nicholas Acocella, *The Biographical History of Baseball* (New York, 1995), 421, and *Baseball: The Biographical Encyclopedia*, 1017–18.

19. Excerpts from decision of Peter Seitz, quoted in press release, MLBPA, December 16, 1974. In his autobiography, Kuhn claims that "Seitz would not have granted free agency, but for Finley's checkered past." Kuhn, *Hardball*, 141–42.

20. Testimony of James Hunter at arbitration hearing, November 26, 1974, p. 73.

21. Evidence entered at arbitration hearing, November 26, 1974, p. 55.

22. Bowie Kuhn to J. Carlton Cherry, October 10, 1974, which prompted a reply from Miller on October 17, 1974.

23. Kuhn, *Hardball*, 140.

24. Testimony of James Hunter at arbitration hearing, November 26, 1974, p. 73.

25. Question by Peter Seitz at arbitration hearing, November 26, 1974, p. 176.

26. Kuhn, *Hardball*, 142–43.

27. Marvin Miller to Bowie Kuhn, October 17, 1974.

28. Closing argument by Barry Rona at arbitration hearing, November 26, 1974, p. 199.

29. Closing argument by Richard Moss at arbitration hearing, November 26, 1974, p. 202.

30. Ruling by Peter Seitz in arbitration hearing, November 26, 1974, p. 16.

31. Press release, MLBPA, December 16, 1974.

32. Kuhn was "troubled by an outside arbitrator [Seitz] seizing the right to punish him [Finley]." Kuhn's philosophy was that "the change [to outside arbitration] was neither necessary or beneficial. . . . There had never been a commissioner whose fairness in disputes could be questioned and, if anything they had probably been more sympathetic to the players' side of disputes." Kuhn, *Hardball*, 141–42.

Chapter 9: Messersmith and McNally

1. Interview with Marshall, March 28, 1991.

2. Interview with Gaherin, March 27, 1991.

3. *Baseball: The Biographical Encyclopedia*, 764.

4. Interviews with Mark Belanger, January 10, 1992, and Brooks Robinson, August 17, 1991.

5. Interview with Dalton, August 17, 1991.

6. Interview with Pappas, June 29, 1987.

7. *Baseball: The Biographical Encyclopedia*, 764. For remarks about the situation in Baltimore by McNally's teammate, Dave Leonhard, see chap. 5, n. 27 above.

8. "History Revisited: Free Agency Began with Baseball," *The Sporting News*, December 23, 2000.

9. Peter Seitz to Sam Kagel, March 24, 1975.

10. Ibid.

11. Peter Seitz to Arthur Swerdloff, September 29, 1982.

12. James Scoville, "Labor Relations in Sports," in *Government and the Sports Business*, ed. Roger G. Noll (Washington, D.C., 1974), 215.

13. Ibid., 215.

14. Interviews with Gaherin, March 27, 1991, and Miller, March 17, 1988. On the twenty-fifth anniversary of the decision, some of the principles still do not agree about what indication Seitz might have given about his intentions. Lou Hoynes, the commissioner's attorney, said, "'We didn't understand Peter to have given us a clear view of what his decision would be.'" Barry Rona, the lawyer who worked with Gaherin, takes a very different view: "'What Seitz was saying Lou chose to interpret and Bowie chose to interpret as Seitz being more flexible. . . . John [Gaherin] and I read it differently. . . . John and I felt he was giving us a negative signal. Marvin [Miller] interpreted

it the same way." "Baseball's Transfer of Power," *New York Times*, December 23, 2000.

15. Peter Seitz to Bowie Kuhn, November 23, 1982.

16. Interview with Gaherin, March 27, 1991.

17. Interviews with Gaherin, March 27, 1991, and Miller, October 19, 1988. In one of Seitz's few public statements about the case, he summarized: "What I did was in the cards. Only the owners were too stupid to see that and they forced me to make a decision." Quoted in the *Baltimore Sun*, December 23, 1976.

18. Quoted in "Baseball's Transfer of Power," *New York Times*, December 23, 2000.

19. Decision by Peter Seitz, Grievances No. 75-27 and 75-28, December 23, 1975.

20. Ibid.

21. Ibid.

22. Ibid.

23. Dick Young, *New York Daily News*, December 26, 1975. The baseball historian and sociologist David Voigt discusses another Brooklyn connection. He makes a convincing case that O'Malley, Miller, and Jackie Robinson were the three most important men in shaping baseball in the period after 1946. David Voigt, "They Shaped the Game: Nine Innovators of Major League Baseball," *Baseball History* 1.1 (Spring 1986): 5–22.

24. "History Revisited: Free Agency Began with Baseball," *The Sporting News*, December 23, 2000, and "Baseball's Transfer of Power," *New York Times*, December 23, 2000.

25. Interview with Gaherin, March 27, 1991. Commissioner Kuhn was an active participant in the efforts to overturn the decision. It is interesting to note that in *Hardball*, Kuhn discusses why he had opposed challenging Seitz's ruling in the Hunter decision because of "the presumption of correctness that the law gives to arbitrators' decisions. Absent capricious, arbitrary, or dishonest conduct, they are difficult to overturn." Kuhn, *Hardball*, 142. This sounds much like the advice that Gaherin gave in 1976, which was ignored by Kuhn, the lawyers for baseball, and the owners.

26. Interview with Kauffman, November 16, 1990. In 2000, Barry Rona claimed, "'We thought it was a conservative court. . . . It was researched pretty carefully going up to the Circuit Court of Appeals.'" "Baseball's Transfer of Power," *New York Times*, December 23, 2000.

27. Interview with Gaherin, March 27, 1991. Early in the proceedings, Judge Oliver demonstrated why the owners should have listened to Gaherin about the appeal and the decision to negotiate with the players rather than forcing Seitz to rule. He rejected the idea that the Flood decision should have any impact on his ruling. He rejected the assertion in the owners' brief that "arbitration should not be permitted to destroy the industry involved in the dispute" and despaired that the plaintiffs had rejected that "the Court

did its level best to lead all of you to the thirst quenching quaff of negotiations." *Kansas City Royals Baseball Corp. v. Major League Baseball Players Association and Golden West Baseball Company, et al.,* United States District Court for the Western District of Missouri Western Division, no. 75-CV-712-W-1 (hereafter *Royals v. MLBPA*), January 26, 1976, pp. 57, 52, and 50.

28. *Royals v. MLBPA*, January 8, 1976, p. 5. Oliver spent a lot of time summarizing the history of labor relations in baseball. He made the point that the Flood decision and its predecessors would play no role in his decision, but he took the opportunity to concur with the remark that the 1922 decision was "written by the great Oliver Wendell Holmes Jr. on one of his not happier days." Ibid., p. 193.

29. Interview with Judge John W. Oliver, November 15, 1990, *Royals v. MLBPA*, January 26, 1976, p. 49.

30. *Royals v. MLBPA*, January 26, 1976, p. 56.

31. Ibid., January 8, 1976, p. 29.

32. Ibid., brief of defendant.

33. Ibid., brief of plaintiff.

34. Ibid.

35. Testimony of Commissioner of Baseball Bowie Kuhn before Ways and Means Committee of the U.S. House of Representatives, March 17, 1978.

36. Peter Seitz to Bowie Kuhn (PERSONAL AND CONFIDENTIAL), November 8, 1982.

37. Bowie Kuhn to Peter Seitz, November 16, 1982. Twenty-five years later, Kuhn was still convinced that Seitz was the wrong man to rule on the case. "'I was not surprised. I had people examine his record. I thought there was a tilt to the players' side.'" Quoted in "History Revisited: Free Agency Began with Baseball," *The Sporting News*, December 23, 2000.

38. Interview with Oliver, November 15, 1990. Oliver made it clear that he was trying to impress upon the baseball leadership that the world in which Commissioner Landis operated had changed.

39. Murray Chass said that "the luck of the draw went against management" and quoted Dick Moss, "'We wound up before Judge John Oliver, one of the most activist federal judges in the country.'" "Baseball's Transfer of Power," *New York Times*, December 23, 2000.

40. *Royals v. MLBPA*, Memorandum and Order, February 10, 1976, Final Judgment and Decree, February 11, 1976, summarized in *409 Federal Supplement*, pp. 245–46.

41. Arbitration Panel Decision No. 29, Grievances Nos. 75-27 and 75-28 (Messersmith and McNally), December 23, 1975, p. 37. Seitz's opinion went into great detail about the precise nature and limits of the subject of his ruling. His job was to rule on the meaning of the phrase in the standard contract, "to renew this contract for a period of one year." He recognized the impact of his ruling, but took pains to point out "it is not for this Panel (and

especially the writer) to determine what, if anything, is good or bad about the reserve system. The Panel's sole duty is to interpret and apply the agreements and undertakings of the parties" (p. 59).

42. *Royals v. MLBPA,* January 27, 1976.

43. Peter Seitz to Bowie Kuhn (PERSONAL AND CONFIDENTIAL), November 8, 1982. Seitz avoided most public comment about the decision, but he broke that silence in March 1976 in an interview with the *Chicago Sun-Times.* He claimed that he had been "muzzled" by baseball, and "as a result everything that has been in the press and the media has been a bunch of nonsense." The point that Seitz wanted to make known was that "he was willing to withhold judgment . . . and the case would still be pending today— or possibly have been withdrawn if the owners had expressed a desire to negotiate on the reserve system." This interview took place in the midst of the work stoppage. Seitz said he was upset by the problems but had no regrets, "since I had a very limited duty to perform and I did it. I'm not the Czar of the baseball industry." *Chicago Sun-Times,* March 3, 1976.

44. *Royals v. MLBPA.* Judge Oliver's ruling reflected the closing arguments made by both sides. Lead counsel for the plaintiffs stated that "He [Seitz] imposed his own brand of industrial philosophy," and associate counsel for the defense, Donald Fehr, said, "In this case the court is called upon to determine whether or not certain grievances relating to certain specific contract provisions in individual contracts with players are subject to grievance." Oliver clearly accepted the latter position. *Royals v. MLBPA,* Memorandum and Order, February 10, 1976, Final Judgment and Decree, February 11, 1976, summarized in *409 Federal Supplement,* pp. 245–46.

45. Peter Seitz to Bowie Kuhn (PERSONAL AND CONFIDENTIAL), November 8, 1982.

46. Bowie Kuhn to Peter Seitz, November 16, 1982. In his reply to Kuhn, Seitz said, "[I] must have developed more umbrage and indignation in respect of my abrupt expulsion from the world of baseball than I had realized." Peter Seitz to Bowie Kuhn, November 23, 1982.

47. *Royals v. MLBPA,* January 27, 1976, p. 30.

48. Ibid., p. 302. Oliver pressed the attorneys for ownership to define precisely what they were willing to include in the "scope of arbitration." The response he elicited was, "The position of the Club Owners in this case is that the core [of the reserve system] is not subject to arbitration." *Royals v. MLBPA,* January 28, 1976, p. 442.

49. *Royals v. MLBPA,* January 27, 1976, pp. 302–3.

50. *Royals v. MLBPA,* January 28, 1976. At one point, Oliver reminded the participants that he had seen similar cases where nothing happened "until the principals agreed with what Jack Cage was reported to have said by Shakespeare that the first thing we do is kill the lawyers and get the lawyers out of the room."

51. Decision of the United States Court of Appeals, Eighth Circuit, in *Kan-*

sas City Royals v. MLBPA, no. 76-1115, March 9, 1976, in *Federal Reporter*, p. 632.

52. Interview with Oliver, November 15, 1990.

Chapter 10: Protecting Free Agency

1. Negotiating Minutes, September 10, 1975.
2. Ibid.
3. Negotiating Minutes, January 30, 1976.
4. Negotiating Minutes, June 20, 1975.
5. Negotiating Minutes, August 15, 1975.
6. Quoted in *New York Daily News*, August 6, 1975.
7. Marvin Miller to John Gaherin, August 20, 1975.
8. Marvin Miller, Memorandum to All Players, August 29, 1975.
9. Ibid.
10. Ibid.
11. For an in-depth study of the situation in the National Football League, see David Harris, *The League* (New York, 1986), esp. 78–82, 181–85, and 255–57.
12. Ibid., 78–82.
13. Marvin Miller, Memorandum to All Players, August 29, 1975. Baseball players, especially members of the Executive Board of the MLBPA, talked a lot about the comparison between their union and the NFLPA. Marvin Miller to WCBS, June 16, 1972. Although there appeared to be some sympathy for the football players and the situation they faced, it was outweighed by the feeling that they had not been willing to show the same resolve as the baseball players in challenging ownership effectively. Football players were fond of using the term "gut check" to evaluate performance. MLBPA members thought the NFL players had failed in refusing to stand together in support of their union.
14. Quoted in Harris, *The League*, 185.
15. *Playbook*, the official publication of the National Football League Players Association (updated September 25, 1995), deals with these issues in a section titled "NFLPA History" (3–24). It notes that in 1976 the players had won in court, "but on the other hand, the players' support for the union had waned. Less than half the players paid dues in 1975, the year after the strike." (10). A problem facing the union in crises in 1982, 1987, and 1990 was the failure of star players to support the union.
16. Red Smith, *New York Times*, August 13, 1975.
17. Negotiating notes, November 1975.
18. Negotiating notes, November 18, 1975.
19. Richards's views were quoted in an article by Dick Young that Miller summarized in a letter to Bill Bradley in which he thanked Bradley for "leaving at my place a copy of Dick Young's article on the reserve rules." Marvin Miller to Bill Bradley, April 19, 1972.

20. Negotiating Minutes, February 3, 1976.

21. Marvin Miller to John Gaherin, December 18, 1975.

22. John Gaherin to Marvin Miller, December 18, 1975.

23. Negotiating notes, January 30, 1976.

24. Marvin Miller to Phil Pepi, April 6, 1976.

25. Bob Feller quoted in Will Grimsley, *Los Angeles Times*, December 12, 1976.

26. Negotiating notes, February 2, 1976.

27. Negotiating notes, February 13, 1976.

28. Negotiating notes, April 1976.

29. Quoted in Bob Hertzel, *Cincinnati Enquirer*, February 26, 1976.

30. Ibid. Howsam used the *Cincinnati Reds-Letter: Official Publication of the Cincinnati Reds, Inc.* to write an "Open Letter to Reds Fans" in which he summarized the current problem and the past history. Baseball had offered "a more lenient reserve rule" in response to the Seitz ruling. This would allow players to play out their option year after eight years. Baseball needed stability in order to survive. Howsam tried to assure the fans that "Baseball is willing to relax the present reserve system," pointing out that it had made concessions in the past with salary arbitration, the ten and five rule, and termination pay. He neglected to mention that he had opposed all of those changes and that they had taken place in response to pressure from the union.

31. Negotiating notes, March 5, 1976.

32. Bowie Kuhn to John Gaherin and Marvin Miller, March 12, 1976.

33. Negotiating notes, March 15, 1976.

34. Negotiating notes, March 16, 1976.

35. See Kuhn, *Hardball*, 161-64.

36. Interview with Steve Rogers, April 10, 1999.

37. Interview with Marshall, March 28, 1991.

38. Helyar, *Lords of the Realm*, 173-74.

39. Interview with Kauffman, November 16, 1990.

40. Quoted in "Baseball's Transfer of Power," *New York Times*, December 23, 2000.

41. Interview with Dalton, August 17, 1991.

42. Interview with Kauffman, November 16, 1990.

43. Interview with Marshall, March 28, 1991.

44. Interview with Miller, March 29, 1989.

45. Interview with Gaherin, March 27, 1991.

46. Interview with Miller, March 29, 1989.

47. Memorandum from Marvin Miller to all players, June 26, 1976.

48. Ibid.

Chapter 11: 1980-The Strike That Didn't Happen

1. "Average Salaries in Major League Baseball, 1967-1992," supplied by MLBPA.

2. For an excellent summary of emotional aspects of the situation in 1980–81, see Koppett, *Koppett's Concise History*, 389–90, 393.

3. Helyar, *Lords of the Realm*, 217–18.

4. Leonard Koppett, *The Sporting News*, May 24, 1980.

5. Negotiating notes, January 25, 1980.

6. Ibid. About six weeks earlier, the Executive Board had discussed the upcoming negotiations and "focused on the apparent belief of many club owners that they have been 'beaten' in the past, and that they need a 'victory' this time around." Whether or not the players were correct in their evaluation, the firmness of their belief meant that any proposal made by Grebey was going to be scrutinized in terms of how it might force the union into a strike. The distrust of the motives of the owners was clear from the start. Miller shared that belief, but did not create it and did not have to foster it.

7. Negotiating notes, January 16, 1980.

8. Negotiating notes, January 25, 1980.

9. Ibid.

10. Negotiating notes, January 16, 1980.

11. Notes of Executive Board meeting, January 25, 1980.

12. Ibid.

13. Ibid.

14. Ibid.

15. Ibid.

16. Ibid. There were twenty-six players who attended this two-day meeting in Houston. Four clubs were not represented. It was a mixture of veteran players who had been on the Executive Board and players who were relatively new to the position of player representative. The participants thought it was necessary to discuss the history of the union as well as the pressing problem. There were a variety of issues raised in addition to the strike. One player talked about how "our owner is backing us," but the general tone was distrustful and reflected the idea that the "Players Association must police owners to prevent owners from paying [players] what they think it's worth." One member of the board stated, "many players believe there should be some compensation." He was the lone voice in this respect. The response to him ranged from "if there are any, let's press them for their reasons" to "we need to educate those who feel compensation may be fair." One member suggested it was time "to call the owners' bluff. . . . If you want compensation, open your books. Show us you need compensation." The board was united behind the conviction that there was a need to fight against compensation, and it recognized that "if they're losing money, we must modify our proposal." The meeting ended with Miller's warning that they "must keep strategy in this room . . . if strategy leaks, no strategy."

17. Notes of Subcommittee Meeting, April 1, 1980.

18. Ibid.

19. Ray Grebey, *The Sporting News*, May 17, 1980.

20. Red Smith, *New York Times*, May 14, 1980.

21. Jim Murray, *Los Angeles Times*, April 3, 1980, and *Los Angeles Times*, May 23, 1980.

22. Marvin Miller to Jim Murray, August 21, 1980.

23. Grebey's statement was distributed in a memorandum from Marvin Miller to All Members of the Players Association, May 29, 1980.

24. Ibid.

25. "Answers to Your Questions," distributed by Major League Baseball, May 1980. "'Union busting' . . . 'Forcing a strike' . . . 'Turning back the clock' . . . 'Settling a score' . . . are some of the terms flung around in these questions. Such questions merit consideration and deserve to be answered. Here are the answers, given on behalf of the 26 Major League clubs and reflecting their policies and objectives."

26. Don Baylor with Claire Smith, *Don Baylor: Nothing but the Truth—A Baseball Life* (New York, 1989), 169.

27. "Answers to Your Questions."

28. Ibid.

29. Interview with Dalton, August 17, 1991.

30. Notes of Executive Board meeting, January 25, 1980.

31. Marvin Miller to C. Ray Grebey, September 29, 1980.

32. Additional Points for Discussion Re: Study Committee Meeting, written by Miller, Fehr, Bando, and Boone, August 5, 1980.

33. Minutes of Joint Study Committee, August 7, 1980. This was the first meeting of the committee. Miller, Fehr, Rose, and Grebey attended in addition to Boone, Bando, Dalton, and Cashen. The comment about the importance of defining the game "from a player's standpoint" was made by Boone. A resolution passed by the Executive Board on July 7, 1980, stated that the committee would have to look "with great care" at the impact compensation would "have on Players and on Baseball" and that the union would not allow the owners to "use the Committee to impose compensation [following] a sham attempt to 'study' the question." See also Minutes of Joint Study Committee, December 29, 1980, and January 22, 1981.

34. Remarks by Commissioner Bowie Kuhn, Dallas, Texas, December 8, 1980, p. 2.

35. Ibid., p. 4.

36. Management Representatives Report: Player Selection Rights Study Committee, February 17, 1981.

37. Report of Player Members of Study Committee, February 19, 1981. Boone, Bando, and Miller spent a lot of time refining the final draft of their report. Two points were changed significantly from the first draft—a detailed historical overview was included to show that baseball had improved in a competitive sense since free agency, and emphasis was placed on the unique talent of major league players (compensation did not mean that a player could

be replaced by one with equal skills, thus why did Grebey make the assumption that compensation would lead to maintained competitive balance?).

38. Management Representatives Report: Player Selection Rights Study Committee, February 17, 1981.

Chapter 12: The Union's Sternest Test

1. Miller, *A Whole Different Ball Game*, 302.

2. Kuhn, *Hardball*, 362. Kuhn is convinced that the strike was the product of Miller's miscalculation of the resolve of the owners and his willingness to mislead the players into thinking that the owners were using compensation to end free agency and that they hoped that a strike might break the union. "Miller was a prisoner of his own ego above all things. . . . The strike was on and we were into what was bound to be a gutter fight. It was the arena where Miller was at his best" (346).

3. Miller, *A Whole Different Ball Game*, 302.

4. Interview with Bando, August 17, 1991.

5. Two examples are a letter from Pat Gillick, vice president of baseball operations, Toronto Blue Jays, to Dear Dick, February 28, 1981, and a letter from Ruly M. Carpenter III, president, Philadelphia Phillies, to Dear Dick, March 3, 1981. Dave Winfield's later analysis was probably typical of the response of the players: "But when the decision [to strike] was made there was never any doubt in my mind that I would abide by it. I knew that without Miller and the Players Association I would have never gotten to where I was." Dave Winfield with Tom Parker, *Winfield: A Player's Life* (New York, 1988), 169.

6. Minutes of negotiating session, May 11, 1981.

7. Doug DeCinces, minutes of negotiating session, May 11, 1981.

8. Kenneth M. Jennings, *Balls and Strikes: The Money Game in Professional Baseball* (Westport, Conn., 1990), 50–59.

9. Notes of negotiating session, June 11, 1981.

10. Interviews with Rogers, April 10, 1999, and Donald Fehr, January 10, 1992.

11. Kuhn, *Hardball*, 347. Kuhn is one of the very few observers who has this view of Miller.

12. Notes of negotiating session, June 26, 1981.

13. Interview with Rogers, April 10, 1999.

14. Major League Baseball Players Association to Grebey and Howard T. Fox Jr., executive vice president, Minnesota Twins, June 23, 1981.

15. Notes of Executive Board meeting, July 7, 1981. The sentiments and the language were similar to a year earlier. The big difference was that more players were outspoken, including some who had been silent in 1980.

16. Mediator's Proposal—Amended, July 10, 1981.

17. Notes of Executive Board meeting, July 7, 1981. A long-serving member of the board who had pushed for some acceptance of compensation in 1980 was adamant in his opposition this time. Other player reps pointed out that now some of the most lukewarm members of the association were "very solid" behind the strike and in opposition to the owners' idea of compensation. Interviews with Marshall, February 28, 1991, and Marvin Miller, July 1, 1991.

18. Earl Lawson, *Cincinnati Enquirer*, July 13, 1981.

19. Notes of negotiating session, July 22, 1981.

20. Congressman Wyche Fowler Jr., writing for himself and fifteen other signatories, to Marvin Miller, July 23, 1981, with copies to Kenneth Moffett, Federal Mediation and Conciliation Service, and Honorable Ray Donovan, Secretary of Labor.

21. Marvin Miller to Hon. Wyche Fowler Jr., August 25, 1981.

22. Notes of Executive Board meeting, July 27, 1981.

23. Ibid. The published Minutes of the Executive Board meeting stated: "While all players felt there was solid and overwhelming support for the bargaining committee, some felt that up-to-date information was not reaching the players quickly enough. Many players indicated that this meeting was helpful to them in understanding the issues and respective positions of the parties. Following these discussions, it was moved and seconded that Mr. Miller and the bargaining committee hold a series of regional meetings with the players."

24. Jerome Holtzman, *Chicago Sun-Times*, July 29, 1981.

25. Notes of Executive Board meeting, July 27, 1981.

26. Quoted by Marvin Miller in draft of an article requested by *New York Times* about "the causes and the significance of the strike and the settlement." Miller sent a copy of the article to all players, appending it to a copy of the statement by August A. Busch Jr. (see below).

27. Statement by August A. Busch Jr. at meeting of owners in Chicago, August 6, 1981. Miller had a long history of using Busch's comments as a way to rally and solidify the players, starting in 1970. That was especially true when the players did something that Busch found completely outrageous like going on strike. In Miller's cover letter to the players, he could not resist using Busch as a foil once more: "Unlike Mr. Busch, my feeling is one of great pride; pride in the solidarity of the players and their principled successful struggle." Marvin Miller, memorandum to all players, August 20, 1981.

28. Quoted in Miller, draft of article for *New York Times*.

29. Minutes of Executive Board meeting, August 1, 1981. A special meeting of the Executive Board had been convened on August 1, 1981, to approve the Memorandum of Settlement and to submit it to the players for ratification. After that action, Miller, Fehr, and Rose were excused from the room, at which time the motion was made, discussed, and approved.

30. John Schulian, *Chicago Sun-Times*, August 2, 1981. For a discussion of

Moffett's tenure as executive director of the MLBPA after Miller retired, see Helyar, *Lords of the Realm*, 322–24.

31. Bill Conlin, *Philadelphia Daily News*, July 27, 1981. In a letter to Hal Bock, Miller contradicted a number of claims made by Ray Grebey in an earlier interview with Bock. The most significant of these were that "the strike was caused by the players' position" and that the owners "got more compensation than we set out to get." For the latter point, Miller asked Bock to "see owners' demands and compare with fragment provided by the settlement" and to read the quotes of Busch about the inadequacy of the settlement. Marvin Miller to Hal Bock, August 31, 1981.

When Miller wrote to Bill Conlin, the letter was in a much more serious tone. Miller was angry at the idea that he had "sold the players on a strike." He could treat Conlin's idea that the strike marked "the end of baseball" as "poetic license," but "not acceptable . . . is your likening of the past fifteen years to the 1919 Black Sox scandal. That paragraph comes under the heading of shameful writing." Marvin Miller to Bill Conlin, September 2, 1981.

32. Hugo Young, *The Observer Monthly Sports Magazine*, December 2000.

33. A. Bartlett Giamatti, *New York Times*, June 16, 1981.

34. Ibid.

35. Marvin Miller to A. Bartlett Giamatti, December 28, 1981.

36. Marvin Miller to A. Bartlett Giamatti, February 4, 1982.

37. Ibid. Shortly after Giamatti was named commissioner, Dave Nightingale, the national correspondent for *The Sporting News*, ran a two-page question-and-answer article about Giamatti, entitled "Meet the New Commissioner." Nightingale headed the article with a reprint of "the impassioned words" that had appeared in the *New York Times* (June 16, 1981) and pointed out that "had they not been written, it is quite possible that A. Bartlett Giamatti would not be ascending to the position of commissioner of baseball." Giamatti was more modest. In replying to a question about how his love of baseball was known to the owners, he said, "Also I used to write some little pieces, here and there, about baseball. I once wrote what I think was probably an annoying Op-Ed piece in the *New York Times*, but that seemed to attract some favorable attention." *The Sporting News, 1989 Baseball Special*, 8–9. One can only wonder if "annoying" referred to Miller's reaction.

The baseball historian Robert F. Burk describes Giamatti's letter as a "diatribe" and points out that the "plague-on-both-your-houses" approach condemned only the actions of one side, the union. Burk also points out that Giamatti, "as N.L. President . . . had been a willing participant in collusion. . . . [And] even before he was formally sworn in as commissioner, Giamatti personally endorsed the lockout idea." Burk, *Much More Than a Game*, 263.

38. Quoted in Richie Ashburn, *Philadelphia Bulletin*, July 26, 1981.

39. Letter from Robin Roberts to Marvin Miller, September 9, 1981.

40. Quoted in Richie Ashburn, *Philadelphia Bulletin*, July 26, 1981. In a 1988 letter to the author, Roberts chose only to discuss broadcast negotia-

tions, the pension fund, and endorsements as reasons for hiring Miller as the first full-time executive director of the MLBPA. "These areas were handled nicely by Marvin Miller who had the support of the players. P.S. The rest developed later." Robin Roberts to the author, August 7, 1988.

41. Robin Roberts to Marvin Miller, September 3, 1981. The issue of Miller's accomplishments have been discussed by a number of journalists in the 1990s, often in the context of whether he should be voted into the Baseball Hall of Fame. One of the first such articles appeared in *Sports National*, January 2, 1990, written by Bob Hertzel, who had been critical of Miller when Hertzel was with the *Cincinnati Enquirer*. The 1990 article was headlined, "Most Deserving of Hall of Fame," and concluded, "He [Miller] was truly the most influential man in baseball over the last 20 years and deserves to have the Veterans Committee, charged with enshrining non-playing personnel, recognize his genius." Frederick Klein of the *New York Times* made the same point about the Veteran's Committee and said that "Missing from the list [of candidates] is someone whose impact on the game, and on American sports in general, exceeded that of all but a handful of people. He's Marvin Miller." Allen Barra (who worked with Miller on his autobiography) discussed the issue in the *New York Times*, February 20, 2000. Barra quoted Bob Costas ("'with the possible exception of Branch Rickey, there is no nonplayer more deserving for the Hall of Fame than Marvin Miller'"), Jim Bunning ("'The Hall of Fame is about players, and Marvin did more for players than anyone else'"), Tom Seaver ("'Miller's exclusion from the Hall [is] "a national disgrace"'"), Henry Aaron ("'Miller should be in the Hall of Fame if the players have to break down the door to get him in'"), and Brooks Robinson ("'This is our fight. . . . Frankly, it's our fault Marvin isn't in the Hall of Fame'"). Barra also pointed out that George Steinbrenner and Buzzie Bavasi "endorse Miller's candidacy."

42. Marvin Miller to Robin Roberts, September 16, 1981.

43. Marvin Miller to Robin Roberts, September 3, 1981.

44. Brooks Robinson to Marvin Miller, August 1981, and Milt Pappas to Marvin Miller, August 22, 1981. Pappas concluded, "Knowing you Marv, you give credit to the players. All I can say is that Marvin gave the players the respect and credibility they deserved."

45. Marvin Miller to Milt Pappas, August 28, 1981.

Conclusion

1. On the first anniversary of the Messersmith-McNally ruling, Peter Seitz characterized the conduct of the owners: "They were like the French barons of the 12th century. . . . They had accumulated so much power that they wouldn't share it with anybody." Quoted in "History Revisited: Free Agency Began with Baseball," *The Sporting News*, December 23, 1976.

2. Bunning was legendary for his fierce competitive instincts. Tim McCarver, a member of the Executive Board with Bunning, discussed how "Bun-

ning would talk with you one day about the 'righteousness of the cause and the need for staying united' and then knock you down with a fastball the next day." Interview with McCarver, August 23, 1989.

3. Interview with Bavasi, November 17, 1989.

4. "Average Salaries in Major League Baseball, 1967–1992" (MLBPA). See also Koppett, *Koppett's Concise History*, 391–94 and 415–16, Helyar, *Lords of the Realm*, Kenneth M. Jennings, *Swings and Misses: Moribund Labor Relations in Professional Baseball* (Westport, Conn., 1997), and Jennings, *Balls and Strikes*.

5. Quoted in AP Dispatch (in files of *The Sporting News*), February 17, 1973.

6. Koppett, *Koppett's Concise History*, 384–85, and Brian Flaspohler, "Player Movement throughout Baseball History," *The Baseball Research Journal* 29 (2000): 98–101.

7. Marvin Miller, Memorandum for Public Release, July 1966.

8. "Bart Giamatti" and "Bowie Kuhn," in *Baseball: The Biographical Encyclopedia*, 407–8 and 628–29. Whitey Herzog expressed serious concerns for the economic problems facing baseball in *You're Missin' a Great Game*, but his evaluation of Miller is that "he explained labor rights to the players. He gave them the tools to negotiate their fair market value" and "Personally, I can't complain about the players' association and its accomplishments. The work Marvin Miller and his followers did brought me and my family the kind of prosperity I could never have imagined." Whitey Herzog and Jonathan Pitts, *You're Missin' a Great Game* (New York, 1999), 204, 223.

9. The comment from Werber was part of an interview on an ESPN broadcast, *The Ten Most Influential People in Twentieth-Century American Sports*. The list was limited to non-athletes. Four baseball personalities were included: Branch Rickey, Judge Landis, Walter O'Malley, and (at number four) Marvin Miller. Hereafter cited as ESPN, *Most Influential*.

Whitey Herzog makes this same point. In a section on collusion, he defends the need of the owners to get some control over their business affairs. Herzog and Pitts, *You're Missin' a Great Game*, 270–71.

10. Probably the most extreme version of the hostile attitude toward so-called mercenary players was the published reaction of a Cardinals fan when the relief pitcher Bruce Sutter went from St. Louis to Atlanta as a free agent: "I hope Sutter develops a rotator cuff injury." The remark was made by George Peach, the St. Louis circuit attorney, the chief law enforcement officer for the City of St. Louis. Other interesting comments on the changing nature of the relationship between fans and players are in Jack Sands and Peter Gammons, *Coming Apart at the Seams* (New York, 1993).

11. Quotes provided by Professor Norman Baker.

12. Voigt, *American Baseball*, vol. 3, 99–100.

13. "Pity Poor Ball Players," *The Sporting News*, April 19, 1962.

14. Giulianotti, *Football*, 118.

15. Dave Anderson, *New York Times*, January 26, 1992.

16. Jim Northrup to Lee MacPhail, February 14, 1976.

17. Quoted in *The Waiting Room*, May 1984, 63.

18. Quoted in "Fans Tired of Bickering, Lane's Warning to Players," *The Sporting News*, January 7, 1956.

19. Kuhn, *Hardball*, 141.

20. "Bowie Kuhn," in *Baseball: The Biographical Encyclopedia*, 628.

21. Interview, circa 1970, with Flood, in ESPN, *Most Influential*.

22. Peter Levine, *A. G. Spalding and the Rise of Baseball: The Promise of American Sport* (New York, 1985), 14–16.

23. Interview with Buzzie Bavasi, in ESPN, *Most Influential*.

24. Tony LaRussa to Marvin Miller, August 27, 1977, Marvin Miller to Tony LaRussa, August 31, 1977.

25. Paul Staudohar, *The Sports Industry and Collective Bargaining* (Ithaca, N.Y., 1986), 25.

26. Paul Staudohar, "The Baseball Strike of 1994–95," *Monthly Labor Review* (March 1997): 24.

27. Miller deposition, 1976, p. 103.

28. Paul Staudohar, report to University of Illinois Press, October 1999.

29. For an excellent discussion of how various versions of history were used in baseball's labor negotiations, see William W. Wright and Mick Cochrane, "The Uses of History in Baseball Labor Disputes," in *Diamond Mines: Baseball and Labor*, ed. Paul D. Staudohar (Syracuse, N.Y., 2000), 62–82. Wright and Cochrane go beyond their title and present an interesting analysis of the political uses of "history" in contemporary American society.

30. Hugo Young, *The Observer Monthly Sports Magazine*, December 2000.

31. Interview with Thomas Boswell, in ESPN, *Most Influential*.

Epilogue

1. Barry Smith, a player with Stockport County, to Graham Lloyd, secretary of the PFA, June 27, 1959, and Graham Lloyd to Barry Smith, August 21, 1959. On October 13, 1959, Smith wrote to Lloyd, "I could not afford to hang on any longer without wages, so I agreed to be transferred to Headington [a much smaller club], thanks for everything."

2. There have been many analyses of the Eastham case. For a good, brief one, see George W. Keeton, *The Football Revolution* (Newton Abbot, 1972), 134–39. For a more detailed history of the PFA, see John Harding, *For the Good of the Game* (London, 1991). The Eastham case is discussed on pp. 276–98. Jimmy Hill was the chairman of the PFA when it fought the Eastham case. After his playing days were over, he became the only man in England to be a player, manager, director, and chairman. He also had a long, distinguished career as a television analyst. Almost forty years after the case, Hill discussed the freedom and enormous wealth of current-day players: "'The sadness is that people ask me whether I worry about the high wages now. They say I've

given birth to a monster. Well, I don't worry about the high wages. If the players have earned that kind of money, they are entitled to be paid it.'" Quoted in Oliver Holt, *The Times* (London), January 13, 2001.

3. Michael Brcarley, *The Guardian*, April 13, 1972.

4. Michael Brearley, *The Guardian*, April 20, 1972. Red Smith used similar language in discussing the situation of one of the first players to take advantage of the ten and five rule in the *New York Times*, December 13, 1973. Over the years, Brearley followed events in baseball. In a 1993 interview with the author, he said that he could not believe how drastically the MLBPA had changed the situation in baseball.

5. David H. Will, "Football and Europe," *Le football et l'europe, Colloquium Paper 97/90* (Florence, 1990). These are the papers from the conference held at the European University Institute, Florence, October 1989.

6. Brian Glanville, *Sunday Times* (London), May 13, 1990.

7. Jessica Larive, "Football and the Europe of 1992," *Le football et l'europe, Colloquium Paper 121/90*. Larive made her remarks long before the Bosman case was started, but she made it clear in the discussion following her presentation that when someone did challenge the transfer regulations, the courts would find that the rules violated both the spirit and the letter of the European Union's rules concerning workers. She offered, in her capacity as an MEP, to work with the football authorities to modify football rules, but her offer was rejected.

8. I attended the meeting in Florence. Glanville made a statement condemning any efforts to convince the football authorities of the need to make changes. The majority of the participants supported his position. Glanville was particularly upset that Larive had said that "under European law, such as it is . . . footballers . . . were no different from doctors or plumbers." During the discussion following Will's presentation, Will's response to questions about competitiveness sounded just like the claims made by baseball owners before 1976. He stressed that any changes in the transfer system that allowed even a limited version of free agency would destroy the competitive nature of top-level football and that a small number of teams would dominate the sport. A member of the colloquium responded by pointing to the results of the past fifteen years. In the English First Division, Liverpool F.C. had finished first ten times and second four times. In the Scottish First Division/Premier League, Celtic had finished first six times and second six times; Rangers had finished first five times and second twice (both clubs are in Glasgow).

9. For the best analysis of the Bosman case, see Herbert F. Moorhouse, "'The Consequences for European Football of Ending the Traditional Transfer System and UEFA's 'Three Foreigner Rule,'" position paper, University of Glasgow, 1995. Moorhouse does an excellent job of using the MLBPA situation for comparative purposes. See also Giulianotti, *Football*, 106–24. Opinion of Advocate General Lenz delivered on 20 September 1995 (Provisional version),

Case C-415/93, *ASBL Union Royale Belge des Societes de Football Associa-tion . . . v. Jean-March Bosman*, p. I-48.

10. Ibid., p. I-81.

11. Ibid., pp. I-81 to I-93.

12. Lenz noted that the UEFA and the Italian government used "'the rule of reason' . . . a doctrine developed in American antitrust law" to support their case and that Bosman "relied in particular on the judgment of the United States Court of Appeals, Eighth Circuit, in *Mackey v. National Football League.*" He noted that there was no reason to discuss in detail how Bosman's decision reflected the American legal position. Ibid., pp. I-105 and I-108.

The governing bodies in each European football nation (there are more foot-ball nations than sovereign states, e.g. Scotland, Wales, Northern Ireland) mounted campaigns to overturn Lenz's ruling. In the United Kingdom, they sent an open letter and an "information leaflet" to members of Parliament, asserting that the ruling would destroy many clubs and damage football at the international level. They also claimed that the only beneficiaries would be "some star players and agents" and that most players opposed the consequences of the ruling. "Open Letter from the Presidents of the 49 National Football Associations of Europe" and *Information Leaflet Concerning the Bosman case,* ca. November 1995. The cover letter to one Member of Parliament conclud-ed, "We are all aware of the significance of football for our country, and thank you for supporting the concerns of football as part of your important activi-ties." D. G. Collins, secretary general of the Football Association of Wales, to Mr. Ted Rowlands, MP for Merthyr Tydfil and Rhymney Constituency, No-vember 2, 1995. I want to thank Mr. Rowlands for supplying these to me.

13. Gordon Taylor, *Football Management,* October 1995 (typescript provid-ed by Mr. Taylor to the author). The results of the Bosman ruling caused some hardships for marginal players, especially those in some of the lower divisions. See Michael Calvin, *Sportsmail on Sunday,* May 17, 1998.

Discussions of the impact of the Bosman ruling have continued to the present day. *Time* magazine featured an article, entitled "Soccer Suicide: Is Big Money Destroying the World's Favorite Sport?" as the cover story in its international edition of June 5, 2000.

Two important analyses of the Bosman ruling and its long-term implica-tions are the F. A. Premier League Seminar on the Bosman Case, held at Middle Temple Hall, London, January 8, 1996, and H. F. Moorhouse, Bren-dan Schwab, Braham Danscheck, Mads Oland, and Jan Munk Plum, *Time for a New Approach: The International Player System,* a FIFPRO Report to the European Commission, February 9, 2001.

14. Quoted in *The Independent* (London), September 1, 2000.

15. Viviane Reading quoted in "Political Football: An Example of the Real Reason Why the EU Is So Unpopular," *Sunday Times* (London), September 2, 2000.

16. Ibid.

17. Taylor quoted in H. F. Moorhouse, "The Distribution of Incomes in European Football: Big Clubs, Small Leagues, Major Problems," paper delivered at the Economics of Sports Conference, Lisbon, Portugal, November 2000. In conversations with the author between 1991 and 1998, Taylor expressed interest in how the MLBPA kept its members in touch with issues and negotiations and how the MLBPA maintained a unified and involved membership. In recent years, he was particularly interested in how the MLBPA established and enforced a set of standards for players' agents.

18. Tim McCarver, *The Perfect Season* (New York, 1999); Mike Lupica, *The Season of '98* (New York, 1999).

19. Koppett, *Koppett's Concise History*, 456–60.

20. Interview with Bob Costas, March 17, 1996. The 1994–95 work stoppage caused an ongoing discussion about the economic structure and the financial future of baseball. Costas's *Fair Ball: A Fan's Case for Baseball* (New York, 2000) attracted much attention from baseball officials and the public.

21. Minutes of Joint Study Committee, January 22, 1981.

22. Koppett, *Koppett's Concise History*, 461.

23. Staudohar, "The Baseball Strike of 1994–95," 23.

24. Koppett, *Koppett's Concise History*, 462.

25. For an interesting discussion of collusion and the ways in which the relationship between the players and owners have changed, see Herzog and Pitts, *You're Missin' a Great Game*, 199–282.

26. Staudohar, "The Baseball Strike of 1994–95," 24.

27. Ibid., 24.

28. Interview with Ted Simmons, April 7, 1995.

29. Wright and Cochrane, "The Uses of History in Baseball Labor Disputes," 69. Wright and Cochrane demonstrate how different versions of the history of baseball have been created and have gained acceptance. They make some interesting comparisons between how various interest groups in baseball and national political figures have used the same approach of creating a convenient version of history.

30. Quoted in ibid., 64.

31. Quoted in ibid., 68.

32. Quoted in ibid., 69.

33. Baylor and Smith, *Don Baylor*, 167–72.

34. Staudohar, "The Baseball Strike of 1994–94," 26. William B. Gould IV presents an important perspective on the strike in *Labored Relations: Law, Politics, and the NLRB* (Cambridge, Mass., 2000), 101–20. Gould is a dedicated fan as well as a historian of baseball and an authority on sports law. He has been a baseball salary arbitrator and was chairman of the NLRB during the 1994–95 work stoppage.

35. Anonymous report submitted to University of Illinois Press, August 2000.

36. Quoted in Roger Ira Berkow, *New York Times*, September 15, 1994.

37. Quoted in Wright and Cochrane, "The Uses of History in Baseball Labor Disputes," 73.

38. William Marshall, *Baseball's Pivotal Era, 1945–1951* (Lexington, Ky., 1999), 438.

39. Paul Staudohar, "The Baseball Strike of 1994–95" in *Diamond Mines: Baseball and Labor*, ed. Paul Staudohar (Syracuse, N.Y., 2000), 60–61. This is a slightly revised version of the article he published in *Monthly Labor Review* in 1997. In the passage quoted about the commissioner, Staudohar recognizes the important change that had taken place between the time of the first article and the revision. The original article concluded, "The biggest remaining problem is the absence of a commissioner. . . . Baseball has had some outstanding commissioners over the years and sorely needs one now." Paul Staudohar, "The Baseball Strike of 1994–95," *Monthly Labor Review* (March 1997): 27.

40. Marshall, *Baseball's Pivotal Era, 1945–1951*, 438.

41. Notes of Executive Board meeting, January 25, 1980.

42. *Report of the Independent Members of the Commissioner's Blue Ribbon Panel on Baseball Economics, July 2000* (distributed by Major League Baseball, 2000; hereafter cited as *Report of the Blue Ribbon Commission*). The *Report* defines the commissioner's Blue Ribbon Panel as "*representing the interests of baseball fans*, formed to study whether revenue disparities among clubs are seriously damaging competitive balance, and, if so, to recommend structural reforms to ameliorate the problem" (emphasis added; p. 1).

The *Report* states that solutions must be based upon a set of postulates, the last of which is, "Any reform of MLB [Major League Baseball] should protect and balance the *interests of players, clubs, and fans*. These three constituencies should cooperate to create an economic structure that promotes a reasonable rate of growth of player salaries, produces competitive balance and preserves baseball as affordable family entertainment" (p. 7). The *Report* defines "competitive balance" as when "every well-run club has a *regularly recurring reasonable hope of reaching postseason play*" (p. 5).

The Blue Ribbon Panel was composed of Richard C. Levin, Senator George J. Mitchell, Paul A. Volcker, and George F. Will, who were described as independent members, and twelve executives-owners, who were defined as "Club Representatives."

The data to support the recommendations in the *Report* deal with salaries and the performances of the clubs. It covers five seasons, 1995–99, and contains no information to make any comparisons with the period before 1995 (pp. 54–57).

43. Ibid., pp. 7, 13.

44. Many pre-1976 players have criticized free agency–driven salaries. Dave McNally played a huge role in obtaining free agency and got no personal benefit from it. His comment on the Rodriguez salary was whimsical rather

than critical: "'My first thought when I saw that was: Did Texas offer him $250 million and he wanted 2 more? . . . How did they get to $252 million?'" Quoted in "History Revisited: Free Agency Began with Baseball," *The Sporting News,* December 23, 2000.

45. *Report of the Blue Ribbon Commission,* p. 37.

Sources and
Further Reading

This book is based primarily on unpublished documents (most of which are in the possession of the Major League Baseball Players Association), interviews conducted by me (in person, unless otherwise noted), and published autobiographies and memoirs of persons involved in the events discussed. There were no restrictions placed on my access to or use of any of the unpublished material listed below.

Agreements between the MLBPA and the Major Leagues

Basic Agreement between the American League of Professional Baseball Clubs and the National League of Professional Baseball Clubs and Major League Baseball Players Association, 1968, 1970, 1973, 1976, 1981.

Agreement, dated as of December 1, 1966, between the major league committee on player relations (herein called the "Committee") and major league baseball players association (herein called the "Association"). Popularly described as the "dues checkoff agreement."

Arbitration Documents

Grievance Nos. 73-16 and 73-18: "Arbitration between American and National Leagues of Professional Baseball Clubs and the Major League Baseball Players Association, April 19, 1974" (Bobby Tolan arbitration decision).

Grievance No. 75-27 and 75-28: "Arbitration between the Twelve Clubs Comprising the National League of Professional Baseball Clubs and the Twelve Clubs Comprising the American League of Professional Baseball Clubs (Los Angeles Club and Montreal Club) and Major League Baseball

Players Association (John A. Messersmith and David A. McNally), December 23, 1975" (Messersmith and McNally arbitration decision).

Correspondence

Director of Major League Baseball Players Association, 1960–1965
Executive Director of Major League Baseball Players Association, 1966–81
Legal Advisor and Counsels of Major League Baseball Players Association, 1960–81
Papers of Peter Seitz, New York State Industrial Relations Library, Cornell University, Ithaca, N.Y.

Draft Reports, Minutes, and Meeting Transcripts

Draft Report of Player Selection Rights Study Committee—"Confidential," January 1981.
Minutes of Meetings of Executive Board of Major League Baseball Players Association, 1960–1981, printed and distributed to all members of the MLBPA.
Minutes of Meeting of Executive Board of MLBPA, December 1969. Ms.
Minutes of Meetings of Joint Study Committees on Reserve System, 1980–81.
Minutes of Negotiating Sessions for Basic Agreements, 1968, 1970, 1973, 1976, 1981. (Lawyer for Major League Baseball usually served as secretary). Ms.
Revised Draft Report of Player Selection Rights Study Committee—"Confidential," January 22, 1981.
Transcript of Meeting of Executive Council of the Pension Committee with Player Reps, June 6, 1966.
Transcript of Proceedings: Meeting of the Executive Council of the Pension Committee with the Player Representatives, June 6, 1966.

Interviews

Broadcasters and Journalists

Bob Broeg (August 27, 1989)
Bob Burnes (August 30, 1989)
Bill Conlin (March 27, 1991)
Howard Cosell (June 15, 1990)
Bob Costas (March 17, 1996)
Red Foley (March 25, 1991)
Bob Hunter (March 26, 1991)
Leonard Koppett (February 14, 1990)
David Lipman (August 27, 1989)

Robert Lipsyte (July 1, 1991)
Paul MacFarlane (August 19, 1989)
Joe McGuff (November 16, 1990)
Hugh McIllvaney (September 20, 1992)

Former Major League Players

Sal Bando (August 17, 1991)
Bob Barton (November 16, 1989)
Mark Belanger (January 10, 1992)
Steve Boros (March 26, 1991)
Clete Boyer (June 20, 1997)
Jim Bunning (June 30, 1987)
Joe Coleman Jr. (March 25, 1991)
Doug DeCinces (May 8, 1992)
Al Downing (March 26, 1991)
Curt Flood (July 1, 1991)
Steve Hamilton (March 10, 1990)
Ralph Kiner (November 15, 1989)
Mike Marshall (March 28, 1991)
Dal Maxvill (March 15, 2000)
Tim McCarver (August 23, 1989)
Dave McNally (by telephone, February 10, 1992)
Milt Pappas (June 29, 1987)
Gary Peters (March 27, 1991)
Robin Roberts (by telephone and correspondence, July 29 and August 6, 1988)
Brooks Robinson (August 17, 1991)
Jackie Robinson (February 17, 1972)
Steve Rogers (April 10, 1999)
Ted Simmons (December 4, 1991, November 20, 1998, April 7, 1995)
Reggie Smith (March 26, 1991)
Joe Torre (March 25, 1991)
Bill White (January 10, 1992)

Officials and Employees of Major League Baseball and/or Clubs

Buzzie Bavasi (November 17, 1989)
Harry Dalton (August 17, 1991)
Bing Devine (April 6, 1989)
Al Fleischman (May 5, 1991)
John Gaherin (March 27, 1991)
Ewing Kauffman (November 16, 1990)
Bud Selig (August 17, 1991)

Officials of the Major League Baseball Players Association

Judge Robert Cannon (August 16, 1991)
Donald Fehr (January 10, 1992)
Marvin Miller (March 17, 1988, October 19, 1988, March 29, 1989, July 1,
1991, April 10, 1999)
Dick Moss (May 7, 1992)

Others

Mike Brearley (September 15, 1993)
Terry Miller (April 10, 1999)
Judge John W. Oliver (November 15, 1990)
Oscar Robertson (March 19, 1990)
Gordon Taylor (October 10, 1993)

Legal Proceedings

U.S. District Court, Southern District of New York, *Curtis C. Flood, Plaintiff, v. Bowie K. Kuhn, et al., Defendants,* 70 Civ. 202, Plaintiff's Memorandum in Support of Motion for Preliminary Injunction.

U.S. District Court, Southern District of New York, *Curtis C. Flood, Plaintiff, v. Bowie K. Kuhn, et al., Defendants,* 70 Civ. 202, Plaintiff's Post-Trial Brief.

U.S. District Court, Southern District of New York, *Curtis C. Flood, Plaintiff, v. Bowie K. Kuhn, et al.,* 70 Civ. 202, Complaint.

U.S. Supreme Court, October Term, 1971, No. 71-32, *Curtis C. Flood, Petitioner, v. Bowie K. Kuhn, et al., Respondents,* Brief for Petitioner and Petitioner's Reply Brief.

U.S. Supreme Court Reports [407 US 258], *Curtis C. Flood, Petitioner, v. Bowie K. Kuhn, et al.,* . . . [No. 71-32], Argued March 20, 1972, Decided June 19, 1972.

In the Matter of Arbitration between THE TWELVE CLUBS COMPRISING THE NATIONAL LEAGUE OF PROFESSIONAL BASEBALL CLUBS AND THE TWELVE CLUBS COMPRISING THE AMERICAN LEAGUE OF PROFESSIONAL BASEBALL CLUBS (LOS ANGELES CLUB AND MONTREAL CLUB) AND MAJOR LEAGUE BASEBALL PLAYERS ASSOCIATION (JOHN A. MESSERSMITH AND DAVID A. MCNALLY), Decision No. 29, Grievance Nos. 75-27, 75-28.

U.S. District Court, Western District of Missouri, *Kansas City Royals Baseball Corp., Plaintiff, v. Major League Baseball Players Association, Defendant, and Golden West Baseball Company, et al., Plaintiff-Intervenors,* No 75CV-712-W-1 (Transcript of Proceedings).

U.S. Court of Appeals, Eighth Circuit, *Kansas City Royals Baseball Corporation, Plaintiff-Appellant, et al. v. Major League Baseball Players Association, Defendant, Counter-Claim Plaintiff-Respondent,* No. 76-1115, 532 F.2d 615 (1976).

U.S. District Court, Eastern District of Pennsylvania, *Fleer Corporation, Plaintiff, v. Topps Chewing Gum, Inc. and Major League Baseball Players Association, Defendants*, Civil Action No. 75-1803, Deposition of Marvin J. Miller, taken on October 6, 1976.

U.S. District Court, Southern District of New York, *Daniel Silverman, Regional Director . . . National Labor Relations Board v. Major League Baseball, et al.*, 81 Civil No. 3291 (H.F.W.).

Negotiating Notes and Notes for Legal Procedings

Negotiating notes of Donald Fehr for Joint Study Committee on Reserve System, 1980–81.

Negotiating notes of John Gaherin for Basic Agreement, 1973, 1976.

Negotiating notes of Marvin Miller, Dick Moss, and Donald Fehr for Basic Agreements, 1970, 1973, 1976, 1980–81.

Reynolds v. Galbreath—Digest of Relevant Information in Minutes of Players Association.

Miscellaneous

Summary of proposed autobiography of Frank Scott, circa. 1990. Ms.

The Waiting Room (magazine), published and edited by Maryanne Ellison Simmons, 1981–84.

Published Sources

Allen, Dick, and Tim Whitaker. *Crash: The Life and Times of Dick Allen.* New York, 1989.

Bavasi, Buzzie, with John Strege. *Off the Record.* Chicago, 1987.

Baylor, Don, with Claire Smith. *Don Baylor: Nothing but the Truth—A Baseball Life.* New York, 1989.

Costas, Bob. *Fair Ball: A Fan's Case for Baseball.* New York, 2000.

Cosell, Howard, with Peter Bonventre. *I Never Played the Game.* New York, 1985.

Dolson, Frank. *Jim Bunning: Baseball and Beyond.* Philadelphia, 1998.

Drysdale, Don, with Bob Verdi, *Once a Bum, Always a Dodger.* New York, 1990.

Flood, Curt, with Richard Carter. *The Way It Is.* New York, 1971.

Greenberg, Hank. *The Story of My Life.* Ed. Ira Berkow. New York, 1989.

Helyar, John. *Lords of the Realm: The Real History of Baseball.* New York, 1995.

Herzog, Whitey, and Jonathan Pitts. *You're Missin' a Great Game.* New York, 1999.

Hunter, Jim (Catfish), with Armen Kateyian. *My Life in Baseball*. New York, 1998.

Kiner, Ralph, with Joe Gergin. *Kiner's Korner*. New York, 1987.

Koppett, Leonard. *Koppett's Concise History of Major League Baseball*. Philadelphia, 1998.

―――. *The New Thinking Fan's Guide to Baseball*. New York, 1991.

Lupica, Mike. *The Season of '98*. New York, 1999.

Kuhn, Bowie, with Martin Appel. *Hardball: The Education of a Baseball Commissioner*. New York, 1987.

MacPhail, Lee. *My Nine Innings: An Autobiography of Fifty Years in Baseball*. Westport, Conn., 1989.

McCarver, Tim, with Ray Robinson. *Oh, Baby, I Love It!* New York, 1987.

Miller, Marvin. *A Whole Different Ball Game: The Sport and Business of Baseball*. New York, 1991.

Peary, Danny, ed. *We Played the Game: Sixty-Five Players Remember Baseball's Greatest Era, 1947–1964*. New York, 1994.

Robinson, Frank, and Beery Stainback. *Extra Innings*. New York, 1988.

Sands, Jack, and Peter Gammons. *Coming Apart at the Seams*. New York, 1993.

Veeck, Bill, with Ed Linn. *Veeck as in Wreck*. New York, 1986.

Winfield, Dave, with Tom Parker. *Winfield: A Player's Life*. New York, 1988.

Wilber, Cynthia J. *For the Love of the Game*. New York, 1992.

Further Reading

In the past fifteen years, there has been a large number of excellent scholarly publications dealing with various aspects of baseball that are directly relevant to this book. In a number of books, edited books, and articles, the economist Paul D. Stauhohar has played a crucial role in developing the field of labor studies in sports. His *Playing for Dollars: Labor Relations and the Sports Business* (Ithaca, N.Y., 1996) is an important introduction to the subject, and his article, "The Baseball Strike of 1994–95," in *Monthly Labor Review* (March 1997): 21–27, is an invaluable study of the subject. A set of essays he edited, *Diamond Mines: Baseball and Labor* (Syracuse, N.Y., 2000) contains the most recent scholarship. William B. Gould IV's *Labored Relations: Law, Politics, and the NLRB* (Cambridge, Mass., 2000) presents unique insights into the strike of 1994–95. Professor Gould is a knowledgeable fan and historian of baseball and one of the nation's leading authorities on sport and the law. He also was the chairman of the NLRB when the strike took place. Lee Lowenfish's *The Imperfect Diamond: A History of Baseball's Labor Wars* (rev. ed., New York, 1980) is the groundbreaking study on the subject. Roger I. Abrams's *Legal Bases: Baseball and the Law* (Philadelphia, 1998), Gerald W. Scully's *The Business of Major League Baseball* (Chicago, 1989), and Kenneth

M. Jennings's *Balls and Strikes: The Money Game in Professional Baseball* (Westport, Conn., 1990) and *Swings and Misses: Moribund Labor Relations in Professional Baseball* (Westport, Conn., 1997) are essential for an understanding of the subject. The latter two have the additional value of exhaustive bibliographies.

Two books by Robert F. Burk are particularly important, *Never Just a Game: Players, Owners, and American Baseball to 1920* (Chapel Hill, N.C., 1994) and *Much More Than a Game: Players, Owners, and American Baseball since 1921* (Chapel Hill, N.C., 2001). In his most recent book, Burk has done a superb job of using secondary and newspaper sources and presents a dynamic picture of the changes that have taken place in baseball. The book contains the best bibliographic essay on the subject.

Other important works include: David Conn, *The Football Business* (Edinburgh, 1997), Warren Goldstein, *Playing for Keeps: A History of Early Baseball* (Ithaca, N.Y., 1989); Richard Giulianotti, *Football: A Sociology of the Global Game* (Oxford, 1999); John Harding, *For the Good of the Game* (London, 1991); Daniel Marburger, ed., *Stee-rike Four! What's Wrong with the Business of Baseball* (Westport, Conn., 1997); William Marshall, *Baseball's Pivotal Era, 1945–1951* Lexington, KY, 1999); James Edward Miller, *The Baseball Business: Pursuing Pennants and Profits in Baltimore* (Chapel Hill, N.C., 1990); Larry Millson, *Ballpark Figures: The Blue Jays and the Business of Baseball* (Toronto, 1987); J. Ronald Oakley, *Baseball's Last Golden Age, 1946–1960* (Jefferson, N.C., 1994); James Quirk and Rodney Fort, *Pay Dirt: The Busines of Professional Team Sports* (Princeton, N.J., 1992) and *Hard Ball: The Abuse of Power in Team Sports* (Princeton, N.J., 1999); Paul M. Sommers, ed., *Diamonds Are Forever: The Business of Baseball* (Washington, D.C., 1992); Neil J. Sullivan, *The Dodgers Move West* (New York, 1987) and *The Diamond Revolution: The Prospects for Baseball after the Collapse of Its Ruling Class* (New York, 1992); David Q. Voigt, *America through Baseball* (Chicago, 1976) and *American Baseball*, vol. 3: *From Postwar Expansion to the Electronic Age* (University Park, Pa., 1983); G. Edward White, *Creating the National Pastime: Baseball Transforms Itself, 1903–1953* (Princeton, N.J., 1996); and Andrew Zimbalist, *Baseball and Billions* (New York, 1992).

Index

Numbers in boldface indicate a photograph on that page.

Aaron, Henry "Hank," 133, 300n.41
Adcock, Joe, 276n.7
Addie, Bob, 47, 55
agents, 3, 62–64. *See also* legal representation
Alexander, Doyle, 287n.1
Ali, Muhammad, 94, 97, 100, 113
Allen, Dick, 87, 281n.47, 287n.1
Allison, Bob, 24–25
All-Star Game: cancellation of, 217; deflated valuation of funds from, 48; grant to MLBPA, 46, 277n.29; office operating funds and, 54; pension funds from, 17, 75, 259
Allyn, Arthur, 58–59
Alvis, Max, 40, 98
American Baseball Guild, 15
American League: dynasties in, 91, 235; on expansion of leagues, 80; negotiations on pension plan and, 75; player rep for, 17, 18–19; reserve system and, 4
Anderson, Sparky, 138
Angell, Roger, 8, 241
antitrust laws, 4, 23, 131, 304n.12
arbitration: commissioner's role in, 144,

163, 164, 176, 263; Eighth Circuit Court and, 160; free agency and, 153; for Hunter, 142–46; importance of, 145; for Johnson, 147–48; Kuhn on, 276n.14; for Messersmith, 7, 149; owners' view of, 72–73; as players' right, 3; reserve system and, 243–44; role of, 232; Seitz on, 153–54
Article 10(a). *See* renewal clause
A's. *See* Athletics
Ashburn, Richie, 227
Ashe, Arthur, 97
Associated Press, 224
Athletics, 186–87, 235
Atlanta Braves, 44, 67, 70, 208
Atlanta Constitution, 34
Atlanta Journal, 43–44
Autry, Gene, 187

bad faith: accusations of, against owners, 47–48, 50, 126, 170; accusations of, against players, 78; dues payment and, 59; funding of central office and, 47–48; layers of, 176; newsletter and, 66; in 1973 negotiations, 126
Baer, George, 57, 275n.9
ballparks, conditions in. *See* stadiums, in conditions

Baltimore Orioles, 152, 186
Bando, Sal: career of, 244; free agency
granted to, 287n.1; free agency study
and, 205, 206–7, 209, 296n.25; on
Miller, 42; on 1981 strike, 211; union
participation of, 174; use of free agency, 187
Barra, Allen, 300n.41
Barrow, Ed, 174
Barton, Bob, 38, 81–82
*Baseball: The Biographical Encyclope-
dia,* 142
baseball cards, 73–74
"Baseball Players Mesmerized by an Old
Smoothy" (Young), 43
Basic Agreements: impact of, 13; of
1996, 262; owners' disregard for, 258;
players' view of, 39
—of 1968: changes in relationships after, 164 (*see also* player/owner relations); grievance procedure of, 131–32,
144, 155–56, 164, 246; impact of, 121
(*see also* power differential); Messersmith-McNally case and, 156, 162–63;
Miller on, 68–69; negotiation of, 68–
72; owners' view of, 165; reserve system and, 153 (*see also* reserve system); role of commissioners since,
144, 163, 164, 176, 263; situation pri-
or to, 233; testing of grievance clause,
138, 140 (*see also* grievances; grievance procedure, impartial)
—of 1973: issues of, 285n.6; Messersmith-McNally case and, 165; negotiation of, 106, 120–23, 126–30
—of 1976: free agency and, 186; negotiation of, 155, 168–71, 175–76, 178–79,
182–83; players' view of, 207
—of 1980: negotiation of, 191–94, 197,
201–2; owners' approach to, 189–91;
trial period of free agency and, 186
Bavasi, Buzzie: on arbitration, 232–33;
articles in *Sports Illustrated* by, 62–
64, 170, 233; on baseball, 60; damage
to owners by, 141; and Miller, 65, 243;
on negotiations, 64–65; on 1972
strike, 112; player grievances and,
140; on players' knowledge of system,

38; salary negotiations by, 62–64, 129;
Tolan and, 141, 149
Baylor, Don: career of, 244; free agency
granted to, 287n.1; on Grebey, 203;
MLBPA and, 152; on 1981 strike, 260–
61; and strike subcommittee, 197
Baylor, Elgin, 37
Belanger, Mark, 152, 197, 244
Bench, Johnny, 90–91, 180
Bender, Sheldon, 138, 140, 288n.14
benefit funds, 74–76, 176, 212
benefits, 17, 39–40
*Biographical Encyclopedia of Baseball,
The,* 149
Biographical History of Baseball, The,
142
Birmingham News, 96
Bisher, Furman, 34, 43–44
Blackmun, Harry, 121–22, 159, 253
black players: barred until 1947, 126;
Dodgers' view of, 65; integration by,
42–43, 241, 282n.67; management
and, 59; participation in union, 95;
the press and, 96–97; racism and, 59.
See also *Flood v. Kuhn; specific black
players*
Black Sox scandal of 1919, 173
Blue, Vida, 187
Blue Ribbon Commission, 264, 306n.42
Bock, Hal, 224
Boone, Bob: career of, 244; free agency
study and, 205–7, 209, 296n.25; on
Grebey's proposal, 195; player rep,
276n.7; and strike subcommittee, 197;
union participation of, 174
Boros, Steve, 27, 42
Bosman, Jean-Marc, 252–56
Bosman case, 252–56, 304nn.12–13
Boston Globe, 262
Boston Red Sox, 111, 112, 187, 235
Boswell, Tom, 247
Brearley, Mike, 250, 303n.4
Brewer, Jim, 26
Brock, Lou, 84
Broeg, Bob, 93, 280–81n.35, 283n.5
Brown, Jim, 97
"bubble gum money," 73–74
Bunning, Jim: Bisher on, 44; Cannon on,

29; on Cannon's refusal of position, 31–32; career of, 244; competitive nature of, 300n.2; Joint Study Committee on the Reserve System and, 77–79; Miller and, 35, 36–37, 268n.36; on Miller's Hall of Fame candidacy, 42, 300n.41; motivations of, 231–32; with Nixon, **30**; on player/owner relations, 12; political philosophy of, 67; racial sensibilities of, 95; at San Juan meeting, 87, 88

Burk, Robert, 2, 299n.37

Busch, Gussie: Anheuser-Busch and, 84; approach to 1976 negotiations, 182; asset to union, 241, 278n.3, 298n.27; Camp David analogy, 219; delay of game by, 134, 136; Flood and, 85; Gaherin's warning to, 141; integration and, 43; Messersmith-McNally case and, 157; new-order owner, 67; on 1981 strike, 222; on pension fund negotiations, 106; press support of, 282n.5; reaction to strike, 111, 115–16; reception of, after strike, 102; Roberts on, 284n.34

bylaws, 56

California Angels, 147, 148, 186–87

Callahan, Tom, 9

Cannon, Raymond, 23

Cannon, Robert C.: approach of, 59; aspirations of, 31, 33–34; bylaws/constitution and, 56; candidate for MLBPA counsel, 23, 31–32; candidate for MLBPA directorship, 28–29; and Cardinals players, **25**; commissioners' and owners' view of, 23–24; correspondence of, 270n.25; on government intervention in baseball, 24; interview with, 10; Martin's disciplinary hearing and, 26; at Miami meeting, 36; on Miller, 48; Oliver on, 166; opinions about, 2–3; Pension Fund Committee and, 25; player/owner relations and, 27–28; and players, 32–33; questionnaire on black players' facilities, 65; role in MLBPA, 32–34

Carlos, John, 94

Carlton, Steve, 134, 206

Carmichael, John, 284n.41

Carpenter, Bob, 282n.67

Carroll, Louis, 163

Cartwright, Alexander, 225

Cashen, Frank, 169–70, 205, 206–7, 296n.25

CBS Corporation, 67

"A Central Office for Major League Baseball Players" (Scott), 21

Chandler, A. B., 22

Cherry, J. Carlton, 142

Chicago Cubs, 235

Chicago White Sox, 58–59

Chiles, Edward, 221

Cincinnati Enquirer: letter to, 8–9; on Miller, 113, 273n.33; Miller's statement to, 45; on 1972 strike, 105, 113

Cincinnati Reds, 186, 187, 288n.14

Clary, Jack, 31

Clemente, Roberto, 95

Clendenon, Donn, 279n.19

club movement, 67, 149

club owners. See owners

Coca-Cola Company, 54–55

Cochrane, Mick, 260, 305n.29

Colavito, Rocky, 240

collective bargaining: for football players, 171; free agency and, 131–32; hiring of Miller and, 246; issues in 1994, 258; Messersmith-McNally case and, 155–56; in 1996, 262; owners' expectations and, 155, 156; pension fund and, 204; reserve system and, 121; Seitz's recommendation for, 154, 158. See also arbitration; grievances

collective bargaining agreement: Koufax-Drysdale holdout and, 63; nature of, 54; negotiation of, 66, 68–69; Richards on, 1; testing of, 138, 140; as weapon for players, 46

collusion (by the owners), 63, 123, 149, 258–59, 299n.37

commissioners: authority of, 58, 144–45, 173, 219, 262–64; Cannon on, 23–24; defense of office, 164; on demise of reserve system, 9; of football, 171, 172–73; on funding for office, 49; fu-

ture of baseball and, 262–63; grievance procedure and, 71; Messersmith-
McNally case and, 153; and Miller,
58; and MLBPA, 57–58; role of, 124,
144, 163, 164, 176; spokesmen for
management, 6; Staudohar on,
306n.39; as unique attribute of baseball, 163; William Marshall on, 263.
See also Eckert, William; Frick, Ford;
Kuhn, Bowie
communications: during 1972 strike,
108–9; during 1973 Basic Agreement
negotiations, 128; during 1980 Basic
Agreement negotiations, 198; during
1981 strike, 212, 220–21, 298n.23; by
Miller and Moss, with players, 65,
170–71; among players, 31
compensation for free agents: Grebey
on, 202; Kuhn on, 208; Miller on, 178,
202; MLBPA proposal for, 213–15;
negotiations on, 213–15, 221; 1980
Basic Agreement negotiations and,
192–96; owners' view of, 209; players'
view of, 203, 216–17, 295n.16,
297n.15; as reserve system in disguise, 194; Rozelle Rule, 171; settlement on, 221; as unbridgeable divide,
211; unilateral implementation of,
212. *See* Joint Study Committee on
Free Agency
competitive balance: after free agency,
194; in Europe, 303n.8; Grebey on,
297n.37; history of, 174; Miller on,
178; reserve system and, 90–91. *See
also* Blue Ribbon Commission
Cone, David, 262
Conlin, Bill, 224, 282n.67, 299n.31
Continental League, 24, 80
contracts: challenges to, 156; changes
in, since 1966, 3; of Downing, 132–33;
of Drysdale and Koufax, 62–64; effect
of free agency on, 187; of football
players, 173; of Hunter, 142–46; of
Kiner, 18; of McNally, 150; of Messersmith, 148, 150, 181–82; of Mantle,
240; multiyear guarantees of, 235–36;
as player issue, 58; playing without
signing, 271n.32; of Simmons, 133–

37; of Tolan, 140–41. *See also* salaries;
salary arbitration
—mutually binding: bubble gum cards
and, 74; Hunter case and, 142, 145;
Johnson case and, 148; Miller on, 59,
75; owners' disregard for, 58–59, 258–
59; Seitz on, 145
control: attitudes engendered by, 241;
Baer on, 57; Bavasi on, 63–64; as crux
of disputes, 6, 233; in European soccer, 250–52; free agency and, 211;
good of baseball and, 79; league expansion and, 80; Miller's challenge to,
48; necessity for owners, 162, 178–79,
183; 1994–95 strike over, 257–58;
owners in position of, 3, 4, 39, 72,
243; pension fund and, 75; players'
challenge to, 103; players' ignorance
of, 38–39; players in position of, 191;
by players of own lives, 37, 38; reserve
system and, 83, 166; union assertion
of, 59–60
corporate involvement, 33, 67, 80, 172
Costas, Bob, 257, 300n.41
courts. *See* judicial system
Cronin, Joe, 25; advice to Miller, 60–61;
letter to Miller, 68; on MLBPA support
of Flood, 97; negotiation of minimum
salary and, 69–70; negotiation of 1973
Basic Agreement and, 126; on pension
fund, 90–91; at players/owners meeting, 28; on reserve system, 89
Culp, Ray, 112
Curt Flood Provision. *See* ten and five
rule
Cy Young Award, 143

Dade, Paul, 131
Dale, Francis, 285n.53
Dallas, Tex., meeting in, 106–12
Dalton, Harry: approach to free agency,
183; as Bando's superior, 211; fined for
statement on negotiations, 191; on
Joint Study Committee for Free Agency, 205, 206–7, 296n.25; on McNally,
150; on Miller, 204; on 1972 strike,
114; on owners' tactics, 119
Daniels, Dan, 269n.10

Dave Winfield Foundation, 205
DeCinces, Doug, 152, 197
Detroit Tigers, 235
Devine, Bing, 42–43, 89, 125, 279n.20
DiMaggio, Joe, 270n.22
direct compensation. *See* compensation for free agents
"Doc Miller's Traveling Road Show," 220–21
Donovan, Ray, 217
doomsday predictions: demand for proof of, 193–94; by Fitzgerald and Cashen, 169–70; by Hadden, 162–63; negation of, 188; by owners, 176, 189
Downing, Al: on being traded, 107–8; compared to Simmons, 136; contract grievance of, 131–33; free agency battle of, 130, 146, 147; on 1972 strike, 110; press portrayal of, 137; on racial issues in Flood case, 95–96
Drabowsy, Moe, 152
Drysdale, Don, 44, 62–64, 76, 77
dues checkoff system, 49–50, 54–55, 58–59, 71

Early, Gerald, 282n.67
Eastham, George, 250
Eastham case (England), 302n.2
Ebony, 97
Eckert, William: candidates for MLBPA directorship and, 35; election of, 34; lecture on Taft-Hartley Law, 47, 48; meetings over finances, 54; at Miami meeting, 36; on player/owner relations, 57–58; removal of, 76
economic structure of baseball, 264–65
Education of a Baseball Commissioner, The (Kuhn), 211
Eisenhardt, Roy, 221
Ellsworth, Dick, 129
endorsements, 22, 54–55
Executive Board of the Major League Baseball Players Association. *See under* Major League Baseball Players Association
Executive Council of the Pension Fund, 47, 57. *See also* Pension Fund Committee

executives: on arbitration, 232–33; on Basic Agreements, 68–69; changes made by, in 1990s, 257; on Flood case, 89; implications of free agency for, 236; on Miller's selection, 43; on players' loyalty, 107–8; threats to players, 16; use of the press to inflame, 169–70. *See also* management; owners

fans: on baseball, 39, 66, 235; baseball cards and, 73; baseball numbers and, 37; changes in attitudes of, 231; concept of baseball, 175; on Fehr, 245; on Flood case, 96; free agency and, 236; Grebey article and, 198; history of baseball for, 39; Howsam's reassurances to, 294n.30; letters to Miller, 284n.41; loyalty to, 234; Messersmith-McNally case and, 178; 1969 World Series and, 82; 1972 strike and, 102, 117–18, 134; 1981 strike and, 217, 222, 228; 1994–95 strike and, 256, 262; on players, 117–18, 238, 239, 301n.10; press influence on, 99–100, 118–19; on reserve system dispute, 87; role of, 2; union participation and, 152
federal courts. *See* judicial system
Federal Mediation and Conciliation Service, 216
Feeney, Chub, 89, 90–91, 97, 126
Fehr, Don: appeal to NLRB, 213; background of, 160–61; director of MLBPA, 245; and free agency, 191, 205, 208–9, 296n.25; Grievance 81-7 and, 215; Messersmith-McNally case and, 292n.44; negotiations on compensation and, 214; at 1993 All-Star Game, 160; on owners' attitudes, 238–39; on players' position, 260; and Ravitch, 259; role of, 11–12, 229, 246; Schulian article and, 223
Feller, Bob, 17, 28, 177
finances: disclosure of, 169–70, 194–95; of MLBPA office, 24–25, 46–50, 54–55; player trading and, 81
fines: changes in, since 1966, 3; Dalton and, 191; of Johnson, 147–48; as player issue, 57; of Tolan, 138, 140

Fingers, Rollie, 131, 187
Finley, Charlie: Bando and, 211; and free
agency, 183, 187–88; Hunter and, 142;
Messersmith-McNally case and, 157;
new-order owner, 67; suit against
Kuhn, 187
Fisher, Ed, 50
Fisher, Jack, 6
Fitzgerald, Ed, 141, 169–70, 181
Flieg, Fred, 69–70
Flood, Curt: background of, 84–85; on
baseball system, 242; basis of case,
128; Busch and, 278n.3; compared to
Bosman, 254; denial of case, 92, 120,
244; determination of, 99; and Devine, 279n.20; disillusionment of, 31;
fate of, 107; goal of, 158; guest at 1995
meeting, 259–60; impact on baseball,
100–101, 131, 254; motives of, 88;
options of, 92; press portrayal of, 84–
85, 137, 278n.4, 280n.34; racial issues
and, 94–97; references to slavery, 84,
87, 94, 96, 281n.46; on reserve system, 282n.67; ridicule of, 207; at San
Juan meeting, 86–89, 124; statement
of, 277n.1; suggestion of contribution
to, 279n.19; suit to overturn reserve
system, 83; supporters of, 281n.37.
See also Flood v. Kuhn
Flood v. Kuhn: basis of, 128; Blackmun
decision on, 121; Bosman case and,
253; denial of, 120–21, 154; Gaherin
on, 122; Hamilton on, 278n.11; impact on football, 171; influence on
Oliver, 161, 290n.27, 291n.28; Kuhn's
use of, 163; MLBPA and, 285n.1; necessity of, 278n.6; press response to,
92–97, 100–101; Seitz's reference to,
157; union tactic after, 176; Veeck's
testimony, 280n.26
Florence, Italy, meeting in, 303n.8
Forbes, Dick, 119
Fort, Rodney, 275n.9
Foster, George, 213
Fowler, Wyche, Jr., 219, 298n.20
free agency: arbitration and, 153; compensation and, 203; essence of, 234–
35; European soccer and, 303n.8; fight
for, 232; financial impact of, 187–89;

first four years of, 186–87; of football
players, 171; history of baseball and,
235; Howsam on, 5–6; Hunter case
and, 142–46; implications of, 236;
Kuhn on, 208; lockout to force restrictions on, 159; Messersmith-McNally
case and, 7–8, 149, 158; in Mexican
League, 16; 1968 Basic Agreement
and, 131–32; 1973 Basic Agreement
negotiations and, 123, 285n.6; 1980
Basic Agreement negotiations and,
195, 200; 1981 settlement and, 222;
1992 negotiations on, 257, 258; owners' opposition to, 179–81; players'
views of, 206; pragmatic concerns
about, 182–83; protection of, 175; salaries and, 80, 181, 234; Seitz's decision and, 178; service time and, 217;
settlement on, 184; Smith's analysis
of, 174; Tolan case, 140; as ultimate
goal, 131. See also compensation for
free agents; Flood v. Kuhn; Joint Study
Committee on Free Agency; Messersmith-McNally case; reserve system
Freeway Series (1980, Los Angeles), 197
Fregosi, Jim, 244
Frick, Ford, 25, 33
Friend, Bob: on Cannon's refusal of position, 32; change in views of, 31; education of, 271n.40; at Miami meeting,
36; and MLBPA study committee, 24–
25; and screening committee, 28; support of Cannon, 23; support of Miller,
35

Gagliano, Phil, 112
gag rule, 169, 191, 193, 221
Gaherin, John: advice on Seitz's employment, 153; on aftermath of strike,
119–20; on arbitration board for Hunter, 143–46; background of, 60; bargaining power of, 169; on baseball,
175; on Bavasi, 141; on changes in
reserve system, 168; on court actions
against Seitz's ruling, 159, 161; on
Flood v. Kuhn, 122; Joint Study Committee on the Reserve System and,
77–82; on Kuhn, 125; Messersmith-
McNally case and, 156–57, 289n.14;

and Miller, 61–62, 189–90; on MLBPA, 60; negotiations lost by, 189; negotiations on pension fund and, 74–76, 114–15; negotiator for PRC, 6–7, **62**; 1966 negotiations and, 66; 1968 Basic Agreement negotiations and, 69, 71–72; 1972 strike and, 105–6, 112–13; 1973 Basic Agreement negotiations and, 122–30; 1976 Basic Agreement negotiations and, 168–70, 175–76, 178, 180, 182–85; on O'Malley, 147, 149; and owners, 60; on player/owner relations, 115, 165; release of, 122, 159, 181; renewal clause and, 133, 140; on reserve system, 4, 166–67; on salary arbitration, 126; on salary disclosure, 129; Seitz on, 158, 165; Tolan case and, 140–41; on Torre, 128; treatment of service time, 217

Galbreath, Dan, 115–16
Galbreath, John, 32
Garner, Phil, 197, 244
Garvey, Ed, 171–72
Garvey, Steve, **150**
Giamatti, A. Bartlett, 224–26, 299n.37
Gibson, Bob, 134
Giles, Warren, 25, 26, 28, 51
Giulianotti, Richard, 240
Glanville, Brian, 252, 303n.8
golden age of baseball, 7, 246
Goldstein, Warren, 2, 39
"good of the game": Cannon on, 24, 27–28; definitions of, 68; free agency and, 15; influence of phrase, 37; Joint Study Committee on the Reserve System and, 79–80; Kuhn's argument for, 163, 164; player protection of, 6, 189; reporters and, 9
Gould, William B., IV, 305n.34
Grant, Donald, 49
Grebey, Ray: approach of, 190; article in *The Sporting News*, 198–99; asset to union, 203–4; and free agency, 205, 208, 296n.25; Grievance 81-7 and, 215; letter from congressmen to, 219; and Miller, 214, 299n.31; MLBPA proposal for compensation and, 213–15; 1980 Basic Agreement negotiations

and, 191–94, 197, 201–2, 295n.6; and players, 215, 296n.25; players' views of, 203; sidelining of, 221; statement after 1980 agreement, 202; unilateral implementation of compensation plan, 212

Greenberg, Hank, 281n.37
Grich, Bobby, 287n.1
Grievance 81-7, 215
grievance procedure, impartial: establishment of, 3, 71–72; free agency and, 131–32; future gains and, 246; key to success, 232; owners and, 72. *See also* arbitration; collective bargaining; grievances

grievances: against Bavasi, 65; of Bosman, 252–56; Cannon's approach to, 32–34; of Downing, 131, 132–33; of football players, 171; of Hunter, 142–46; increase in, with procedure for, 73; as player issue, 57; of Johnson, 147; of Messersmith and McNally, 131, 155–56; Miller's attitude toward, 137, 141; of Simmons, 131, 133–37; of Tolan, 131, 137–41. *See also* grievance procedure, impartial

Griffey, Ken, Jr., 256
Griffith, Clark, 125
Guardian, The, 250

Hadden, Sandy, 52, 162, 163
Hall, Dick, 152
Haller, Tom, 49, 244
Hamilton, Steve: career options of, 37; and committee studying Astroturf, 125; on Flood case, 95–96, 278n.11; on Mexico City meeting, 86; Miller on, 40; on Miller, 41–42; negotiations for minimum salary and, 71; on 1972 strike, 111–12; reason for joining union, 67; at San Juan meeting, 87
Harnish, Pete, 260
Harrelson, Ken "Hawk," 279n.19
Harvey, Brian, **160**
Helyar, John, 133, 190
Henscha, 206
Hertzel, Bob: correspondence with Miller, 8, 284–85n.41; on Miller, 273n.33, 300n.41; on Moss, 52

Herzog, Whitey, 301nn.8–9
Hill, Jimmy, 302n.2
history of baseball: Bourdieu on, 13;
    competitive balance and, 90–91; dis-
    parity in versions of, 6, 39, 305n.29;
    dominance of teams in, 174; grievance
    procedure and, 72; longest winning
    streak in, 3, 193; Messersmith-
    McNally case and, 160–62; Miller's
    knowledge of, 36; Oliver on, 166;
    owners' appeal to, 246–47; owners'
    disregard for, 257; Seitz's appeal to,
    154; Selig and, 7; and union strength,
    193
history of labor relations, 155, 259–60
holdouts, 62–63, 76
Holmes, Oliver Wendell, 4, 159, 253,
    291n.28
Holtzman, Ken, 187
Houston, Tex., meeting in, 295n.16
Houston Astros, 206
Houston Chronicle, 93
Howard, Elston, 132
Howsam, Bob: approach to 1976 negoti-
    ations, 179, 181, 182; and committee
    studying Astroturf, 125; on golden age
    of baseball, 7; on 1972 strike, 105;
    1981 strike and, 216–17; on owners'
    position in reserve system negotia-
    tions, 294n.30; on reserve system, 5–
    6; on salary arbitration, 123; on the
    union, 137–38
Hoynes, Lou: on changes to reserve sys-
    tem, 166; on Kuhn's role in Messer-
    smith-McNally case, 163–64; on
    Messersmith-McNally case, 159,
    289n.14; on reserve system, 77–78
Hunter, Bob, 40, 45, 96, 118
Hunter, Jim "Catfish," 142–46, 181, 187

Jackson, Reggie: at Dallas meeting, 109;
    free agency of, 131, 187; Hunter's ref-
    erence to, 142; at San Juan meeting,
    95; and strike subcommittee, 197
Jackson, "Shoeless" Joe, 23
job opportunities, 5, 37–38, 80
Johnson, Alex, 147–48
Johnson, Davey, 244
Johnson, Samuel, 191

Joint Study Committee on Free Agency,
    205; compensation statement and,
    204; establishment of, 202; impossible
    task of, 206–7; players' view of,
    296n.33; players' report for, 297n.37;
    sessions of, 208–9; stalemate, 211
Joint Study Committee on the Reserve
    System: discussions during, 77–83;
    Flood case and, 88–89; Messersmith-
    McNally case and, 166; 1973 Basic
    Agreement negotiations and, 285n.6;
    owners' recalcitrance and, 243,
    279n.22; press silence about, 93
Jones, Randy, 197
judicial system: antitrust exemption in,
    4, 23; Bosman case (Europe), 253;
    Eastham case (England), 250; Flood v.
    Kuhn, 120–22, 154; Messersmith-
    McNally case, 7, 153, 159–67, 175;
    owners' views of, 89, 157, 158, 159,
    241; reserve system and, 4, 154, 155

Kaat, Jim, 99, 180, 181, 244
Kansas City Royals, 81, 186, 206
Kansas City Royals v. Major League
    Baseball Players Association, 161
Kansas City Star, 107
Kauffman, Ewing, 33, 113, 159, 183
Killibrew, Harmon, 98–99
Kiner, Ralph: career of, 18; on Mexican
    League, 16; on owners' part in union
    decisions, 269n.11; player rep, 17; on
    players' position in 1950s, 19–20; on
    unions in baseball, 18–19
Kirby, Clay, 140
Klein, Frederick, 300n.41
Koosman, Jerry, 215
Koppett, Leonard: on Miller, 45; on 1972
    strike, 112, 113, 118–19; on 1980 ne-
    gotiations, 191–92; on 1994–95 strike,
    256; on players' thankfulness, 37; sup-
    port of Flood, 93
Koufax, Sandy, 44, 62–64, 76, 77
Kranepool, Ed, 279n.19
Kuenn, Harvey, 22, 36, 244, 270–71n.32
Kuhn, Bowie: on arbitration, 289n.32;
    on baseball, 6; on commissioner's
    role, 6, 36, 242, 289n.32; congression-
    al testimony of, 164; on demise of

reserve system, 9; on economics of free agency, 207–8; election of, 76; firing of, 166; on free agency, 144, 159; grievance procedure and, 72; on Hunter case, 142, 144, 145, 287n.3, 288n.19; intervention in player sales, 187–88; intervention in player trading, 279n.19; letter from Flood to, 84; letter from Fowler to, 219; letter from Seitz to, 156; lockout and, 180–81; Messersmith-McNally case and, 153, 157, 162, 163–64, 290n.25; Miller and, 125–26, 127, 210–11, 214, 286n.18, 297n.2; on Miller-Eckert relationship, 58; on Moss, 274n.51; negotiations on pension plan and, 75; with Nixon, 30; and players, 124–25; referred to as "Ayatollah Kuhn," 196; on reserve system, 5, 164; response to Flood's letter, 89; on San Juan meeting, 86; as scapegoat, 263; on Seitz, 166, 291n.37; on union actions, 244

labor issues, 52–53
labor law: Eckert's lecture on, 47, 48; Miller's knowledge of, 37; use of, 4, 60; as weapon for players, 46
Labor Management Relations Act, 58
Landis, Kenesaw Mountain: ambiguity of powers under, 1; Cannon on, 33; creation of commissioner's office and, 144; office under, 26, 163–64, 242, 263; Oliver on, 291n.38; reserve system and, 280n.26
Lane, Frank, 242
Lansing Leader (Kans.), 280n.34
Larive, Jessica, 252, 303nn.7–8
LaRussa, Tony, 244
legal representation: denial of, in 1950s, 19–20; for Flood, 88–89; for Hunter, 142; for Koufax and Drysdale, 62–64; for Kuhn at Messersmith-McNally case, 162; for Messersmith-McNally case, 160; Miller on, 46; for MLBPA, 50–51; 1968 Basic Agreement and, 233; for owners at negotiations on salary increases, 69–70; for owners at pension plan negotiations, 75; for owners in Messer-

smith-McNally case, 153, 159–60; for players, 3
length of career, 1–2, 5, 37–38, 107
length of season, 39, 58, 71
Lenz, Aloys-Michael, 253, 304n.12
Leonhard, Dave, 91–92, 249
Levin, Richard C., 306n.42
Lewis, J. Norman, 19, 20–21, 48, 269n.6
Lipsyte, Robert, 45
Lloyd, Graham, 302n.1
lockout(s): free agency negotiations and, 159; Giamatti on, 299n.37; 1973 Basic Agreement negotiations and, 126–28; in 1976, 179–81; 1980 Basic Agreement negotiations and, 197; owners' assumptions about, 193; players' response to, 185; threats of, 181
Lords of the Realm (Helyar), 190
Los Angeles Angels, 186–87
Los Angeles Dodgers: on black players, 65; contract negotiations of, 62–64; domination of, 91, 186, 235; executives' view of, 147; Messersmith-McNally case and, 148–49, 155–56; move of, 67, 242
Lupica, Mike, 256

Mack, Connie, 91, 188
MacPhail, Larry, 16–17
MacPhail, Lee, 36, 54, 221
Major League Baseball: after free agency, 226; assault on structure of, 2; Brearley on, 250; expansion of, 80; history of, 225; reserve system and, 89–91; sole spokesman for, 36; structure of, 64, 82, 247; transition period of, 187–89
Major League Baseball Players Association (MLBPA): accomplishments of, 245; approach of, 12, 189, 244; assumptions about, 11; Cannon as candidate for executive directorship, 28–34; Cannon as legal counsel, 23–28; changes in baseball relationships by, 152–53; compared to National Football League Players Association, 171–74; constitution of, 56; counsel for, 2–3, 4 (see also Cannon, Robert C.; Fehr, Don; Moss, Richard); European interest in, 305n.17; financing of, 54–55; as

first sports union with collective bargaining agreement, 172; fiscal standards of, 55; function of, 10; gains by, after 1966, 228–30; historical background of, 15–20, 243; issues dealt with, 2 (see also under players); Lewis's role in, 18–20; master plan of, 232; nature of, 201; newsletter, 65–66; 1972 strike of, 102–20; 1981 victory of, 221–22; owners' attempts to break up, 258; participation in, 40; the press and, 238; readiness of players to seek help from, 86, 131, 132, 136, 137; on reciprocally binding contracts, 145, 148; on reserve system, 7–8, 280n.35; Scott's role in, 18, 21; Seitz's ruling and, 176–77; strength of, 203; support of Flood case by, 88–89; transformation of, 3, 9, 245–46; as "union by another name," 1, 45, 60, 66, 275n.15; validation of, 144–46. See also Miller, Marvin J.; player representatives; players
—central office of: constitution and, 56; financing of, 24–25, 47–50, 54–55; function of, 21–22; ratification of, 41; Roberts's suggestion for, 28, 31
—director of: constitutional recognition of, 56; Eckert on, 57–58; full-time, 28–35; Miller approved as, 36; owners' reaction to Miller as, 47–50; press reaction to Miller as, 43–46; role of, 4, 21–22; selection of, 28–36. See also Miller, Marvin J.
—Executive Board: baseball card contracts and, 74; compensation negotiations and, 215, 218; Dallas meeting of, 106–12; on direct compensation, 296n.25; endorsement agreements and, 55; function of, 56; on Grebey's proposal, 195–97; Joint Study Committee on Free Agency and, 205; meeting after Washington, D.C., sessions, 219; meeting on collective bargaining, 66; modern baseball labor relations and, 245; 1973 Basic Agreement negotiations and, 287n.37; 1980 Basic Agreement negotiations and, 295n.6; 1980 strike recommendation,

198; 1981 strike decision, 211–12; pension plan negotiations and, 76; preparation for fight, 174; reward for Miller and attorneys after 1981 strike, 223, 298n.29; role of, 4, 229; San Juan meeting of, 86, 94, 98, 242
—legal counsel of, 22; Lewis as, 19–20, 21, 269n.6. See also Fehr, Don; Moss, Richard
—opinions about: Bisher's, 44; Brearley's, 250; criticism of, 229, 238–39; Herzog's, 301n.8; Oliver's, 166; owners', 20; players', 297n.5; the press's, 43; in The Sporting News, 268–69n.1; Staudohar's, 244
Major League Executive Council, 270–71n.32
management, 73; contract writing and, 271n.33; of English football teams, 251; Johnson case and, 148; Oliver and, 161–62; players' view of, 235; reserve system and, 5; role in meetings with Miller, 40, 41. See also executives; owners
Mantle, Mickey, 240
Marion, Marty, 17
Maris, Roger, 256
marketing of players: before 1966, 3; bubble gum cards and, 73; compensation and, 194; endorsements by, 22, 54–55; Hunter case and, 145–46; reserve system and, 81, 83; salaries and, 194. See also players: selling of; trading of players
Marshall, Mike: Camp David analogy and, 219; on free agency, 183, 184; on minor league experience, 67; renewal clause and, 148; and strike subcommittee, 197
Marshall, William, 263
Martin, Billy, 26, 240
Martinez, Buck, 244
Mathews, Eddie, 26
Maxvill, Dal: attitude of, 134; career of, 244; during 1972 strike, 104; player rep, 283n.22; at San Juan meeting, 87
Mays, Willie, 85
McCarver, Tim: on Bunning, 300n.2; career of, 244; competitive imbalance

and, 90–91; Flood case and, 87; on
1972 strike, 108; on players' knowledge of system, 38–39; reason for joining union, 67
McCormick, Mike, 125
McCovey, Willie, 131
McGeary, William R., 116–17
McGuff, Joe, 57, 107, 118
McGwire, Mark, 256
McHale, John, 152
McNally, Dave: career of, 149–50; with
Expos, **151**; grievance of, 131, 141,
152; reserve system and, 92, 137; on
salaries, 306n.44. See also Messersmith-McNally case
media: attitude toward players and, 239;
coverage in 2000, 265; and Fehr, 245;
on reserve system, 4–5; role of, 8–9;
and Tolan incident, 140. See also
sportswriters; specific sportswriters
"Men of Baseball, Lend an Ear" (Giamatti), 225
Messersmith, Andy: career of, 147; contract of, 150, 152; as free agent, **150**,
181, 182, 208; grievance of, 131, 141;
personal situation of, 177; reserve
system and, 92, 137. See also Messersmith-McNally case
Messersmith-McNally case: aftermath
of, 189, 227; arbitration of, 141–59;
Bosman case and, 253; court proceedings, 159–67; English view of, 256;
impact on baseball, 168, 175, 184,
209; impact on Basic Agreement negotiations, 168, 169; Miller on court
resolution of, 176; union on, 246. See
also McNally, Dave; Messersmith,
Andy
Mexican League, 16
Mexico City meeting, 69–70, 86
Meyer, Dick, 141
Miami, Fla., meeting in, 35–36
militancy: Cannon on, 29, 31; fans angered by, 134; 1981 strike and, 210;
Rickey and, 80; Torre on, 87; of
unions, 233
Miller, Marvin J.: All-Star Game funds
and, 277n.29; appeal to NLRB, 213;
approach of, 10, 39–40, 59–60, 65–66,

237–38; article on Reinsdorf, 222–23;
assertion of independence by, 58–59;
attitude toward player grievances,
141; background of, 36; baseball card
contracts and, 73–74; candidate for
MLBPA directorship, 28, 35; changes
credited to, 42–43; commissioners
and, 264; contributions of, 189, 232;
at Dallas meeting, 106–7; demand for
financial disclosure, 170; director of
MLBPA, 1, 61; Downing case and,
132–33; fiscal standards of, 55; Flood
case and, 97; focus of, 56; free agency
and, 205, 296n.25; Hall of Fame candidate, 300n.41; Hunter case and, 143–
46; impact on baseball, 290n.23,
301nn.8–9; impact on players, 67;
Joint Study Committee on the Reserve System and, 77–83; leadership
of, 172; Messersmith-McNally case
and, 162, 289n.14; misconceptions
about, 11–12, 175; names called, 39,
43, 191; 1966 tour of training camps,
39–40, 177; 1972 strike and, 102–3,
105–6, 108; 1976 Basic Agreement
summation, 184–85; 1990 address to
players, 259; on pension fund,
284n.41; personal appearance of, 36,
44, **61**, 116, 272n.4, 273n.24; philosophy of, 45–46; player support of, 36–
37; referred to as "labor goon" and
"vulture," 39, 42; Richards and, 13;
Roberts's introduction of, 29, 271n.38,
299n.40; role of, 229, 246; Simmons
case and, 136; use of Bavasi article, 64
—correspondence of: after 1981 strike,
224–29, 284n.41; with Braves on Richards, 70; with congressmen, 219; with
Cronin, 68–69; with a journalist, 8–9;
with Leonhard, 91–92; with Murray,
202; post-strike response to the press
and the public, 116–17; with Yastrzemski, 98
—negotiations by: on Basic Agreements,
69–72; on compensation, 213–19; on
finances, 54–55; in 1966, 66; on 1973
Basic Agreement, 122–30, 287n.37; on
1976 Basic Agreement, 168–71, 175–
76, 178–79, 182–85; on 1980 Basic

Agreement, 189–90, 191–94, 197, 201–2, 295n.16; on pension funds, 74–76, 114–15
—opinions about: Bisher's, 34; Cannon's, 32, 48; Dalton's, 204; Gaherin's, 113; Giamatti's, 227; Herzog's, 301n.8; Kuhn's, 58, 210–11, 214, 297n.2; McGuff's, 107; Murray's, 200–201; O'Malley's, 48; owners', 191; players', 40–42, 229–30, 300nn.41, 44; the press's, 43–45, 113–14; Roberts's, 92, 228; Seitz's, 158; sportswriters', 11, 36, 37, 43, 44–45, 56, 59, 113, 273nn.24, 33, 300n.41; Staudohar's, 9, 244, 245; Veeck's, 9; Yawkey's, 234; Young's, 93–94, 158
—relationship with: Bavasi, 65; Eckert, 58; Gaherin, 6–7, 61–62, 189–90; Grebey, 214, 215; Moss, 51–52; players, 39, 41–42, 223, 229–30, 234, 237, 297n.5, 300n.44; the press, 8–9, 45, 117–18, 273n.33
—views on: accomplishments of union, 245; baseball labor relations, 272n.1; Cannon, 2; changes in reserve system, 168–69; commissioners, 60, 71, 124, 125–26, 144, 164, 176; court resolution of problems, 176; events since 1966, 226–27; Gaherin, 125–26; Kuhn, 6, 286n.18; MLBPA, 275n.15; National Football League system, 280n.32; 1972 strike, 115–16; 1981 strike, 210–11, 222, 223, 224, 298n.27, 299n.31; owners, 46; players, 6, 60–61, 298n.27; press coverage, 284n.41, 285n.53; public acceptance of union actions, 236–37; reciprocal contractual obligations, 60, 75; reserve system, 4, 81; topics at spring training, 131; unity of players, 203
Miller, Terry, 108, 116
Milwaukee Brewers, 169, 211
minimum salary: changes in, since 1966, 3–4; establishment of principle of, 17; negotiations for increase in, 69–71; negotiations in 1992 and, 258; 1980 Basic Agreement negotiations and, 195; 1981 increase in, 222; as player issue, 44, 57, 58

minor leagues, 1, 15–16, 37, 67, 173
Mitchell, George J., 306n.42
MLBPA. *See* Major League Baseball Players Association
Moffett, Ken, 216
"Money Makes the Players Go" (Bavasi), 64
Montreal Expos, 150–52
Montreal Star, 102
Moss, Richard: approach of, 59–60, 65–66; assertion of independence by, 58–59; baseball card contracts and, 73–74; candidate for MLBPA counsel, 22; commissioners and, 264; on Flood case, 97; on grievance procedure, 72–73; on Hunter's position, 145; impact on players, 67; Joint Study Committee on the Reserve System and, 77–80; Kuhn on, 274n.51; leadership of, 172; letter from Scott to, 274n.49; letter to players on free agency, 131; letter to Seitz on appointment as arbiter, 141; Messersmith-McNally case and, 156, 162–63, 291n.39; negotiations on pension plan and, 74–76; 1972 strike and, **103**, 106, 108; 1973 Basic Agreement negotiations and, 122–30; 1976 Basic Agreement negotiations and, 182; personality of, 50–52; and players, 52, 237; and the press, 52–53; public relations and, 236–37; resignation of, 160–61; role of, 11–12, 229, 246; use of Bavasi article, 64
"Most Powerful Sports Figures in the Century" (Bisher), 45
Murphy, Johnny, 17
Murphy, Robert F., 15–16
"Murphy money," 17
Murray, Jim, 116, 199, 200–201, 285n.42
Musial, Stan, 43

National Labor Relations Board (NLRB), 127, 208, 213, 261
National League: dynasties in, 91, 235; expansion of, 80; negotiations on pension plan and, 75; player reps for, 17, 23; reserve system and, 4
New York Mets, 82
New York Times: Giamatti article in,

225, 299n.37; on Miller, 45, 300n.41; Miller article on Reinsdorf in, 222–23; post-strike analysis of, 118

New York Yankees: domination of, 91, 235; Kansas City and, 81; 1998 record win total, 256; owners of, 67; reasons for success of, 174; return to glory of, 186–87

NLRB. *See* National Labor Relations Board

Niekro, Joe, 213

Nightingale, Dave, 299n.37

Nixon, Richard M., 30

Nordbrook, Tim, 131

Northrup, Jim, 240–41

Nunn, Bill, Jr., 97

Oliver, John: approach of, 291n.39; on commissioner's role, 163, 164, 242, 291n.38; decision of, 164, 291n.28, 292n.44; on lawyers, 292n.50; Lenz's argument and, 253; Messersmith-McNally case and, 161–65, 290n.27; owners' position and, 292nn.44, 48; on reserve system, 166–67; ruling on Messersmith's arbitration hearing, 153

O'Malley, Walter: decision making of, 149; on facilities for black players, 65; on funding central office, 49; Gaherin on, 147, 149; impact on baseball, 290n.23; Koufax-Drysdale holdout and, 63; on lockout, 181; on Miller, 48; moving of Dodgers by, 84; on 1972 strike, 130; on player/owner relations, 115

owners: accusation against Seitz, 165; accusations against players seeking reforms, 20; approach of, 240–42; as asset to union, 9, 39, 47–50, 69, 106, 112–13; attitude toward commissioners, 173; attitude toward players' lawyer, 19–20; Blue Ribbon Commission and, 300n.42; business interests of, 178–79; and Cannon, 2; Cannon on, 23–24, 32–33; change in business practices of, 60; on collective bargaining, 69; control over players, 3, 4 (*see also* control); destructive acts of, 175;

division among, 180, 182; Finley suit and, 187–88; on *Flood v. Kuhn*, 92, 120, 122; of football teams, 172–73; free agency and, 144, 159, 178–80, 183, 187–89; grievance procedures and, 72 (*see also* grievance procedure, impartial; grievances); on Hunter decision, 145–46; immutability in reserve system negotiations, 178, 278n.6, 279n.20, 292nn.43–44 (*see also* reserve system); independence of MLBPA and, 58–59; Joint Study Committee on the Reserve System and, 77–83, 97, 279n.22; on judicial system, 159–60; Koufax-Drysdale holdout and, 62–64; lockouts and threat of lockouts, 126–28, 159, 179–81, 193, 197; on Messersmith-McNally case, 153, 157, 290n.17; Miller on, 46, 126; on Miller, 106, 203; on Miller's Hall of Fame candidacy, 300n.41; on Miller's selection, 47–50, 74–75; Murphy's impact on, 16; new types of, 67; 1972 strike and, 104–5, 111, 112–13, 114–16; 1980 Basic Agreement and, 190–91, 193, 196, 202, 203–4, 295n.6; 1981 strike and, 185, 211, 216–17, 221–22; on 1994 negotiations, 257; Oliver and, 161–62, 164–65, 166–67, 290n.27; on pension fund control, 75; on players, 245–46; players' view of, 1–2; and the press, 8–9, 93, 118–19; reaction to strikes, 104–5, 216; renewal clause and, 133; representation at Miami meeting, 36; on reserve system, 33, 89–91, 154, 155–56, 157, 176; response to Flood's letter, 89; response to newsletter, 65–66; revolution and, 231; role of, 2; on salary arbitration, 123; Seitz on, 300n.1; self-perceived function of, 6; tactics in negotiations, 170–71; unilateral implementation of compensation plan, 212; on the union, 106, 243–44; unity of, 114, 180, 191, 221–22; use of the press to inflame, 118–19. *See also* executives; management

—attitudes of: toward players, 134; doomsday for baseball, 1, 162–63,

169–70, 176; as French barons, 300n.1; toward union, 75
—invulnerability of: assurances of, 157, 159, 241; in European football and, 253–54; Flood case and, 89, 120; Messersmith-McNally case and, 160; slaying of, 165–67, 177

Pagliaroni, Jim, 71
Pappas, Milt: at Dallas meeting, 109–10; on Miller, 300n.44; MLBPA and, 152; reason for joining union, 67; on support for Flood, 87
Parker, Wes, 110
Pasqual, Alfonso, 16
Pasqual, Jorge, 16
paternalism: of Bavasi, 64; death of, 80–81; of Eckert, 57; of Grebey, 204; of Kuhn, 125; Miller and, 48, 244; nature of, 113; need for challenge to, 31–32; players' response to, 232; Simmons and, 136. See also "we'll take care of you" attitude
Peach, George, 301n.10
Pension Fund Committee, 17–20, 25–26, 47, 56. See also Executive Council of the Pension Fund
pension fund/plan: Cannon on, 23; Miller on, 47–48; MLBPA and, 2; negotiations on, 74–76, 105–6; owner control of, 75; ownership of, 47–49, 54; owners' view of, 90; players' knowledge of, 39; players' view of, 204; the press on, 283n.5; Roberts on, 25, 271n.38; strike of 1972 and, 103–4, 105, 115–16; withholding of, in 1994, 259. See also Executive Council of the Pension Fund; Pension Fund Committee
Pepe, Phil, 113
Perini, Lou, 16–17
Perry, Gaylord, 142
Perry, Jim, 128
Peters, Gary, 87, 109, 111, 112
Peters, Jesse, Jr., 97
Philadelphia Daily News, 224, 299n.31
Philadelphia Phillies, 186, 206, 282n.67
Pipp, Wally, 2
Pittsburgh Pirates, 15, 186

player/commissioner relations, 32–33, 57–58, 164, 187–88
player/fan relations, 241, 301n.10. See also fans
player/owner relations: All-Star Game grant and, 46–47; Basic Agreements and, 165; Bunning on, 31; Cannon on, 23, 26, 27–28; changes in, after Seitz ruling, 176–77; committee studying Astroturf, 125; confrontation with Kuhn and, 164; continued struggles in, 260–61; demonization of players, 241; Eckert on, 57–58; factors shaping, 245; Flood's legal challenge and, 86; funding for central office and, 47–50; grievance procedure and, 72, 155; in Mexican League, 16; Miller on, 45–46, 56–57; Miller's impact on, 237; nature of, 103; 1946 talks and, 16–17; 1972 strike and, 111; players' knowledge of, 39; players' view of, 27; PRC and, 6; salary arbitration and, 123–24; Scott on, 21–22; support for Kuhn and, 187–88; Tolan grievance and, 140. See also power differential
player/press relations, 8–9, 100, 116, 118. See also sportswriters
Player Relations Committee (PRC): creation of, 6, 60; firing of Seitz, 153, 157; MLBPA action on reserve system and, 122; negotiations lost by, 189; 1972 strike and, 105–6, 112; 1976 Basic Agreement negotiations and, 168; 1976 lockout and, 180; 1980 Basic Agreement negotiations and, 190–91; 1981 strike and, 185, 221; players' view of, 203; unilateral implementation of compensation plan, 212. See also Gaherin, John; Grebey, Ray; owners
player representatives: Bavasi's articles and, 64; at Dallas meeting, 108; election of, 56; funding of office and, 49, 54; housing for blacks and, 42; impact of 1972 strike on, 112; meeting agendas of, 26–27; at Miami meeting, 36; MLBPA study committee and, 25; public relations role of, 43; role of, 40, 106–12, 212, 216, 220; at San Juan

meeting, 92; selection of, 17; support of union, 41

players: on baseball, 39; Bisher on, 43–44; careers of, 244; compensation negotiations and, 213–15; control of, before 1966, 3; disillusionment with management, 64, 65; facial hair and, 138; faith in MLBPA, 170; of football, 173; on free agency, 187–89; on Grebey, 199, 203; initial interest in union, 271n.33; interpretation of changes in baseball business, 80; marginal, 38, 80–82, 111–12; Mexico City meeting and, 69; and Miller, 177, 229–30, 234, 237; Miller on, 6; on Miller's Hall of Fame candidacy, 300n.41; and MLBPA, 1, 5, 48; motivations of, 243; negotiations on compensation and, 217–18; on new salary structure, 189; 1972 strike and, 111, 114, 115; 1980 Basic Agreement negotiations and, 195–97; 1981 strike and, 210, 211–12, 216, 297n.5; on 1992 negotiations, 258; readiness to seek union help, 86, 131, 132, 136, 137; reality of game for, 37–38; relationship with the press, 8–9; replacements for, 15, 259, 261; reserve system and, 7–8, 91, 168; revolution of, 231; role of, 2; salary disclosures for, 129; selling of, 3, 187, 188. *See also* grievances; legal representation; player representatives; *specific players*

—attitudes of/toward: accused of arrogance and ingratitude, 20, 84, 85, 118, 134; accused of greed, 117–18, 152, 238, 301n.10; accused of selfishness, 113–14, 118, 152, 238; anger over treatment by owners, 19–20, 69, 71, 107; antiestablishment, 13, 231; challenge for Miller, 41; changes in, since 1966, 12, 275n.8; commissioners, 125; disillusionment, 31; distrust of management, 49–50, 192, 193, 219, 258–59, 295n.6; in football, 173–74; insecurity, 1–2, 15–16, 18–19, 20, 111–12, 173; "lucky to be playing," 5, 37–38; need for change in, 41; in 1959, 270–

71n.32; in 1960s and 1970s, 275n.9, 287n.32; during 1972 strike, 110–11; perceived as greedy, 43–44; "playing for keeps," 2, 4; pragmatism, 10, 237; press representation of, 136–37; sacrifice and teamwork, 107; self-respect, 106; self-satisfaction, 19–20; "that's baseball," 27

—competitiveness of: Joint Study Committee's understanding of, 78–79; Miller's use of, 60; 1980 Basic Agreement negotiations and, 192, 196; owners' underestimation of, 111; player/owner relationships and, 1, 4

—issues of concern to: inherent in sports, 37–38; legal representation, 19–20; length of season, 39, 58; Miller's focus on, 42, 57; moving expenses, 44; in 1959, 23; in 1960s, 26–27, 58; in 1966, 39; in 1967, 58; in postwar era, 16, 17; racial concerns, 42–43, 56, 59; scheduling, 58, 270–71n.32; split double headers, 58, 71; stadium conditions, 26–27; trading/selling players, 1–2. *See also* compensation for free agents; free agency; reserve system; salary arbitration

—unity among: in American Baseball Guild, 15; building of, 55; Flood case and, 88, 101; in football, 173–74; gains from, 185; Kaat on, 99; Mexico City meeting and, 69; in 1972 strike, 110, 175; 1980 Basic Agreement negotiations and, 195; in 1981 strike, 216, 217, 220–21, 223, 224; owners' actions and, 50; the press and, 282–83n.5; union concessions and, 178

Players Association. *See* Major League Baseball Players Association (MLBPA)

Porter, Paul, 49–50

Povich, Shirley, 19

power differential, 78; evidence of changes, 137–38, 140, 144–45; 1972 strike and, 103; 1973 Basic Agreement and, 123; 1976 negotiations and, 155; Oliver on, 165; players and, 251; Seitz's ruling and, 176–77; Torre on, 87, 98. *See also* control pragmatism: Miller's, 176; O'Malley's, 130; players', in negotiations on free agency, 182–83; Seitz's, 154; union's, 10, 237; Veeck and O'Malley's, 180

PRC. *See* Player Relations Committee

public relations: apathy toward players' concerns, 26–27; Hertzel's suggestion on, 273n.33; Miller on, 236–37; MLBPA and, 22, 204; Moss and, 52–53; need for, 99–100; in 1959, 21–22; 1981 strike and, 216; pension plan negotiations and, 76; player reps' role in, 43; support for commissioner and, 188

Quinn, John, 92, 282n.67
Quirk, James, 275n.9

racial issues: barring of black players, 126; Bavasi and, 65; in Flood case, 94–97, 282n.67; integration of players, 42–43, 56; MLBPA constitution and, 56; segregation of players, 42–43, 241; union participation and, 95; White Sox and, 59
radio, 239–40
Ravitch, Richard, 259
Rayburn, Sam, 136
Regan, Phil, 125
regional meetings, 220–21, 298n.23
Reinsdorf, Jerry, 222–23
renewal clause (Article 10[a]): Downing and, 132, 133; Flood case and, 163; Gaherin's concerns about, 122; Hunter case and, 142–46; McNally and, 150; Messersmith-McNally case and, 7, 156, 157; owners' view of, 155–56; pathway to reserve system changes, 130; Seitz on, 141–42; Tolan case and, 140
Report of the Blue Ribbon Commission, 265
reserve system: American Baseball Guild and, 16; Cannon's approach to, 32–33; change in, 92; demise of, 7, 9–10; discussion of, at San Juan meeting, 86, 89; Drysdale-Koufax holdout and, 63; expansion and, 80; Flood and, 254, 282n.67; *Flood v. Kuhn* and, 285n.1;

function of, 4–5; Gaherin's attempt to save, 122–23; grievance procedure and, 155; inception of, 4; Messersmith-McNally case and, 149, 156–57, 162; Miller on, 79, 83; MLBPA on, 280n.35; 1973 Basic Agreement negotiations and, 121–22, 126–27, 128, 130, 287n.37; 1976 Basic Agreement negotiations and, 168; owners' recalcitrance on, 278n.6, 292n.48; owners' view of, 89–91, 155–56, 241, 243–44; players' leverage in, 64; questionnaire on, 98; renewal clause and, 163; salaries and, 77–83, 80–81, 145, 153; salary arbitration and, 127; Seitz on, 154, 156, 158; Smith's analysis of, 174; Spalding and, 243; stalemate in negotiations on, 175, 279n.22; Veeck on, 280n.26. *See also* Joint Study Committee on the Reserve System; renewal clause
revenue sharing, 258, 262
Reynolds, Allie, 17, 18–19
Richards, Paul: on collective bargaining, 1; Miller and, 13; reserve system and, 82; Torre and, 276n.7; on union goals, 70
Richmond, Milton, 94, 281n.46
Rickey, Branch, 18, 80, 300n.41
Rizzo, Frank, 140
Roberts, Robin: Cannon on, 29; career of, 244; central office and, 21–22, 28, 31; concerns about union actions, 226–28; election of Scott and, 269n.6; Major League Executive Council meeting and, 270–71n.32; at Miami meeting, 36; on Miller's role in Flood case, 92; MLBPA study committee and, 24–25; recommends Miller for directorship, 29, 35, 271n.38, 299n.40; role in MLBPA, 21; suggestion to Miller on Flood case, 280n.32; testimony before Senate committee, 29
Robertson, John, 113, 284n.34
Robinson, Brooks: career of, 244; on Miller's Hall of Fame candidacy, 300n.41; MLBPA and, 152; reason for joining union, 67; reception of, after strike, 102; union participation of, 174

Robinson, Jackie: impact on baseball, 290n.23; on press coverage, 8; racial hatred toward, 96, 281nn.37, 47
Rodgers, Bob, 244
Rodriguez, Alex, 265, 306n.44
Roebuck, Ed, 129
Rogers, Steve, 215, 244
Rona, Barry: approach to 1980 Basic Agreement negotiations, 194, 207; free agency study and, 205, 208–9; Grievance 81-7 and, 215; on Hunter case, 145; on Messersmith-McNally case, 289n.14; Oliver on, 167; on Oliver, 290n.26
Rose, Pete, 206
Rose, Peter (MLBPA attorney), 296n.25
Roush, Ed, 162
Rozelle, Pete, 172
Rozelle Rule, 171, 194
Rudi, Joe, 187
Russell, Bill, 97
Rustin, Bayard, 97

salaries: American Baseball Guild and, 16; changes in, since 1966, 3–4; compensation and, 193; free agency and, 181, 188–89, 234; historical view of, 233; Joint Study Committee on the Reserve System and, 77–83; managers' percentage of, 65, 271n.32; minimum, in 1946, 17; negotiations about, in 1992, 257; pre-1976 players' view of, 306n.44; proposed cap on, 258; reserve system and, 4, 63, 80–81, 145, 153; scale for, 194–95; ticket prices and, 284n.36
salary arbitration: Finley and, 187; 1973 Basic Agreement negotiations and, 128, 130, 285n.6, 286nn.24, 28; 1973 negotiations about, 122, 126–27; 1980 Basic Agreement negotiations and, 195, 196; 1992 negotiations about, 258; reserve system and, 168; Seitz on, 153; service time and, 217; technology used for, 215; as whipping boy, 232
salary disclosure, 128–30, 233–34, 287n.32
San Francisco Giants: domination of,

91, 235; move of, 67, 242; opposition to central office and Miller by, 40, 41
San Juan, P.R., meeting in: agenda for, 86–89; Flood at, 87–88, 92; Kuhn at, 124–25, 164, 242
Schmidt, Mike, 206
Schulian, John, 223–24
Score, Herb, 240
Scott, Frank: Bavasi's complaints to, 65; Cardinals and, 25; Coca-Cola deal and, 54–55; Devine's letter to, 43; election of, 269n.6; letter to Moss, 274n.49; letter to Williams, 270n.22; in locker room with Cannon, 25; at Miami meeting, 36; MLBPA administrator, 21–22, 28; on MLBPA prior to 1966, 2; MLBPA study committee and, 25; Roberts on, 24–25; role of, 18
Scoville, James, 154–55
Season of '98, The (Lupica), 256
Seaver, Tom, 128, 300n.41
Seitz, Peter: on arbitration, 153–54; appointment of, 141–42; approach of, 291n.41; firing of, 153, 157, 165–66, 292n.46; on free agency/arbitration, 153; Hunter case and, 143–46, 153; impact on baseball, 192, 244; Kuhn on, 291n.37; on Kuhn's role as commissioner, 164; Messersmith-McNally case and, 131, 156–58, 289n.14, 290n.17, 292n.43; Oliver on, 165; owners' attack on, 159, 165; on owners' attitude, 300n.1; on reserve system, 154, 166–67; Young on, 158
Seitz decision: appeal to courts, 161–62; essence of, 157–58, 291n.41; impact of, 155, 175, 176, 178, 184; Kuhn on, 9, 288n.19; 1976 Basic Agreement negotiations and, 168, 169; Oliver's decision and, 165; owners' response to, 7; Selig on, 9
Selig, Bud: on demise of reserve system, 9; Gaherin's warning to, 141; on history of baseball, 7; on owners' position, 260; selection as commissioner, 263; strike of 1994–95 and, 211
service time, 217, 221
Sewell, Rip, 15, 52
Shecter, Leonard, 5

Short, Bob, 123

Simmons, Ted: career of, 244, 288n.10; compared to Downing, 136; contract grievance of, 131, 133–37; contract negotiations of, 162; free agency battle and, 130, 146, 147; at 1976 Basic Agreement negotiations, 180; playing without contract, **135**; press portrayal of, 137

Slaughter, Enos, 234

slavery: compensation as, 207; Flood's references to, 84, 87, 94, 96, 281n.46; free agency and, 209; references to, 141, 177, 250; reserve system as, 96–97; Seitz's reference to, 157

"Slave Trade with a Pension Scheme, The" (Brearley), 250

Smith, Barry, 302n.1

Smith, Red: analysis of historical evidence, 174–75; on Flood case, 94; as "Gee Whizzer," 239; on possible strike in 1980, 199–200; support of Flood, 93; support of union, 273n.24; on ten and five rule, 303n.4

Smith, Reggie, 40, 99, 111

Smith, Tommie, 94

Sondereggar, John, 282–83n.5

Sosa, Sammy, 256

Sotomayor, Sonia, 261

Spalding, A. G., 242–43

Sporting News, The, 268–69n.1; on Cannon, 24; on guild members, 16; Miller's response to, 46; on player salaries, 239; post-strike analysis in, 118; on 20-percent suggestion, 20

Sports Illustrated, 62, 63–64, 84

Sports Industry and Collective Bargaining, The (Staudohar), 244

Sports National, 300n.41

sportswriters: on Cannon, 24, 31, 34; concept of baseball, 175; English football players and, 240; first mentions of Players Association, 20; on Flood, 89, 92–93, 97, 100–101; impact on fans, 8–9, 99; on issues involving players, 6; Johnson and, 147, 148; Joint Study Committee on Free Agency and, 208; on Kiner and Reynolds, 19; knowledge of contract negotia-

tions, 271n.33; labeling of players by, 136–37; letters from Miller to, 8–9, 116, 284n.41; on Messersmith, 177, 292n.43; Mexico City meeting and, 69–70; on Miller, 11, 36, 37, 44–45, 59, 273n.24; on Miller's Hall of Fame candidacy, 300n.41; on Miller's mustache, 272n.4, 273n.24; on Miller's selection, 43; Miller's use of, 127; Moss and, 52–53; 1972 strike and, 104–5, 112, 113–14; 1973 Basic Agreement negotiations and, 127; 1976 Basic Agreement negotiations and, 169–70; 1980 Basic Agreement negotiations and, 190; 1981 negotiations and, 214; on 1981 strike, 217–18, 220, 223–24, 228; on 1994–95 strike, 262; objectivity of, 39; on owners' attitudes, 18; owners' use of, 118; on pension fund, 283n.5; on pension plan negotiations, 76; and players, 238; portrayal of blacks, 96; portrayal of players, 20, 43–44, 204–5, 236, 239; on possibility of strike in 1980, 199–200; on reserve system, 5, 87; role of, 8–9; Seitz and, 158; on Simmons, 136; supportive of players, 174, 199–200; threats of, toward players, 16. *See also specific sportswriters*

stadium conditions, 16, 26–27, 39

standard player's contract: grievance procedure and, 72; negotiations on pension plan and, 76. *See also* renewal clause

Stargell, Willie, 180

Staub, Rusty, 244

Staudohar, Paul: on commissioners, 306n.39; on Miller's role in revolution of baseball, 245; on 1994–95 strike, 263; on union success, 9, 244

Steinbrenner, George, 182, 187

Steinem, Gloria, 97

Stillman, Royce, 131

St. Louis Browns, 67

St. Louis Cardinals, 42–43, 91, 235, 241

St. Louis Post Dispatch, 85, 93, 282n.67

Stock, Wes, 57

Stoneman, Bill, 244

strike insurance: 1980 negotiations and,

191, 193, 199; 1981 strike and, 216, 221
strikes: Cannon on, 33; first reference to, 89; of football players, 171–72; Grebey on, 198–99; 1980 Basic Agreement negotiations and, 196, 197–98, 201; owners' assumption about, 193; Pirates' 1946 vote on, 15; Roberts on, 227, 271n.38; threat of, in 1976, 175; union on, 228–29
—of 1972: credibility of union and, 246; Dallas meeting about, 106–12; essence of, 119; important aspects of, 103–4, 105; issues of, 261–62; lessons from, 114–15; Miller's warnings about, 108–9; 1976 Basic Agreement negotiations and, 169; owners' assumption about, 193; owners' views of, 113, 115; players' enthusiasm for, 109–10; players' views of, 110–12; press's views of, 113–14; reaction of fans to, 102; reaction of press and owners to, 104–5; and "Sacco-Vanzetti document," 108; settlement of, 114; Simmon's incident and, 134; solidarity in, 175; union on, 229
—of 1981: aftermath of, 221, 222; congressmen's letter on, 219; declaration of, 214; "Doc Miller's Traveling Road Show" and, 220–21; impact of, 211, 216, 228; issues of, 261–62; Kuhn on, 297n.2; Miller on, 210; Miller's summation of 1976 Basic Agreement and, 185; negotiations during, 214–18, 221; union on, 229, 246, 297nn.5, 15
—of 1994–95: aftermath of, 305n.20; impact of, 255; issues of, 223, 256, 261–62; Marshall on, 263; Miller's influence and, 244; Selig and, 211; settlement of, 261; Taylor's reference to, 256; union on, 246; World Series and, 9–10
suspensions, 3, 56, 138, 140
Sutter, Bruce, 301n.10
Sutton, Don, 213, 244

Taft-Harley Act, 47, 48
Taylor, George, 35
Taylor, Gordon, 255, 256, 305n.17

Tebbetts, Birdie, 40
television, 239–40
Tenace, Gene, 287n.1
ten and five rule, 3, 128, 130, 148–49, 168
Ten Most Influential People in Twentieth-Century American Sports (ESPN broadcast), 301n.9
Terry, Bill, 19
"that's baseball" attitude, 7, 26–27, 99, 129
Times, The (London), 255
Tolan, Bobby: collective bargaining and, 131; contract negotiations of, 162; on the field, 139; free agency battle and, 146, 147; grievance action of, 137–38, 288n.14; renewal clause and, 140
Tomlin, Dave, 140
Topps Chewing Gum, 73–74, 76
Torre, Joe: attitude of, 134; on Cannon, 2–3; career of, 244; on Miller, 42; 1972 strike and, 102, 104, 111; 1973 Basic Agreement negotiations and, 128, 180; player rep, 276n.7, 283n.22; reason for joining union, 67; reserve system and, 82, 98; at San Juan meeting, 87; on Simmons, 136; trading of, 69–70; union and, 12, 174
trading of players: Carlton and, 134, 206; changes in, since 1966, 3; Clendenon and Harrelson and, 279n.19; difficulties in, 78; in disguise, 194; Downing and, 107–8, 133; Flood and, 84, 86, 87, 128; Friend and, 31; Holtzman and, 187; impact on union participation, 152; issue in 1973 negotiations, 123; Jackson and, 187; Marshall and, 148; McCarver and, 87; McNally and, 150; Messersmith and, 147, 148; occupational hazard, 1–2; owners' view of, 81; reasoning behind, 234, 250; refusal by owners, 91–92; retaliation, 18, 111–12, 206; Slaughter and, 234; threats of, to Mantle, 240; Tolan, Tomlin, and Kirby and, 140; Torre and, 69–70
tradition(s) of baseball: basis of negotiations by owners, 183; Cannon and, 3, 34; commissioner's role as, 144; griev-

ance procedure and, 72; Howsam on, 7; lockouts and, 179; masking of self-interest with, 126; Oliver on, 166–67; players' break with, 67; Rayburn's dictum, 136; reserve system as, 5, 90; salary disclosure and, 129; strikes and, 33; union and, 9
Tresh, Tom, 132
Turner, Ted, 182, 208

Uebberoth, Peter, 63
U.S. Congress, 122, 164

Veeck, Bill, 9, 91, 180–81, 241, 280n.26
Vincent, Fay, 263
Voigt, David, 239, 290n.23
Volker, Paul A., 306n.42

Walker, Dixie, 5, 17, 19
Walker, Harry, 5, 96, 281n.47
Wallace, George, 59
Wall Street Journal, 92
Washington, D.C., meeting in, 216–17
Washington Post, 47, 55, 280n.34
Washington Senators, 67
Weiss, George, 65, 174, 240
Wells, David, 256
"we'll take care of you" attitude: Eckert and, 57 (see also paternalism); Gia-matti and, 225; grievance procedure and, 71; influence of the phrase, 37–38; post–World War II and, 16; reality of, 38–39, 48
Werber, Bill, 238
Werker, Henry, 213
Whole Different Ballgame, A (Miller), 211
Will, David, 251–52, 303n.8
Will, George F., 306n.42

Williams, Edward Bennett, 22–23, 221, 270n.22
Williams, Ted, 93
Winfield, Dave, 297n.5
Woodward, Woody, 244
working conditions, 2, 21, 26–27, 39
work stoppage. See lockout(s); strikes
World Series: cancellation of, 9–10, 256–57, 261; Hunter's grievance and, 143; McNally's wins in, 149; in 1976, 187; Phillies win, 206; strike proposal and, 197
—radio and television revenue from: deflated valuation of, 48; financing of MLBPA office and, 24; negotiations on pension plan and, 75; ownership of, 54; pension funds and, 17
World War II, return of players from, 15–16
Wright, William, 27, 260, 305n.29
Wynn, Early, 269n.6

Yastrzemski, Carl, 98, 111
Yawkey, Tom, 20, 27, 111, 233, 234
Young, Dick: on Cannon's aspirations, 33; on changes in society, 113–14; changing of newspapers, 84; criticism of Flood, 93; criticism of players' union, 21; on Flood case, 93–94, 96; on Messersmith-McNally decision, 158; on Miller, 43; Moss's remark to, 52; on players participating in decision making, 270n.16; on reserve rules, 293n.19; on ticket prices, 284n.36
Young, Hugo, 224, 247
You're Missin' a Great Game (Herzog and Pitts), 301n.8

CHARLES P. KORR is a professor of history and Fellow of the Center for International Studies at the University of Missouri–St. Louis. His published work in sports history includes *West Ham United: The Making of a Football Club* and numerous articles dealing with political, economic, and legal aspects of twentieth-century sports. He is working on a book dealing with the important role of sports in the lives of South African political prisoners on Robben Island.

For the past twenty-four years, BOB COSTAS has covered every major sport for NBC-TV, including Major League Baseball, the National Football League, and the National Basketball Association, and has anchored prime-time coverage of the last three summer Olympiads and the 2002 Winter Games. The winner of thirteen Emmy Awards, he has also been honored eight times by his peers as the National Sportscaster of the Year. His book *Fair Ball: A Fan's Case for Baseball* (2000) attracted wide attention from baseball officials and fans and was on the *New York Times* bestseller list.

SPORT AND SOCIETY

A Sporting Time: New York City and the Rise of Modern Athletics,
   1820–70   *Melvin L. Adelman*
Sandlot Seasons: Sport in Black Pittsburgh   *Rob Ruck*
West Ham United: The Making of a Football Club   *Charles Korr*
Beyond the Ring: The Role of Boxing in American Society
   Jeffrey T. Sammons
John L. Sullivan and His America   *Michael T. Isenberg*
Television and National Sport: The United States and Britain
   Joan M. Chandler
The Creation of American Team Sports: Baseball and Cricket, 1838–72
   George B. Kirsch
City Games: The Evolution of American Urban Society and the Rise
   of Sports   *Steven A. Riess*
The Brawn Drain: Foreign Student-Athletes in American
   Universities   *John Bale*
The Business of Professional Sports   *Edited by Paul D. Staudohar and
   James A. Mangan*
Fritz Pollard: Pioneer in Racial Advancement   *John M. Carroll*
Go Big Red! The Story of a Nebraska Football Player   *George Mills*
Sport and Exercise Science: Essays in the History of Sports
   Medicine   *Edited by Jack W. Berryman and Roberta J. Park*
Minor League Baseball and Local Economic Development
   Arthur T. Johnson
Harry Hooper: An American Baseball Life   *Paul J. Zingg*
Cowgirls of the Rodeo: Pioneer Professional Athletes
   Mary Lou LeCompte
Sandow the Magnificent: Eugen Sandow and the Beginnings
   of Bodybuilding   *David Chapman*
Big-Time Football at Harvard, 1905: The Diary of Coach Bill Reid
   Edited by Ronald A. Smith
Leftist Theories of Sport: A Critique and Reconstruction
   William J. Morgan
Babe: The Life and Legend of Babe Didrikson Zaharias   *Susan E. Cayleff*
Stagg's University: The Rise, Decline, and Fall of Big-Time Football
   at Chicago   *Robin Lester*
Muhammad Ali, the People's Champ   *Edited by Elliott J. Gorn*
People of Prowess: Sport, Leisure, and Labor in Early Anglo-America
   Nancy L. Struna
The New American Sport History: Recent Approaches and
   Perspectives   *Edited by S. W. Pope*

Making the Team: The Cultural Work of Baseball Fiction
  Timothy Morris
Making the American Team: Sport, Culture, and the Olympic
  Experience   *Mark Dyreson*
Viva Baseball! Latin Major Leaguers and Their Special Hunger
  Samuel O. Regalado
Touching Base: Professional Baseball and American Culture in the
  Progressive Era (rev. ed.)   *Steven A. Riess*
Red Grange and the Rise of Modern Football   *John M. Carroll*
Golf and the American Country Club   *Richard J. Moss*
Extra Innings: Writing on Baseball   *Richard Peterson*
Global Games   *Maarten Van Bottenburg*
The Sporting World of the Modern South   *Edited by Patrick B. Miller*
The End of Baseball As We Knew It: The Players Union, 1960–81
  Charles P. Korr

REPRINT EDITIONS

The Nazi Olympics   *Richard D. Mandell*
Sports in the Western World (2d ed.)   *William J. Baker*

The University of Illinois Press
is a founding member of the
Association of American University Presses.

Composed in 9.5/13 Trump Mediaeval
with Jute display
by Jim Proefrock
at the University of Illinois Press
Designed by Dennis Roberts
Manufactured by Thomson-Shore, Inc.

University of Illinois Press
1325 South Oak Street
Champaign, IL 61820-6903
www.press.uillinois.edu